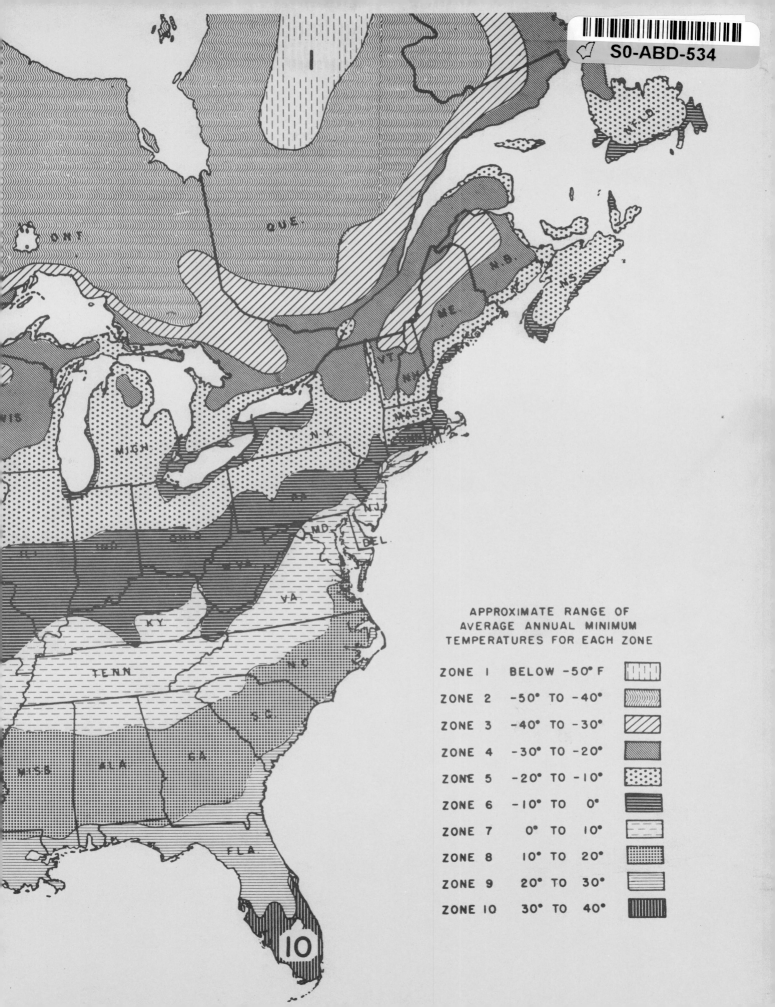

S0-ABD-534

APPROXIMATE RANGE OF
AVERAGE ANNUAL MINIMUM
TEMPERATURES FOR EACH ZONE

ZONE 1   BELOW −50° F
ZONE 2   −50° TO −40°
ZONE 3   −40° TO −30°
ZONE 4   −30° TO −20°
ZONE 5   −20° TO −10°
ZONE 6   −10° TO   0°
ZONE 7   0° TO 10°
ZONE 8   10° TO 20°
ZONE 9   20° TO 30°
ZONE 10   30° TO 40°

McGraw-Hill Series in
LANDSCAPE AND LANDSCAPE ARCHITECTURE

Albert Fein, Ph.D., A.S.L.A.(hon.) *Consulting Editor*

Bring and Wayembergh ■ Japanese Gardens: Design and Meaning
Gold ■ Recreation Planning and Design
Hudak ■ Trees for Every Purpose
Landscape Architecture Magazine ■ Landscapes for Living
Landscape Architecture Magazine ■ Water and the Landscape
Simonds ■ Earthscape

Trees for Every Purpose

Joseph Hudak

Drawings by
Artemas Partridge Richardson

McGraw-Hill Book Company
New York St. Louis San Francisco Auckland
Bogotá Hamburg Johannesburg London
Madrid Mexico Montreal New Delhi
Panama São Paulo Singapore
Sydney Tokyo Toronto

This book is dedicated to all who enjoy trees and especially to Kenn Stephens.

Library of Congress Cataloging in Publication Data

Hudak, Joseph.
  Trees for every purpose.

  Bibliography: p.
  Includes index.
  1. Ornamental trees. 2. Trees. I. Title.
SB435.H84   635.9'77   79-22578
ISBN 0-07-030841-1

*The editors for this book were Jeremy Robinson and Joan Matthews,
the designer was Naomi Auerbach, and the production supervisor
was Thomas G. Kowalczyk. It was set in Souvenir Light
by The Clarinda Company.*

It was printed and bound by Halliday Lithograph.

*Black and white photographs are by The Arnold Arboretum and numbers
44, 46, 47, 58, and 59 are by the author; the color photographs as credited.*

Contents

1 View in Hemlock Hill,
The Arnold Arboretum.

We have many satisfying reasons for learning about trees. As the largest plant life known, they contribute to worldwide comfort and convenience by providing many usable materials for construction and industrial purposes, attractive foods for our tables, potent medicines for healing, fuels for heating, and valuable sustenance for all types of wildlife. Trees are permanent in habit with their persistent, woody, usually single stems and are generously set around the globe in natural—and now man-made—stands we call forests. These have served as sources of untold wealth from primitive times to today, while also functioning as botanic treasure troves and wilderness retreats of great recreational appeal. People readily learned to benefit from having trees around.

Even from those dawn-of-history, agricultural societies to today's superspeed, mechanistic cultures, trees have been intelligently welcomed—if not always utilized properly. Their appreciated, utilitarian assets gradually expanded, however, to another value when trees were deliberately placed as ornaments of beauty for the sensory enrichment of our lives. That unrecorded moment in the haze of thousands of years past was a horticultural milestone.

Trees give us shelter from wind, provide buffering shade from intense sun, add bafflement from noise, ensure privacy, and contribute importantly to erosion control and to removing dust from the air. Their seasonal appeals include showy blossoming, contrastingly colorful foliages and bark, intriguing fragrances, decorative fruiting, striking winter silhouettes, and graceful movements. As major landscape design elements, trees add immeasurably to architectural and natural settings by their potentially grand size and generous variety of decorative forms and textures. Trees and people are naturally companionable.

The main objective of this book is to provide reliable, comprehensive guidance for both professional and amateur users of trees in landscape developments, as well as to present this relevant material conveniently in one publication. The special graphics and detailed descriptions hopefully include all the information about trees needed by any reader. May you enjoy using this book as much as I have enjoyed compiling it for you.

Joseph Hudak

Acknowledgments

Grateful thanks are extended to all who assisted with this effort in any way, and especially to the staff of the Massachusetts Horticultural Society's library, to The Arnold Arboretum, and to the shared responsibility of typing the manuscript by both Margaret and Kathleen Clover.

Trees grow from the remarkable interaction of their roots, stems, and leaves. None is more important than another, but damage to one can lead to a loss of function in the other two. Although trees produce flowers regularly, these uniquely specialized parts of the plant serve a separate, reproductive function only. Any tree can effectively expand without having flowered, but it cannot maintain its health with any severe loss of roots, stems, or leaves.

Roots

Roots are located hidden in the earth (although some semitropical trees carry secondary, aboveground, appendage rooting, too, for extra support of the trunk or branches) and have several important life functions: absorbing water and dissolved minerals from the soil, anchoring the plant against the stress of wind thrusts, storing necessary nutrients, and serving in the potential reproduction of the tree. Contrary to a long-held, popular belief, tree roots do not often venture very deep since there is little oxygen or water available for growth beyond the first 5 feet of soil.

The two main types of roots are *tap* and *fibrous*. A tap-rooted tree has a deep, downward-reaching, thick set of main roots with few lateral branchings close to the surface. Their search for water in the lower levels of soil, however, gives them a substantial edge in drought resistance. Such trees are nevertheless very difficult to transplant except when very young, and even then they may require extra time and attention to adjust satisfactorily after being moved. Of necessity, their earth ball, when dug, has a narrowly elongated shape.

Fortunately, most trees have crisscrossing, shallow, fibrous rooting and therefore transplant far more simply than tap-rooted plants. Here the network of dense roots is regularly set around the trunk and extends to the tip of the branches at a point called the *drip line,* where rain sheds abundantly from the foliage to the concentrated root system below. These horizontal, much divided, finely elongated roots are usually within the first foot or so of the surface in the humusy, loose part of the soil in order to gain the most water quickly. Below them develop the heavier support roots.

Obviously, these surface feeding roots can be severely hampered in their work by soil compaction from heavy equipment or from concentrated foot traffic. They also resent deep cultivation and excessive fill deposits over them. Since roots expect to roam freely for water and food and need a free interchange of oxygen with the soil, they either have to adapt to or suffer damage from such less-than-ideal conditions as waterlogged, contaminated, or hardpan soils, and they do not enjoy being replanted at a lower depth than they were originally growing.

It may come as a discovery to learn that only the very minute, growing tip of a tree root absorbs water and nutrients from the soil or that older root structures act mostly as food and water conductors as well as support mechanisms for the upright, woody trunk and heavy branching. This vital absorptive process is adroitly managed for even the largest specimen towering hundreds of feet into the sky by an incredible number of microscopic *root hairs* terminating each root tip. Without them a tree will die. Curiously, they have an individual life span of

2 Massive trunk of the world's tallest tree: redwood *(Sequoia sempervirens).*

only a few days, but their constant replenishment during the normal growing season by an active, healthy tree is ensured. This replacement factor answers the question of how trees take up water as well as how they manage to repair the shock damage from transplanting or from any disruption to the root system from nearby construction.

Roots continue to expand in temperate climates as long as the soil—not the air—temperature remains above freezing. Then all root activity slows appreciably, and the tree enters a resting period called *dormancy,* a reliable time for safe transplanting. In temperate zones this dormant season arrives in late autumn and continues until early spring, but where the local climate produces consistently frozen ground and heavy snowfalls, any transplanting activity is then greatly hampered or even stopped until mild weather returns. Whether late autumn or early spring is the better moving time for trees is variable with the locale and personal experience; foliage damage to deciduous trees is obviously less bothersome in autumn, while spring is a hectic, unsure time for reliable temperatures and ground thaw. In any event, roots are usually able to cope with your decision.

Subtropical and tropical plants pause, too, but their resting period is much shorter and moving them is often best arranged to take advantage of the beginning of the normal rainy season. Even full-foliaged trees can be moved in late summer with reasonable success if competently managed by professionals, but this abnormal scheduling is not recommended with enthusiasm since known chemical changes occur in the plant if the aftercare maintenance is mishandled. For both your economy and peace of mind, dormant transplanting is still preferred.

Since exposure to air, wind, and bright sunlight dries out dug roots easily, always avoid delays in completing the transplanting and always shield the fragile, exposed roots adequately with moist coverings while they are out of the ground. Although young deciduous trees are often planted as *bare-rooted* saplings, none of the evergreens accept such treatment. They must be dug with a firm ball of earth around the roots, a process generally known as *balled and burlapped* (or perhaps *balled and plasticized* today since synthetic wrapping fibers are less costly and more durable than burlap). Very small trees may also be available as *containerized* material, but larger ones are normally handled with the balled and burlapped technique.

Stems

Tree stems are the strongly upright, aboveground parts of the plant which support the leaves, flowers, and fruit. There are three main types: *columnar,* like palm, with a long, unbranched trunk topped by a heavy crown of foliage; *excurrent,* like spruce, with a conical shape from a tapering trunk and horizontally radiating branches; and *deliquescent,* like maple, with a heavy main trunk, rounded outline, and constantly divided upper branching that "melts away" to fine twig ends.

A tree is here defined as having one main stem rising upright from the ground, while its woody counterpart, the shrub, has a multitude of mostly equal-sized stems arising from a common, ground-level point. Although some may define a tree as also having a certain height, there never can be any precise definition, whether a plant is a tall shrub or a short tree, just by height alone. Since this is a book about the pleasurable aspects of trees, some shrubby types are occasion-

3

4

3 The trunk and buttress roots of cypress *(Cupressus).*

4 Even this huge trunk of a beech *(Fagus)* is given water and food only by tiny root hairs in the soil.

5 The *excurrent* stem of a nikko fir *(Abies homolepis).*

6 The *deliquescent* stem of a black tupelo *(Nyssa sylvatica).*

ally included for their special contributions to landscape beauty. It would be foolish to eliminate them just because of a still-faulty system for classification.

Another main function of tree stems is to act as conduits for transferring water and dissolved minerals to all parts of the plant in a special mix called *sap.* With cone-bearing trees there is an extra ingredient in the sap called *resin,* a gummy substance often with a mildly-pungent odor, and this resin has the unusual quality of acting as a natural antiseptic on the surfaces of cut or damaged branches to curtail serious inroads from insects and diseases.

Living stems are always full of water in winter and summer, but in their dormant stage such water is static. There is no truth to the myth that sap moves down a plant in autumn and up again in spring; sap is always handy in all stems. Its constant presence, however, does caution against pruning some trees in late winter or spring since sap can then bleed profusely, to the tree's detriment. Late summer is usually the preferred pruning time.

Woody plants have a thin layer of dead cells called *bark* on the outer portion of older stems for deflecting wind, heat, cold, insects—and perhaps vandals—from disrupting an extremely shallow but vital ring of very thin, moist cells called the *cambium layer,* which lies just beneath the bark. Cambium alone forms the new stem tissues yearly, and any serious damage to it will cause deformity or total loss of existing branches and new twigs. When functioning properly, cambium creates *xylem* tubes for moving sap upward and *phloem* tubes for returning the sap to the roots. The marvel of it all, not yet explained fully, is how this delicate and intricate process works so effectively over great distances and on such a regular basis.

5

6

If a cut is made *horizontally* into the cambium around the entire stem, all growth above the cut will shortly wither and die; yet if a *vertical* slash should occur—or a *circular* one during pruning—the tree will continue functioning satisfactorily as it slowly repairs the wound. One of the disheartening discoveries about tree health is that the quick kill of large branches often comes from the girdling habits of insect pests solely interested in the stem cambium.

The annual expansion of the cambium produces a layer of woody stem enlargement called *sapwood,* which occurs as a two-season spurt in spring and late summer. The rapid need for springtime sap in the upward and outward growth of a tree brings about the development of mostly thin-walled cells. Once this surge of expansion is over by midsummer, buds for next year's foliage and stems then develop, and by late summer the tree trunk and older stems expand *laterally* in an increase of stem *caliber.* This change in girth exerts pressure on the inflexible outer bark, causing it to crack, peel, or furrow in characteristic patterns often useful for identification. Inside the trunk the conclusion of this yearly expansion, called an *annual ring,* is marked by dark-colored cells. Counting these rings on a felled tree gives the age of the plant.

Because sapwood moves naturally outward from the center, the older cells left behind slowly lose their sap-carrying capacities and convert to inert wood called, logically enough, *heartwood.* Its main function, then, is to strengthen the trunk to support an ever-increasing weight of new twigs and leaves. While all this is going on above ground, the main roots also thicken in the same rhythm. There is always a balance in nature.

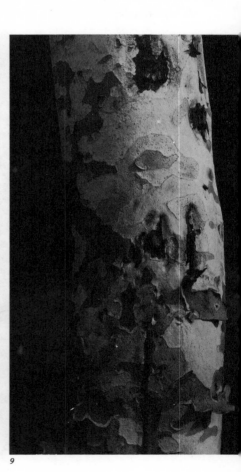

7

8

9

10

11

12

7   The bark of a shagbark hickory
(Carya ovata).

8   The bark of a paperbark mapel
(Acer griseum).

9   The bark of a lacebark pine
(Pinus bungeana).

10   The bark of a cedar of lebanon
(Cedrus libani).

11   The bark of Japanese flowering cherry
(Prunus serrulata).

12   The bark of an Italian stone pine
(Pinus pinea).

Every plant stem has tiny breathing pores called *lenticels* generously spread from ground level to the topmost twigs. They act as vents for the necessary exchange of gases, much like the stomata of leaves. On some plants, such as cherry, they are not only visibly prominent but also decorative as they form horizontal lines along the trunk. Exactly where lenticels begin at ground level is unclear, and it is always unwise to pile anything—even temporarily—against a trunk since it may cause some degree of suffocation in the tree. Decorative painting of tree trunks is no help to this breathing process either.

Some trees carry stiff thorns along their stems as protection from animal inroads of feeding and abuse. When they are branched, such thorns are botanically considered modified stems; but if they are only simple elongations, they are classed merely as epidermal growths. Either way, thorns can be formidable obstacles to safety for humans and should be carefully evaluated when considered for public spaces.

Leaves

Often the most noticeable part of a tree is the foliage. Each young stem always develops the leaf buds in the previous summer—not, as so many believe, in the spring—and these buds are found nestled at the axils where the leaves join the stem. Any topmost bud is called *terminal* by its position and is often larger than others on the stem since it usually contains the embryo of a flower along with the rudiments of new leaf and stem forms. Buds regularly given a secondary position on the stem are called *axillary* and act as replacement growth if anything should seriously damage the terminal bud. Some of these are unused and become enveloped by the expanding stem tissue as time passes: but if older branches (or even the trunk) are accidentally scarred or damaged, these buds, which are then called *adventitious,* suddenly spring into action. Such bud stimulation often occurs after heavy pruning work is done on some trees, and it is one of nature's ways of quickly shielding bark from too much strong sunlight or wind.

All leaves are importantly involved with a mystifyingly complex process called *photosynthesis,* where sunlight and carbon dioxide unite to create both the energy for growth and the carbohydrates for plant enlargement. Since leaves receive their basic stimulus to emerge from dormancy by the pressure of spring sap flowing up the stem, they also must shed themselves—even on evergreens—at some point, or else they would pump the roots dry. Annual leaf drop is normal for all plants, although the degree varies between the total shedding of deciduous trees and the limited removal of old leaves on evergreen plants. Leaf loss in summer, while abnormal, is often a safety valve for the tree in prolonged drought.

The largest part of any leaf, however small, is the *blade,* that flattened, broadened surface jutting away from the stem. It is secured in place by a flexible, sap-carrying stalk called a *petiole,* which has the unique ability to twist and turn to bring the blade, that factory for photosynthesis, to meet the greatest concentration of the sun's rays. Some leaves have only a bare fragment of petiole and are then called *sessile,* a common leaf arrangement with many needled evergreens that gives them a densely solid appearance very useful for year-round privacy screens.

Because the petiole moves the blade to face the strongest light, large trees on city streets often develop lopsided trunks from the shift in foliage weight away

13

13 Noticeably horizontal lenticels exist on the trunk of many birches *(Betula).*

14 The dormant appearance of deciduous oaks *(Quercus).*

15 The year-round appearance of needle evergreens like firs *(Abies).*

16 Broadleaf evergreens are well represented by the many forms of holly *(Ilex).*

17 The simple and multicolored foliage of the variegated kousa dogwood *(Cornus kousa variegata).*

18 The palmately compound leaves of red horse chestnut *(Aesculus x carnea).*

19 The pinnately compound leaves of European mountain ash *(Sorbus aucuparia).*

20 The bipinnate leaves of silk tree *(Albizia).*

from the shading effect of tall buildings. Symmetrical tree shapes can develop only where there is equal light intensity on all sides of the plant. In natural settings, crowded trees tend to become unusually slender as their leaves stretch constantly upward to find the sun.

There are two main types of leaves as defined by their persistence: *deciduous* and *evergreen*. Deciduous foliage sheds entirely at the conclusion of the growing season and is often assisted by rapidly cooling night temperatures, while an evergreen maintains its greenery even after consistent frost. Evergreen trees are further divided by the shape of their leaves into *needle* and *broadleaf* forms. Does all this mean that unfrosted, tropical plants never drop foliage? Hardly. Such leaves eventually lose resiliency with age and draw less and less stem sap to keep them pliant. Eventually their sagging weight ruptures the sap tubes entirely, and then the leaf withers and finally drops. Nothing lasts forever, even in the jungle.

Leaf outlines are either *simple* or *compound;* and compound leaves are additionally separated into *palmate* forms, where all the leaflets radiate from a common point on the petiole (much like fingers spreading out from your wrist), or *pinnate* forms, where the elongated petiole, now renamed a *rachis,* carries sets of leaflets up itself in ladder fashion. Occasionally, pinnate foliage develops double divisions—palmates never do—to become *bipinnate* and potentially sizable in spread. Pinnate leaves have duality in the placement of the leaflets since they can be either *opposite* or *alternate* to one another on the petiole. Trees certainly offer leaf variety.

Leaves are arranged on the twigs mostly in an opposite or an alternate way. As you might expect, nature also includes a variation called a *whorl,* where more than two leaves sprout from a common junction around the stem, but this is very uncommon. Since every fallen leaf shows a stem scar where it was formerly placed, identifying the arrangement—if not the style—of the foliage helps in plant identification when a deciduous tree is leafless. By their nature, evergreen trees are always ready for leaf identification.

Leaves provide useful shading for tender, emerging stems and also cool the surrounding air in summer by expelling oxygen and water vapor in a process called *transpiration.* These gases discharge from myriad, tiny openings called *stomata* located mostly on the underside of the leaf so that dust and other pollutants have little chance of clogging this necessary mechanism. Quite a few trees, however, carry foliage with a topside, waxy coating called *cutin* that sheds dirt readily with every rainfall. Such glossy-leaved trees have long been valued as choice landscape elements.

14

15

16

17

18

19

20

Because a small tree can disperse up to 60 gallons of water vapor *per day* during its growing season, the availability of replacement soil moisture has a definite influence on total plant vigor and health. In times of excess heat, wind, or dryness—and most likely when all these combine—leaves lose their normal stiffness and show *wilting,* a sign that insufficient water is available for daily functions. Combating this with artificial watering is then appropriate to forestall leaf drop and internal damage, but only deep penetration of this rescue moisture will be helpful since shallow irrigation tends to bring the feeder roots even closer to the surface. Because dry soil tends to take longer to absorb water effectively, it is wise to maintain a consistently moist condition for trees even before drought takes its toll.

Living foliage usually has a high percentage of green coloring matter called *chlorophyll,* and when leaves turn unnaturally yellowish during the growing season, they are said to be suffering from *chlorosis,* or lack of sufficient chlorophyll. Unfortunately, there is no single cause of this dilemma since it may result from inadequate moisture, a superabundance of moisture, infertility of the soil (especially trace elements), the inroads of disease or insects, soil contamination by chemicals, compaction of the roots, accidental spray poisoning from weed killers, and a variety of other potential difficulties. Always investigate the cause before applying any remedies since a sick tree can be made worse by random treatment of its ills.

Along with the dominant green pigments of leaves are smaller percentages of yellow and red ones that usually remain hidden until the leaf is ready to drop. When the production of chlorophyll diminishes, the emergence of these potentially bright colors gives us the splendor of deciduous foliage displays in autumn. Some foliages are already differently tinted through the growing season naturally in bronze, yellow, gray, or plum tones, and these rarely change color further before shedding. In any event, the color of dead plants is brown.

Flowers

The remarkable reproductive mechanism of plants is located in their flowers, and after the successful fertilization of the female member by the male, the final stage of a plant is formed: its fruit. Without flowers there can be no fruiting; and because the blossoms are fragile and short-lived, any deviation from the normal pattern of development caused by frost, drought, insects and diseases, or excessive rain has a long-lasting effect on the full value of a tree as an ornamental.

Flowers are usually found in larger, terminal buds formed the previous summer and appear along with the developing spring leaves; others are axillary in location and bloom in late spring when the foliage is already developed; a few more blossom as the final statement of the current growth in mid- to late summer without any special budding arrangement. There is so much variation and complexity in the size, shape, position, coloring, and special function of flowers in plants that the information could fill a book of its own. Suffice it to say that flowers are unique attributes of trees which are capable of grand showiness, vibrant colors, heady fragrances, and dramatic, but brief, sparkle in the annual parade of landscape effects from trees. Life would indeed be dull without them.

Flowers are *perfect* if they have both the female and the male reproductive parts close together for easy fertilizing by insects or wind. When these sexual partners are separated by nature but still appear on the same tree (as in the

21

22

21 The waxy coating of cutin on the foliage of a sawtooth oak *(Quercus acutissima).*

22 The gloss from cutin on the leaf surface of holly *(Ilex).*

24

23

25

23 Flowers of pear *(Pyrus).*

24 The flower of tulip tree *(Liriodendron).*

25 Flowers of Korean mountain ash
(Sorbus alnifolia).

26 Flowers of sourwood *(Oxydendrum
arboreum).*

26

27

27 Flowers of amur maackia *(Maackia amurensis)*.

28 Flowers of southern catalpa *(Catalpa bignoniodes)*.

29 Flowers of Japanese snowbell *(Styrax japonicus)*.

30 Flowers of American yellowwood *(Cladrastis lutea)*.

28

29

30

cone-bearers like pine), then the plant is called *monoecious* ("one house"); but when, in an unusual twist, they appear on completely different plants (as in holly), then the trees are called *dioecious* ("two houses"). Obviously, dioecious plants require more landscape space to accommodate their special diversity.

Flowers, like leaves, have flexible supports attached to the stem, and these are called *peduncles.* They move, too, and often elongate after flower fertilization is completed and the fruit development begins. Both deciduous and evergreen trees have flowers and peduncles, and here, too, peduncles can be *sessile* as in leaves.

While some stems and leaves have scent only when crushed or bruised, flowers usually develop some strength of perfume—not always likeable—without any extra effort of discovery on our part. This odor comes from a liquid called *nectar* and is used by the flowers to attract pollinating insects—not by the fragrance itself, which is unknown to the insect, but by the increase in air density that somehow becomes comprehensible and acts as a navigational guide to the blossom. Flowers with little or no fragrance are mostly pollinated by wind action, and such trees often have only bland flower colors. The majority of trees have brightly reflective blossoms that radiate visual attractions for passing insects.

Plants with minute, odorless, pallid flowers may also develop a peculiar helpmeet from the leaves by a device called a *bract,* which is a modified leaf that colors brightly to draw insects for pollination of the flowers. Tree dogwoods are a fine example of this cooperative venture, and they are commonly admired for their large, conspicuous flowers which, in truth, are only leaves.

Flower appearance on any tree is arranged in nature by age, not by size. Most trees wait until their surge of establishment growth is past before moving into the complexity of flower production and seed development. There is no established age when flowering begins, but once started, it is not always annually repeated. Bumper displays of flowering can exhaust the nutrient storehouse of the plant so that it occasionally rests and recuperates for a full season before reblooming in a spectacular way. Such trees are called *alternate bearers,* and this behavior is not influenced by external effects of cold or drought. It is simply the natural rhythm of the plant.

The classification of plants into families is arranged primarily by using the flowers (and the later fruit) for identification. Knowing this relationship for landscape purposes may seem initially remote, but understanding it gives greater assurance of what ornamental effects to expect. Pines do not have fleshy fruit and crabapples do not have cones, but once you know the reverse is true, then you can expect to find that spruce, fir, umbrella pine, and hemlock have cones because they are all members of the same family, *Pinaceae.* Perhaps more useful is the simple observation that if a member of the same family thrives in your locale, then other members might also do well. The easy growing association among ash, lilac, privet, and forsythia—all from the *Oleaceae,* or olive family—in so many landscapes across the United States provides a simple illustration of the value which can be derived from knowing about plant families.

Fruit

Fruit is possible on plants only when fertilization of the flowers has successfully occurred. Botanically, fruit is the most important plant part since it is the guarantee of the future by its production of fertile seeds within it. For decorative pur-

31

31 Leaf bracts of kousa dogwood *(Cornus kousa)* surround the true flowers.

poses, however, the fruit of trees has a more intriguing landscape interest by its size, color, shape, time of appearance, and persistence. Generous and showy fruiting can add a later summer or autumn bonus that flowering cannot quite match for long-lasting effectiveness. Such noticeability, nevertheless, may be of short duration since attractive fruit is often a staple in the diet of birds and other wildlife and can rapidly disappear if their other rations are in short supply.

Fruits are mainly categorized as being *fleshy* or *dry* by their mature appearance. There are many subdivisions of each, but they are first classified by how the seeds are released from their protective coverings. Where the seed jacket splits open neatly along a *suture*, or seam, that fruit is called *dehiscent*; where it cracks irregularly or not at all, it is labeled *indehiscent*. All the fleshy fruits are indehiscent, an easily made observation, and the location or quantity of seeds in fruits botanically separates them into a *pome* (crabapple), a *drupe* (the "stone" fruits like cherry), a *berry* (holly), a *aggregate* (strawberry), and a *multiple* (mulberry).

The dry fruits are either dehiscent or indehiscent with far too many botanic subdivisions to recount here. A dry, dehiscent type generously represented throughout the world, however, is the *legume*, whose characteristic pod is easily recognized in trees by the fruit of honey locust, laburnum, albizia, yellowwood, and poinciana, to name but a few examples. A dry, indehiscent fruit well known to all is the acorn fruit of oaks, which is extraordinary for its special development of a cap-like shield—not considered an official part of the fruit—called a *cup*, which is only a compressed series of tiny leaf bracts.

Fruit on trees can be small or large, clustered or singly distributed, persistent or fast-withering, bright-colored or dull, a nuisance or a boon, occasionally poisonous to humans, and, like its forerunner the flower, of fascinating appeal for landscape embellishment. Of course, the superabundance of some fruit crops and their seeds can present an expensive maintenance cost from litter, volunteer seedlings, and general decay odors; and it behooves any designer to investigate such details, which this book attempts to present faithfully, before endorsing any tree for general landscape use. By their fruits you shall know them.

34

35

32

33

32 The fruit of northern catalpa *(Catalpa speciosa).*

33 The fruit of hawthorn *(Crataegus).*

34 The fruit of cedar of lebanon *(Cedrus libani).*

35 The fruit of flowering dogwood *(Cornus florida).*

The Botanic Naming of Plants

Official labels for plants are organized botanically into a system of *scientific* names formulated today by the International Union of Biological Sciences and issued through their publication *International Code of Nomenclature for Cultivated Plants.* This scientific congress meets with irregular frequency to revise and update plant names as additional specific information about their true histories is uncovered. There is no formal code in existence for the *common* names of plants, but current botanic preference in writing them is to use only lowercase lettering, except for geographic locations and personal names.

The system itself is based on the formula developed by the celebrated eighteenth-century Swedish botanist-taxonomist Carl Linnaeus, whose *Species Plantarum,* published in 1753, together with his *Genera Plantarum* of 1754, has generally been accepted internationally as the starting point for the stabilization of modern plant names. His achievement rests on a keen observation of the *sexual* interrelationships of flowers and their fruits, where the number and placement of these related sexual characteristics brought unsuspected unity to the enormous quantities of plants throughout the world. Today, over 600,000 different plants are properly identified and cataloged by his system.

Linnaeus used Latin or Latin-formed words for his descriptions of plants—not to be obscure or difficult but to be accurate—since Latin was the language of scholars in his day and was also a tongue no longer in common use and therefore not subject to further change. (In setting out to stabilize a confusion of names, one benefits from using a stable language.) In later generations, Greek words also were included, but to a lesser degree.

A major link between plants of broadly similar nature is represented in the *family,* which is identified by its scientific *-aceae* ending, as in *Fagaceae,* or beech family, containing such diverse but sexually related trees as beech, chestnut, and oak. To use the more-obvious plant foliage as a primary guide for establishing a family relationship would soon prove chaotic (as many botanists before Linnaeus discovered) since leaves vary from evergreen to deciduous, from simple to compound, from having entire leaf margins to being deeply lobed, and from tiny to sizable. Flowers and fruit, however, remain noticeably consistent in appearance from plant to plant within a group for anyone to recognize a family tie.

Each plant within a family is provided with a *genus* name, and its first letter is capitalized, as in *Fagus* (beech). These *genera* (the plural of *genus*) are major divisions with deep-seated flower and fruit similarities but do not have identical representations of them. Since nature is always abundant with variations, there are also, as you might expect, subdivisions within all the genera, and these are categorized as *species* (plural: *species*), descriptive words that help to differentiate noticeable but *secondary* characteristics between plants of the same genus such as leaf shape, flower color, fruit size, or geographic location. The species are preferably written with all-lowercase lettering, and the former practice of capitalizing the first letter when the species is derived from the names of people or from former generic names is no longer recommended and therefore was not used in this book.

A final category of naming is the *variety,* a plant identical in all major botanic aspects to the parent species except, for example, that it has flowers, foliage, or fruits differently colored or that its silhouette is weeping instead of erect. A true variety can be found growing in the wild and will reproduce accurately from seed. In more common use today is the coined word *cultivar* (from "cultivated variety"), representing plants with horticultural appeal and extensive nursery planting that offer noteworthy form, color, rate of growth, or other landscape interest on an attractive basis. These are usually propagated asexually by cuttings to guarantee exact duplication since seed is unreliable for this purpose. Cultivar names are normally set apart by single quote marks and can be given in any modern language; a true variety is usually listed in Latin only.

The scientific names of *hybrid* plants, those hoped-for improvements created by deliberate human intervention in the fertilization of flowers between members of the same family, are preceded by the multiplication sign—×—which is not pronounced in conversation, and its presence can tell either of two stories about the new plant. If the × comes *before* the genus, then the hybrid came about through the pollination of two separate *genera* within the family; but if the × *follows* the genus, then the fertilizing took place between two (or perhaps even more) *species* members of that genus. In talking about such hybrids, the × translates into either "hybrid genus" or "hybrid species."

Using the full scientific name—genus, species, and variety or cultivar—is essential for both clarity and accuracy as well as for saving time in discussing or ordering plants. Common names are wholly unreliable for describing plants since the names vary greatly throughout the world, opening the way for obvious misunderstandings that can be costly in time and money with all landscape activities. Professionals internationally, however, comprehend and appreciate the use of complete scientific names from Alaska to Zambia. Join them in this useful pursuit.

37

38

36

36 The pea family has many members such as redbud *(Cercis)*.

37 The pea family has many members such as locust *(Robinia)*.

38 The pea family has many members such as pagoda tree *(Sophora)*.

The needs of plant growth remain constant: light, water, air, nourishment, a fixed temperature range for durability, and soil. Woody plants like trees have identical requirements, of course, but because of their long persistence in the landscape, they usually need our closer attention to their individual behavior over the passing years so they may reach maturity with assurance and natural vigor. Any plant with a potential life span of several hundred years deserves more than a casual glance.

A tree is the tallest plant type but is also the slowest to reach its full development. As it continues upward and outward, its root search for water and nutrients remains keen, and dominant, older trees seldom allow the successful introduction of any other major planting competition into their root domain. Tree saplings, on the other hand, always seem to be struggling amicably for the same root space in a ballet of frenetic harmony, but eventually one—or perhaps several—of these will achieve superiority and begin the long ascent toward noticeable stature. Survival of the fittest includes the plant kingdom, too.

Light and Shade

The sun is the source of all natural light and is an essential partner of photosynthesis, where leaves covert sunlight and carbon dioxide into growth energy for the entire plant. This process ceases at nightfall (and is only minimally active during the dormancy of evergreens in winter), but it can be reactivated—in a harmful way—by high-intensity, artificial lighting nearby which burns all night. This round-the-clock light stimulation can affect all the mechanisms of tree functions abnormally since the usual daily resting period, and even dormancy, is now disallowed. Excess winter damage is known to occur under these circumstances because soft plant tissues fail to ripen or harden completely before the harshness of seasonal weather changes suddenly occurs. Someday we are going to have to reevaluate whether safety illumination is worth the loss of normal tree development nearby.

While the majority of plants enjoy a maximum of sunshine throughout the year, some have a decided preference for reduced light—shade—during some part of the day. By its degree of intensity, shade can be divided into full, deep, half, and light. Full shade is year-long dimness at ground level from the light-screening effect of tall buildings or from heavy-foliaged, large evergreens. Deep shading usually comes from the dense summer foliage of deciduous trees, but here some stronger light penetrates to the ground from late autumn until early spring when these plants are leafless. Half shade is an equalized proportion of full sun and shade, but it is important to know when the sunlight appears since the heat and light most productive to strong growth come between 10 A.M. and 3 P.M. in summer. Light shade, the easiest type to utilize in landscape developments, is simply filtered light that reduces some of the intensity and heat of the sun for brief periods.

Normal plant growth and hardiness are sometimes noticeably affected by an increase in shading. Such plants often become less vigorous or have stems which elongate and become thinner as they push their leaves farther upward to reach the light. Constantly shaded soil often remains cold far longer into the spring;

39 Most evergreen trees prefer full sun for best growth.

may compact easier because useful, aerating animal life in them is less prolific; or may hold surface water longer to become soggy and oxygen-deficient, producing a well-known condition called "sour" soil. These soil adjustments from heavy shade can markedly affect plant behavior.

Shade and dryness, however, can often go hand in hand since the competition from the roots of large trees causing the shady situation usually leads to localized dryness and to spindly, weak growth on any introduced planting not readily adaptable to such trying conditions. Trees, by their tall nature, give great amounts of useful shading, but they can create some troublesome problems, too.

Water

Trees require great quantities of water for growth and without sufficient water will eventually die or become so misshapen and weak that they may lose their landscape appeal. Since water can be made available to plants only through the roots, the moisture content of the soil, especially in the active growing season, is critical to continued good growth. A constantly moist—not wet—soil is ideal.

40

Natural irrigation comes from rain and winter snowfalls, yet this may need to be supplemented by artificial watering during prolonged summer drought. Only deep penetration of water is valuable then in order not to bring the roots too close to the surface. For whatever reason, if roots are only shallowly set into the earth, they are weakened links of tree support and cannot long resist the constant buffeting of wind, especially when the tree becomes very large.

Air

Air is essential for proper root activity because root hair development depends on the easy availability of oxygen in the soil for survival. The aboveground parts of a tree are not so influenced since air is readily available to them at all times, but more so because leaves produce and release oxygen as part of their daily routine. Waterlogged, compacted, or clay hardpan soils are oxygen-deficient, and only a few stalwart trees can adapt successfully to such negative growing conditions. Roots prefer humusy, loose, well-drained sites because these are also oxygen-rich.

Nourishment and Fertilizer

The natural nutrients for tree growth are found only in the soil as minerals dissolved by rainfall into weak salt solutions available for quick absorption by the root hairs. Some of these nourishments also come from a layer of decayed vegetable and animal remains atop the soil surface—at least in a natural setting—in a system where life returns to life.

When a tree grows well and fulfills all expectations readily, it can be assumed to be fully supplied with its nutrient requirements; yet if it shows some growth or color deficiencies, unrelated to physical problems, it may require supplemental fertilizing. First, the soil should be professionally analyzed to determine if the three primary nutrients of *nitrogen, phosphorus,* and *potassium* are in sufficient quantities and in balance with one another. Nitrogen is used by plants mostly for stem and foliage development, phosphorus is involved with root enlargement

40 Moss-draped live oaks *(Quercus virginiana)* enjoy streamside locations.

and extension, and potassium provides the stimulus for flower and fruit production. Because a tree has greater quantities of stems and leaves, the nitrogen of the soil is quickly exhausted, and in tree fertilizer formulas nitrogen usually represents the largest percentage of the ingredients.

Although a chemical analysis of soil is often satisfactory when limited to these three basic nutrient ingredients, recent investigations of how plants grow now suggest that also determining the presence of *trace elements* such as iron, boron, magnesium, and copper is well worth including. For reasons that are as yet unclear, even minute percentages of these special soil ingredients are somehow essential for maximum growth in trees.

Fertilizers are commonly available in slow-acting, organic, natural forms as well as in synthetic, quick-acting chemical combinations. Even more specialized are the liquid and foliar nutrients. Each has a valid use somewhat different from the other, but with any of them always follow the manufacturer's or supplier's instructions for application carefully, keeping in mind that if a little is good, a lot is not always welcomed. Concentrations of fertilizer can damage delicate feeding roots all too quickly, defeating the whole purpose of the operation, and several light doses of nutrients are often more effective in the long run than one heavy application. In general, trees are best fertilized as they start growing in spring, but in some cold-climate areas, autumn applications work just as well.

Hardiness Zones

Hardiness in plants is primarily related to a satisfactory adjustment toward extended *cold* temperatures since most heat appears to be acceptable to plants within reason. As useful guides to this range of low-degree tolerances, authoritative maps (included in this book) are now available for most of the temperate regions of the world showing these *zones of hardiness.* The worst conditions exist in zone 1, where the winter temperatures can range down to −40 degrees Fahrenheit (−40 degrees Celsius), and the warmest are in zone 10 with usual cold snaps measured as 40 degrees Fahrenheit (5 degrees Celsius). The largest quantity of trees exist comfortably between zones 3 and 8. So does most of the world's population.

Since plants recognized as adaptable to a certain zonal range can be grown commercially throughout that spread of distance, plants with the same name can also behave differently when transplanted to other locations within the zone. By now it is recognized that plants originating in the northerly limits of the zone often develop greater hardiness, while southerly plants, because of their extended growing season and milder growing conditions, often fail to adapt easily when brought north. This is especially noticeable with evergreens.

Trees taken south from northern nurseries can usually cross the boundaries of *two* zones of hardiness without undue stress, but plants brought northward often do not behave satisfactorily beyond *one* zone unless they are very small. Moving plants from east to west—and the reverse—seems to be more workable as long as the soil conditions and moisture requirements for the plant are nearly identical in the new location. Locally grown material, however, still remains a wiser choice for landscape developments.

Microclimate areas exist in all these zones, creating those unusual growing situations that either raise or lower the normal temperature expectations for that particular zone. The protection from sheltering buildings, topography, fences,

41

42

41 The Scots pine *(Pinus sylvestris)* grows well from hardiness zones 3 to 8.

42 The deodar cedar *(Cedrus deodara)* is limited to growing in the warm side of zone 7 through zone 10.

and other plants can moderate the wintertime temperatures and wind conditions enough to encourage good response from plants not usually found in the vicinity. However, in reverse, exposure to excessive cold or wind can debilitate plants usually considered hardy for the geographic location.

Even with all these basic hardiness considerations, some other factors can also influence successful adaptation: air, soil, and water pollution; prolonged drought and consistent flooding; unsought shading; major alterations in soil alkalinity, acidity, or salt content; and, of course, vandalism. Benevolently, nature has somehow provided us with certain trees that are capable of enduring any and all of these problems.

Soil

Soil is that loose layer of the earth in which plants grow, and it is composed of varying amounts of minerals, humus, water, air, pieces of decomposed rock, and minute animal life all mixed harmoniously. The three dominant soil types are *sand, silt,* and *clay,* and a plant-productive soil is a balanced mix of all three.

Soil is found throughout the world in natural layers of varying thickness. The uppermost layer, *topsoil,* usually has a darker color from the decayed animal and vegetable matter it contains known as *humus.* It is remarkably rich in necessary nutrients, has an open, loose composition, and generally is uniform in quality. Having topsoil in any reasonable depth encourages rapid root and stem development, but too much—usually in excess of 9 inches—can sometimes produce negative effects from its tremendous water-holding qualities. The next soil level is *subsoil,* a denser, often rock-strewn layer that acts as a reliable reservoir of moisture and as a stockpile of additional nutrients. Its depth is often measured in feet. Below this level may lie gravel, clay hardpan, pure sand, or even rocky ledge. How quickly and how deeply gravitational water drains through the upper two layers largely determines how far roots finally penetrate and endure. This soil water mostly equalizes at about 5 feet of depth.

Since soils are often unequal in their texture and nutrient content, they can be improved by both physical and chemical means. Mixing coarse sand with heavier clay soils can aerate the wet stickiness of the clay enough to improve drainage greatly, while adding animal manure, peat moss, compost, or leaf mold to sandy soil can upgrade its poor water-holding nature appreciably. Because soils of any type can be negatively altered in texture by weather conditions, always move either frozen or very muddy soil as little as possible.

Soils are either acidic or alkaline, and the degree of either greatly influences how well roots adapt after transplanting. Soil acidity is given more notice since the majority of the world's soils are of that balance, and its percentage is measured by testing soil samples for the *potential of hydrogen ions,* more commonly called *pH,* on a scale calibrated from 1 (extremely acid) to 14 (very alkaline) with 7 established as the *neutral balance* between the two. Most trees grow contentedly within a range of 4 to 7. Since the difference of one full point here means the soil is ten times as acid (or alkaline) as the next number on the scale, altering the condition is difficult to arrange easily. Yet there are ways.

Adjusting any reasonable imbalances in pH for growing plants can be handled by applying dry amounts of chemicals to the soil (in quantities that may prove astounding) and then disking or harrowing or hand-digging the materials. For changing acid conditions, apply ground limestone; for altering alkaline soils, use sulfur. Both materials are only *catalysts*—not fertilizers by any means—since they do not enter into any chemical reactions themselves but merely *arrange* for the reactions to take place. Because they are independent of providing nutrients and have their own peculiar natures, always spread and incorporate catalysts well in advance of fertilizer programs.

Spacing Trees

Although the method of properly spacing trees for any landscape development can become as variable as the number of people who plant trees, there are some guidelines to observe from the beginning in order to achieve the expected timetable of mature results. Both the ultimate size and the annual rate of growth obviously should have prime importance, yet these factors are modified somewhat by the purchase size and the length of the growing season where the tree is installed.

Any fast-growing tree deserves ample room from the start, regardless of its initial size, and any tree's response can be improved by attentive maintenance while it is becoming adjusted to the new surroundings. Naturally, site exposure, the normal moisture and nutrient content of the soil, and disease and insect afflictions have some effect on the speed with which trees perform their usual growth patterns. Evergreens are generally slower to mature than deciduous trees, especially when in close root competition with them, but any tree expresses some resentment to crowding by slowing its rate of growth. As always, a little foreknowledge about how plants behave can go a long way toward gaining all their landscape attributes without strain on their (or your) part.

43 Incorrect spacing of evergreens can eventually overwhelm a site.

For over 2500 years the methods of caring intelligently for trees have been recorded throughout the world by practitioners of this necessary art; and although the variations of technique have been constantly modified right to the present, the basic premise remains the same of first recognizing what a tree *naturally wants* in terms of its site exposure, soil conditions, water requirements, need for sunlight, and tolerance of cold. This natural adaptation of trees offers us remarkable information for how any might succeed if transplanted beyond the usual limits, and such specific and hard-won data have been the basis for centuries of planting experimentation that has revealed either great delight or grave disappointment about our handling of trees for landscape purposes. Once this background information is completely understood, its use can only lead to mutually satisfactory response for all concerned, especially the tree.

Caring for Existing Trees

Any site with trees on it has a visual appeal that barren surroundings can never hope to match. Since trees give us personal pleasure, they deserve more than slight attention for their preservation when development has to take place near them. Because there is always a financial involvement as well, the care and enhancement of existing trees should be thought of as *protecting the investment.*

Initial survey   An important initial step is to survey the grounds to determine the location, condition, and worth of the trees in relation to their removal or retention in the final design scheme for the property. All types of trees at this investigatory stage are worth the same since they coexist in natural harmony, and it is only after a thorough, on-site review of the plant materials by a landscape architect, arborist, or other skilled tree professional that a realistic appraisal can be made about their future value. Identification of the genus and species of all trees is best handled by recording them permanently on a topographic map that also plots their individual locations and sizes. (In dense woodlots of appreciable acreage, only trees with stem calibers of 4 to 6 inches and above can sensibly be fitted to the small scale of most maps and still be legible.) Such mapping, which ought to include contour elevations as well, becomes especially useful if extensive grading changes near trees are to occur on the site. After the survey is completed, certain trees will emerge as being more valuable than others by their size, uniqueness, location, character, and health. These should then have the highest priority for preservation, and the layout scheme should be modified to protect them as necessary.

Since the locations of existing trees are fixed but some trees are rarely positioned to avoid being sacrificed to the construction development, only a staking out of the intended roadway and building sites on the grounds can clearly show how much effect grade changes will have on trees intended to be salvaged. Disrupting even a small percentage of the roots can produce a decline in stem and leaf growth, and with older trees, any abrupt dismantling of the intricate balance between tree parts can have enduringly negative results that defeat the whole preservation effort. While young trees seem to tolerate change with greater ease, no disturbed tree, if treated casually, can fulfill its usual growth functions for the immediate future. As a living entity, each tree has demands that must be met, or it will sulk into decline.

Grading influences Probably earth grading has the most influence on the health of existing trees since both *cut* and *fill* operations, if carelessly handled, have important plant drawbacks. Excessive soil removal near the spread of a tree exposes the delicate feeder roots to additional air and sunlight they do not require, and cutting the support roots can seriously weaken the sturdiness of the plant in storms. Deep filling of earth around the trunk can quickly interrupt the lenticel breathing system of the stem and cause slow suffocation, while at the same time placing an extra burden on the roots for the normal oxygen and moisture exchange ratio with the surrounding soil. Trees such as beech are so immediately sensitive to any important grading changes that even the largest specimen can die within two years if disturbed by either large-scale filling or cutting within its root range.

44

Couple the action of grading with the unusually heavy equipment normally needed for accomplishing it and you can increase the tree's survival problems manyfold by adding compaction of the soil, the threat of accidental damage to the bark and its vital cambium layer, the funneled heat discharge into the foliage from the exhaust pipes, soil contamination by oil leaks, and limb breakage resulting from the size and handling of the equipment. Close supervision of all clearing operations should readily become a professional responsibility of the designer throughout the site work.

Protective fencing Protecting trees to be saved by erecting sturdy fencing around them is worth the cost during construction, but it is also important that this fencing be located properly. Ideally, such protective barriers ought to be set out at the drip line of the branches, but if this is impossible to arrange, then the fencing should be placed as far away from the trunk as it can be. Trees growing in close quarters to development alternatively might be well wrapped around their trunks with heavy burlap mats secured with rope or wire and further reinforced with regularly spaced wood slats on the outside of the blanket cover. Nothing, of course, should be nailed into the trunk or piled against it.

Soil cut procedures Existing trees in areas to be graded lower require hand labor—not mechanical equipment—for removing the soil from the root areas. At best, only a few inches of soil can safely be taken away from the feeder roots here, and unfortunately the nutrient-rich topsoil is being removed. While it is potentially feasible to induce these feeder roots to grow deeper by trenching in a circle at the branch drip line well before grading begins, this complex and time-consuming operation needs a full growing season to achieve any noticeable results. Most work schedules will not allow such a luxury of time, and wherever possible, it is wiser to rearrange the grading design and not skim off the topsoil around the trees.

Entirely removing major anchor roots by grading necessities on any side of the tree can upset the weight balance of the trunk enough that windstorms and ice storms can cause toppling, a dismal prospect for trees worth preserving. Digging trenches for underground utilities close to a trunk creates similar damage, too, but excavations through the smaller roots at the drip line are less harmful to tree health since the smaller roots at least have the capacity for speedier repair. Any severed main roots should be cleanly sawed off and then chemically painted to encourage quick healing. Open trenches through root zones also should be backfilled with earth as quickly as possible to forestall evaporation of soil mois-

44 This terrace tree soon died from an excess of filling against its trunk.

ture and dehydration of the root system. When such filling cannot be achieved readily, the exposed roots should be protected with wet burlap sheets.

Trees used for street decoration are often plagued with constant root interruptions from the laying of repair or utility lines, and they frequently show their displeasure at these intrusions by insipid growth, an understandable response to being frequently hacked apart underground. A wise designer avoids this conflict by never deliberately mixing the two at close quarters.

While not a wholly endorsed procedure, removal of a portion of the top growth to compensate for losing some roots to trenching or other construction is often recommended to maintain the normal balance of roots to stems and leaves. Thinning out of secondary, minor branches is the place to begin, while still maintaining a natural silhouette, but the work must be done in an appropriate season to avoid excessive sap flow from the cuts. Stem reduction is far simpler to achieve with deciduous trees than evergreens since different foliage densities need to be maintained. Evergreens are really not cooperative candidates for root invasions or compensating branch removals.

Soil fill procedures   Filling against the trunk of a tree is detrimental both from the closing off of the breathing pores along the stem (plus the likely rotting of the bark below grade) and from the greatly increased density of soil cover over the feeding roots. These important surface roots are located when they are by necessity and function, and to place them suddenly far deeper than nature intended can upset the oxygen-water relationship of the soil severely enough to cause suffocation of many roots. Any earth used for such filling near trees should be very limited in depth and should also be porous, light in composition, and rich in humus. Anything less will prove harmful in the long run.

Some professionals are known to advise publicly that fill of several feet at the trunks of trees will do no serious harm, but it is my belief that this is wishful thinking and that only certain tropical palms can tolerate such abnormalities with aplomb. Other trees will surely decline to become eventually worthless as the tonnage of such gross filling smothers the struggling roots. Even adding the well-intentioned technique of mechanical aeration by ventilating pipes through the soil cannot fully compensate for such basic plant mismanagement, and its use illustrates a simplistic understanding of how trees grow at their best. Drastic as it may seem, complete removal of the tree is no worse than forcing it to a slow death.

A useful construction device to keep soil fill intelligently away from a trunk is the masonry wall that creates a wide, open well around the plant while supporting the new grading. It is important, of course, to keep this construction out of the main support roots, but if this is impossible to achieve, then bridging over the roots with the wall is more advisable than severing them for convenience. Because accumulated rainfall in a totally enclosed well is often harmful to the roots, a three-quarter enclosure allows quicker water drainage. Full-circle tree wells can also become collectors of odd debris troublesome to remove and often turn into compost heaps of sodden leaves in quantities not always favorable to tree growth. To be effective, a tree well should be kept clean to ground level at all times.

Site modifications   Trees are often forced to make an unusual adjustment in their growth response when paving is brought right up to the trunks by sidewalk and parking lot construction. Not only do reflected heat and light, plus automobile pollution, become more concentrated beneath the tree, but natural rainfall is greatly curtailed from reaching the roots. Any hope that a tree will survive in good health under these circumstances is rarely based on a sound understanding of plant needs.

Nevertheless, satisfactory future growth can be encouraged from existing trees, at least those which are not overly abused, by fertilizing annually and by removing any dead or diseased wood. Spray programs for insect pests and diseases should be added as these problems become important to tree health, while clearing out unneeded volunteer seedlings aids in maintaining the display merits of specimen trees and reduces the need for supplemental watering during extreme dry spells.

Woodlot trees that once provided bark shading to one another can suffer *sunscald damage* when suddenly exposed to greater wind and light intensity by site-clearing operations. Shaded trunks often develop slightly thinner bark than isolated trees in full sun and cannot adjust rapidly enough here to forestall some dehydration of the stems and some leaf scorch (especially noticeable with evergreens) as the bulldozer removes its former neighbors. There is, unfortunately, little help any of us can offer to alleviate these distress signals except to hope for rapid adjustment with a minimum loss to the tree's silhouette. Violent storm damage in forests throughout the world creates the same stress conditions for the still-standing trees, and even in nature not all living plants make successful adjustments.

Grading operations often modify the surface drainage flow to pocket water around trees at depths they cannot long endure. Such change is especially harmful in already low-lying areas and more so if the soil drains sluggishly. Any increase in the volume of water standing around tree trunks soon changes the oxygen content of the soil and promotes slow disintegration of the roots. Deep grading cuts near trees have the reverse effect by opening channels that drain away soil moisture too rapidly, and here the roots suffer dehydration and an eventual decline.

Tall, isolated trees with high sap content are often attractors of electric energy during storms and are frequently struck by lightning bolts. Protection of choice specimens requires adding wire cables—lightning rods—from the crown down the trunk into the ground. As the stems expand upward, these rods must also be regularly extended if they are to do much good.

Selecting and Transplanting Trees

Trees chosen for site development additions usually come from commercial nursery grounds because planned cultivation allows greater selection and buyer convenience, plus some stated guarantee of performance by the nursery. Such plants will already have had root pruning, fertilizing, cultivation, irrigation, spraying, and some shaping—all meant to produce compact rooting, uniform growth, and better health than material collected in the wild state.

Inspection of major nursery stock choices by the designer before they are dug should become an expected procedure in order to avoid delivery of trees with scarred bark, weak stem crotches, lopsided silhouettes, abnormal growth habits, or noticeable disease afflictions. The important selection of *specimen* material—those scarce plants with unusually desirable growth characteristics or great size—certainly deserves personal attention.

Plate 1 Mainly evergreen and continually colorful, the *Arbutus* clearly shows its flower relationship to the blueberry.

Plate 2   The noticeable
leaf bracts of *Cornus
florida rubra* vary
naturally from
pale pink to rose.

Carola Gregor

Plate 3   Attractively scented,
the sizeable blossoms
of *Magnolia soulangiana*
cultivars create showy
springtime displays.

Morris Arboretum

Plate 4 This prolific flowering
from *Malus* reasonably
guarantees an abundance
of long-lasting fruit
in autumn.

Philip Keenan

Plate 5 Handsomely placed,
this avenue of *Betula pendula*
is stimulating to see
in any season.

Grant Heilman

Plate 6 Spectacular effects
are consistent hallmarks
of spring from
the double-flowered
Oriental cherries.
Ralph Gates

Plate 7 Readily adaptable
to container growing,
the *Podocarpus
macrophylla maki* offers
sedate companionship
for contemporary
settings.
Guy Burgess

Digging operations   The majority of nursery-grown trees are handled *balled and burlapped;* that is, the roots will be dug with a full ball of earth around them and be wrapped with either burlap cloth or plastic sheeting that is tied with rope or pinned with balling nails for delivery to the job site. Young sapling trees can safely be handled *bare-rooted* when fully dormant or *containerized* when in leaf. Very large tree balls may also require sturdy wooden platforms—or even full crating—for safe handling and transport.

Having the correct width and depth of a ball is important for gaining a maximum number of feeder roots. Landscape industry standards have long been established by the *American Association of Nurserymen,* to which the major percentage of nurseries in the United States belong and contribute information about plants. They distribute up-to-date periodicals providing sensible guidelines for this critical digging operation since they know skimpy balls leave too many roots in the ground and fail to encourage rapid readjustment. Trees dug with loose balls also are suspect because they indicate that earth is not clinging adequately to the roots and that air is reaching them to cause dehydration. All dug plants, of course, should be well watered regularly while out of the ground and should be placed away from extreme wind and sun. Some nurseries even use a *constant-mist,* overhead watering system to curtail undue evaporation from foliaged trees awaiting transfer to the new planting site. This is called *hardening off* of the plant.

Transport to the site   Handling a very large tree usually requires a truck with a heavy-duty winch for both collecting the material at the nursery and depositing the tree conveniently at the site. Skids and rollers are also useful transfer tools. Smaller trees are generally lifted by a hydraulic tailgate elevator attached to the rear of the truck body. Under no circumstances should a balled plant be tossed from a truck to land unassisted since this will crack the ball. While in transit, all plants should be covered with canvas or other wind-protective shielding to avoid dehydration.

Using collected trees   Another method of finding trees for a site is to search out and collect them from the wild, but while this may appear to offer sizable cost savings initially, the drawbacks of using *collected material* cannot be easily overlooked. In the first place, the major roots of wild trees have probably meandered all over in search of water and nutrients. While young saplings can be transplanted relatively simply because all their roots are usually within a short distance of the stem, any large-caliber tree may not prove so cooperative. Also, woodlot trees often develop irregular root arrangements to avoid underground obstructions such as other tree roots, boulders, rock ledge, and hardpan soil. To dig such trees without spending time on prior root pruning can quickly lead to disappointment in their behavior now and later, and under no circumstance should living trees be scooped up with the bucket of a bulldozer for planting purposes.

Preparing wild trees for transplanting involves encircling the intended root ball with a deep trench, roughly 18 to 24 inches deep and wide as a minimum, and then backfilling with a prepared mix of topsoil and peat moss, compost, rotted manure, or leaf mold. The intention is to encourage rapid and dense fibrous rooting in this trench for safer and easier transplanting later, but the technique often requires at least a full year to accomplish and even then offers no assurance that *beneath* the trunk some large rock or sand deposit may not still present problems for digging an adequate ball. Collected trees present risks all the way,

Plate 8   Vibrant bark and generous distribution in northern woodlots give *Betula papyrifera* well-deserved marks for landscape value.

Ouy Burgess

and contractors should not be freely allowed to utilize them, especially since none ever comes with a guarantee of future performance.

Occasionally, trees are also available for sale from private grounds, and since these already have had some root pruning just to reach their present site, they offer less risk than trees taken from the wild. Transplanting costs here may become higher than for nursery stock because access to the tree is very often restricted entirely to hand labor in moving it off the old site.

Transplanting timetables   When, precisely, any tree should be moved is still hotly disputed and probably never will be resolved to everyone's satisfaction. The time of year, the age, condition, and location of the plant, the weather at the time of transplanting, the type of plant (deciduous or evergreen), and the anticipated aftercare maintenance all influence the success of the operation. What remains constant is that some plants favor one season over another for making quick root adjustments after being moved.

Unfortunately, common knowledge about plant preferences varies sufficiently throughout the zones of hardiness to be incohesive for generalization, so that local rules and methods for transplanting should be learned and understood. What is considered standard procedure in a cold area is not necessarily useful in more southerly locations for the same-named plant. Since the livelihood of both nurseries and landscape contractors depends on their successful handling of local planting operations, relying on their judgment and experience cannot be far from the best advice.

Too often clients insist that tree planting be done when conditions are unfavorable to success. It should be the responsibility of the designer to evaluate and redirect such mistaken programs, especially where constant visual annoyance from shabby appearance and weak-looking growth will benefit no one. As a rule, reputable nurseries and contractors will refuse to accept such out-of-season planting commissions, and they should be applauded for their wisdom.

Trees are best dug and handled when they are fully dormant since then there is no soft, new growth to damage and their immediate water demands are lessened. Early spring weather conditions are often troublesome, however, because of gooey mud and suddenly high temperatures, at both the nursery and the job site. Autumn planting schedules, though, can be thwarted by early freezing of the ground or even deep snowfalls. Fortunately, most needle evergreens allow easy transplanting by the end of summer (or whenever they locally become autumn-dormant). Broadleaf evergreens, on the other hand, often suffer foliage damage from drying winds and cold when transplanted late in the year. In general, deciduous trees can usually be moved in either spring or autumn, and their leafless winter condition presents far fewer problems from weather damage.

Protective coatings   Those thin wax coatings mechanically sprayed on leaves to prevent excess dehydration from winter cold are called *antidesiccants* and are valuable aids in helping autumn-planted, broadleaf evergreens protect themselves from injury. They should be used with caution, however, since heavy coatings can clog the breathing pores of leaves and stems. Normal plant flexing and weathering action usually dislodges the wax by early spring. These foliage-protecting agents are also used widely on deciduous material transplanted during the heat of summer for the same water-loss reduction purposes, but here they have an occasionally odd side effect of gluing leaves to the stems far longer than normal; and so when the annual leaf drop arrives, such trees are often still verdant. The first heavy snowfall usually knocks them free of foliage in a rush.

Preparing the planting hole   The planting *hole,* or *pit,* for a new tree should be dug and prepared well before the arrival of the plant. The excavation should be made at least 1 foot wider than the tree ball diameter, and the excavated material should be placed so that all topsoil is reserved conveniently for reuse as *backfill.* All subsoil should either be discarded or disposed elsewhere on the site. The bottom of the hole need be only 6 inches deeper than the ball since the feeder roots are always well above this depth. Bare-rooted trees should have planting pits with the same dimensions.

Extraneous material uncovered in the digging, such as the various types of construction debris, large rocks, clay hardpan, and dead tree roots or branches, should be removed and discarded as restrictive to normal root growth. When rock ledge or immovable boulders become importantly evident in the pit excavation, the location of the tree should be moved. Once the pit is dug, the drainage should be checked by adding water to a depth of several inches and then verifying the time required for complete removal below the bottom of the pit. Extremely sluggish drainage has to be considered enough of a high risk for the tree's immediate health that the pit should be abandoned. On the other hand, tree holes with very rapid drainage can be adjusted by excavating the pit somewhat deeper and adding water-holding, natural materials such as peat moss, compost, well-rotted manure, or leaf mold. What matters here is that water around the tree ball be made available for use without causing growth problems.

Before depositing the tree in the hole, spread at least a 6-inch cushion of conditioned topsoil (a mix, by volume, of topsoil and some humus-producing material—but no fertilizer) evenly over the bottom of the pit. Frozen or very muddy soil should never be used for fill. Allow for some slight settlement from the weight of the tree ball by raising the center portion of this topsoil fill slightly higher than the rest of the bottom soil layer. The hole is now ready to accept the new tree.

Installing the tree   Set the tree so that it will have a finish grade identical with its original condition and so that its main trunk will be straight or at least perpendicular to the eye. Add some backfill to make sure the ball doesn't move out of plumb and then cut back the top—not the support sides—of the ball covering and discard it away from the hole. Now complete the backfilling with more conditioned topsoil in 6-inch layers either tamped carefully with a log or else puddled with hose water to remove any detrimental air pockets, since roots want close contact only with moist earth. Finish the operation by creating an earthen collar several inches high and deep around the dimensions of the pit to concentrate water directly into the root ball; then soak the roots thoroughly. (Slope plantings especially benefit from having these water saucers.) If the tree now settles too low or becomes out of plumb, immediately reset it correctly, or else it will continue that way and prove a future disappointment.

Trunk wrapping   At this juncture in the work, many designers recommend wrapping the exposed trunk with heavy paper or burlap to reduce stem evaporation during the lengthy period of root adjustment. Because such covering is not only unsightly but becomes progressively shabby-looking, and because this dense shield often creates moist, soft bark and an excellent hiding place for insects and their activities, it is not a recommended process here. Trees have been transplanted successfully for generations without this awkward treatment, and in over twenty-five years of professional practice I have never found it worth the effort to use it.

Guying and staking   Most newly planted trees require support by either *guying* or *staking* to hold them erect and firmly in place during high winds. When the crown of a transplanted tree vibrates from air movement through it, the as-yet unanchored root ball can easily separate from the backfill enough to allow damaging sleeves of air to enter the root zone. *Guying* involves setting either three or four evenly spaced lengths of double-strand, galvanized (zinc-coated) wire into rubber or plastic hose lengths, which are then slipped around the trunk as shields and fastened about 6 feet from ground level, usually just above the first branch junction. The loose ends are then attached securely to either wooden or metal peg stakes driven into the ground beyond the pit excavation to form a 45-degree angle with the trunk. For very large-caliber trees, use buried logs, called "dead men," laid horizontally with the finish grade instead of surface staking. For trees installed in an aboveground planter box or tub, anchor the guy wires to eye hooks drilled inside or into the rim of the container. In order to tighten these guy wires when they go slack, insert turnbuckles into the middle of the span and arrange for frequent inspection of guy-wire tautness during the year these supports are usually left in place. With trees installed at ground level in public spaces, add brightly colored warnings flags of plastic or wood to avoid collisions with the nearly invisible wires.

Tree guards   In many urban situations, metal tree guards are usually added to protect the trunk from vandalism, animal urine, and accidental abrasions from trucks or snowplows. They must be designed, however, to allow for many years of trunk expansion, or else they can do more harm than good if the tree matures and rubs against this nonexpansive metal cage. A recent handicap in their use comes from the unneeded film of paint left on the trunk from spray-painting maintenance work—more common now than the preferred hand painting—that fails to include a temporary bark shield.

Trees in containers   Planters, tubs, boxes, or pots for plants artificially isolate the roots from natural contact with earth and pose the continuing dilemma of making these plants largely dependent on humans to survive. No containerized plant flourishes as it would in nature, and all such material must eventually be replaced even with the finest maintenance. Trees installed in planters require more regular attention because the soil ages and dries out more quickly, the roots eventually exhaust the size limits of the container and may often turn to girdling themselves harmfully, the humus and nutrient content of the soil continually diminishes, while the increasingly matted development of the root ball excludes any generous reserve of soil water and also increases their demand for supplemental watering. In brief, a well-grown containerized plant often outdistances its "home grounds" in a briefer time than we prefer. Once a tree reaches this situation, it can only decline in performance and then needs a larger container.

Because elevated containers have continually exposed sides, the roots are also brought into more contact with cold and drying winds as well as increased dehydration from the heat-absorbing pavements on which they rest. The necessary drainage holes in the bottom of the pot also contribute to water loss. Reflected light and heat from nearby buildings and roadways, while often useful in modifying winter's harshness, can prove detrimental, too, by summer as they increase the transpiration of water vapor out of the tree by the general aridness. Evergreen trees especially suffer from these overheated conditions during summer and also dislike the accompanying stagnancy of the air. In many ways, deciduous trees in planters are a wiser choice for urban locations.

Pruning adjustments   Pruning of trees should always be delayed until the installation is well underway—or even completed—since damage to the plants can occur in all the handling stages. One curious and well-promoted system of encouraging adjustment for a tree is to compensate for the loss of some roots in transplanting by both thinning out and limbing back the main branch structure. The concept is to help the tree recover more quickly by reasonably balancing the roots with the top growth, but the treatment is far from attractive and has no fully verified justification. While there can be no question that weak or damaged stems should be taken away as a matter of course, reducing the tree to a "hat rack" of stiff branches should not be recognized as the only sensible way of managing successful new growth. Careful handling and thoughtful maintenance are just as productive.

Understandably, the new leaves and stems are likely to be smaller and thinner than normal from one season to another, but simply observation of recovery rates with transplanted trees shows that an overwhelming percentage manage to become adjusted by the second season without any need for pruning abnormalities. Adequate and faithful watering can probably do as much good for a tree's recovery as any hacking away of its branches. Excessive pruning of evergreens is known to be erroneous, so why are deciduous trees so frequently subjected to the oddity of being trimmed unnaturally? They need not be.

After-Planting Maintenance

Once a tree is satisfactorily growing in its new location (usually about a year after installation), remove the guy wires or support stakes completely. Never leave any part of the wire collar in place around the trunk since normal caliber expansion will soon engulf it and cause permanent constriction to the internal plumbing. By now the earthen water saucer can be removed, too, and the mulch refreshed with more material to retain about a 3-inch depth. Deep watering should continue, of course, if drought occurs.

Fertilizing   Regular fertilizer programs should be arranged after the first year to stimulate the fullest root growth—now that the severed roots are well along in repair and can accept fertilizer treatments without damage—but how long they should be maintained is still a moot question. Any vigorous, healthy tree is not a likely candidate for any additional growth improvement, but an average-looking tree is. Sickly plants, on the other hand, rarely benefit from overstimulation by concentrated fertilizing—their problems usually rest elsewhere—although *liquid* feeding compounds, when used during the growing season with discretion, have a commendable record of helping ailing trees. Dry, granular fertilizers should be the mainstay of tree-feeding programs, and local experience will dictate whether early spring or late autumn timing is better. These annual applications usually involve drilling or digging small holes in a series of concentric circles beneath the main spread of the branches and then filling the excavations with the fertilizer compound. Convenient cylinders of prepared tree food are currently available which eliminate handling loose fertilizer for this operation.

Insect and disease control   Insect pests and plant disease (which are minute plant life attacking other, larger plants) are a normal part of every environment; and while there is supposedly a natural predator or antidote for all these ailments, none seems to arrive on any schedule convenient for our purposes. Drastic leaf defoliation or disease disfigurement of any tree is a severe shock to its current health and future growth, besides becoming a visual disappointment in the landscape, and timely applications of protective sprays are worth both the cost and the time. No tree is known to have died simply of old age, but many millions have died because of marauding insects and fungal infections. As you might expect, maintaining vigorous, normal health is the key to all planting success, but when problems arise, treat them quickly and thoroughly with proved chemical remedies. As with other health aids, always follow the manufacturer's or distributor's instructions explicitly. All are poisonous to some degree for humankind, and some even have the annoying side effect of staining or disfiguring painted or porous construction materials.

A wise consideration about tree selection is to choose only those with minimum attractions locally for either pests or diseases, but neglected plants, even those with the highest credentials, are always prone to more problems than well-maintained ones. This detail of plant health is emphasized in the tree listings of this book and also accounts for some of the eliminations made in compiling it.

Corrective pruning techniques   Pruning damaged or dead wood as soon as it is discovered is wise practice. Any breaks in the bark lead to hidden internal decay, and the prompt removal of diseased, broken, cracked, rubbing, or dead limbs allows the tree to heal more quickly and safely. Prune also to increase light penetration and air circulation through the crown, to control unwanted growth habits, to forestall interference with other plants and overhead utility lines, and to reshape—but not butcher—for personal aims. In all pruning, maintain the natural shape and habit as much as possible. Creating the special shapes of *topiary,* while visually intriguing, leads to a maintenance nightmare that, once begun, can rarely be abandoned easily, and their upkeep is a luxury few can afford on any grand scale.

In all pruning, always make only flush cuts against the trunk or main branches and never leave unsightly stub ends that can bring decay or insects into the heartwood of the tree. Cambium repair cells cannot grow over these unwanted projections until they rot away, and then the repair unfortunately seals the damage from view. Trimming small twigs can be managed with well-honed hand clippers; but, again, prune only with a smooth cut at a junction of the branching. Large limb removal requires sawing with either a sharp, specially toothed pruning saw or a powered chain saw. Using a carpenter's fine-toothed saw is both tiring and inefficient since the small teeth quickly become clogged with sawdust and sap.

The preferred technique for branch removal is first to *undercut* the limb about 1 foot from the main stem to a depth of several inches; then make a top incision another foot or so outward from the undercut, so that the weight of the falling branch will force the limb to crack cleanly at the undercut and not rip into the adjacent bark, creating unnecessary injury. Finish by severing the branch stub flush with the main stem and painting the open wound with an asphalt-based tree

45

46

45   A flush cut on this amur cork tree *(Phellodendron amurense)* trunk shows repair cells at work covering the open wound.

46   "Decandling" the new growth on pine for more compact growth.

paint. Some recent studies, however, now suggest that such painting is more cosmetic than healing and may actually inhibit the cambium repairs, but this scientific evidence has yet to gain international acceptance for all trees. Oddly enough, needle evergreens produce an antiseptic, natural repair covering on their own from their resin sap, making any painting superfluous since it will only flake or float off in a short time.

Watering   Newly planted trees benefit from deep watering at all times of prolonged dryness during the growing season to encourage continual root repair, but consistent saturation of the soil can quickly lead to occasional root rot, notably with trees having limited fibrous rooting systems. In planting areas remote from hydrant water, plan for pumped irrigation from tank trucks on a regular basis until adequate rainfall resumes. In both drought situations always keep in mind that other nearby plants are also thirsty and will likely intrude their own root needs into the program, and then more frequent watering may be necessary.

At the beginning of the autumn dormancy period, transplanted trees, especially evergreens, seem to enjoy generous and regular irrigation, whether it comes from the sky or the end of a hose, to prepare them adequately for the rigors of winter. Throughout the growing season all containerized trees need watchful attention about watering since they are always isolated from finding additional moisture as their ground-installed brethren can. Maintenance is an ongoing requirement for landscapes with distinction.

Landscape design is a visual fine art with a long and distinguished history in human affairs. It all began when people deliberately planted trees in cultivated spaces for use and enjoyment, and these condensed statements about it are intended to be no more than a generalized guide. The continuing use of these basic principles for creating attractive outdoor surroundings is constantly undergoing modification.

Design of any sort is a problem-solving *process* which serves functional needs, creates meaningful forms, and conserves economic means. Landscape design differs from all other art forms in its broadened scope, its unique materials, and in the effect of time on its components. It is the least static art because it involves plant growth, and it is the only profession largely concerned with *living* elements and their skillful placement on the land. All landscape designers are unusually restricted since only *existing* plant colors, textures, and shapes are available for the work. New plant materials cannot be ordered or created simply on demand.

Because landscape design is primarily involved with the creation of *usable* outdoor space, it often incorporates both planting and architectural devices to define and explain the intended use and function of the layout. It is also very concerned with the effects of light and of the third-dimensional volume of space. While *horticulture* is growing plants well, planting *design* means arranging them well. Combining both attractively and enduringly is the sought-after formula for a memorable landscape setting. Since trees are the largest plant type, their use on a site often establishes the major emphasis and visual influence of the space for public use and appreciation.

Trees are a valuable tool for the harmonious and practical resolution of many physical site problems along with, of course, the client's aesthetic satisfaction. They offer the noticeable, large-scale effects of screening, cooling, privacy, enhancement of architectural lines, enframement of views, erosion management, sun and wind control, sound deadening, horticultural focus and emphasis, and potentially reduced maintenance costs. They further contribute *sensory* attractions during the year by individual or blended colors, fragrances, moving shadow patterns, seasonal foliage and fruiting changes, and stimulating silhouettes and textures. The generous variety of tree types in most growing areas allows for a wide range of designer interpretations of their special qualities.

Because trees are often used as a canopy of foliage, they can define upper space by their leafy enclosure and become a "ceiling" outdoors. When planted to define boundaries, trees act as "walls." They can assume dramatic emphasis as specimens standing majestically alone or as complements to architecture, and if massed, they can become background foils for other landscape elements. Both the branching and the foliage textures can provide fine, coarse, or intermediate accents, while the *character* of an individual tree—the sum of all its inherent mannerisms of yearly growth coupled with the variable site influences shaping its mature appearance—can produce an emotional response ranging from ruggedness to delicacy, from flamboyance to somberness, and from wistfulness to stately elegance. Trees have conveyed mood and symbolism to human existence since the dawn of time.

The natural silhouette *forms* of trees are usually arranged along these lines of description: columnar to fastigiate, conical to pyramidal, round to oval, vase-

47 Evergreen specimens offer privacy screening and become effective sound barriers.

shaped to inverted pyramid, dense to open-headed, pendulous to weeping, and irregular to distorted. By selective and patient pruning, any tree can be modified into an artificial or *topiary* shape to suit special landscape purposes, such as *espaliering* for flat wall display, *pleaching* by intertwining top branches into a thick canopy as an archway over a walk, or *pollarding* by severe architectural shaping of those branches close to the trunk for a dense, third-dimensional form. All these pruning techniques are expensive in time and skilled effort, are needed on an annual basis, and fit only a limited number of landscape settings well. They are hardly wise pursuits for the novice.

Since a tree is an elastic design element of potentially great size, the designer has to recognize and define from the start what will be the ultimate contribution of trees in the development. A thorough analysis of the intended *use* of the space, the established *proportions* of the total area under development, and the *form* of the design scheme influences the site enrichment potential of trees both now and in the future. Of course, careful site analysis has to evaluate what existing items are to remain on the site as well as what influence neighboring uses, exposure, soil conditions, air movement, utility lines, and human concentrations will have on plant growth. Only by clarifying and utilizing all these background data can the designer or client hope to achieve the finest results. Both need a keen sensitivity to the site conditions and to plant material, but unfortunately not everyone is born with it. When in doubt, hire a specialist for professional guidance.

Planting compositions have principles of *order:* repetition, sequence, and balance. *Repetition* is the most fundamental and is achieved easily by duplicating ad infinitum any of the the following: color, shape, texture, size, position, or quantity. For increased visual harmony, however, repetition must be accompanied by both sequence and balance since the overuse of repetition soon brings monotony and a dulling of anyone's interest and appreciation. While *variety* is at least a relief from monotony, it is not a principle of order but merely a welcomed gratification of the mind to what is seen. Introducing variety often leads quickly to excess and then to a lack of specific focus that degenerates into visual chaos. Variety may be the spice of life, but it was never intended to become the meal.

50

48

49

51

52

55

53

56

54

48 The narrowly erect form of a columnar sugar maple *(Acer saccharum monumentale)*.

49 A weeping Norway spruce *(Picea abies pendula)* is often irregular in outline.

50 The conical outline of the dwarf hinoki cypress *(Chamaecyparis obtusa nana)*.

51 The oval silhouette of a European hornbeam cultivar *(Carpinus betulus 'Columnaris')*.

52 A contrast between the open-headed Japanese pagoda tree *(Sophora japonica)* on the right and its compact weeping form nearby *(Sophora japonica pendula)*.

53 An espaliered southern magnolia *(Magnolia grandiflora)*.

54 A pleached allee of American beech *(Fagus grandifolia)*.

55 The inverted-pyramid shape of the autumn-flowering higan cherry *(Prunus subhirtella autumnalis)*.

56 The slender, pendulous branching of a weeping willow *(Salix)*.

Sequence is arranging the diverse attributes of plant material to lead the eye easily and comfortably in one main direction. It involves a *progressive change* of at least one plant characteristic, perhaps shape or color or size, in all partners of the series. Subtly arranging a transformation of foliage from coarse to fine is one example of sequence, and when well-handled, the interconnected rhythm of the planning can elevate even a mundane setting to a memorable experience. Here, variety is not only deliberately used but also deliberately controlled.

Because we are more accustomed to recognizing and accepting objects that have equally distributed parts on a vertical axis, we refer to this visual satisfaction as *balance,* and there are two main types. When both sides of an axis are identical, or mirror images of each other, they are in *symmetry,* a design formula long distinguished by its ever-popular use for thousands of years in landscape developments. It often shows a crisply architectural influence and is frequently known as "formal" design. Its opposite is *asymmetry,* or *occult* balance, and is popularly called "informal." Either type can be visually agreeable as long as each suits the total landscape concept. Throughout history the fads and fancies of landscape design have waxed or waned between these two types of presentations, and our contemporary design resolutions in architecture and engineering today appear to favor the informal approach. The *style* of a design, which is nothing more than a fixed combination of materials and the arranged form given them in any historical period, is often identified with a known personality, such as the *Victorian* with Queen Victoria of England. When influential enough, the expressions of one artistic discipline eventually emerge in all the others, as painting often influences sculpture and even architecture.

All design elements in a landscape have characteristics of *size* and relative *scale.* As you might imagine, living plants create some bothersome problems here since they are constantly expanding in size and may become disproportionate with their surroundings if they are not selected with adequate knowledge about their natural habits. People are the scale by which all things are measured, and the phrase *out of scale* refers to our own expectations of how compared items visually relate to one another and whether the comparison is acceptable. In

57

58

57 Portugal laurel *(Prunus lusitanica) readily adapts to tight shearing or pollarding.*

58 A well-designed sequence of needle evergreen foliages.

far too many home landscape efforts, unwise tree selections have led to either a jungle of overwhelming growth or shapes mangled by constant and abnormal pruning. Proper plant judgment here could have reduced the effort and enhanced the effect of plant growth.

Distance and *perspective* alter the outline and true shape of all objects. The uncountable, fine leaves of a hemlock, for example, disappear completely from our attention when viewed from far away, so that only the conical silhouette and feathery outline offer clues to its identity. Close-at-hand planting, alternatively, reveals all the intricacies of growth but little of the total outline, and this relationship of placement provides a useful way of enlarging or diminishing outdoor space. Fine-textured trees at a distance will seem optically farther away than they are physically, while nearby coarse-textured plants will appear even closer. This effect is also evident with colors, where "cool" ones such as blue and purple recede from us while the "hot" colors like orange and red seem to advance.

Design *values* are several: proportion, emphasis, accent, and unity. *Proportion* in outdoor design is the distribution percentage of any element and soon dictates how many shapes, colors, sizes, textures, or positions can be comfortably acknowledged before clutter sets in. *Emphasis* is uniqueness and is created by a noticeable contrast between two objects or characteristics of those objects. It should be used sparingly since we all tire easily from constant visual stimulation, especially on a dramatic basis. *Accent* is a collection of low-keyed, *secondary* objects arranged into a flowing procession toward a main focus; it has a relationship with *sequence*. *Unity* is the successful harmonizing of all elements in a design toward a commonly understood statement of purpose. It is the one landscape value prized most by every designer since it illustrates true skill in landscape artistry. Such an end result should be so appealingly organized that the resolution becomes the only possible choice for the situation. Such genius is unevenly distributed in the world.

Because flowering on woody plants lasts only a few weeks at best, having trees with a dual seasonal appeal becomes invaluable for most planting designs. Summer foliage variations, attractive and persistent fruiting, autumnal leaf

59

59 Distance alters leaf size to show only the silhouette of evergreen trees.

changes, and noticeable wintertime bark all add welcome visual stimulation beyond the blooming time. Contrasting deciduous tree silhouettes against an evergreen backdrop add yet another worthwhile effect throughout the year.

Although evergreen plants have rightly been labeled the aristocrats of the landscape scene, designs filled exclusively with them tend in time to become gloomy, dull, and perhaps overpowering. Groupings of all deciduous trees, on the other hand, often appear sparse, leggy, or fuzzy-outlined during winter defoliation. An agreeable mix of the two usually provides the most satisfactory appeal, especially where the interplay of texture and color is both noticeable and noteworthy.

Color in the landscape can make the difference between calmness and excitement since color is a *motivating* element in personal response. Take away all color by reducing light to pitch blackness, or by adding intense brightness that completely dazzles the eye, and you will become disoriented. Color is naturally associated with light, and all objects reflect light to some degree by their structure and color pigments. With trees, the size and quantity of the leaf, stem, flower, and fruit surfaces dictate how much light we receive and therefore what color we perceive. Minute blossoms or tiny foliage need to be massed together to be fully appreciated, especially at a distance.

We can alter the quality of color in natural light by changing the *intensity* of the source (such as filtering sunlight with foliage), by changing the type of *surface* catching the light (glossy foliage is reflective while hairy leaves are light-absorbing), and by a *contrast* of colorings (white flowers intermixed with dark-toned ones enliven them). The time of day also influences color intensity, where morning light adds a yellowish overtone, the white brilliance of noontime sun dilutes all but the most intense color values, and sunset hours bring a reddish or purplish cast to the scene.

The nearness of similar color values creates "richness" in landscape effects, and monochromatic schemes tend to unite diverse areas in a simple but effective way. The usually consistent foliage of street trees is a good example of how one

60

60 An attractive balance of deciduous and evergreen tree shapes.

color can provide a unifying bonus of visual appeal. Of course, the dominant color of plant material is green, but which green? In spring the emerging foliage of both evergreen and deciduous trees is thin-walled and filmy with a fresh, yellow-green coloring. By summer the leaves thicken and become both opaque and deep-toned. Aging further modifies the color and reduces the sheen of the foliage. Every season offers some variation in the color a plant is said to be.

Intriguing color combinations in the landscape can be readily created from using the *harmony of triads.* These are three related colors assembled in proportions guided by personal preferences, the site conditions, and client reactions. A reasonable division is to pair two for emphasis and retain the last as a dash of accent. Beginning with the primary colors of red, yellow, and blue, consider using their tones of russet, citrus, and slate; with the secondary colors of purple, orange, and green, evaluate plum, buff, and sage as cooperative blendings. White usually works well to separate intense colorings, while gray-toned plants are an attractive foil for increasing the clarity and intensity of other colors.

With all its potentialities, planting design will always offer a paradox: seeing a plant as an individual while finding ways to incorporate its assets into a larger picture. There can be no totally fixed set of rules for using trees in the landscape— only options for your experiments with them.

While all trees have some purposeful, natural use, not all have distinguished landscape value. Since the quantity of known trees in the temperate parts of the world is calculated in many thousands, some deliberate—and personal—reduction of this vast array to manageable size had to be made for this book. Certain eliminations came about because the plants were noticeably inferior to their neighbors in some important ornamental quality, were grown mainly for their commercial fruit crop, were consistently shrubby in their nature, were prone to be scarce in cultivation, or were just too challenging to grow well without constant attention.

The several hundred trees that remained for inclusion ought to supply enough choices, nevertheless, to satisfy all the known purposes for using trees in our landscapes, especially since the additional *varieties*—those distinct novelties of a species found growing wild in nature and which come true when grown from seed—and the even more extensive listing of current nursery *cultivars*—those horticultural selections which are *cultivated variants* of the parent plant and which are reproduced only from cuttings—further expand the possible tree options to remarkably generous proportions. Without a doubt, even a reduced list such as this can provide an attractive tree for every planting need in the zones of hardiness from 2 to 10.

This portion of the book is in three divisions logically based on the major leaf types (both simple and compound) of *deciduous, needle evergreen,* and *broad-leaf evergreen.* Regretfully, space restrictions and the very limited warm areas where they thrive eliminated having the palms and the tall succulents as part of these data.

Each division is alphabetically arranged by the currently acceptable scientific name as published in the new *Hortus Third.* If the name has had a recent change, then the older name appears in brackets beside it. Each entry carries the most usual common naming as well (and you will notice that botanic authority now recommends using a minimum of capitalization for these names), along with the expected range of its hardiness limits, the average height in cultivation and its potential height in the wild, plus the family to which each tree belongs, an association not always plainly evident between plant relatives in either foliage or plant size but always present in the type of flowers and the later fruit development.

Those plant categories with many species are given as enlarged, introductory statement when the genus first appears to avoid needless repetition of the same data for each entry; nevertheless, all entries carry an individual paragraph about the landscape merits of each species as well as its native origin. To complete the word pictures, each entry has detailed notes about growth habit, rate of expansion, seasonal appearance, cultural preferences, growing difficulties, pest and disease afflictions, along with any varieties or cultivars currently available in the United States and Canada.

The graphics are unique. Never before has any plant book showed the comparison of growth patterns between a *10-year-old* tree and its *25-year-old* counterpart, nor has any publication provided the root system usual for all the species described. Since the 10-year-old plant is a commonly used size in landscape work, it is drawn with a ball of earth—if it can successfully be transplanted at this age. If not, then its root system is shown. Except for a few tap-rooted and unusual desert trees in this book, most trees rarely penetrate the soil beyond a 5-foot depth, and this point is indicated by the 5-foot grid intervals with each drawing.

While none of these tree outlines should be considered a faithful representation of an actual specimen—a futile gesture considering the wide geographic distribution of any tree—the graphic information is useful for determining the evolving silhouette changes, the eventual branching pattern, and the necessary space required for full growth.

The sketches also show an unusual departure by illustrating only the foliage and the fruit of each tree, and these scale drawings are accompanied by either a vertical or a horizontal bar representing 1 inch of measurement. Attractive as they are, flowers offer only a brief landscape asset in the year-long visual aspect of trees as design elements and are not included in the drawings. Both the blossoming and the autumn foliage changes, however, are described in the text accompanying each entry.

In assessing these tree selections, always match the plant to the site conditions beforehand since it is wiser to grow a commonplace tree well than to force adaptation on a specimen ill fitted for its surroundings. It is this author's hope that by the skilled use of this information you will increase the worth of your landscape developments aesthetically and horticulturally.

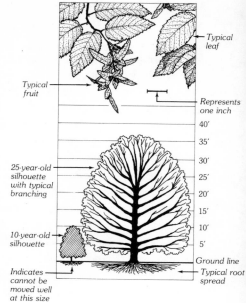

Broadleaf Evergreens

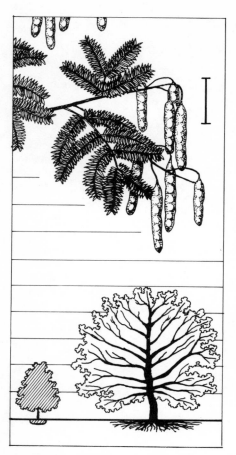

Acacia baileyana (Cootamundra wattle, Golden mimosa, Bailey acacia)

Zones 9 and 10   20' to 30'   Pea family

Although *Acacias* tend to be short-lived (thirty years at most) and have brittle stems easily damaged by high winds, they offer showy flowering for a long period and are drought-tolerant when established. This native from southeastern Australia is especially popular in southern California as an accent tree, where it does well even at seaside locations when protected from wind. Its vivid colorings make it an outstanding selection from the fifty *Acacias* usually found in nurseries there. None requires fertilizing to do well.

HABIT: Generally rounded and spreading with a natural tendency to be shrubby if left unpruned at the base; fast when young.

SEASONAL APPEARANCE: Grayish twigs carry compound, twice-divided foliage in a striking steel blue to gray-green color alternately or spirally arranged on the stems; brilliant yellow, fragrant, globular but tiny blossoms appear in dense 3-inch terminal or axillary clusters from mid-January to March; fruit develops as a gray-toned, slender pod up to 4 inches long with noticeable constrictions between the seeds; bark is grayish tan.

PREFERENCES AND PROBLEMS: Provide full sun and rich soil with copious and regular watering initially to encourage deep rooting; avoid very windy sites since all *Acacias* have weak wood and tend to be shallow-rooted; this species may be shy to flower in subtropical heat.

PESTS AND DISEASES: Notably free of both.

VARIETIES AND CULTIVARS: Cultivar 'Purpurea' with new foliage tinged purple but later turning gray-green; somewhat rare.

Acacia dealbata (Silver wattle, Mimosa)

Zones 8 (warm) to 10   40' to 50'   Pea family

Longer-lived than most other *Acacias,* highly scented, and very colorful in bloom, this visitor from Tasmania and southeastern Australia is set out extensively as a desirable street tree. Its cut branches are marketed to florists throughout the country for sale as Mimosa.

HABIT: Narrowly erect and quick-growing.

SEASONAL APPEARANCE: Twigs are gray-green with doubly compound, feathery leaves of silvery, crowded leaflets; golden yellow, ball-like heads of noticeably fragrant flowers profusely appear during February and March; fruit pods are narrow and between 2 and 4 inches long; bark color is silvery.

PREFERENCES AND PROBLEMS: Same as *A. baileyana.*

PESTS AND DISEASES: Inconsequential.

VARIETIES AND CULTIVARS: None, but some botanic authorities consider this to be only a variety or cultivar of *A. decurrens.*

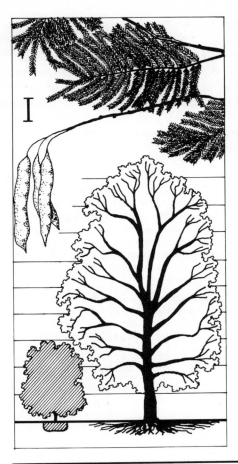

Acacia decurrens (Green wattle)

Zones 8 (warm) to 10   40' to 50'   Pea family

Here the eastern Australian plant is highly valued as a street tree or specimen for the large garden, especially for its fine-textured foliage and late winter flowering.

HABIT: Upright and somewhat narrow-headed; rapid in growth.

SEASONAL APPEARANCE: Dark green, bipinnate leaves have from sixteen to seventy leaflets; flowers are bright lemon yellow in heavy clusters to 4 inches long in February and March; seed pods are between 3 and 4 inches in length; trunk evolves with age from olive green to dark gray.

PREFERENCES AND PROBLEMS: See A. baileyana.

PESTS AND DISEASES: Unimportant.

SPECIES AND CULTIVARS: None, but A. dealbata is frequently sold as a variety or cultivar of this species; Hortus Third claims most material cultivated under this category is actually A. mearnsii (Black wattle), which is unhappily prone to wood borer attacks.

Acacia pruinosa (Frosty wattle, Bronze wattle)

Zones 9 and 10   30' to 60'   Pea family

Yet another southeastern Australian native, this plant has also proved attractively useful as a specimen or street tree for its graceful appearance and neat silhouette. Flowering is less showy than others.

HABIT: Wide-spreading and dome-shaped with speedy growth.

SEASONAL APPEARANCE: New foliage emerges bronze but turns light green later in the season; the 2- to 4-inch compound leaves provide a lacy, fern-like texture; flowers appear occasionally throughout the summer and autumn in pale yellow, 3-inch clusterings; seed pods are thin, between 3 and 4 inches long; the bark is smooth and gray with a purplish overcast.

PREFERENCES AND PROBLEMS: Similar to A. baileyana with the addition of needing regular watering to grow best.

PESTS AND DISEASES: Of no consequence.

VARIETIES AND CULTIVARS: None.

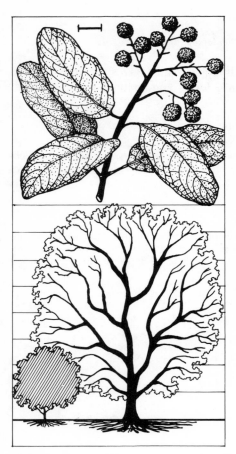

Arbutus menziesii (Madrona, Madrone, Madrono)

Zones 7 to 9   25' to 100'   Heath family

Attractively colorful and interesting in all seasons, this tree is native from British Columbia to southern California and the Baja Peninsula of Mexico, which explains the wide range of its possible growth heights. Unfortunately, it does not transplant easily unless very small, and its new location should be well considered since it will be permanent. Although mostly evergreen, it defoliates—colorfully—for a short period in late summer.

HABIT: Globular but open with a moderate growth rate.

SEASONAL APPEARANCE: New leaves unfold pinkish green or copper-toned but soon turn shiny, dark green with dull gray undersides and become leathery; old foliage colors red, yellow, and orange in late summer before shedding briefly; the small, honey-scented, urn-shaped blossoms (similar to blueberry flowers) appear as erect groups up to 9 inches tall in white to pale pink from midwinter to spring; pea-sized fruit clusters soon follow with orange to red, wrinkled berries for yet another burst of color interest; bark is terra cotta and smooth when young, peeling off in thin flakes later to reveal a roughened, dark brown trunk.

PREFERENCES AND PROBLEMS: Plant in either full sun or semishade on a consistently moist but very well-drained, acid soil where winters tend to be cool; water regularly if needed and protect from high winds; does not grow well in eastern United States; troublesome to move except as puny, 2-foot seedling; prone to litter spent flowers, fruit, leaves, and bark all year long.

PESTS AND DISEASES: On sprinkler-irrigated sites, overwatering can induce root rot; insect pests are not bothersome.

VARIETIES AND CULTIVARS: None.

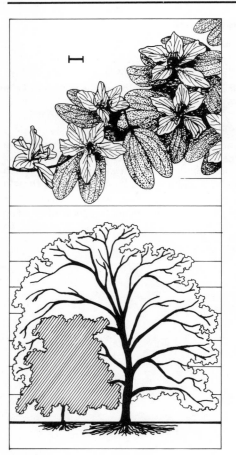

Bauhinia blakeana (Hong Kong orchid tree)

Zones 9 (warm) and 10   20'   Pea family

Few flowering trees have as much conspicuousness and persistence of bloom as this unusual plant, which came known from a single tree discovered growing alone in Canton, China several generations ago. All plants today are from this lone discovery. Both the flower and foliage shapes are novel, and the cleft leaf outline logically, if somewhat whimsically, honors the twin Swiss botanists, Jean and Gaspard Bauhin, responsible for cataloging this special plant genus.

HABIT: Irregularly rounded and spreading; fast-growing.

SEASONAL APPEARANCE: Kidney-shaped leaves are gray-green, 6 to 8 inches wide with a lower cleft up to one-third of the length; some older foliage drops when the plant flowers; blossoming is spectacularly lengthy from late autum to spring with fragrant, red-toned (from cranberry to rose-purple), orchid-like flowers veined with white in long, 6-inch-wide displays; since all flowers are sterile, fruiting is impossible; bark is grayish.

PREFERENCES AND PROBLEMS: Full sun is best, but light shade is tolerated; a slightly acid soil is desirable along with reasonable moisture at all times; unfortunately, it is difficult to transplant easily except when only a few feet tall.

PESTS AND DISEASES: None of importance.

VARIETIES AND CULTIVARS: None.

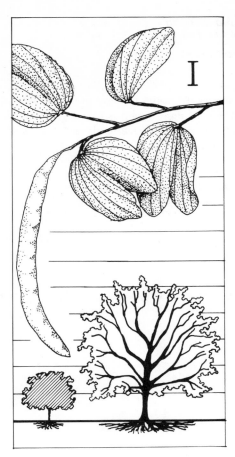

Bauhinia variegata (Orchid tree, Mountain ebony, Buddhist bauhinia)

Zones 9 (warm) and 10   20′ to 30′   Pea family

Native to both India and China, here the species is almost as flamboyant in flowering effect as *B. blakeana* except that the blooming period is shorter. More importantly, it tolerates sudden cold better and also offers a pure white cultivar.

HABIT: Upright and dome-shaped but ragged in outline; slightly more vigorous than *B. blakeana* when young.

SEASONAL APPEARANCE: The grayish green leaves are smaller and less deeply cleft than *B. blakeana;* the flowers are between 4 and 5 inches across and appear as lavender or magenta with the central petals (of five) dark purple; blooming time begins in early April and lasts only to May with, again, some old leaves dropping as flowering commences; fruit is a half-inch, flat pod up to 8 inches in length; gray bark.

PREFERENCES AND PROBLEMS: Enjoys constant heat but will take kindly to a sudden drop in temperature; prefers a well-drained, almost neutral soil in a nonwindy location; especially showy in bloom following a mild, dry winter; problematic to move satisfactorily unless quite small.

PESTS AND DISEASES: Not worth mentioning.

VARIETIES AND CULTIVARS: Cultivar 'Candida' has strikingly white flowers veined delicately with light green; usually shorter in height.

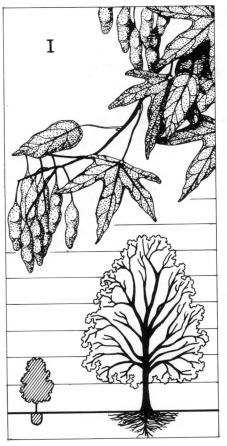

Brachychiton acerifolus [*Sterculia acerifolia*] (Flame tree)

Zones 9 and 10   25′ to 60′   Sterculia family

These Queensland and New South Wales, Australia, flamboyantly flowered trees can reach the gigantic height of several hundred feet, but in cultivation they stay much more manageable. Their unique foliage and vivid bloom recommend featuring them for specimen use.

HABIT: Generally cone-shaped crown, densely twiggy; moderate growth rate.

SEASONAL APPEARANCE: Foliage is variable even on the same tree, but the usual form is fan-shaped with five to seven lobes, light green and glossy and between 10 and 12 inches long; leaves on flowering branches tend to drop as bloom starts; flowers are glistening, bright scarlet, tubular bells, three-quarters-inch across in large, loose, terminal spikes supported by leafstalks of the same vivid color; main flowering displays are in May and June with sporadic color into autumn; ornamentally attractive, smooth, woody, black pods follow; bark is gray-green, smooth, and up to 2 inches thick on mature trunks.

PREFERENCES AND PROBLEMS: Full sun and deep, rich, moist soil best, but drier conditions are tolerated since this plant has long tap roots; dislikes windy sites; patience is required because young plants take seven years for first bloom; tends to litter something of itself most of the year; can be moved only when very juvenile because of deep rooting.

PESTS AND DISEASES: None of consequence.

VARIETIES AND CULTIVARS: None.

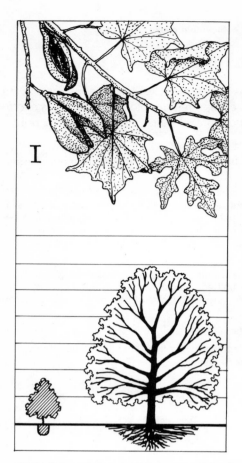

Brachychiton discolor [*Sterculia discolor*] (Scrub bottle tree, Queensland lacebark, Hat tree, Pink flame tree)

Zones 9 and 10   30' to 90'   Sterculia family

Popular in the warmer reaches of Florida, this species differs from its cousin *B. acerifolius* in most respects. At home in New South Wales, Queensland, and northern Australia, it often expands to 100 feet, but here it varies from coast to coast in growth rate and eventual height. It even can become deciduous in the cooler parts of its hardiness zones.

HABIT: Dome-shaped outline with variably slow to moderate growth.

SEASONAL APPEARANCE: Dull, dark, green, 4- to 7-inch-wide maple-like leaves have three to seven lobes and are wooly white or yellowish beneath; flowering is terminal and first appears as warty, cinnamon-colored, almond-shaped buds opening into 2-inch, rose-pink or pale red cups for six weeks of summer; the 5- to 6-inch fruit clusters are densely covered with rusty hairs and carry yellow, corn-like seeds; bark is gray.

PREFERENCES AND PROBLEMS: Likes deep, moist soil in sheltered, sunny locations; where chill winds and fog are common, poor foliage and fewer flowers result; if very cool, tree will even defoliate and become deciduous in its annual behavior; tap roots prevent easy transplanting except when small.

PESTS AND DISEASES: Unknown.

VARIETIES AND CULTIVARS: None.

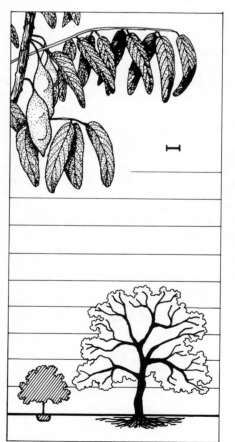

Castanospermum australe (Moreton Bay chestnut, Black bean)

Zones 9 (warm) and 10   25' to 60'   Pea family

Handsome foliage throughout the year, plus unusual flower color, promotes this as an accent tree readily. In cultivation here the plant usually grows between 25 and 40 feet, but in its natural habitat of eastern Australia it might even exceed the 60-foot upper limit.

HABIT: Broadly rounded, open, often more wide than tall with slow growth.

SEASONAL APPEARANCE: Compound, leathery, glossy, dark green foliage remains attractive year-round; pea-like, 1-inch flowers appear on second-year wood (and somewhat disguised by leaves) as deep orange shaded with yellow and red in loose clusters to 6 inches from June to August; noticeable, woody, brown, fruit pods up to 9 inches long contain large, rounded, chestnut-like seeds; bark is grayish.

PREFERENCES AND PROBLEMS: Best flowering comes from abundant heat on an average-fertility, moist soil in full sun or partial shading; tolerant of drier conditions; appears to be nonproblematic.

PESTS AND DISEASES: Unafflicted.

VARIETIES AND CULTIVARS: None.

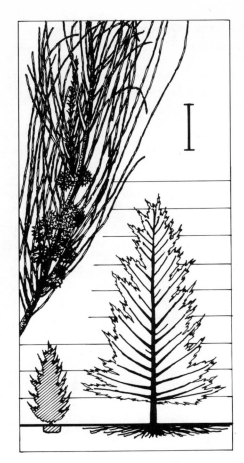

Casuarina cunninghamiana (River oak, River she-oak, Cunningham beefwood)

Zones 9 and 10   30' to 70'   Casuarina family

Even though it is not remotely related, the tree resembles a pine in its silhouette. Originally native to the eastern shores of Australia, where early settlers used the hard, durable, red-toned wood as an oak substitute, this species has now become naturalized in many dry parts of Florida and California. Easily grown and useful as a specimen or in a grove, all *Casuarinas* can aid in dune stabilization at beaches from their widespreading, surface rooting, rapid growth, and easy adaptability to salt spray. The separate species are troublesome to differentiate, however, since most produce only juvenile foliage types in cultivation, even on older trees. This particular one is often planted as a specimen and is frequently mislabeled as *C. equisetifolia* in nurseries.

HABIT: Erect with usually upturned branching; airy-looking with only light shade; very fast.

SEASONAL APPEARANCE: Has no true leaves but eight minute, green scales turning white near the tips and found whorled around wiry, gray-green stems; in summer, masses of female flowers give a rose-red glow to the plant; the woody, grayish, half-inch, cone-like fruit is studded with pyramidal bumps; bark is brown.

PREFERENCES AND PROBLEMS: While most *Casuarinas* readily take to brackish, wet sites as well as dry ones, this species prefers moist soil near fresh water in full sunlight; roots are still typically greedy and invasive.

PESTS AND DISEASES: None of importance.

VARIETIES AND CULTIVARS: None.

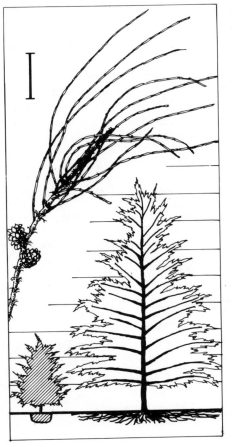

Casuarina equisetifolia (Horsetail tree, South Sea ironwood, Mile tree, Common beefwood)

Zones 9 (warm) and 10   40' to 70'   Casuarina family

Because the appearance of the whorled leaves on the needle-like stems of this well-distributed tree of southeastern Asia and Australia suggests the foliage of the ground-cover plant *Equisetum* (horsetail), its common name logically came to pass. It differs from *C. cunninghamiana* by having fewer leaf scales and by its spreading or drooping habit. Both are much confused in nurseries.

HABIT: Slender, erect stem with mostly horizontal branching or downturned branch tips; often with an open, ragged top; fast-growing with 2 feet annually.

SEASONAL APPEARANCE: Here the branchlets are barely gray-green, the scale count is between 6 and 7, and the foliage is fully green without any fading at the tips; female flowers are deep rose in summer; grayish cones can be up to three-quarters inch long; bark color is brownish.

PREFERENCES AND PROBLEMS: Tolerant of almost every situation with full sun from seashore to desert; invasive roots; only light shading produced.

PESTS AND DISEASES: Inconsequential.

VARIETIES AND CULTIVARS: None.

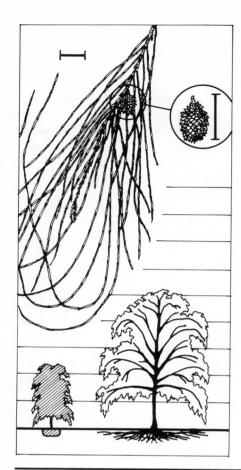

Casuarina stricta (Drooping she-oak, Coast beefwood)

Zones 9 and 10   25′ to 35′   Casuarina family

Novel in form, this species from Tasmania and eastern Australia offers dense shade and the longest and coarsest branches of any *Casuarina*. It is usually planted in parks and gardens as a specimen.

HABIT: Weeping crown, unusually quick-growing.

SEASONAL APPEARANCE: Leaf scales are dark green and arranged ten to twelve at a node; summer flowering is rosy-toned; cones can be up to 1¼ inches long in dark, glossy brown or black; bark is brown-toned.

PREFERENCES AND PROBLEMS: Grows well in sandy, shoreside locations and also tolerates brackish soil; becomes lopsided from coastal prevailing winds; has surface, greedy roots.

PESTS AND DISEASES: Unimportant.

VARIETIES AND CULTIVARS: None.

Ceratonia siliqua (Carob, St. John's bread, Algarroba bean, Locust bean)

Zones 9 and 10   25′ to 50′   Pea family

Supposedly, this eastern Mediterranean plant is the Biblical tree John the Baptist used for nourishment while living in the desert wilderness since the palatable fruit pulp is known to be full of concentrated sugar and protein. A long-lived tree tolerant to drought when established, it is much used today as a decorative street tree and as a specimen in parks and gardens.

HABIT: Dense, compact, often wider than tall; slow-growing.

SEASONAL APPEARANCE: Evenly pinnate leaves are glossy, dark green, leathery, and slightly wavy-margined on crooked stems; springtime flowers are on separate trees with the inconspicuous male blossoms disagreeably scented and blooming from highly conspicuous, chunky knobs regularly protruding from the many branches; red female flowers are stalked up to 3 inches tall and appear on older wood (occasionally even on the trunk); the black-brown, leathery pods sometimes individually elongate to 12 inches, but usually they cluster in a modest 6- to 8-inch size; the edible pulp surrounding the seeds has a mild chocolate taste; bark is dark brown.

PREFERENCES AND PROBLEMS: Sun-loving and adaptable to any well-drained soil in its hardiness zones; endures considerable drought, urban pollution, poor and alkaline soils, plus desert heat; tolerant of heavy wintertime pruning for controlled shapeliness; may require extra pruning attention to maintain single trunk.

PESTS AND DISEASES: Generally free of both, but a fatal root rot can be forestalled (usually) by watering infrequently—but deeply—during warm months.

VARIETIES AND CULTIVARS: None.

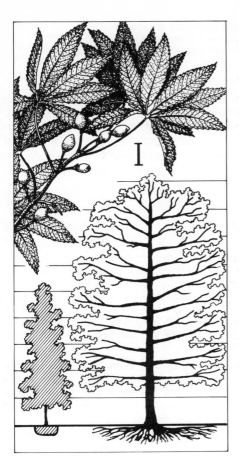

Chorisia speciosa (Floss-silk tree)

Zones 9 and 10   30′ to 60′   Bombax family

Bizarre for its spine-studded trunk but elegant when flowering, *Chorisia* captures the imagination throughout the year and is widely planted for specimen use. Native to the subtropical and tropical areas of Brazil and Argentina, the plant is apt to lose all or most of its foliage from sudden cold here, making it only semievergreen—or even deciduous—in some growing areas.

HABIT: Arrow-straight, slender stem when young; usually twice as tall as wide with maturity; fast-growing as a juvenile.

SEASONAL APPEARANCE: Palmately compound leaves with light green, lanceolate leaflets to 5 inches; large, upright, profuse clusters of ball-like buds develop into 3- to 5-inch, hibiscus-shaped flowers with widely flared, ivory petals tipped conspicuously with light orchid, purple-rose, mulberry, or even burgundy color from late September to December; the oval fruit capsules eventually burst into fluffy balls up to 8 inches wide resembling cotton floss (once used to stuff pillows); the bright green, smooth trunk, which turns gray and base-swollen with age, is closely studded with many brown-red, broad-based spines about 1 inch tall.

PREFERENCES AND PROBLEMS: Full sun, quick drainage, and infrequent—but deep—watering promote success; reducing water with established trees encourages greater flowering; difficult to reproduce from seed of cultivated plants or even from cuttings.

PESTS AND DISEASES: None worth mentioning.

VARIETIES AND CULTIVARS: None.

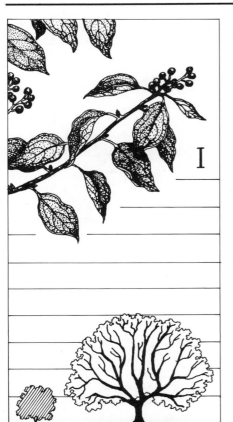

Cinnamomum camphora [Camphora officinalis] (Camphor tree)

Zones 9 and 10   20′ to 50′   Laurel family

Well established now as indigenous in southern California and most of the southerly parts of the United States, this aromatic tree originally was native to China, Taiwan, and Japan. Useful as a slow-growing street tree or, when pruned, as a solid hedge and windbreak, the tree has unfortunately become afflicted with a serious outbreak of verticillium wilt from a root rot fungus, and no cure is in sight yet. Existing trees might outgrow the wilt attack, however, with prudent care. This tree is too valuable in the landscape to forgo, even with its disease problem.

HABIT: Round-headed, dense, often wider than tall; slow-growing.

SEASONAL APPEARANCE: Stout, yellow-brown branches carry green twigs and glossy, yellow-green foliage with whitened undersides and two characteristic glands at the base of each leaf; old leaves drop in early spring but are quickly replaced by new leaves of pink or bronze; foliage has strong camphor scent when crushed; flowers are tiny, fragrant, and greenish yellow in May and June; the ineffectual fruit is globose, shiny black, about a half-inch, and poisonous if eaten in any quantity; the bark is dark brown to gray-black and fissured into small plates like some oaks.

PREFERENCES AND PROBLEMS: Enjoys full sun, any well-drained soil, and great summer heat; water heavily to encourage deep rooting; fallen leaves are slow to decompose; troublesome to move except when small and containerized; has vigorous, competitive, surface rooting and dense shade that eliminate most underplanting.

PESTS AND DISEASES: Verticillium wilt is most problematic, but quick, sanitary pruning of diseased parts, followed by a high nitrogen fertilizing program, may induce complete recovery.

VARIETIES AND CULTIVARS: None.

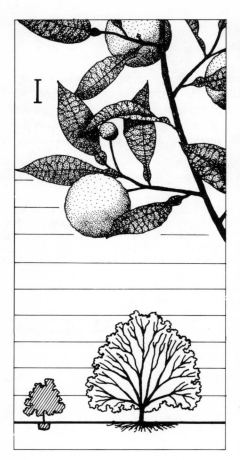

Citrus aurantiifolia (Lime), ***Citrus aurantium*** (Sour orange), ***Citrus limon*** (Lemon), ***Citrus*** × ***paradisi*** (Grapefruit), ***Citrus reticulata*** (Tangerine), ***Citrus sinensis*** (Sweet orange)

Zones 9 and 10   15′ to 30′ (except sweet orange: 40′)   Rue family

A well-known group of attractive plants native to southeastern Asia and the Malay Peninsula, *Citrus* has long been used for its colorful, desirable fruit and ornamental flowering throughout the semitropical parts of the world. For best blossoming and fruiting, each individual type's heat requirements and cold tolerance must be understood; but even so, all need consistent and proper fertilizing along with spraying programs to give their best performance, as is true with many other popular fruit trees.

HABIT: Shapely, symmetrical, compact, round-headed, except *C. sinensis,* which is more pyramidal and usually taller than the others; moderate growth rate.

SEASONAL APPEARANCE: Glossy, oval, dark green, thick leaves are dotted with aromatic glands and have winged petioles evolved from ancient compound leaves; occasionally the green twigs carry spiny projections; flowering varies in the group from winter through spring, but all have highly fragrant, waxy, white or purple-toned blossoms in clusters; some cultivars bloom sporadically throughout the year; the persistent and showy fruit is a leathery berry with juicy pulp botanically called an *hesperidium* (a reference to mythology and one of Hercules' labors) in yellow, orange, and green.

PREFERENCES AND PROBLEMS: Best in bright sun with a deep, mellow, sandy soil having consistent moisture and excellent drainage; cannot tolerate stagnant water since root rot develops; needs fertilizing two or three times yearly and regular pest spraying for best development; can be pruned at any time, and even older, unkempt trees can be reshaped easily.

PESTS AND DISEASES: Host to many of both with black scale, aphids, mealybugs, rust mites, and whitefly prominent, along with an array of fungal and bacterial diseases, but not all become major difficulties in ever growing area.

VARIETIES AND CULTIVARS: A sizable collection of cultivars is usually available in nurseries for each of the many species listed here.

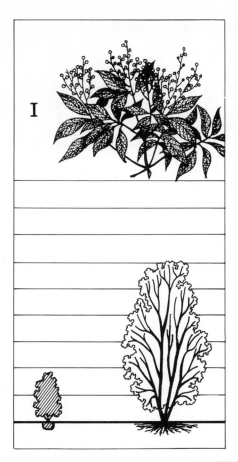

Clethra arborea (Lily-of-the-valley clethra)

Zones 9 and 10   20' to 30'   Clethra family

Neat and shapely, this attractive tree from the coastal African island of Madeira is valued for its cascades of summer bloom and absence of problems. Botanically it is closely allied in flower appearance to the Heath family.

HABIT: Dense, narrowly upright, often multistemmed; moderate-growing.

SEASONAL APPEARANCE: Shining dark green foliage, paler beneath, with serrated edges first appears as reddish new growth; flowers generously cover the plant during the late summer in large, nodding, terminal clusters up to 6 inches long of fragrant, white to pale pink, bell-shaped, half-inch blossoms; the fruit is a tiny, rounded capsule of no special decorative value.

PREFERENCES AND PROBLEMS: Likes a rich, acid, moist, and well-drained soil in sun to semishade located with shelter from high winds and with abundant humidity; suffers noticeably from drought and arid air conditions; apt to be tender in all but the mildest areas.

PESTS AND DISEASES: None of significance.

VARIETIES AND CULTIVARS: None.

Crinodendron patagua [*Tricuspidaria dependens*] (Lily-of-the-valley tree)

Zones 9 and 10   25' to 45'   Elaeocarpus family

Visually similar in foliage to some evergreen oaks, *Crinodendron* alters that image when in flower during most of the summer. It adapts well to specimen use in almost wet as well as shaded conditions.

HABIT: Compact, bush, rounded; slow to moderate growth.

SEASONAL APPEARANCE: Oval, 2-inch, dark, dull green leaves have light fuzz beneath; pendant flowers are three-quarters inch, fringed bells of waxy white set singly in the leaf axils and appear from mid-June to October; the oval, green fruit carries a slender, elongated end wisp and turns orange-red and woody later with many shiny, black seeds visible.

PREFERENCES AND PROBLEMS: Very moist, acid-humus soil and semishading suit it best; water heavily monthly to encourage deep roots; fallen seed capsules become a maintenance nuisance on walks; may require consistent pruning attention when young to grow as a tree form.

PESTS AND DISEASES: Unimportant.

VARIETIES AND CULTIVARS: None.

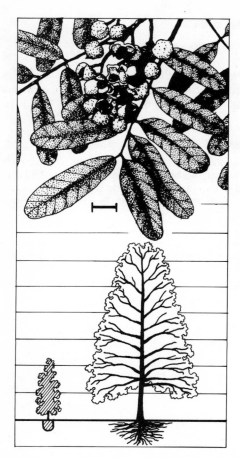

Cupaniopsis anacardiodes [Cupania anacardiopsis]
(Carrotwood, Tuckeroo)

Zones 9 (warm) and 10   25' to 40'   Soapberry family

Another sturdy Australian import, carrotwood offers easy adaptability to almost any growing situation of its hardiness range and is commended as a specimen or street tree.

HABIT: Slenderly erect and open when juvenile but becoming dense and widely dome-shaped with age; moderate to fast growth.

SEASONAL APPPEARANCE: Evenly pinnate leaves carry between five and ten shiny, medium green, leathery leaflets up to 6 inches in length with an indented tip; flower spikes are white and inconspicuous during December; strings of abundant seed capsules may follow (fruiting is often haphazard) with three-lobed, quarter-inch, yellow coverings opening to reveal nests of shiny, orange-red, fleshy fruit; bark is light gray.

PREFERENCES AND PROBLEMS: Likes full sun in an average soil but adapts well to poorly drained sites, salt-laden air, and hot, drying winds; in rich soil and adequate moisture it may climb to 40 feet; has deep roots and moves best when small.

PESTS AND DISEASES: Seldom bothered by either.

VARIETIES AND CULTIVARS: None.

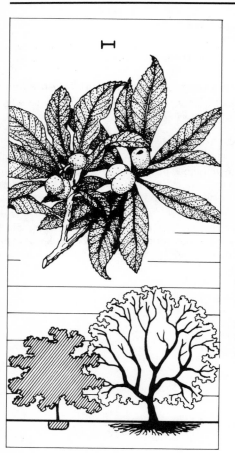

Eriobotrya japonica   Loquat, Japanese medlar, Japanese plum)

Zones 7 (warm) to 10   20' to 30'   Rose family

Adaptable as a terrace shade tree, hedge, or even an espalier, this native of China and south-central Japan takes any amount of pruning well and is a desirable fruiting staple of gardens and parks where it is hardy.

HABIT: Broad and rounded with upright, spreading, heavy branches in sun but slender and narrow if overly shaded; fast-growing.

SEASONAL APPEARANCE: Prominently veined, stiff, leathery, dark to bright green, glossy leaves are rusty pubescent beneath on rust-colored new stems; foliage is variable in length from 6 to 12 inches and appears somewhat crowded toward the branch ends; upright clusters of half-inch, white, sweetly fragrant (like vanilla) blossoms are obvious but not showy in mid-November to January; the edible, tartly sweet, bunched fruit is either round or pear-shaped and colored orange to yellow-orange; fruit is generously produced, however, only in frost-free locations.

PREFERENCES AND PROBLEMS: Needs deep, well-drained, moist soil in full sun to half shade; adaptable to seaside locations; acid fertilizing encourages rapid growth; high-quality fruit more likely from grafts of known desirability than from seed; rabbits tend to gnaw on young bark.

PESTS AND DISEASES: Red spider mites and mealybugs are often problematic, and fireblight dieback can be a serious disease.

VARIETIES AND CULTIVARS: None yet with any botanic standing.

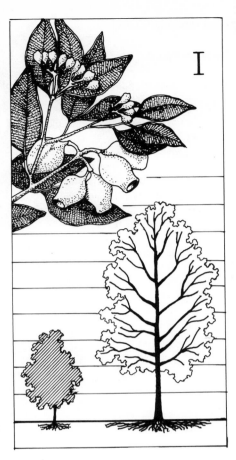

Eucalyptus calophylla (Marri, Red gum, Port Gregory gum)

Zone 10   40' to 60'   Myrtle family

The Eucalyptuses are novel and intriguing landscape contributions introduced—and now well-enough adapted here to have become natives—over one hundred years ago from Australia, New Zealand, and Tasmania. They are noted for their bark, their aromatic fragrance after rainstorms, their generous flowering, their explosive growth, their long life, and their wealth of sizes and silhouettes as specimens, street trees, windbreaks, and screens. Over 700 separate types have been identified, and valid separation is complicated by their habit of issuing oppositely placed, petiole-less, juvenile foliage on occasionally squared stems, while also producing mature foliage with definite leafstalks alternately set on the twigs. One useful aid for identification can be the bark type: those which shed in flakes, strips, or large patches (usually called *gums*) and those with tight, checkered, or furrowed bark (labeled *ironbarks*). Flowers on all are masses of stamens, and their various colors help in identification, too.

Remarkably, none is prone to pest or disease nuisances, and because they all grow so fast, small containerized plants adjust better to transplanting than older specimens. Be cautioned, however, that potted material in garden centers is apt to become root-strangulated from such zesty growing habits. It is a wise planting procedure, therefore, to wash away all container soil, to spread out the fan-like roots carefully in a moistened pit, and to water generously after refilling until new growth begins again. Any *Eucalyptus* is likely to suffer chlorosis (a lack of sufficient chlorophyll in stems and leaves) from alkaline soils, and the simple treatment is merely to apply chelates of iron solutions at regular intervals. Even with these drawbacks, their ornamental place in the landscape is ensured and deserved.

HABIT: Narrowly erect, symmetrical, fast-growing.

SEASONAL APPEARANCE: Dark green, glossy foliage, lighter beneath, up to 6 inches long and 2 inches wide; clustered flowers are white to slightly pink (with some dark-toned pink possible) from greenish white buds during early spring and summer; the woody fruit capsules are pear-shaped and over 1 inch long; bark is rough, flaky, gray, and irregularly and shallowly grooved.

PREFERENCES AND PROBLEMS: Deep, moist soil with good drainage and full sun is best; avoid overwatering.

PESTS AND DISEASES: Of no importance.

VARIETIES AND CULTIVARS: None with botanic authority endorsement.

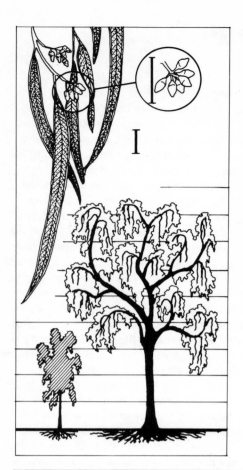

Eucalyptus camaldulensis [*rostrata*] (Murray red gum, River red gum)

Zones 8 (warm) to 10   50′ to 120′   Myrtle family

An excellent shade tree for large spaces, this Australian species is especially decorative when visible in its entirety.

HABIT: Open, spreading crown, gracefully weeping branches, curved trunk, bare of lower branching for half its height; rapid growth.

SEASONAL APPEARANCE: Thin leaves, medium to dull green on both sides, from reddish twigs; foliage between 4 and 10 inches long and 1 inch wide; white flowers in clusters of five to ten on half-inch stalks from May to July; quarter-inch, bell-shaped fruit; trunk is thick with mottled, ashy, blue-toned bark exfoliating in patches.

PREFERENCES AND PROBLEMS: Sun-loving, tolerant of alkaline soil without chlorosis, takes routine lawn irrigation well.

PESTS AND DISEASES: None.

VARIETIES AND CULTIVARS: None.

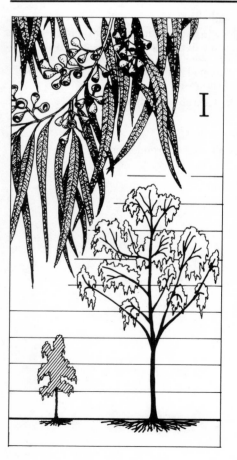

Eucalyptus citriodora [*maculata citriodora*] (Lemon-scented gum)

Zones 9 (warm) and 10   50′ to 100′   Myrtle family

The well-behaved roots here promote its use for streets and boulevards, while its profuse flowering in late summer attracts bees as a source of honey.

HABIT: Slender-trunked with feathery, arching branches and a sparse crown; trunk usually barren of wide branches for one-third to one-half its height; speedy growth.

SEASONAL APPEARANCE: The pendant, strongly lemon-scented foliage is yellow-green on both surfaces and can be up to 10 inches in length; the three-quarter-inch flowers are creamy white in generous, terminal clusterings during August and September; urn-shaped, half-inch fruit capsules appear on half-inch stalks; the thin, peeling bark leaves attractive, smooth, yellow-white to flesh-colored patches on the narrow trunk.

PREFERENCES AND PROBLEMS: Best grown in moist, sunny, coastal areas free from heavy frost; adaptable to varied amounts of soil moisture; young trees are apt to be weak-stemmed and need support.

PESTS AND DISEASES None.

VARIETIES AND CULTIVARS: None.

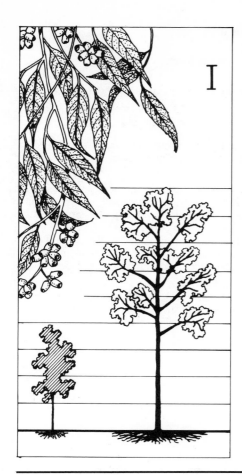

Eucalyptus cladocalyx [*corynocalyx*] (Sugar gum)

Zones 9 (warm) and 10   50′ to 80′   Myrtle family

Very common in southern California as a roadside tree of some distinction, this tree's well-proportioned silhouette promotes its further use as a set-apart specimen viewable from all directions.

HABIT: Straight, slender trunk with widely separated branching and puffy foliage; rapid-growing.

SEASONAL APPEARANCE: Red-toned twigs carry shiny, dark green, 3- to 6-inch leaves, dull-colored below; white blossoming only sporadic during late winter into early summer from slender, cylindrical buds in clusters from six to sixteen; the small, half-inch fruiting capsules are chalice-shaped; its rough, gray trunk sheds noticeably to reveal creamy white to yellow-brown inner bark.

PREFERENCES AND PROBLEMS: Easily grown in full sun on any average soil; very drought-resistant; dislikes heavy frost areas.

PESTS AND DISEASES: None.

VARIETIES AND CULTIVARS: A dwarfed form called 'Nana' is often sold in nurseries but has no botanic credentials.

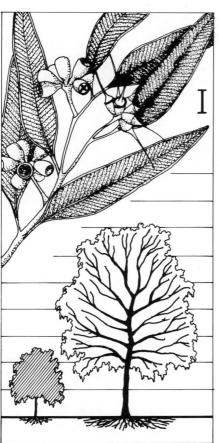

Eucalyptus cornuta (Yate tree, Yate)

Zones 9 (warm) and 10   35′ to 100′   Myrtle family

This tough, adaptable *Eucalyptus* species thrives equally well on coastal sites or dry, interior valleys with mild frost, to become a desirable tree with good shade and shapely appearance.

HABIT: Profusely branched with a spreading, dense crown; wavy trunk; quick to grow.

SEASONAL APPEARANCE: Slender, shiny leaves are medium green on both sides and up to 4 inches long; tightly grouped flower buds have an 1-inch-long, slender beak and open as greenish yellow blossoms from mid-June to August; the seed capsules are only one-third to one-half inch long and also sport a beak-like projection; the persistent, deeply furrowed bark is dark brown.

PREFERENCES AND PROBLEMS: Sunny locations in a variety of soil types, including alkaline, provide good growth patterns; adapts to dry or moist sites well; cannot endure prolonged or severe frost.

PESTS AND DISEASES: None.

VARIETIES AND CULTIVARS: None.

Eucalyptus ficifolia (Red-flowering gum, Scarlet-flowering gum)

Zones 9 (warm) and 10   15′ to 40′   Myrtle family

Brilliant, showy masses of flowering occur throughout most of the year—but spectacularly in midsummer—to make this small-sized tree a worthy addition to almost any landscape layout for its climate zone.

HABIT: Compact and round-headed with a short trunk and dense foliage; slower-growing than many other species; has some leaf and flower similarities with *E. calophylla* but different bark.

SEASONAL APPEARANCE: Foliage thick, dark green above and much lighter below, 3 to 5 inches long and between 1 and 2 inches wide, turning red before dropping; abundant clusters of 1½-inch flowers in very large, terminal projections can range from flaming red (the most common) to salmon, orange, coral, and even cream; bloom is year-round but shows most generously from June to August; the persistent fruit is a thick, woody, vase-shaped capsule untypically containing red-brown, winged seeds; its brown-gray, rough, persistent bark is furrowed and occasionally fluted.

PREFERENCES AND PROBLEMS: Grows best in light, well-drained, rich soils with summer watering and full sunshine; seems to thrive near the coast; tolerant of smog, heat, alkalinity, and drought; intolerant of frost and wet, slow-draining soil.

PESTS AND DISEASES: None.

VARIETIES AND CULTIVARS: None.

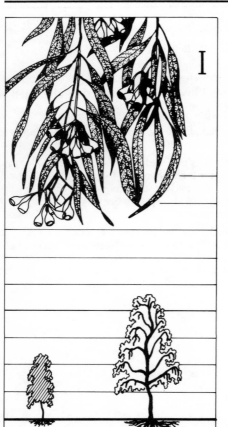

Eucalyptus leucoxylon (White ironbark)

Zones 8 (warm) to 10   25′ to 80′   Myrtle family

Easily at home in most soils where it is hardy, this species has several attractive cultivars and a slow growth rate welcome in small spaces.

HABIT: Slender in silhouette with drooping, mottled branches, it often has a crooked trunk; slow to moderate growth.

SEASONAL APPEARANCE: Foliage is sickle-shaped, narrow, willow-like, gray-green, and up to 6 inches in length; terminal flowers are noticeably white or faintly pink-toned during most of the winter months; its fruit capsules are only one-half inch long; the irregularly flaking bark is mottled in creamy white and gray-blue.

PREFERENCES AND PROBLEMS: Adapts well to heat, wind, and salt spray in full sun and adjusts also to heavy, light, and even rocky soils comfortably.

PESTS AND DISEASES: None.

VARIETIES AND CULTIVARS: Cultivar 'Purpurea' with bright purple flower stamens; cv. 'Rosea' with bright, rose-red, inch-wide blossoms; often multistemmed with a pink-toned, gray bark and shorter in height.

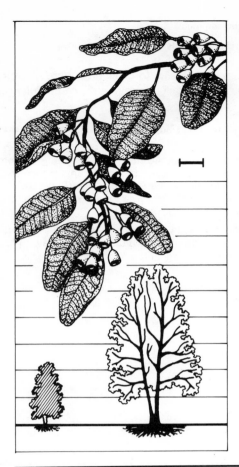

Eucalyptus polyanthemos (Silver dollar gum, Australian beech)

Zones 9 and 10   40′ to 70′   Myrtle family

Unfazed by highway and street conditions, here the species offers sturdy durability as a windbreak and erosion controller, plus a pleasantly slender silhouette with blue-toned foliage valued ornamentally for cutting. The common name derives from juvenile color and its rounded leaf outline.

HABIT: Upright, often multistemmed and low-branched with a neat outline; fast-growing.

SEASONAL APPEARANCE: Initial foliage oval, grayish blue and blunt-tipped; mature leaves more wedge-shaped and blue-green or dull, gray-green on both sides; flowers are small, creamy, and less than showy during March and April; its cup-shaped capsules are a quarter-inch and appear in clusters of 3 to 6; the gray, fibrous bark is shallowly grooved.

PREFERENCES AND PROBLEMS: Readily adaptable to heavy, shallow, dry, or alkaline soils as well as to desert and coastal growing conditions as long as it is in full sun; gives poor response in wet soils.

PESTS AND DISEASES: None.

VARIETIES AND CULTIVARS: None.

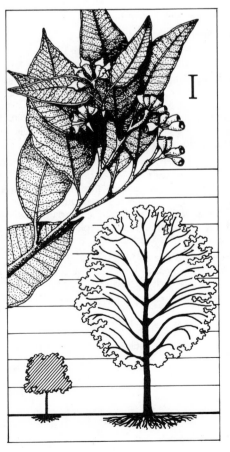

Eucalyptus robusta (Swamp mahogany, Brown gum)

Zones 8 (warm) to 10   40′ to 80′   Myrtle family

Stately as a specimen for good shading, the plant's heavy foliage and easy adaptability to any soil recommend it also as a versatile windbreak.

HABIT: Dense, rounded crown with spreading branches starting halfway up the trunk; fast-growing.

SEASONAL APPEARANCE: Shiny, leathery, dark green leaves are lighter-toned beneath and up to 6 inches long with a middle width of about 2 inches; the small but abundant, creamy white flowers appear from pink buds in January to May but are more profuse in winter; the goblet-like capsules which follow are up to a half-inch long; its strongly furrowed bark is rusty brown, fibrous, and rough.

PREFERENCES AND PROBLEMS: Takes readily to any soil, including alkaline and saline, in full sun as long as it is moist; requires watering regularly if planted on dry, interior sites.

PESTS AND DISEASES: None.

VARIETIES AND CULTIVARS: None.

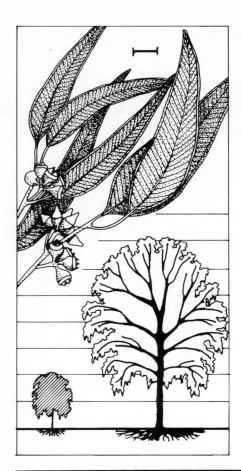

Eucalyptus rudis   (Desert gum, Swamp gum)

Zones 8 (warm) to 10   30' to 60'   Myrtle family

The common names tell the story of its ability to grow anywhere since it is nearly failure-proof. This species occasionally resembles *E. camaldulensis* in appearance.

HABIT: Upright and spreading for the most part but often weeping or at least with downturned branching; speedy growth.

SEASONAL APPEARANCE: Thin, sickle-shaped leaves are dull green to gray-green on both sides and up to 4 inches long; the white flowers are fuzzy in appearance and appear clustered in branches of four to ten during June through August; the woody capsules are about three-eighths inch long and show four projecting valves at the top; bark is persistent, rough, dark gray, and tightly fissured.

PREFERENCES AND PROBLEMS: Especially durable in hot, dry locations in full sun but also tolerant of wind, any soil (including saline), both much and less water, plus desert and coastal sites; hardiness improves with generous watering.

PESTS AND DISEASES: None.

VARIETIES AND CULTIVARS: None.

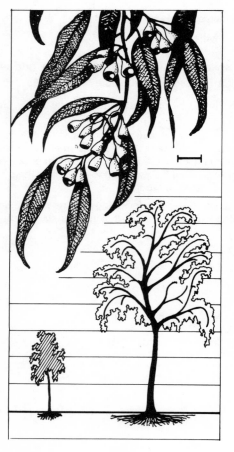

Eucalyptus sideroxylon   (Red ironbark, Pink ironbark)

Zones 9 and 10   30' to 80'   Myrtle family

Greatly variable for height and silhouette, it has wide acceptance for its ready adjustment to difficult roadway sites and harsh exposures. The unusual, reddish black bark is distinctive.

HABIT: Can be open-headed or dense but mostly slender-trunked; varies as well as from erect to weeping in form and is inconsistent for mature height; usually unbranched for some distance up the trunk; moderate to fast in expansion.

SEASONAL APPEARANCE: Slim, curved, 4- to 6-inch, wavy leaves are gray-green on both surfaces but may change to blue-green with a bronze tint in winter; dark-foliaged plants commonly have the deepest flower colors; the intermittent blossoming from October to May varies from light to rich rose-red but may also be cream-white on some trees, all from drooping clusters of half-inch, creamy buds; its cup-shaped fruit is about a half-inch long, the thick, hard, deeply furrowed, deep red-brown and black-toned bark is especially noteworthy.

PREFERENCES AND PROBLEMS: Thrives on sunny coastal, inland, or desert locations with all soil types, including alkaline; adjusts well to smog and street or highway pollution; resistant to wind damage and very dry growing conditions; requires little maintenance except staking when young to encourage an erect stem; develops chlorosis on heavy, wet soils.

PESTS AND DISEASES: None.

VARIETIES AND CULTIVARS: None, but many nurseries still erroneously list this as *E. sideroxylon rosea.*

Eucalyptus viminalis (Manna gum, Ribbon gum)

Zones 9 and 10   50' to 100'   Myrtle family

Commonly cultivated for its graceful, pendulous habit and imposing specimen value.

HABIT: Grand in height with a somewhat open head and elegantly weeping branchlets; rapid-growing.

SEASONAL APPEARANCE: Willow-like, narrow, 4- to 9-inch leaves are pale green on both sides and appear on long, dropping branchlets; small, white, globe-shaped flowers blossom from June to September; its tiny, quarter-inch fruit has four conspicuous valves at the top; the lowest bark is rough, persistent, furrowed, and dark gray, but the upper stem exfoliates attractively in long ribbons to show smooth white or yellow-white patches of inner bark.

PREFERENCES AND PROBLEMS: Readily grown with full sun in a wide variety of soils and exposures; does especially well even on poor, dry soil.

PESTS AND DISEASES: None.

VARIETIES AND CULTIVARS: None.

Ficus benjamina (Benjamin tree, Weeping fig, Java fig, Tropic laurel, Weeping laurel)

Zones 9 (warm) and 10   15' to 50'   Mulberry family

Conveniently adaptable for either outdoor planting in mild areas or indoor, potted display where conditions are colder, this semitropical tree from India, southeastern Asia, and north Australia has a wide-ranging appeal in its natural form or as sheared topiary and wall espaliers. All types ooze milky sap when pruned.

HABIT: Rounded and broadly spreading with weeping branch ends; may be gracefully irregular in outline; moderate growth rate; often taller in Florida than in California.

SEASONAL APPEARANCE: Thin, shiny, wavy-edged, oval to elliptical, dark green foliage up to 5 inches long with a noticeably tapered point; the flowering effect is totally inconspicuous; fruiting is rare with this species but, if produced, will appear as pairs of globose, half-inch, inedible, greenish red fruit in the leaf axils; bark is smooth and grayish tan.

PREFERENCES AND PROBLEMS: Requires a consistently moist soil in either full sun or half shade and good drainage; tolerant of salt air if well protected from high winds; readily damaged by frost.

PESTS AND DISEASES: Mealybugs are the worst affliction.

VARIETIES AND CULTIVARS: *Variety benjamina,* the typical form with leaves 2½ inches wide and up to 5½ inches long, plus bright red fruit (if it occurs); variety *nuda (comosa),* with narrower, longer foliage and red-brown to whitish fruit; cv. 'Exotica', having twisted leaf tips on slender, more dropping branchlets.

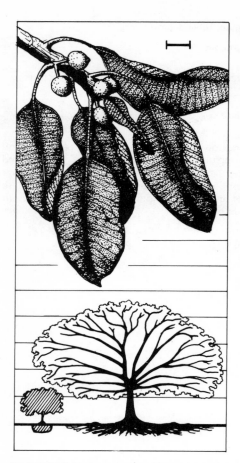

Ficus macrophylla   (Moreton Bay fig, Australian Banyan)

Zones 9 (warm) and 10   40′ to 60′   Mulberry family

Massive in spread, this species from Australia requires a generous growing space since it creates a network of large, buttress roots at the surface. The largest known specimen in this country was planted in 1877 at Santa Barbara, California, and today spans 160 feet!

HABIT: Dome-shaped, spreading, dense crown usually twice as broad as high with stout branching and invasive, surface roots; grows reasonably fast.

SEASONAL APPEARANCE: Thick, oval, 6- to 12-inch, dark green leaves, glossy above and silvery to rusty beneath; flowering is not noticeable; the rounded fruit in the leaf axils can be up to 1 inch wide and dark red-brown to purple with speckled skin; bark is smooth and gray.

PREFERENCES AND PROBLEMS: Wants either full sun or partial shading on an average soil with good drainage and lots of moisture; tolerant of more frost than other figs; surface rooting eventually eliminates any other growth beneath it.

PESTS AND DISEASES: None of importance.

VARIETIES AND CULTIVARS: None.

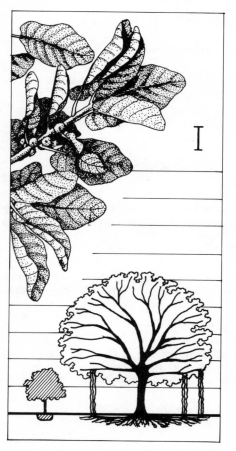

Ficus rubiginosa [australis]   (Port Jackson fig, Rusty fig, Littleleaf fig)

Zones 9 and 10   30′ to 60′   Mulberry family

Since this native of New South Wales and Queensland, Australia, is prone to send down clusterings of slender, aerial roots to the ground, they hamper its use in many landscape settings; just the same it enjoys popularity as a tropical novelty in parks and gardens of southern California.

HABIT: Dense, rounded broadly spreading to become as wide as tall with maturity; massive branching, occasionally with several trunks and many descending aerial roots from lower limbs; moderate growth rate.

SEASONAL APPEARANCE: Young twigs rusty-haired with thick, leathery, elliptical, dark green leaves having rust-colored undersides in sizes up to 4 inches; blossoming is nondescript; the paired, tasteless, warty fruits are oval and about a half-inch wide and appear at the tips of the twigs; they color from green to yellow as they mature; the bark is dull gray.

PREFERENCES AND PROBLEMS: Enjoys light shading or full sun in a moist location but will tolerate sandy, beach soil and salt-wind positions satisfactorily; very hardy in drought and reasonable heat; cannot tolerate frost; may drop old foliage frequently on some sites.

PESTS AND DISEASES: Not bothered by much.

VARIETIES AND CULTIVARS: Cultivar 'Variegata', has attractive mottling of foliage with cream-yellow streaks; may revert in part to all-green leaves, which can be pruned out as discovered; occasionally this form may grow with a columnar habit.

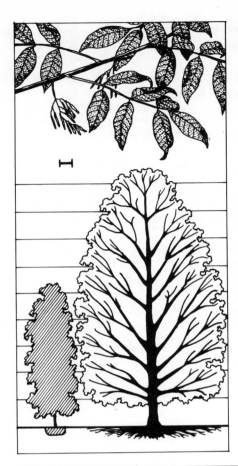

Fraxinus uhdei (Shamel ash, Everygreen ash)

Zones 9 and 10   50' to 70'   Olive family

One of the few evergreen ashes know, the tree usually loses most of its foliage briefly where frost occurs during January and early February. Its sturdy, erect, young growth and handsome, vase-shaped silhouette at maturity ensure its continued use as a notable shade and street tree for hot summer climates.

HABIT: Upright, dense, and narrow while young with ascending branches; becomes round-topped and more fountain-shaped with age; grows rapidly.

SEASONAL APPEARANCE: Dark green, wavy-margined, compound leaves have five to nine shiny, toothed leaflets; panicled flowers are nonshowy in midspring; the pendulous fruit culsters of winged seeds are conspicuous by midautumn for size but not for any special colors; bark is grayish tan.

PREFERENCES AND PROBLEMS: Does best in full sun on a rich, moist soil; tolerant of low temperatures to 15 degrees Fahrenheit (−9 degrees Celsius) and to alkaline conditions; its leaves scorch in hot, dry winds; the natural, shallow-rooting habit can be altered by consistent, deep watering; requires some pruning when young to maintain a sturdy and full outline.

PESTS AND DISEASES: Fusarium wilt is serious on parent, but cultivars show improved resistance to this disease.

VARIETIES AND CULTIVARS: Cultivar 'Sexton', with darker and larger leaflets and a more compact, rounded crown; cv. 'Tomlinson', with more leathery foliage and a denser, strongly upright, juvenile growth habit; both are usually grafted plants.

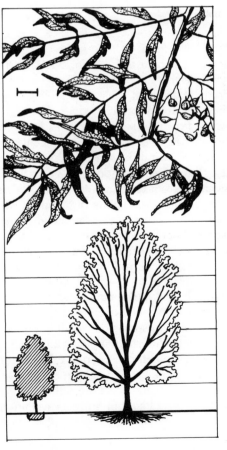

Grevillea robusta (Silky oak, Silk oak)

Zones 9 (warm) and 10   50' to 75'   Protea family

In Australia, where it is native and apt to grow to 150 feet, this tree is extensively used as a street and shade specimen for its worthy tolerance to heat, drought, and neglect. It has now found the same practical and decorative use in Hawaii, Florida, and California.

HABIT: Narrowly upright but not heavily branched; moderate to fast growth.

SEASONAL APPEARANCE: Young twigs velvety with rusty hairs; the fern-like, compound, leathery foliage can stretch to 9 inches and is dark green above and white, silky beneath; in April and May generous 3- to 6-inch sprays of small, comb-like orange tubes appear on leafless branches followed by oval, woody, half-inch fruit with a noticeable, slender beak; the bark is dark gray-brown and fissured.

PREFERENCES AND PROBLEMS: Likes a sunny location and rich, moist, deep soil but is tolerant to poor, sandy soil as well; usually will not set flowers in cool, foggy areas; has brittle branches.

PESTS AND DISEASES: Free of both.

VARIETIES AND CULTIVARS: None.

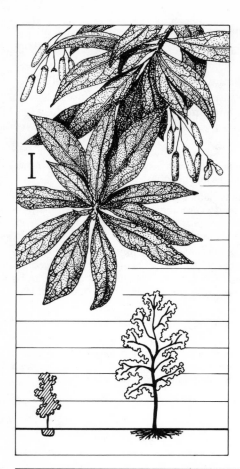

Hymenosporum flavum   (Sweetshade)

Zones 9 and 10   20' to 40'   Pittosporum family

Yet another Australian transplant, this heavily fragrant ornamental offers an irregularly open structure as a garden accent, but it presents more impressiveness when several are grouped.

HABIT: Slender with a recurved trunk and very open silhouette from widely spaced branching; moderate to fast growth rate.

SEASONAL APPEARANCE: Wavy-margined, richly glossy, light green leaves are up to 6 inches long and have a finely tapered tip; they are alternately set and usually crowd toward the ends of twigs in a rosette formation; the 1½-inch, trumpet-shaped, richly fragrant (like orange blossoms), golden yellow flowers have a red throat and appear in generous, terminal clusters from April to September; the flattened, 1-inch fruit capsule has numerous, papery seeds; bark is grayish tan.

PREFERENCES AND PROBLEMS: Shade-tolerant and undemanding of any special soil except that it be well drained; apt to sulk in windy locations; foliage drops with erratic watering and sudden cold.

PESTS AND DISEASES: Unbothered by either.

VARIETIES AND CULTIVARS: None.

Ilex × altaclarensis   (High Clere holly)

Zones 7 to 10   20' to 50'   Holly family

Hollies have worldwide distribution and appear as both deciduous and evergreen trees or shrubs of varying heights and spreads. They have been ornamentally cultivated for hundreds of years for their glossy foliage, showy fruit, and ability to take severe pruning well as hedges. The nondescript male and female flowers grown on separate plants, however, requiring close-at-hand installation of both to produce the persistent clusters of colorful female berries admired on most species. One male, nevertheless, can pollinate about a dozen neighborhood females; and if the flowers open at the same time, even different types can fulfill this necessary function. Since male involvement is of short, springtime duration, these plants usually expand more rapidly than females of the same age.

All holly types are tolerant of some shading, yet the best fruiting and most compact growth occur in full sun with the right growing conditions. Most like a rich, consistently moist, slightly acid, well-drained soil and protection from drying winds (all are unsuited to lower midwest and southwestern United States), along with acid mulching instead of cultivation because of surface, fibrous rooting. The evergreen tree selections described here transplant readily in spring but require a generous earthball and careful handling to succeed. Transplanting shock often defoliates either sex of older leaves when plants are beyond a few feet tall, even with the best attention; yet they fully adjust in a season or two with renewed vigor. Holly leaf miner, mealybugs, and scale are often troublesome insect pests, while leaf and twig blight in humid areas are the main disease afflictions.

The High Clere holly is a hybrid cross between *I. aquifolium* and *I. perado* of the Azores and Canary Islands which evolved as a nonfruiting male plant often listed now in catalogs as a form of *I. aquifolium*. Its lustrous foliage makes it a good candidate for a high hedge or screen.

HABIT: Densely foliaged and conical; vigorous rate of growth.

SEASONAL APPEARANCE: Rich green, thick, elliptic leaves have fewer spines than *I. aquifolium* and are between 2¹/₂ and 4 inches long; inconspicuous flowering appears in early summer; fruiting unimaginable on this male plant; bark is purple-toned.

PREFERENCES AND PROBLEMS: See introductory remarks.

PESTS AND DISEASES: Review introduction for this species.

VARIETIES AND CULTIVARS (some have reverted to having fruit): Cultivar 'Atrovirens variegata', male with leaves blotched with gold in the center; cv. 'Camelliifolia', vigorous and solid with few-prickled leaves turning bronze in winter plus bright red fruit; cv. 'Eldridge', leaves large and flattened with prominent spines and profuse, sizable, red fruiting; cv. 'Hodginsii', dark green foliage up to 4 inches long with bold spines on the margins; cv. 'J. C. van Tol' ('Polycarpa'), with an almost spineless, dark green, glossy leaf and heavy crops of dark red berries; cv. 'Wilsonii', compact in form and vigorous with thick, very glossy foliage 5 inches long and 3 inches wide along with generous red fruit and an easy adaptability to seaside and polluted locations in any soil and exposure from sun to semishade, making it a remarkable hybrid superior to other cultivars.

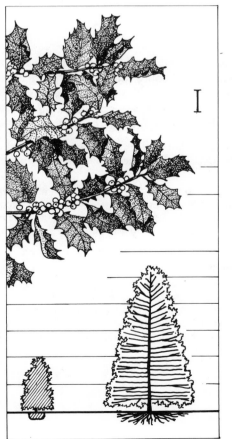

Ilex aquifolium (English holly, European holly, Oregon holly)

Zones 6 (warm) to 9   20' to 50'   Holly family

Probably the most variable of all the hollies, this well-liked native of the British Isles, southern and central Europe, north Africa, and western Asia is particularly admired for its winter-persistent, large fruit, adaptability to clipping, and low maintenance requirements. Its lists of cultivars is especially large.

HABIT: Stiff, pyramidal, densely branched; slow to moderate growth.

SEASONAL APPEARANCE: Twigs green or purplish with 1- to 2-inch, leathery, dark green leaves having thick margins and stiff, spiny teeth; white, fragrant flowers appear in late spring on second-year growth; bright red, round fruit up to three-eighths inch in diameter persists all winter; bark is smooth and gray.

PREFERENCES AND PROBLEMS: See *I.* × *altaclarensis*.

PESTS AND DISEASES: See *I.* × *altaclarensis*.

VARIETIES AND CULTIVARS (a sampling of some noteworthy ones): Cultivar 'Argenteo-marginata', male and female plants have silver-edged leaves and a variety of named clones such as 'Silver Beauty'; cv. 'Argenteo-marginata pendula' carries bold, creamy white leaf margins on weeping twigs; cv. 'Aurea regina', male, leaves variegated with deep gold; cv. 'Bacciflava', bright green foliage and yellow fruiting; cv. 'Ferox', male with hunchbacked leaves and short spines; cv. 'Ferox argentea', male, silver-white spines and margins on green leaves; cv. 'Fructu-aurantiaca' displays deep orange fruit often flushed with scarlet; cv. 'Muricata', leaves heavily streaked with greenish yellow or silver-gray, plus red fruit; cv. 'Smithiana', male, dense growth of thin, spineless, narrow foliage.

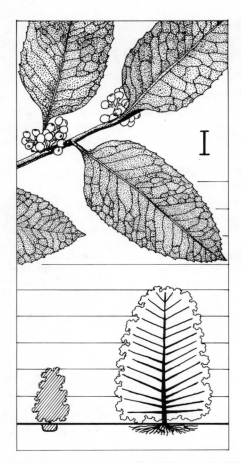

Ilex latifolia   (Lusterleaf holly, Tarajo)

Zones 7 (warm) to 10   50′ to 60′   Holly family

Here is the holly with the largest leaves and an impressive size. Native to eastern China and Japan, it is often found in ancient shrine gardens of the Orient as a specimen or in hedges.

HABIT: Broadly stout and dense with a rounded crown and heavy, upturned branching; slow growth when small.

SEASONAL APPEARANCE: Thick, leathery, dark green leaves are glossy above and dull, yellowish green beneath, 3 to 7 inches long and up to 3 inches wide with fine, margin serrations and unprickly, black teeth on green stems; yellowish flowers appear on previous year's growth; broadly oval, dull orange-red to red, clustered fruit of quarter-inch size follows; bark is greenish gray.

PREFERENCES AND PROBLEMS: See *I.* × *altaclarensis;* tolerant of more shading than most.

PESTS AND DISEASES: See *I.* × *altaclarensis.*

VARIETIES AND CULTIVARS: Cultivar 'Variegata' has yellow-streaked foliage.

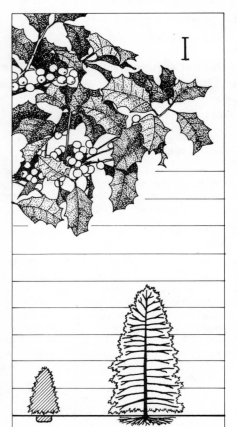

Ilex opaca   (American holly)

Zones 6 to 9   40′ to 50′   Holly family

Native to the coastal United States from eastern Massachusetts to Florida and westward into Texas and parts of Missouri, the parent plant is less glistening for its foliage and produces less fruit than most other hollies but does have landscape appeal as a sturdy specimen, screen, or clipped hedge. Over 1000 cultivars have been named, to the confusion of us all.

HABIT: Dense and pyramidal when young but changing to irregularly conical or even columnar with age; has short, spreading branches and a moderate growth rate.

SEASONAL APPEARANCE: Foliage is semiglossy to dull above, thick, leathery, sharp-spined, flattened, keeled or even twisted in shape; tiny, cream-white flowers blossom on current growth; fruit single, up to a half-inch, round, from scarlet to crimson; bark is smooth, light gray and apt to become warty with age.

PREFERENCES AND PROBLEMS: See *I.* × *altaclarensis.*

PESTS AND DISEASES: See *I.* × *altaclarensis.*

VARIETIES AND CULTIVARS (only a minute sample of hundreds is possible): Both cv. 'Fructu-luteo', with yellow fruit and cv. 'Xanthocarpa', with sparse, yellow fruiting, offer some novel winter color; the most widely distributed red-berried cultivars, known for their improved fruiting habits and foilage, are 'Bountiful', 'Croonenburg', 'East Palatka', 'Merry Christmas,' 'Miss Helen,' 'Mrs. Santa,' 'Old Faithful,' 'Old Heavyberry', and 'Yule'.

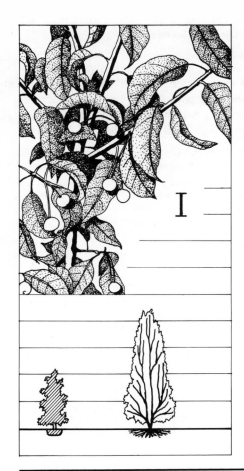

Ilex pedunculosa (Longstalk holly)

Zones 6 and 7   15′ to 30′   Holly family

Often multistemmed and shrubby in form, this introduction from Japan and China is not yet common in nurseries but deserves a closer look for its long-lasting, bright red fruit and unusual leaf outline for a holly.

HABIT: Narrowly pyramidal with ascending branches; silhouette open to dense; moderate in growth.

SEASONAL APPEARANCE: Thin, ovate, 2- to 3-inch leaves have a slender tip and vary from dull to glossy, dark green with a slightly wavy, *entire* margin; flowers are creamy; the quarter-inch, single or clustered, bright red fruit appears on the current growth and is supported by long peduncles up to 2 inches in length; bark is light gray.

PREFERENCES AND PROBLEMS: See *I. × altaclarensis;* appears to tolerate Midwestern heat and winds satisfactorily.

PESTS AND DISEASES: See *I. × altaclarensis;* seems unfazed by leaf miner.

VARIETIES AND CULTIVARS: None.

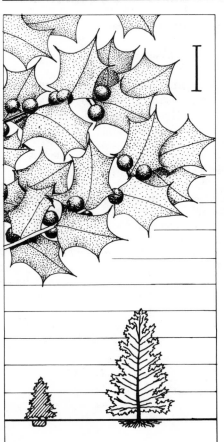

Ilex pernyi (Perny holly)

Zones 6 and 7   15′ to 30′   Holly family

Discovered in central China, this plant is often shrub-like in some growing areas here, but its showy fruit crop is meritorious just the same.

HABIT: Narrowly pyramidal when young but apt to become open with age; moderate rate of growth.

SEASONAL APPEARANCE: Novel, triangular-tipped, glossy, olive-green foliage is from ¹/₂ to 1¹/₄ inches long and appears on noticeably hairy twigs; flowers are yellow-toned; round, scarlet, quarter-inch fruit is generously paired in the leaf axils for an enduring display; bark is dark gray.

PREFERENCES AND PROBLEMS: See *I. × altaclarensis.*

PESTS AND DISEASES: See *I × altaclarensis.*

VARIETIES AND CULTIVARS: Cultivar 'Compacta', has dense habit and slow growth.

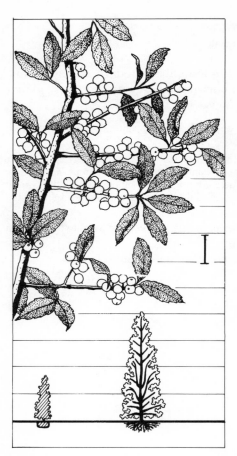

Ilex vomitoria (Yaupon, Cassina, Cassena, Cassine)

Zones 7 to 10   20′ to 25′   Holly family

Native to the United States from southeastern Virginia to Florida and west to Texas, it is a prolific fruiting tree or broad shrub often with multiple stems (and subsequent wide-spreading growth for solid hedge making), unusually adaptable to drought and slightly alkaline soils.

HABIT: Generally compact and slender with stiff branching in cultivation but often open and loose-limbed in the wild; moderate to fast growth rate.

SEASONAL APPEARANCE: Un-holly-like, narrow, grayish green, glossy foliage has only scalloped margins without spines on hairy twigs; blossoms are white on second-year wood; lustrous, red, rounded, tiny fruit clusters generously line the twigs to outproduce almost any other holly for colorful showiness; has smooth, grayish white bark.

PREFERENCES AND PROBLEMS: See *I.* × *altaclarensis;* takes some prolonged dryness and less-than-acid soil conditions well.

PESTS AND DISEASES: See *I.* × *altaclarensis.*

VARIETIES AND CULTIVARS: Many nursery cultivars often are available, but the most popular types seem to be cv. 'Nana', a nonfruiting dwarf to 4 feet, and cv. 'Yawkeyii', a yellow-fruiting, tall selection; others display weeping branches or compact growth.

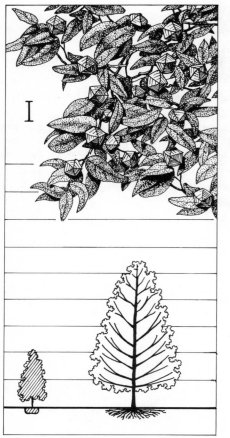

Lagunaria patersonii (Pyramid tree, Patterson sugarplum tree, Primrose tree, Cow-itch tree)

Zones 9 (warm) and 10   25′ to 50′   Mallow family

A colorful specimen or street tree from the Lord Howe and Norfolk Islands of the south Pacific, as well as eastern Australia, the plant has many attributes but one important drawback: The seed capsules are lined inside with needle-sharp hairs highly irritating to animal skin.

HABIT: Densely pyramidal and slow-growing when young with regularly spaced, low branching; more spreading with age and then moderate in growth rate.

SEASONAL APPEARANCE: Thick, leathery, 3- to 4-inch leaves are dull, olive-green above but noticeably whitened beneath and appear on new growth covered with rough scales; generous summer flowers are five-pointed stars, about 2 inches wide in pale rose fading to white from July to September; the ovoid fruit is first light green and then tawny, 1 inch long, persistent, and densely filled with short, stiff hairs very irritating to humans and other animals; bark is dark gray-brown.

PREFERENCES AND PROBLEMS: Enjoys full sun and deep, rich, moist locations but will tolerate drier soils; adjusts satisfactorily to desert heat and alkaline soil conditions as well as to shore sites open to ocean winds and salt spray; moderately frost-hardy.

PESTS AND DISEASES: Unbothered by either importantly.

VARIETIES AND CULTIVARS: None.

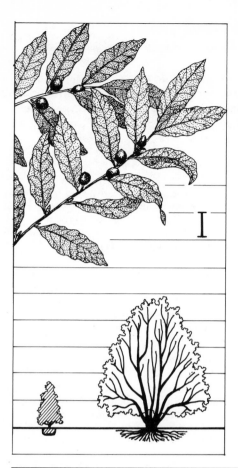

Laurus nobilis (Laurel, Bay, Sweet bay, Grecian laurel)

Zones 8 to 10   30′ to 40′   Laurel family

Here is the pungent, Mediterranean bay leaf of cookery and the honor wreath material for the brows of noteworthy Greeks and Romans in ancient times. Currently it is popular for formal, sheared hedges and tubbed, topiary displays.

HABIT: Slender and conical when juvenile with ground-level branching and often multiple stems; broad and densely pyramidal when older; slow at all stages of growth.

SEASONAL APPEARANCE: Stiff, dull green, 2- to 4-inch foliage is redolent with a distinct, aromatic odor when crushed; the nonshowy, clustered flowering in February and March is creamy yellow to greenish white; its half-inch, oval berries are dark green, turning deep purple to black; bark is smooth and gray.

PREFERENCES AND PROBLEMS: Likes full sun but filtered shade in the afternoon; adapts easily to any soil as long as drainage is very good; enjoys plentiful moisture in spring but can tolerate much dryness for the rest of the year; damaged by heavy frost but not tender otherwise.

PESTS AND DISEASES: None of consequence.

VARIETIES AND CULTIVARS: Cultivar 'Angustifolia', with narrow, willow-like, wavy-edged, pale green leaves and hardier than the parent; cv. 'Aurea', with golden-yellow foliage but rare; cv. 'Undulata', with noticeably wavy leaf margins.

Leptospermum laevigatum   (Australian tea tree)

Zones 9 and 10   15′ to 30′   Myrtle family

This long-lived importation from southeastern Australia and Tasmania has the ability to grow suitably in almost pure sand (making it useful for dune stabilization) and develops a picturesque, gnarled trunk when mature.

HABIT: Shrubby when young (to make a dense, solid hedge) but becoming upright and contorted with gracefully weeping branchlets when older; moderate-growing.

SEASONAL APPEARANCE: Foliage is fine-textured from stiff, leathery, elliptical, 1-inch leaves in light green to gray-green; solitary, white, half-inch, rose-like blossoms appear in masses from February through April; has abundant, flat-topped, quarter-inch, woody seed capsules; bark is gray-brown and shreds in stringy flakes to show red-brown, inner bark.

PREFERENCES AND PROBLEMS: Provide full sun and a well-drained, neutral to acid soil; readily adaptable to drought, salty winds, and sandy or gravelly locations; water established trees infrequently; chlorosis develops in alkaline soils; prune for tree shape only to branches with foliage since bare twigs do not develop further.

PESTS AND DISEASES: Free of both.

VARIETIES AND CULTIVARS: Cultivar 'Compactum', with compact habit and a 3-foot height.

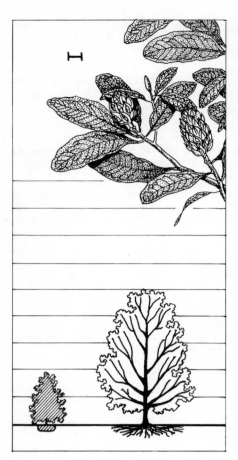

Magnolia grandiflora (Southern magnolia, Bullbay)

Zones 8 to 10, 7 in northwest United States   60' to 100'   Magnolia family

Magnificent as a lawn specimen for its size, flowering, and glistening foliage, our native U.S. tree grows wild from North Carolina to Florida and west to parts of Texas. Small plants can be trained as wall espaliers or limbed high for street use, while the leathery foliage dries well when cut to become a persistent indoor decoration.

HABIT: Ground-hugging if unpruned; usually pyramidal but often round-topped with stout, ascending branches; slow to moderate growth.

SEASONAL APPEARANCE: Shiny, dark green, leathery foliage can be up to 8 inches long and 4 inches wide with rust-colored, downy undersides (if in full sun) on new twigs with the same pubescence; from April to August many waxy, goblet-shaped, cream-white, 8-inch, terminal blossoms perfume the air with a strong but pleasant lemon scent; the erect, 4-inch, cone-like fruit has stacked sets of shiny, red-brown seeds; its thick bark is brownish gray.

PREFERENCES AND PROBLEMS: Adaptable to full sun or semishade on a consistently moist, well-drained, rich soil from neutral to slightly acid and out of high winds; needs generous root ball when transplanted; its thick, fleshy roots are prone to rot if damaged by cultivation or moving; soil or irrigation water that is alkaline causes leaf chlorosis; resents crowding; nursery stock raised from seed consistently shows great variation in habit, leaf size, and shape.

PESTS AND DISEASES: Remarkably unbothered by either.

VARIETIES AND CULTIVARS (many cultivars, of which these are some choice selections): Cultivar 'Cairo', with very glossy and flexible leaves plus early and enduring flowering; cv. 'Exmouth', with narrow leaves and a conical silhouette; cv. 'Gloriosa', having blossoms up to 1-foot wide; cv. 'Goliath', flowers up to 12 inches across and ongoing longer than most; cv. 'Majestic Beauty', with larger foliage and 12-inch blooms; cv. 'Samuel Sommer', carrying enormous, 14-inch flowers and leaves covered with soft, brown hairs; cv. 'St. Mary', low-branched and slower than other types with 10-inch-long leaves and rusty-red fuzz beneath plus 5-inch, cupped flowers.

Melaleuca linariifolia (Flaxleaf paperbark, Snow-in-summer)

Zones 9 and 10   20′ to 30′   Myrtle family

As a group, these Australian trees have the novel habit of producing new growth from the tops of their showy flower spikes, thereby tightly surrounding the twigs later with decorative and persistent seed capsules. Their spongy, peeling bark makes them additionally attractive for specimen or street tree use.

HABIT: Open, willowy, and upright when young, when growth is very rapid; becomes dome-shaped and dense with maturity.

SEASONAL APPEARANCE: Pale beige new growth produces 1- to 1¹/₂-inch, rigid, needle-like foliage of bright green or bluish green; densely set, terminal spikes of fuzzy, cream-white flowers (which also produce the new stem extensions) cover the entire plant like snow from July to September; tiny, woody, cup-like fruit cling to several inches of the stems for many years; bark is white and spongy when young but becoming honey-brown, papery, and exfoliating on older limbs and the trunk.

PREFERENCES AND PROBLEMS: Wants full sun and an average, moist soil but accepts almost any growing condition of heat, wind, poor soil, or drought; tends to be less than content if placed directly at the seashore; juvenile stems are weak and require staking if desired as tree forms.

PESTS AND DISEASES: None of consequence.

VARIETIES AND CULTIVARS: None.

Melaleuca quinquenervia [*leucodendron*] (Paperbark tree, Punk tree, Tea tree, Swamp tea tree, Cajeput tree)

Zones 9 (warm) and 10   20′ to 40′   Myrtle family

One of the tallest of the *Melaleucas,* this species is also found natively in New Guinea and New Caledonia as well as coastal Australia. The tree has found wide acceptance in central and southern Florida for decorative and windbreak use.

HABIT: Generally erect with an oval or rounded, open crown and weeping branch tips; quick-growing.

SEASONAL APPEARANCE: New growth is coppery and covered with silky hairs; leaves are stiff, narrowly oval, between 2 and 4 inches long, dull green above and gray-green below; has conspicuous, bottlebrush-looking flower spikes usually from 2 to 3 inches tall in yellow-white but may also be seen in pink or purple tones on some trees; the quarter-inch, cylindric fruit capsules are woody and persistent; thick, spongy, light brown to nearly white bark peels in long, papery layers.

PREFERENCES AND PROBLEMS: Enjoys sun and average soil; has admirable tolerance for poor drainage, salt air and spray, drought, wind, and even grass fires; may re-seed vigorously to become a pest on consistently moist sites.

PESTS AND DISEASES: Unbothered.

VARIETIES AND CULTIVARS: None.

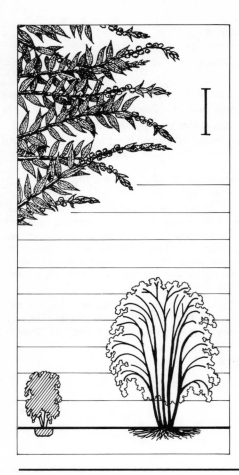

Melaleuca styphelioides (Rigidleaf melaleuca, Prickly-leaved paperbark)

Zones 9 and 10   25′ to 50′   Myrtle family

In contrast with *M. quinquenervia,* its texture is finer and its habit is usually multistemmed with decidedly weeping branchlets. *Melaleuca decora,* a less desirable species, is often confused with this plant.

HABIT: Dense with gracefully pendant branching but mostly carrying several erect trunks; generally fast-growing.

SEASONAL APPEARANCE: Rigid, narrow, three-quarter-inch leaves are bright green, partly twisted and taper to a prickly point; bloom appears from April to June as 2- to 3-inch, brush-like spikes of yellowish white, tiny flowers; the globular, one-eighth-inch, fruit capsules clasp the stems; its spongy bark is white when young but becomes light tan or charcoal gray and flakes with maturity.

PREFERENCES AND PROBLEMS: Treat as for *M. quinquenervia.*

PESTS AND DISEASES: None known.

VARIETIES AND CULTIVARS: None.

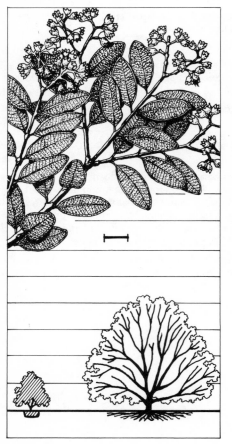

Metrosideros excelsus [tomentosus] (New Zealand Christmas tree)

Zone 10   20′ to 35′   Myrtle family

Native to the shores of New Zealand, this is a vivid-flowering evergreen thriving in the salty blasts of tropical ocean air to make an ideal hedge or specimen focus for seaside garden developments.

HABIT: Multitrunked and heavily branched from shrubby youth to wide-spreading maturity; very sluggish to grow and bloom.

SEASONAL APPEARANCE: White, wooly new growth; recurved foliage thick, leathery, shining dark green with gray, velvety hairs beneath, sometimes bronzed in the juvenile stage; flowering very conspicuous from mid-May to July as 2- to 4-inch-wide, fluffy masses of terminal, dark scarlet stamens with yellow tip ends; woody fruit becomes clustered on projecting stalks and totally covered with white down; bark is grayish tan.

PREFERENCES AND PROBLEMS: Prefers shore sites in full sun with open exposure to salt spray and any wind condition; dislikes dry winds and frost; may unfortunately take twenty years for initial blossoming.

PESTS AND DISEASES: Not nuisanced by either.

VARIETIES AND CULTIVARS: Cultivar 'Aurea', with pale, lemon-yellow flowers.

Olea Europaea   (Common olive)

Zones 8 (warm) to 10   25' to 30'   Olive family

Cultivated since the dawn of history throughout the areas of the eastern Mediterranean, the olive has amazing longevity with ancient survivors there documented to be almost 2000 years old. In California today are gnarled trees still growing and producing fruit as they did when early Spanish missionaries first planted them in the 1700s. Such durability, along with stalwart drought tolerance and a pleasingly sweet bloom, easily promotes this small tree for street use and garden decoration.

HABIT: Densely rounded in poor soil but asymmetrically open in good soil; low-branched with generally upthrust limbs and a contorted trunk with age; moderate for expansion growth but very slow to fill out.

SEASONAL APPEARANCE: Leathery, fine-pointed, 1½-to 3-inch gray-green leaves are silvery beneath; tiny, pleasantly scented yellow-white flowers appear along the second-year twigs in April and May; glossy fruit about 1 inch long is first green, then purple, and finally black but is ripe only when wrinkled (and edible, however, only when processed); bark smooth and gray when juvenile but rough, scaly, and dark brown with maturity.

PREFERENCES AND PROBLEMS: Shapeliest silhouette comes with dry, hot, sunny locations, but better growth occurs on protected sites having deep, fertile, well-drained soil and regular watering; unfazed by considerable drought and tolerant of shallow, rocky, poor and alkaline soils; suckers profusely at the base; dislikes high humidity (and flowers and fruits much less in Florida for that reason); fallen fruit stains pavements but the crop can be greatly reduced with a spring application of a sterilizing hormone spray on the flowers.

PESTS AND DISEASES: Scale occasionally bothersome along with gall distortion on branches.

VARIETIES AND CULTIVARS (many grown but these are the most common): Cultivar 'Ascolano', used mostly as a commercial orchard tree with generous fruiting; cv. 'Barouni', suitable for areas with high summer heat; cv. 'Fruitless', an almost fruitless type; cv. 'Manzanillo', wider-spreading than usual; cv. 'Mission', taller and more compact than others; cv. 'Sevillano', generally planted for its abundant fruit crop.

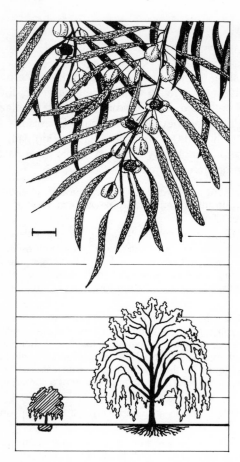

Pittosporum phillyraeoides (Narrow-leaved pittosporum, Willow pittosporum)

Zones 9 and 10   15′ to 30′   Pittosporum family

What all these Australian natives have of special note is desirable evergreen foliage that is clean-looking and plentiful, plus neat habit and a rewarding flower fragance. This species is a handsome choice for specimen use where its weeping habit can be fully seen and appreciated.

HABIT: Upright, somewhat distorted trunk with long, thin, trailing branches; slow growth rate.

SEASONAL APPEARANCE: Dusty green, 2- to 4-inch, slender foilage ends with a hooked point; nicely scented, yellow, quarter-inch blossoms appear singly along the twigs from January to April; the half-inch, oval fruit is deep yellow and shiny; bark is gray.

PREFERENCES AND PROBLEMS: Likes full sun and an average, well-drained soil with occasional watering during drought; adapts satisfactorily to seaside winds, great heat, and almost any soil type; rarely requires fertilizing.

PESTS AND DISEASES: Aphids and scale are sometimes troublesome.

VARIETIES AND CULTIVARS: None.

Pittosporum rhombifolium (Queensland pittosporum)

Zones 9 and 10   30′ to 50′   Pittosporum family

In its homeland of eastern Australia it can stretch to 80 feet, but its smaller size here is no drawback for street tree or specimen use, especially when it is covered with bright fruit in late summer and autumn.

HABIT: Erect, open, usually symmetrically oval; slow-growing.

SEASONAL APPEARANCE: Glossy, uniquely rhomboid or diamond-shaped, 2- to 4-inch, dark green leaves are rust-colored and fuzzy beneath; flowers arrive in late spring as terminal clusterings of quarter-inch, white, fragrant blossoms producing heavy bunches of half-inch, glossy, yellow to orange, round fruit persistent for many months; its bark is smooth and gray.

PREFERENCES AND PROBLEMS: See *P. phillyraeoides*.

PESTS AND DISEASES: Scale infestations and aphids are occasionally bothersome.

VARIETIES AND CULTIVARS: None.

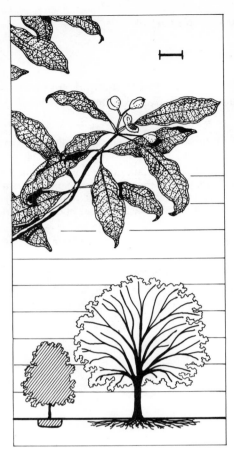

Pittosporum undulatum (Victorian box, Mock orange, Orange pittosporum)

Zones 9 and 10   20' to 40'   Pittosporum family

Especially attractive as a specimen when it develops a wide-spreading crown equal to its height, this species from Australia and Tasmania unfortunately has shallow, surface rooting, denying much room for luxuriant underplanting. It does perform well as a tall screen or low, clipped hedge.

HABIT: Dense, dome-shaped with spreading branches; rapid until 20 feet tall, then slows to moderate growth rate.

SEASONAL APPEARANCE: Glossy, rich green, 4- to 6-inch leaves have wavy edges and often are crowded toward the branch tips; heavily scented (similar to orange blossoms), half-inch, creamy yellow flowers appear generously in terminal clusters from February to April; its pear-shaped, half-inch fruit is orange-yellow, then brown, and splits to reveal many sticky seeds; bark is gray-toned.

PREFERENCES AND PROBLEMS: See *P. phillyraeoides*; develops heavy mat of surface rooting; fallen fruit often a sticky nuisance.

PESTS AND DISEASES: May be troubled by aphids and scale insects.

VARIETIES AND CULTIVARS: None.

Prunus caroliniana [*Laurocerasus caroliniana*] (Cherry laurel, Wild orange, Mock orange, Carolina cherry laurel)

Zones 7 to 10   20' to 40'   Rose family

Native from North Carolina to Texas, it is cultivated as a street and park tree for its glossy foilage, drought resistance, and adaptability to heavy shearing for hedges and topiary displays in containers.

HABIT: Single-trunked or multistemmed with slender, horizontal branching and a dense, broad, somewhat pyramidal crown; moderate rate of growth.

SEASONAL APPEARANCE: Shiny, leathery, 2- to 4-inch, bright to dark green foliage is bronze-colored when new; loose, terminal, one-inch spikes of creamy white flowers from February to early May offer little decorative value; its shiny, black, oval, half-inch fruiting persists most of the year; bark is dark gray-brown.

PREFERENCES AND PROBLEMS: Adaptable from full sun to half shade in humus-rich, consistently moist, well-drained soil; established trees highly drought-resistant; suitable for shore locations exposed to salt spray; highly alkaline soils produce scorching of foliage margins; fruit litter bothersome on pavements.

PESTS AND DISEASES: Susceptible to scale insects and fire blight.

VARIETIES AND CULTIVARS: Cultivar 'Bright 'n' Tight', shrub-like and compact; cv. 'Compacta', denser and shorter-growing.

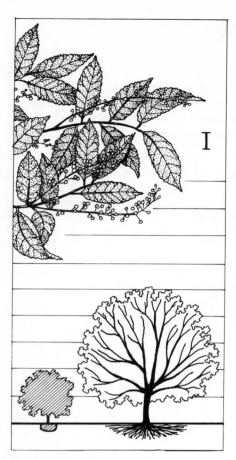

Prunus lusitanica [Laurocerasus lusitanica]
(Portugal laurel)

Zones 7 to 10   15' to 40'   Rose family

Showy flowering and dependable tolerance to hot sun and strong winds give this native of Portugal, Spain, and the Canary Islands a well-deserved landscape appeal.

HABIT: Dense, round-topped, single-trunked or multistemmed with spreading branches and moderate growth.

SEASONAL APPEARANCE: Thick, glossy, 2½-to 5-inch, dark green leaves are lighter-colored beneath and appear with red petioles; quarter-inch, cup-shaped, cream-white flowers bloom from April to July on 10-inch spikes held conspicuously beyond the foilage; oval, quarter-inch fruit is red in late summer and turns dark purple or black later; bark is grayish brown.

PREFERENCES AND PROBLEMS: Similar to *P. caroliniana* but more adaptable to poor or alkaline soils and hot, windy sites.

PESTS AND DISEASES: Seemingly unbothered by any of importance.

VARIETIES AND CULTIVARS: Cultivar 'Angustifolia', limited to 15 feet with smaller foliage and a dense, conical shape; cv. 'Variegata', leaves streaked with creamy white markings.

Quercus agrifolia   (California live oak, California field oak, Coast live oak, Encina oak)

Zones 9 and 10   30' to 100'   Beech family

Success with evergreen oaks often relies heavily on the conditions existing when the plants are young. Majestic specimens found natively growing usually have had only winter rainfall and greatly resent constant artificial irrigation to become seriously afflicted by a fatal root rot. Young, wild trees, on the other hand, adapt readily to automatic sprinkler systems as easily as nursery-grown stock. Old trees also object to cut-and-fill operations around their roots.

This species from California and the Baja Peninsula of Mexico is a long-lived, commonly planted tree for its heavy shading and sturdy, far-reaching branches as a terrace ornament or as a durable street tree where it has room to expand properly.

HABIT: Dense, picturesquely dome-shaped or round-topped with a stout, short trunk usually divided into low, wide-spreading branches often touching the ground; grows moderately fast when young if watered regularly.

SEASONAL APPEARANCE: New growth pale green or pinkish bronze; mature foilage variable from tree to tree but usually semiglossy, stiff, 1½ to 3 inches long, oval and convex in form with spiny margin tips resembling holly, dark green above with short, grayish hairs on the veins beneath; flowers are catkins of no special notice; the acorn fruit can be up to 1½ inches long and matures the first year; bark is smooth, light gray changing with age to rough, dark gray-brown with slight fissuring.

PREFERENCES AND PROBLEMS: Takes full sun or light shade equally well and likes a rich, moist soil with a sandy or gravelly subsoil able to hold adequate moisture at that root level; needs no fertilizing; old trees cannot tolerate artificial watering near their trunks; trees collected from the wild do poorly unless transplanted several times; root system is eventually greedy and close to the surface; nut drop may become problematic.

PESTS AND DISEASES Caterpillars, oak moths, and borers often need control; old trees suffer from root rot if overwatered.

VARIETIES AND CULTIVARS: None.

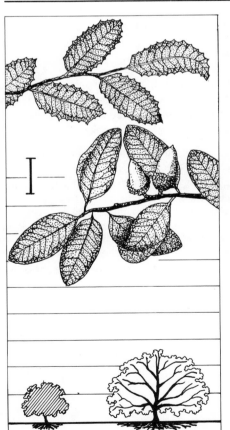

Quercus chrysolepis (Canyon live oak, Canyon oak, Mauri oak)

Zones 7 (warm) to 10   60' to 90'   Beech family

Odd in leaf because young plants have spiny foliage while older trees are spineless, this wide-spreading, long-lived Pacific coast native grows wild from Oregon to the Baja Peninsula of Mexico and is occasionally given room in cultivated spaces for its attractive bark and foliage.

HABIT: Round-headed and very wide-spreading with age, occasionally with pendulous twigs; generally develops a thick, short trunk; slow-growing.

SEASONAL APPEARANCE: Has variable oval foliage with young trees carrying spines on the leaf margins but older plants showing entire edges; leaves up to 4 inches long, stiff and leathery, at first down-covered, then shiny, medium green with grayish, yellowish, or whitish felt on the undersides; its catkin flowering is nondescript; inch-long acorns are egg-shaped, and the cups are thickly covered with golden yellow hairs; fruit matures the second year; bark is gray-brown and tinged with red, exfoliating with age as small scales.

PREFERENCES AND PROBLEMS: Thrives in full sun on moist, average, well-drained soil; can tolerate dryness; does not transplant well unless very young.

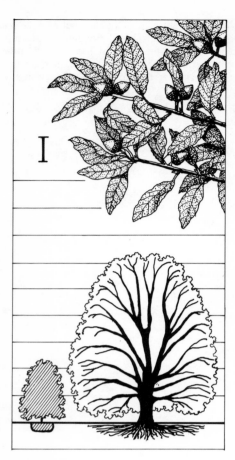

Quercus ilex (Holly oak, Holm oak)

Zones 7 to 10   40' to 70'   Beech family

In southern Europe and the British Isles, where this Mediterranean native is very popular as a shade tree, the height is often greater than listed, while its dense, twiggy growth and symmetrical outline allow for easy shaping into distinctive topiary forms.

HABIT: Dome-shaped or rounded with a regular outline, dense with spreading or ascending branches forming a large crown; tends to retain lower branching well into old age even in woodlots; moderate growth rate.

SEASONAL APPEARANCE: Foliage variable in having entire or spiny-toothed leaves on downy new growth; leaves stiff, up to 3 inches long, shiny, dark green above and covered with yellowish or whitish fuzz below; its springtime flowering is unimportant; the oval, inch-long acorn fruit is often clustered in threes and matures the first year; bark nearly smooth or rough-checked and light gray.

PREFERENCES AND PROBLEMS: Enjoys full sun but tolerates semishading well on an average-fertility, well-drained, sandy soil; adjusts happily to windy sites at oceanside; loses all its old foliage in late spring to create a maintenance problem since the leaves are rot-resistant.

PESTS AND DISEASES: None of consequence.

VARIETIES AND CULTIVARS: Variety *rotundifolia* carries smaller leaves, grows better in zones 8 to 10, and has a crop of edible, large acorns; cv. 'Fordii' has a pyramidal form and narrower foliage.

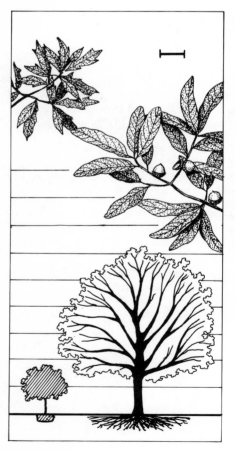

Quercus laurifolia (Laurel oak, Darlington oak, Swamp laurel oak)

Zone 8   60' to 100'   Beech family

Extensively used as a street tree in the moist, southern parts of the United States, the plant is native to wet areas from Virginia to Florida and west into eastern Texas, but has to be considered as only a semievergreen since it defoliates in spring and remains bare for several weeks.

HABIT: Erect, broad-crowned, and dense with slender branching; moderate rate of growth.

SEASONAL APPEARANCE: New stem growth dark red; thin foliage variable between entire or slightly lobed leaves from $2^{1}/_{2}$ to 6 inches in length, glossy, dark green above and light green beneath with a noticeably raised, yellow midrib; flowering generous yearly but nonshowy; egg-shaped, half-inch acorns are dark brown to black and have a hairy cup; fruit matures in the second year; its juvenile bark is dark brown, maturing to nearly black with shallow fissures.

PREFERENCES AND PROBLEMS: Likes full sun and very moist sites; intolerant of lime soils.

PESTS AND DISEASES: Inconsequential.

VARIETIES AND CULTIVARS: None.

Quercus suber (Cork oak)

Zones 8 to 10   **40' to 60'**   **Beech family**

Its thick bark is the cork of commerce, and it is stripped from living trees without harm every ten or fifteen years in Portugal and Spain, the center of the industry. Native to north Africa and southwestern Europe, its wide-spreading but low-branched silhouette suggests some use as a specimen in parks or other large spaces.

HABIT: Compact, round-topped, somewhat open and leaning with age; has short trunk often divided into several stout stems with lower branches touching the ground; moderate growth.

SEASONAL APPEARANCE: Oval, shiny, prickle-toothed leaves, dark green above and gray-wooly beneath from 1 to 3 inches long; inconsequential flowering; inch-long acorns are oval and encased in a thick cup with recurved scales; the fruit matures in one year; bark is pale gray, rugged-looking, corky, up to 3 inches thick, and deeply furrowed.

PREFERENCES AND PROBLEMS: Full sun best on a gravelly soil in hot locations with low humidity; dislikes any cold exposure; fruit not likely in areas with constantly humid conditions.

PESTS AND DISEASES: Unbothered by either.

VARIETIES AND CULTIVARS: None.

Quercus virginiana (Live oak, Southern live oak)

Zones 8 to 10   **50' to 60'**   **Beech family**

Although native from Virginia to Florida and down to Mexico, this tree is deciduous in its northern limits and will shed appreciable foliage elsewhere if winter cold snaps arrive suddenly. Usually twice as wide as high, it is a sizable tree favored as a street or shade plant in the most southerly parts of the United States, where it usually is festooned with scarves of Spanish moss.

HABIT: Fine-textured, dense, broadly dome-shaped with heavy, horizontal branching and a buttressed trunk; fast-growing where summers are consistently hot but grows only moderately in warm areas.

SEASONAL APPEARANCE: New stems covered with fine hairs; foliage variable with both thick and thin, egg-shaped leaves from 1¹/₂ to 5 inches long, glossy, dark green above and white-hairy below with the edges slightly rolled under; spring flowers of no significance; long-stalked, oval acorns are dark, chestnut brown, one inch long and capped with a red-brown cup; the thick, dark brown bark is tinged with red and deeply furrowed.

PREFERENCES AND PROBLEMS: Enjoys full sun on a deep, rich, consistently moist soil but tolerant of many soil types, including alkaline; easily transplanted when young.

PESTS AND DISEASES: None of consequence.

VARIETIES AND CULTIVARS: None.

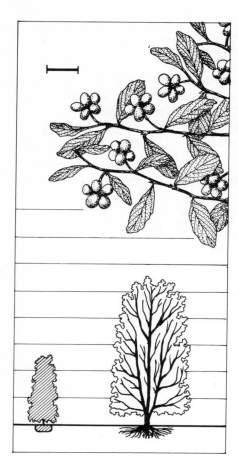

Quillaja saponaria (Soap-bark tree)

Zones 8 (warm) to 10   30′ to 60′   Rose family

Oddly, few South American plants transpose successfully to our hemisphere with ease, but this native of Chile has done just that. As a slender accent tree, it provides interesting flowering and fruit.

HABIT: Upright, narrow, multistemmed, and dense when young with drooping branchlets; older plants have broad, flattened, open crowns; growth is moderate.

SEASONAL APPEARANCE: Lustrous, oval, leathery foliage, between 1 and 2 inches long, is bright green with slightly toothed edges on the forward tips; yellow-white, half-inch flowers appear generously at the twig ends during May and June as star-shaped clusters with separate male and female blossoms on the same plant; the one-inch fruit has five brown, leathery projections; bark is grayish tan.

PREFERENCES AND PROBLEMS: Likes sun and an average, moist, well-drained soil; drought-tolerant when fully established; may require staking when young.

PESTS AND DISEASES: Unknown.

VARIETIES AND CULTIVARS: None.

Schinus molle (Pepper tree, California pepper tree, Peruvian pepper tree)

Zones 9 and 10   20′ to 50′   Cashew family

A curious native from the Andes Mountains of Peru that has readily adapted to the conditions of life here, the handsome pepper tree offers a gracefully weeping form, abundant fruiting, and billowing, fine-textured foliage—along with a few drawbacks detailed below.

HABIT: Round-topped and wide-spreading with long, pendulous branching and a gnarled, knobby trunk; vigorous in growth.

SEASONAL APPEARANCE: Pinnately compound foliage is 6 to 12 inches in length with twenty to sixty one- to 2-inch, very narrow, light green leaflets giving off a peppery scent when crushed; male and female flowers are on separate plants, and the tiny blossoms in early summer are equally nonshowy as yellowish white in terminal clusterings; conspicuously pendant bunches of quarter-inch, rose or red fruit generally appear from November through May; bark is brownish gray.

PREFERENCES AND PROBLEMS: Thrives in full sun on an average, well-drained site; takes remarkably well to poorly drained situations, great heat, dry and low-fertility soils, plus neglect; prone to constant litter of fruit, twigs, and old leaves; young plants require firm staking for upright growth; has rapidly invasive, shallow rooting well able to lift paving and clog nearby drainage lines; pollen drift gives an allergic reaction to some people.

PESTS AND DISEASES: Highly susceptible to disfiguring aphid infestations and attacks of black scale, which bans its placement anywhere near citrus groves.

VARIETIES AND CULTIVARS: None.

Schinus terebinthifolius (Brazilian pepper tree, Christmasberry tree)

Zones 9 and 10   15′ to 40′   Cashew family

Very ornamental with its bright red fruiting (on female plants) from December through March, this native of Brazil has now become naturalized over much of the Florida peninsula and the Hawaiian Islands. Less graceful than *S. molle,* it offers desirable compactness for terrace and street use.

HABIT: Dense and rounded in outline with broadly spreading, stiff, horizontal branching; often multistemmed; fast to moderate growth.

SEASONAL APPEARANCE: Compound foliage between 6 and 8 inches long, composed of five to thirteen broad leaflets with the odor of turpentine when crushed; leaves are shiny, leathery, and dark green above but lighter-colored beneath; late summer, white-toned flowers (sexes are on different plants) appear terminally; highly conspicuous, 4- to 5-inch, pyramidal clusters of bright red to dull rose-red, one-eighth-inch berries develop from late autumn to spring on female plants; its bark is rough, gray-brown, and checkered shallowly.

PREFERENCES AND PROBLEMS: Grows best in full sun on any well-drained site; adjusts well to dryness; apt to be surface-rooted unless watered deeply but infrequently; its pollen may cause allergies; in windy areas thin out the heavy crown for less branch damage; appears to become dominantly weedy if allowed to seed indiscriminately; seed-grown plants highly variable for fruit colors.

PESTS AND DISEASES: Unbothered.

VARIETIES AND CULTIVARS: None.

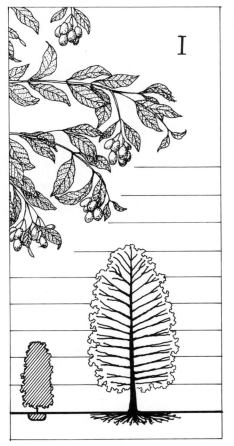

Syzygium paniculatum [Eugenia myrtifolia] (Australian brush cherry)

Zones 9 (warm) and 10   30′ to 50′   Myrtle family

Its consistently columnar form and tolerance to heavy pruning readily recommend this western Australian tree as a high hedge or a topiary accent in an outdoor tub. Showy, edible, but ground-messy fruit adds a bonus.

HABIT: Upright, dense-foliaged, and strongly columnar when young but broadening to an oval silhouette with age; moderate in growth.

SEASONAL APPEARANCE: New growth is noticeably attractive in glistening, reddish bronze; leaves glossy, leathery, from 1 to 3 inches long, and rich, dark green above but lighter beneath; both flowers and fruit are produced throughout the year; the cream-white blossoms are round heads of fluffy stamens up to one inch wide in terminal clusters; the scented, edible (some say bland) fruiting is a shiny, bright rose-purple, fleshy berry about three-quarters-inch in diameter that stains pavements when it drops; its light gray bark is shallowly grooved.

PREFERENCES AND PROBLEMS: Enjoys either sun or partial shade in any well-drained soil that is watered regularly; cannot tolerate freezing weather, salt spray, or drought; sometimes quite variable in habit, leaf appearance, and flower size.

PESTS AND DISEASES: Mealybugs, aphids, and scale can prove bothersome, but diseases are unknown.

VARIETIES AND CULTIVARS: Cultivar 'Compacta' is denser and smaller.

Umbellularia californica (California bay, California laurel, California olive, Pepperwood, Oregon myrtle)

Zones 7 to 10   30' to 70'   Laurel family

Highly ornamental for its silhouette and foliage, this slow-growing native of coastal California and southwestern Oregon can have a life span of several hundred years (an ancient specimen with a 100-foot spread is in Santa Barbara). Desirable as a street tree, specimen, or hedge plant, this tree is the only representative of the laurel family indigenous to this part of the United States.

HABIT: Dense, rounded crown with ascending branches and a swollen trunk base; apt to be appropriately compact and cone-shaped on highly windy, open sites; very slow growth.

SEASONAL APPEARANCE: Smooth, leathery, dark green foliage between 3 and 5 inches of length has a heavily pungent odor of bay rum or camphor when bruised (and can be safely substituted for the true bay leaf, *Laurus nobilis,* in cookery); tiny flowers appear in winter and early spring as yellow-green, cup-shaped clusterings of minor importance; its bunched fruit is olive-shaped, one inch long, shifting from yellow-green to dark purple at maturity; the bark is dark gray, changing to scaly, deep reddish brown with age.

PREFERENCES AND PROBLEMS: Best in full sun but tolerant of much shading (with even slower growth) on a deep, rich, constantly moist site; greatly wind-tolerant and sturdy; moderately injured by frost; tends to a shrubby nature on dry, rocky, shallow soils.

PESTS AND DISEASES: Occasionally bothered by scale.

VARIETIES AND CULTIVARS: None.

**Needle
Evergreens**

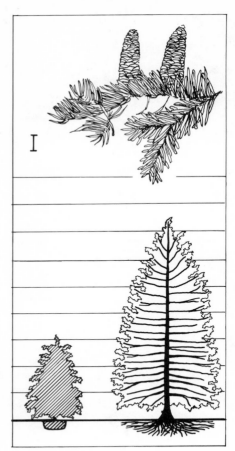

Abies concolor (White fir, Balsam fir, Colorado fir)

Zone 5 to 8   50′ to 100′   Pine family

Firs are splendidly symmetrical trees with single, straight trunks and narrowly pyramidal silhouettes of stiffly horizontal branching. All hold their needle leaves for several years to produce both dense foliage and tight outlines. They prefer moist, acid, cool-in-summer locations but greatly dislike air pollution. For the most part they are unbothered by insects or diseases.

The nondescript male and female flower parts on second-year twigs of firs are always separated on the same plant. Later, erect female cones develop on the topmost limbs and always on the upper side of branches. These cones mature in one season but have the unique habit of totally disintegrating when ripe, leaving only a pencil-thin, upright woody core by winter. Cone production, while noticeably worthwhile as a summer landscape effect, is obviously not a durable attraction.

Of all the needle evergreens, firs and spruces have enough look-alike similarities to become confusing at times. To separate them, make a simple comparison of some fresh twigs and needles. Firs have flattened needles (usually with blunted tips) and whitened undersides; spruce foliage is squared in cross section (and rolls easily between fingers) with sharply pointed ends and is green on both surfaces. Fir twigs are relatively smooth when leaves drop and show rounded leaf scars, but spruce twigs are rough from woody, peg-like bases remaining after needles shed. Further, fir twigs are somewhat brittle and carry rounded winter buds protected by a waxy covering, while spruce twigs are tough and flexible with pointed, scaly buds not usually resin-coated.

The fir described here is native to much of the western and the southwestern United States and is a well-liked ornament for large, open spaces because of its very long, soft, gray-toned foliage, nearly conical shape, and tolerance for semishading. It also withstands summertime heat and dryness better than any other fir.

HABIT: Narrowly conical when young but broadening with age into a dome-shaped crown; growth varies from moderate to rapid.

SEASONAL APPEARANCE: As with all firs, the needles are single and arranged in whorls around the twigs; here the 2-inch needles twist upward to appear to be all from the top, are gray-green to blue-green on both surfaces, and appear on yellow-green twigs; needles can remain from five to ten years before shedding; the 5-inch, short-duration cones are silvery olive-green to purple-toned; its bark has the resin blisters common to firs and is pale to ashy gray with deep furrows.

PREFERENCES AND PROBLEMS: Best grown on deep, rich, acid loam (but not clay) in either full sun or semishade; adapts better when transplanted in spring but August moving is also workable if followed by regular watering; adapts well to the warm, humid conditions of the northeastern and southeastern United States; very drought-tolerant but intolerant to polluted air; protect from dry, summer winds.

PESTS AND DISEASES: Usually free of both but occasionally bothered with the sawfly larva or the larva of the fir needle miner.

VARIETIES AND CULTIVARS: Cultivar 'Argentea' ('Candicans') with silvery white needles; cv. 'Aurea' with golden yellow new growth, rare to locate; cv. 'Brevifolia' with short, stout foliage; cv. 'Compacta', densely branched but irregular in outline and only 3 feet tall, scarce; cv. 'Conica', dwarfed and cone-shaped, rare in cultivation; cv. 'Globosa', short-branched and rounded in outline; cv. 'Pendula' with strongly curved and drooping branches; cv. 'Violacea' with conspicuously silver-white needles; cv. 'Wattezii' with pale yellow new growth turning silver later.

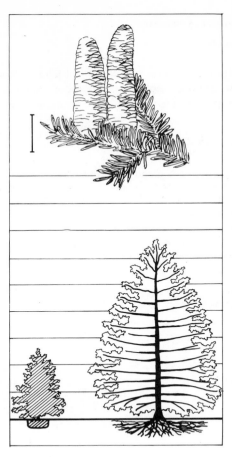

Abies homolepis [*brachyphylla*]   (Nikko fir)

Zones 5 to 8   80′ to 100′   Pine family

Native to the mountains of Japan, the special appeal of this fir as a specimen comes from the foliage color with its strikingly white lines on the underside of each needle, plus its tough adaptability to some degree of air pollution.

HABIT: Broadly pyramidal with branching usually retained to ground level; moderate-growing.

SEASONAL APPEARANCE: Dark green, glossy, one-inch needles have bright silver-white banding beneath; foliage arranged in a V formation on whitened twigs showing unique (with fir) stem grooving between new leaves; cones are cylindrical, up to 4 inches tall in purple coloration that turns deep brown with aging; its scaly bark is pale gray with pink toning and becomes purple-gray at maturity.

PREFERENCES AND PROBLEMS: Enjoys a moist, sunny, well-drained site with cool, humid summer air; transplants best in spring; tolerant to moderate pollution; best adaptable to northeastern and eastern United States growing conditions.

PESTS AND DISEASES: None of consequence.

VARIETIES AND CULTIVARS: Cultivar 'Scottiae', a dwarfed type; cv. 'Tomomi' with shorter leaves and fewer branches, rare; cv. 'Umbellata' with green young cones, scarce.

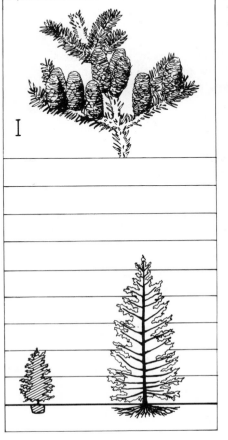

Abies koreana   (Korean fir)

Zones 5 to 7   30′ to 50′   Pine family

Sedate in growth habit, this inhabitant of the mountain slopes of south Korea is less likely than other firs to overwhelm garden spaces in a short time. It also has the attractive habit of producing showy cones (however briefly) at an early age.

HABIT: Uniformly but stiffly pyramidal and somewhat open in silhouette; slow growth.

SEASONAL APPEARANCE: Glossy, three-quarter-inch, deep green, older needles carry silvery lines beneath but first emerge as bright silver-gray on yellowish twigs; erect, cylindrical, prominent, 2-to 3-inch, violet-purple cones are often abundant even in youth; the bark is smooth, reddish brown turning gray and splitting with age.

PREFERENCES AND PROBLEMS: Likes full sun on a well-drained, moist, rich soil; does not take well to pollution or great heat.

PEST AND DISEASES: Unimportant.

VARIETIES AND CULTIVARS: Cultivar 'Flava' with yellow-green cones; cv. 'Prostrata', low and spreading with many cones.

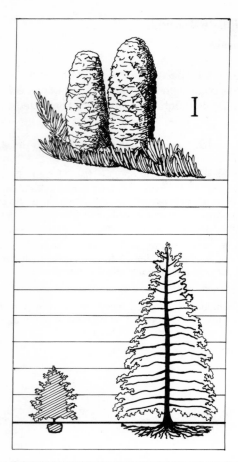

Abies nordmanniana (Nordmann fir, Caucasian fir)

Zones 5 to 8   50′ to 60′   Pine family

In its wild state of growing in the coolness of the high mountains of Asia Minor, Armenia, and Greece, its mature height can become a majestic 150 feet. In lowland cultivation this specimen is usually less dominant in size and adjusts well to warm areas.

HABIT: Narrowly pyramidal to conical and dense; slow when juvenile but moderate when established.

SEASONAL APPEARANCE: Needles are shining, dark green with white lines beneath and up to 1¼ inches long on bright, yellow-green twigs; when bruised, its foliage gives off the odd scent of orange peel; its 5- to 6-inch cones are green and then red-brown; the gray-brown bark is mostly smooth.

PREFERENCES AND PROBLEMS: Thrives best in areas which are consistently cool and sunny and have constantly moist but well-drained soil; adaptable to warmer climates easier than most other firs; enjoys regular watering.

PESTS AND DISEASES: Seemingly resistant to both.

VARIETIES AND CULTIVARS: Cultivar 'Aurea' with golden yellow foliage; cv. 'Nana', a dwarfed form; cv. 'Tortifolia' with some leaves twisted and curled inward.

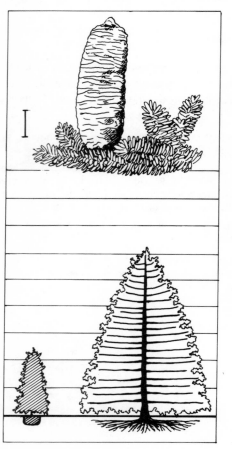

Abies pinsapo (Spanish fir)

Zones 6 to 8   50′ to 80′   Pine family

Common to the mountains of southern Spain, its solid growth and squat form at maturity readily give this evergreen an ornamental appeal. The stiff needles are more densely packed along all sides of its twigs than on any other fir.

HABIT: Narrow when young but broadening widely with age; slow to expand, expecially on dry sites.

SEASONAL APPEARANCE: Brown twigs carry tight rows of dark green, rigid, three-quarter-inch needles with pale gray lines below; cones are 4 to 5 inches tall and purple-brown; the brown-gray juvenile bark is smooth and becomes grooved and flaky later.

PREFERENCES AND PROBLEMS: Does well in full sun on any moist soil (except boggy), including chalky; sluggish growth results where air is very warm and soil conditions consistently dry.

PESTS AND DISEASES: Unfazed by either.

VARIETIES AND CULTIVARS: Cultivar 'Argentea' with silvery white or gray foliage; cv. 'Glauca' with very gray leaves; cv. 'Nana', a dwarfed type; cv. 'Pendula' with drooping branches, rare in cultivation.

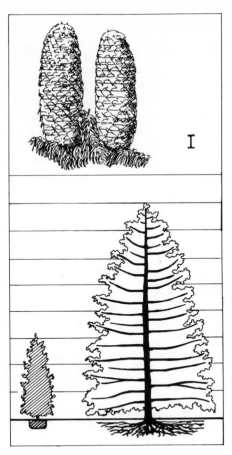

Abies procera [nobilis] (Noble fir, Feathercone, Red fir)

Zones 6 to 8   100' to 150'   Pine family

Achieving grand size even in lowland garden spaces, the noble fir of the hills and mountains in Washington, Oregon, and northern California carries the largest and most interesting cones of any fir, usually in generous quantities. Unfortunately, like all fir fruiting, they fall apart quickly by autumn.

HABIT: Conically slender and dense with branches at right angles to the trunk and often persisting to ground level; generally rapid-growing except in very warm locations.

SEASONAL APPEARANCE: Rich, blue-green, thick needles up to 1½ inches long with grooved tops appear on rusty-haired twigs; cones are oblong, between 4 and 10 inches high, in green tones changing to purple-brown with unusual sharp-pointed bracts overhanging the scales; its bark is thick, dark gray becoming cinnamon-brown and deeply grooved.

PREFERENCES AND PROBLEMS: Best grown at high elevations in either sun or part shade on deep, acid, well-drained, cool, consistently moist soils; tolerates lower, warmer elevations but shows less growth response; dislikes chalk soils; only fair-growing in eastern United States.

PESTS AND DISEASES: Unbothered by insects but occasionally contracts fungal diseases.

VARIETIES AND CULTIVARS: Cultivar 'Glauca' with silver-blue needles and heavy cone crops once its 15-foot mark is reached.

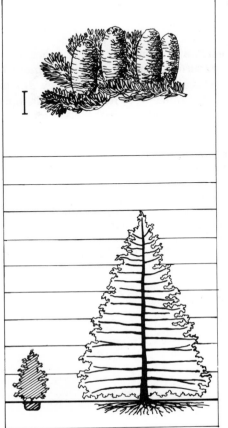

Abies veitchii (Veitch fir)

Zones 4 to 7   50' to 75'   Pine family

Widely planted and easy to establish, this fir is content on both ocean coasts of the United States as a slow-growing, pyramidal specimen.

HABIT: Broadly pyramid-shaped at maturity with ground-hugging branches; slow to moderate growth rate.

SEASONAL APPEARANCE: Twigs are densely hairy and red-brown with shiny, dark green, tip-notched needles up to one inch in length showing broad banding of white beneath (but not as bright-colored as *A. homolepis);* cones are blue-purple turning brown and about 3 inches tall; the smooth bark is a light gray with brown flecks; normally develops depressions beneath all branches where they join the trunk.

PREFERENCES AND PROBLEMS: Takes sun or semishading on a moist, acid, well-drained site; intolerant of alkaline soils; seems to adapt well to unpolluted locations on both east and west coasts of the United States.

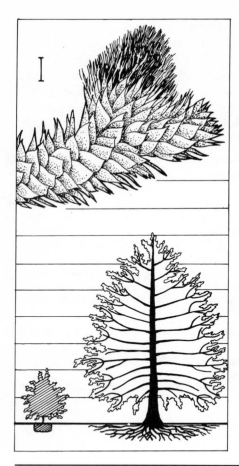

Araucaria araucana [*imbricata*] (Monkey-puzzle, Monkey-puzzle tree, Chilean pine)

Zones 7 to 10   70′ to 100′   Araucaria family

A native to the western Andes slopes in Chile and to southwestern Argentina, this odd-shaped tree supposedly gets its common name from a growth habit of sending all its sharp needles pointing upward to allow a monkey to climb up but not descend—comfortably. Often planted for its novelty, it gives an impression of being from another planet with its strangely stiff, rope-like branching. Place it very carefully since a female plant has heavy fruit approaching the size of a small coconut. Falling fruit weighing up to 10 pounds can make quite a dent in cars and people.

HABIT: Oval to round at first but becoming broadly spreading and pyramidal with age; its heavy branching is widely spaced in whorls of five with upturned ends; the brittle limbs often drop off in storms or with aging; slow to start but moderately rapid in growth later.

SEASONAL APPEARANCE: Its awl-shaped, overlapping, glossy, leathery, bright green leaves range from 1 to 2 inches long and carry sharpened tips; sexes are on separate trees with erect male flowers in cone-shaped heads up to 5 inches tall at the branch tips; female cones generally appear in pairs (but occasionally to five) as woody, scaly ovals about 7 inches tall of substantial weight; its thick, resin-filled grayish bark is ringed with shallow grooves.

PREFERENCES AND PROBLEMS: Provide full sun and a rich, moist, acid loam in locations with high humidity and free of winds; tolerant of all but very dry or boggy soils; female fruit drop can become hazardous; will grow only in zones 9 and 10 on the east coast of the United States.

PESTS AND DISEASES: Inconsequential.

VARIETIES AND CULTIVARS: Cultivar 'Variegata' with straw-colored leaves intermixed with green ones on young growth; rare.

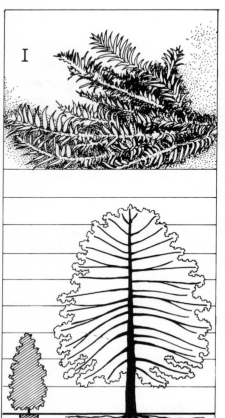

Araucaria bidwillii (Bunya-bunya, Bunya-bunya pine)

Zones 9 and 10   80′ to 150′   Araucaria family

Certainly better-looking from a landscape standpoint than its cousin *A. araucana,* this native from northeastern Australia carries its ornamental foliage in bunches arranged only at the tip ends of its pleasantly drooping branches. The sizable, heavy fruit on female trees resembles a pineapple but has the drawback of being quite a danger to nearby pedestrians and automobiles when is unexpectedly falls—as it will.

HABIT: Narrowly columnar in youth but broadly conical with age; may become free of lower branching to half its mature height; generally rapid-growing.

SEASONAL APPEARANCE: Carries two kinds of foliage when older; its juvenile leaves are thick, narrow, glossy, very sharp-pointed, dark green, up to 1½ inches long, and clustered at the branch tips; mature foliage is oval, half-inch long, very stiff, dark green, and spirally set to overlap each other on the twigs; the short-lived, male-flowering cones are 3 to 5 inches high while the hefty female ones are up to 9 inches tall with a marked similarity to a pineapple fruit; its gray-toned, thick, resinous bark peels off in thin layers.

PREFERENCES AND PROBLEMS: Same as *A. araucana.*

PESTS AND DISEASES: Fairly resistant to both.

VARIETIES AND CULTIVARS: None.

Araucaria heterophylla [excelsa] (Norfolk Island pine, Australian pine, House pine)

Zone 10   50' to 100'   Araucaria family

Adaptable when juvenile to potted culture as an indoor plant, this native from the Norfolk Island of the Pacific can become a 200-foot giant in its wild state. In outdoor culture here it usually remains within reasonable size, while its incredibly straight stems and absolutely symmetrical, tiered branching contribute handsomely for is use as a specimen of special beauty.

HABIT: Perfectly straight, rugged stems carry regularly spaced whorls of stiffly erect foliage to form an open, narrow pyramid of unusual distinction; moderate growth rate.

SEASONAL APPEARANCE: Develops two types of closely spaced foliage with age; its young leaves are slender, half-inch, recurved, light green, and soft; the older foliage becomes somewhat triangular, rigid, stiff-pointed, only a quarter-inch in length, and set densely and overlappingly on the twigs; male flowering is about 2 inches tall, and the female cones are round and up to 6 inches in diameter; its gray-brown bark scales off with age in thin flakes.

PREFERENCES AND PROBLEMS: See A. araucana.

PESTS AND DISEASES: Untroubled.

VARIETIES AND CULTIVARS: Cultivar 'Albospica' with leaves and new stems variegated in silver but often reverting to all-green foliage.

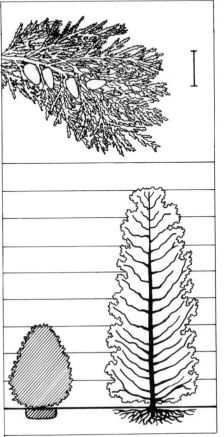

Calocedrus decurrens [Libocedrus decurrens, Heyderia decurrens] (California incense cedar)

Zones 5 to 10   70' to 100'   Cypress family

Outstandingly attractive as an accent, hedge, or windbreak for its tightly columnar silhouette in cultivation (it grows chunkier in the wild), along with distinctive foliage for color and scent, this native evergreen from western Oregon to Mexico deserves far greater use than it now receives since it is surprisingly hardy throughout much of the United States.

HABIT: Fat and rounded when young, maturing (in cultivation) to a tall, narrow, completely dense column with neat foliage to the ground if unshaded; wild plants tend to be irregular in shape and broadened in the middle; growth is moderate to fast, varying with its hardiness zone.

SEASONAL APPEARANCE: Foliage is composed of flat sprays of glossy, dark green, eighth-inch, scale-like, highly aromatic leaves held upright on flattened, red-brown twigs; flowering is on separate parts of the same plant with male pollen bearers yellow-toned, tiny, and terminally produced; the pendant, 1-inch, female cones are tapered urns in shape and first appear green, then reddish brown, and finally yellow-brown; the almost-hidden bark is cinnamon-red, thick, and deeply furrowed.

PREFERENCES AND PROBLEMS: Enjoys full sun but is tolerant of light shade on a moist, well-drained loam; dislikes shallow, dry soil and smoggy, windswept sites; watering deeply but infrequently instills drought resistance.

PESTS AND DISEASES: None of importance in cultivation, but heart-rot fungus often attacks forest specimens.

VARIETIES AND CULTIVARS: Cultivar 'Compacta', a dwarfed, tight-foliaged form; cv. 'Intricata', an erect dwarf of very dense branching and foliage with leaves tip-colored bronze in winter.

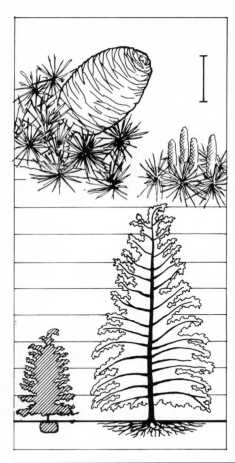

Cedrus atlantica (Atlas cedar, Atlantic cedar)

Zones 7 to 10   50′ to 120′   Pine family

Now widely cultivated apart from its homeland in the Atlas Mountains of Algeria and Morocco, this popular plant—at least in its striking blue-foliaged form—has a worldwide appeal for both its simple gracefulness and simple care.

HABIT: Cone-shaped with upright branching and very open when young but flat-topped and widely spreading with maturity; reasonably fast-growing.

SEASONAL APPEARANCE: Blue-green, needle foliage about 1 inch long appears in clustered groupings of seven to ten leaves on short, stout spurs; flowering is on different portions of the same plant with small, male flowers erect and cone-like; the 3-inch female cone is also erect but oval, first green, then purplish, and takes two years to mature; its upright, straight trunk has brown bark.

PREFERENCES AND PROBLEMS: Enjoys full sun and a well-drained, loamy soil; tolerant of heavy clay if not overly wet.

PESTS AND DISEASES: None of importance.

VARIETIES AND CULTIVARS: Cultivar ‘Argentea’ with leaves silvery white (and similar to ‘Glauca’); cv. ‘Aurea’ with golden yellow foliage, shorter height, and slower growth; cv. ‘Fastigiata’ with dense, upswept branching to create a narrow, conical form; cv. ‘Glauca’ with silver-blue leaves and gray bark; cv. ‘Pendula’ with gracefully drooping branchlets spilling over the ground like a prostrate waterfall unless propped up early as a weeping tree form.

Cedrus deodora (Deodar, Deodar cedar, Himalayan cedar, Indian cedar)

Zones 7 (warm) to 10   80′ to 150′   Pine family

Perhaps the lightest-textured cedar, this native of the northwestern Himalaya Mountains keeps a conical shape well into maturity. Its gracefully pendulous limbs provide an attractive accent for a large garden space.

HABIT: Generally pyramidal to conical with pleasantly drooping branching; fast-paced in growth.

SEASONAL APPEARANCE: Twigs are usually heavily covered with short hairs and carry generous bundles of dark blue-green needles up to 2 inches long; female cones are barrel-shaped, violet, turning red-brown, and up to 5 inches tall; the bark is gray-brown.

PREFERENCES AND PROBLEMS: Needs full sun and an acid, well-drained, moist soil; difficult to transplant except when young; warm, humid climate conditions encourage a greater weeping silhouette; needles become sickly yellow on alkaline soils.

PESTS AND DISEASES: No problems.

VARIETIES AND CULTIVARS: Cultivar ‘Aurea’ with golden yellow new growth fading to greenish yellow; cv. ‘Compacta’, slow-growing, dense, and rounded in outline; cv. ‘Fontinalis’ with elongated, very flexible branching, rare in cultivation; cv. ‘Glauca’ with noticeably blue-gray foliage; cv. ‘Pendula’, carrying long, drooping branches and needing stem support to become an erect tree; cv. ‘Prostrata’, a dwarfed, spreading, low form; cv. ‘Robusta’ with greater vigor and stiffer, dark gray-blue foliage; cv. ‘Verticillata’, a compact form with blue-white leaves; cv. ‘Viridis’ with vivid, deep green foliage.

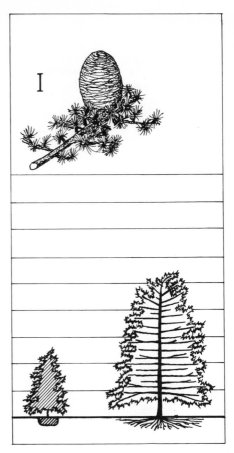

Cedrus libani (Cedar of Lebanon)

Zones 7 to 10   80' to 100'   Pine family

Enduring is a fitting word for this evergreen from the Lebanon Mountains of Syria. Known to cultivation for over 2500 years, it has exerted an exotic appeal since King Solomon used the timber for his famous Temple. The initial plantings of 1646 in Great Britain attest to their longevity as these plants are still very much alive, if not exactly shapely. Not as much used today as the other *Cedrus* species, it still can hold its own as a specimen of landscape distinction.

HABIT: Dense and narrow when juvenile but flat-topped, open, and wide-spreading with age from stiffy horizontal branching; slow-growing when young and moderate-growing when established.

SEASONAL APPEARANCE: Foliage rosettes hold up to forty stiff, 1-inch needles which are bright green when young but dark gray-green with age; male flowering is non-descript, but the tan female cones are 4 inches tall and stand erect on the topside of the limbs after developing for two seasons; its thick bark is blackish gray and eventually splits and divides.

PREFERENCES AND PROBLEMS: Does best on a rich, well-drained soil in bright sun with reasonably consistent moisture.

PESTS AND DISEASES: Unbothered.

VARIETIES AND CULTIVARS: Variety *stenocoma* is more cold-tolerant than the parent and will grow well in zone 6; cv. 'Aurea' has smaller, yellow-green foliage; cv. 'Compacta', a dense form; cv. 'Glauca' with blue to silver-white leaves, uncommon in cultivation; cv. 'Nana', slow, compact, and dwarfed with bright green foliage; cv. 'Pendula' with drooping branches, rare; cv. 'Sargentii' with dense, pendulous branching requiring support for tree form and very slow-growing.

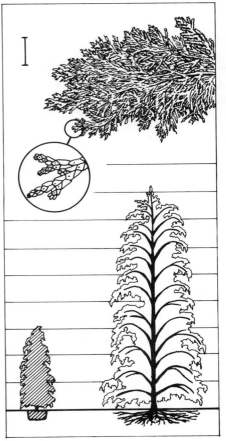

Chamaecyparis lawsoniana [Cupressus lawsoniana]
(Lawson cypress, Port Orford cedar, Lawson false cypress, Oregon cedar)

Zones 6 to 9   60' to 100'   Cypress family

Half of the four ornamentally popular species of this genus are native to the high-humidity areas along the Pacific coast of this continent, while the other two are from inland Japan. Our native plants thrive also in much of Europe but grow less well on the drier east coast of the United States (yet the Japanese introductions there do very well). As a total group, *Chamaecyparis* presents a bewildering array of hundreds of sizes, colors, forms, and needle types exceedingly troublesome to separate clearly.

Chamaecyparis greatly resembles *Thuja* (Arborvitae) in most aspects of growth, especially in their common foliage sprays of flattened, scale-like needles, but false cypress has white lines on the leaf undersides while arborvitae foliage is green on all surfaces. Cone production separates them, too, with *Chamaecyparis* showing rounded ones and *Thuja* carrying bell-shaped, slender fruit.

Like *Cupressus,* the true cypresses, *Chamaecyparis* has mature foliage composed of tiny, scale-like leaves tightly overlapping one another on very slender twigs, but it varies from cypress by producing juvenile growth with needle-like foliage as well. *Chamaecyparis* further differentiates itself by carrying its branchlets in flat sprays.

This species from southwestern Oregon to northwestern California can grow to 175 feet in its wild state, but under cultivation it remains nicely manageable for many decades. The normally columnar habit promotes its attractive use as a hedge or windbreak.

HABIT: Narrowly pyramidal with gracefully drooping branches and a moderate growth rate.

SEASONAL APPEARANCE: Carries frond-like, lacy sprays of flat, bright green to bluish green foliage composed of sixteenth-inch scales on drooping branchlets; flowering is separated on the same plant with the tiny male parts pink or crimson while female cones become half-inch, berry-like and turn dark russet-brown; the bark is thick, fibrous, and red-brown.

PREFERENCES AND PROBLEMS: Grows well with high humidity in full sun or semishade on a consistently moist but well-drained site of average fertility; intolerant of dusty and polluted air, salty wind, high heat, and drought; dislikes grass at its base.

PESTS AND DISEASES: Spider mites are occasionally bothersome, and root rot is common in very wet soils.

VARIETIES AND CULTIVARS: (over 200 have been named and this is only a mere sampling of tree forms): Cultivar 'Allumii' with foliage of a blue, metallic hue, compactly columnar; cv. 'Ellwoodii', slow-growing with thick, soft, gray-green leaves; cv. 'Erecta', densely columnar with rich, green foliage; cv. 'Lutea' with stiff, yellow new growth turning blue-gray later; cv. 'Pendula' with dark green leaves on drooping branchlets; cv. 'Stewartii', cone-shaped and broad in outline with golden yellow new foliage changing to dark green in summer.

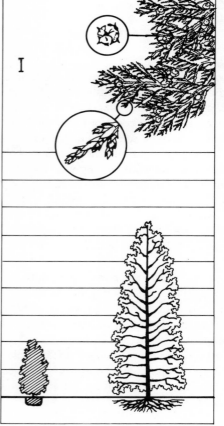

Chamaecyparis nootkatensis (Nootka cypress, Alaska cedar, Nootka false cypress)

Zones 5 to 9   70' to 100'   Cypress family

Noted for its cold hardiness and adaptability to poor soil conditions, this native from southeastern Alaska, British Columbia, and northern Oregon is more coarse in foliage texture and has stiffer branching than *C. lawsoniana,* yet if offers a landscape appeal in naturalistic settings.

HABIT: Narrowly columnar with sturdy, irregular branching and pendant tip ends; moderate in growth.

SEASONAL APPEARANCE: Foliage dark green but without the characteristic white markings on the undersides; leaves emit a distinctive odor when bruised; leading shoots have foliage with spreading points that are harsh to the touch; male flowering minute and yellow; female cones purple-green and a half-inch in diameter; its bark is brownish gray and separates into thin scales.

PREFERENCES AND PROBLEMS: Enjoys full sun on a constantly moist, well-drained, acid soil but tolerates almost any other conditions satisfactorily; needs winter wind protection in its zone 5 limits.

PESTS AND DISEASES: See *C. lawsoniana.*

VARIETIES AND CULTIVARS: Cultivar 'Aurea', pyramidal with bright yellow new growth turning yellow-green later; cv. 'Compacta', a dense, globose dwarf showing dull, light green foliage; cv. 'Glauca', pyramidal with gray-green leaves; cv. 'Pendula' with noticeably drooping, widely spaced branches and dull green foliage; cv. 'Viridis', narrowly columnar with bright green leaves.

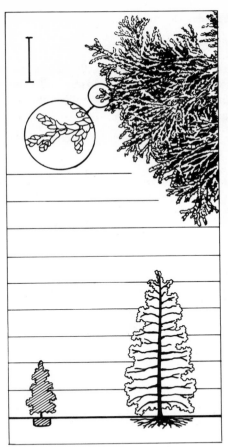

Chamaecyparis obtusa [*Cupressus obtusa*] (Hinoki cypress, Hinoki false cypress, Japanese false cypress)

Zones 5 to 9   75′ to 120′   Cypress family

In central and southern Japan, where it is found natively in vast forests, this evergreen is an important timber tree. With the most ornamentally attractive foliage of any *Chamaecyparis,* its landscape appeal is consistent and deserved (especially so for its myriad compact and dwarf shrubby forms popular in Oriental gardens and for containers). This species adapts well to the eastern United States.

HABIT: Dense, compact, broadly conical, and irregular in outline with horizontal branching; slow-growing.

SEASONAL APPEARANCE: Thick, glossy, blunt-tipped, bright green leaves are unequal in size and have showy but tiny white lines beneath; branchlets are fern-like, flattened, and gently pendulous; male flowering is terminal and inconspicuous; globose female cones vary in size up to three-eights inch but are nonshowy and orange-brown at maturity; the smooth, red-brown bark peels in thin strips.

PREFERENCES AND PROBLEMS: Provide full sun or partial shade with good humidity on a moist, acid, well-drained soil; tolerant of some soil dryness but dislikes reflected heat and light from nearby buildings.

PESTS AND DISEASES: None of consequence.

VARIETIES AND CULTIVARS: Variety *formosana* from Taiwan is limited to zones 8 and 9 and has smaller, more slender foliage; cv. 'Aurea' with young leaves a rich, golden yellow; cv. 'Breviramea', narrowly tall with short branching and thick, very glossy foliage lacking white lines beneath; cv. 'Caespitosa', dense, very dwarf with dark green leaves; cv. 'Crippsii' with a loose, open habit and pale yellow foliage later darkening to green; 'Ericoides', dwarfed, slow, with glossy, light green leaves; cv. 'Filicoides' with very deep green, lustrous, fern-like foliage on shortened branches and an open, irregular habit; cv. 'Gracilis', narrowly pyramidal with dark green leaves; cv. 'Magnifica' with bright green, lustrous foliage and vigorous growth.

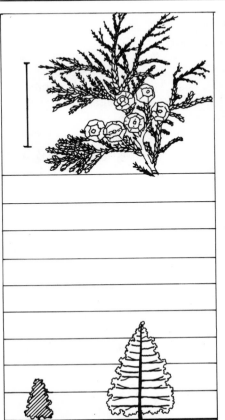

Chamaecyparis pisifera [*Cupressus pisifera,* *Retinospora pisifera*] (Sawara cypress, Sawara false cypress)

Zones 5 to 9   70′ to 120′   Cypress family

In this instance the parent has been completely overshadowed by the cultivars since they are now exclusively planted for specimen appeal in its place. These Japanese importations grow very well in the eastern parts of this country.

HABIT: Narrowly conical with horizontal branching and a loose, open silhouette; slow in growth.

SEASONAL APPEARANCE: Long-pointed, slightly flared, dark green leaves with whitened undersides appear on flattened branchlets; male flowering almost invisible, but female cones are up to a third-inch wide and yellow-brown; its smooth, reddish brown bark exfoliates in slender strips.

PREFERENCES AND PROBLEMS: Sunny, moist, well-drained, rich, acid soil is preferred; tolerant of considerable shading and polluted air; dislikes dry soil, heavy clay, lime, and windy exposures.

PESTS AND DISEASES: Of no special consequence.

VARIETIES AND CULTIVARS: Cultivar 'Aurea' with golden yellow foliage at its best in summer; cv. 'Cyanoviridis' ('Boulevard') with soft, mossy, silver-green to bluish green needle foilage turing bronze-toned in winter, compact but broadly conical form; cv. 'Filifera', pyramidal to conical with widely spaced branching and graceful sprays of thread-like, drooping foliage; cv. 'Filifera Aurea', slower than 'Filifera' with golden yellow leaves; cv. 'Plumosa' with feathery, dull green foliage and a conical, dense shape and upright branching, fast-growing; cv. 'Squarrosa' with gray-mossy, woolly, soft, needle-like leaves projecting from the twig, irregularly branched with a dense but still open silhouette.

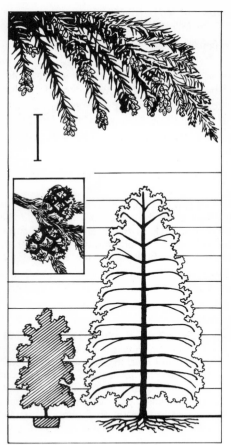

Cryptomeria japonica (Japanese cedar, Cryptomeria)

Zones 6 to 9   75′ to 150′   Taxodium family

A stately contribution from central and southern Japan, the *Cryptomeria* is a hardy (but not fast-growing) specimen tree even in Boston, offering an unusual tint of bronze foliage during winter, along with noticeably cinnamon-brown, peeling bark as it matures.

HABIT: Narrowly conical when young with drooping branch tips; openly broad and flat-topped later; fast-growing in warm zones.

SEASONAL APPEARANCE: Awl-shaped, half-inch needle foliage is spirally set on horizontal, decurved branching; leaves bright green or blue-green in summer and bronze-tinted through the winter; yellow, male flowering clustered at branch tips; round, light brown female cones up to 1 inch across persist for several years; the red-brown bark peels in long, vertical strips.

PREFERENCES AND PROBLEMS: Thrives in full sun on a deep, fertile, moist soil; transplants easily when young; seldom likes windy sites or polluted air.

PESTS AND DISEASES: None of consequence.

VARIETIES AND CULTIVARS: Variety *sinensis* from south China is tender, belongs in zones 8 and 9, and has both slender branches and a less formal outline; cv. 'Elegans' with 1-inch, gray-green, feathery foliage turning rosy bronze in winter on drooping branchlets, slow-growing; cv. 'Lobbii', narrowly upright and conical with lighter green leaves remaining that color all year in warm zones.

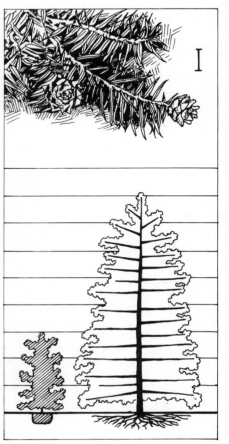

Cunninghamia lanceolata [sinensis]   (China fir)

Zones 7 to 9   60′ to 120′   Taxodium family

While a botanic cousin of *Cryptomeria,* the tree has a stronger resemblance to *Araucaria* (which has its own family) with its similarly styled, sharp-pointed foliage. Native to most of China, this graceful evergreen often assumes a deep bronze wintertime color where the climate is consistently cold. It is well liked here as a decorative lawn specimen.

HABIT: Heavy-trunked with radial branching and slightly downturned tip ends; assumes a conical shape usually with foliage to ground level; moderate in growth rate.

SEASONAL APPEARANCE: Leathery, very sharp-pointed, glossy leaves are about $2^1/_2$ inches long, richly green above with noticeable white banding beneath, and arranged radially on green twigs; leaves often bronze in winter; male flowers are clustered at the branch tips; the female, oval cones are red-brown and between 1 and 2 inches wide with diverging scales; its brown, scaly bark reveals red inner bark coloring.

PREFERENCES AND PROBLEMS: Adjusts well from full sun to light shade on a well-drained, acid soil; dislikes windy sites, especially if wind is dry and hot; has the unusual ability to regrow as a dense shrub if all top growth is killed by heavy frost.

PESTS AND DISEASES: None known of consequence.

VARIETIES AND CULTIVARS: Cultivar 'Glauca' has blue-green foliage and greater cold tolerance.

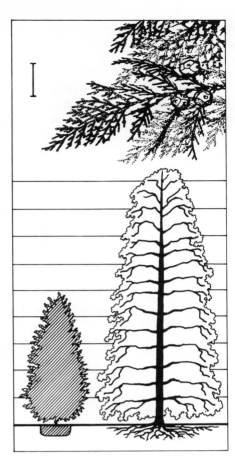

× *Cupressocyparis leylandii* (No common name)

Zones 5 to 10   65′ to 100′   Cypress family

A fascinating hybrid of *Chamaecyparis nootkatensis* and *Cupressus macrocarpa,* resembling the former in habit and foliage, this valuable tree can spring up to 50 feet in only twenty years! Its spectacular growth is unfazed by pests and diseases, has the hardiness of its *Chamaecyparis* parent, and willingly adjusts to just about every soil type around. It has a decidedly bright future as a high hedge, screen, or windbreak.

HABIT: Dense with foliage to ground level and broadly columnar with long, slender branching turning down at the ends; extremely rapid growth.

SEASONAL APPEARANCE: Flattened foliage sprays are composed of gray-green, tiny leaf scales overlapping one another; minute male flowering is inconspicuous; the round, brown female cones vary up to three-quarters inch; its bark (mostly invisible) is thick, brown-gray.

PREFERENCES AND PROBLEMS: Full sun best on any average-fertility soil from very wet to dry in cool, moist, hot, or dry climates; seemingly impervious (so far) to having cultural problems.

PESTS AND DISEASES: Nothing bothers it.

VARIETIES AND CULTIVARS: Cultivar 'Haggerston Gray' with open growth and foliage sage-green above and gray-green beneath; cv. 'Leighton Green', narrowly columnar with flattened sprays of gray-green leaves darkening with age on branches with upturned ends; cv. 'Naylor's Blue', slenderly columnar with gray-blue leaves shaded gray-green beneath.

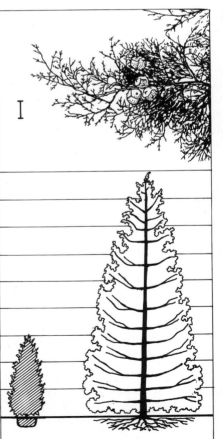

Cupressus arizonica (Arizona cypress, Rough-barked Arizona cypress)

Zones 6 to 10   40′ to 50′   Cypress family

Thriving best in its dry, western homeland from southern Arizona to Texas and south into Mexico, this durable tree has great use there as a windbreak or screen and for erosion control of mountain slopes.

HABIT: Narrowly pyramidal with an open silhouette and a very straight trunk; fast-growing.

SEASONAL APPEARANCE: Pale green to gray-green, scale-like leaves (with a strong odor when crushed) are acutely pointed and appear on light green twigs; male flowering inconspicuous; the 1-inch female cones are round, woody, dark red-brown, and prominently stalked away from the twigs; cones turn gray with age and persist for several years; its bark is variable in color with younger trunks having reddish brown bark separating in thin strips while older trees can show rough, thick bark from light to dark gray.

PREFERENCES AND PROBLEMS: Wants full, hot sun and a well-drained location without added fertilizer treatments; greatly drought-tolerant; sulks if overwatered; fast growth sometimes discourages deep rooting, and plants may topple on windy sites if not staked.

PESTS AND DISEASES Not problematic.

VARIETIES AND CULTIVARS: (some of these may later be assigned to *C. glabra*): Cultivar 'Compacta', very slow-growing, narrowly conical with gray-green foliage; cv. 'Gareei' with silver blue-green leaves; cv. 'Glauca', having new growth silvery gray, rare in cultivation; cv. 'Oblonga' with markedly horizontal growth and gray-green foliage; cv. 'Verhalenii', softer-looking silhouette and bright, gray-blue leaves; cv. 'Watersii' with a dense, narrowly pyramidal outline and silver-green leaves.

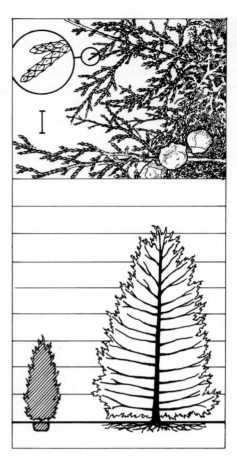

Cupressus glabra (Smooth Arizona cypress, Smooth-barked Arizona cypress)

Zones 7 to 10   40' to 70'   Cypress family

Long confused with its kinsman *C. arizonica,* this native of central Arizona has its outer bark shedding *annually* to show very smooth, cherry-red inner bark. Unfortunately, it has only shallow rooting and can easily blow over in high winds if the soil becomes supersaturated.

HABIT: Irregularly branched but dense with a broadening, pyramidal shape; moderate-growing.

SEASONAL APPEARANCE: Foliage waxy, sharp-pointed, blue-green to gray with a noticeable resin gland on each scale; male flowers yellow but unnoticeable; oval, brown-toned female cones are over 1 inch in size and carry a prominent point at the center of each scale; bark is thin, very sleek, peeling yearly to show cherry-red inner bark.

PREFERENCES AND PROBLEMS: See *C. arizonica.*

PESTS AND DISEASES: None.

VARIETIES AND CULTIVARS: Because of a long-standing confusion between this species and *C. arizonica* in nurseries and botanic collections, further research may eventually reassign some of the present cultivars to *C. arizonica.*

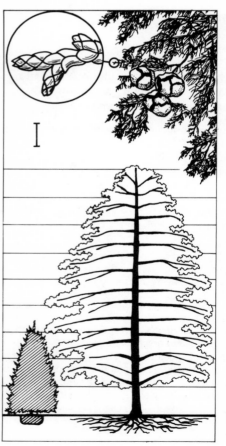

Cupressus macrocarpa (Monterey cypress)

Zones 8 to 10   40' to 70'   Cypress family

Long renowned as a durable and hardy tree for direct shoreline sites battered by storms and salt spray, it is curiously native only to Monterey County in California. Excellent when used as a garden specimen, windbreak, or a clipped hedge, the tree now suffers from a quickly destructive canker disease for which there is yet no known cure. It will be a discouraging landscape loss if this picturesque tree finally disappears.

HABIT: Neatly symmetrical and narrowly pyramidal when young; loosely broadens with age to a wide-spreading, rounded outline; fast-growing when young but moderate later.

SEASONAL APPEARANCE: Scale-like leaves from dark to bright green (possibly yellow-green) have blunted ends and appear on long, jutting branches; male flowering insignificant; round female cones are purple-brown and up to $1^1/_2$ inches in diameter; the thick bark is gray on the surface but irregularly fissured to show red-brown inner bark.

PREFERENCES AND PROBLEMS: Full sun best on a well-drained soil of average fertility; shaded branching soon dies and falls off; mature trees do not transplant satisfactorily.

PESTS AND DISEASES: Incurable canker fungus can kill readily; with it the foliage turns yellow, then red-brown; and soon the canker destroys the plant; wood borer is occasionally bothersome, especially near San Francisco.

VARIETIES AND CULTIVARS: Cultivar 'Aurea', erect with strikingly attractive golden leaves and irregularly horizontal branching; cv. 'Crippsii', narrow-growing with very white new development on short, rigid branching; cv. 'Donard Gold', narrowly conical with upswept branching and pure, golden yellow foliage; cv. 'Lutea', narrowly pyramidal with bright yellow leaves turning green with age, has yellow cones; cv. 'Stricta', very slender and columnar.

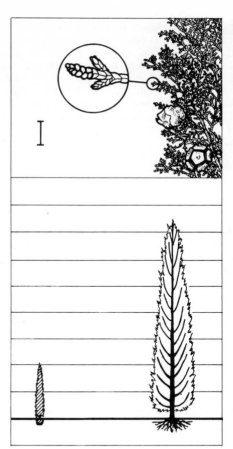

Cupressus sempervirens   (Italian cypress, Pencil pine)

Zones 8 to 10   50' to 80'   Cypress family

Perhaps most of you will be surprised to learn that the well-known Italian cypress is not necessarily shaped like an exclamation point but that it varies in the wild to being as wide-spreading as a cedar of Lebanon. The pencil-slim form seen here which excites the most comment is cv. "Stricta', a type once greatly used by ancient Greeks and Romans as graveyard adornments signifying immortality. Since these trees are documented to be long-lived, there may be something significant in that analogy.

HABIT: Densely columnar to widely spreading in the wild; moderate to fast in growth, depending on the cultivar.

SEASONAL APPEARANCE: Tightly set dark green to gray-green scale-like leaves adhere to horizontal branching and have hidden bud formation; the new growth comes from beneath the topmost leaf scales, leaving no bare twig between seasonal expansion; male flowering is nondescript; the 1-inch female cones are first shining green, then gray-brown, usually with a jutting point at each scale; its thin, mostly smooth bark is grayish brown.

PREFERENCES AND PROBLEMS: Best grown in full sun on a well-drained, average soil; enjoys hot, dry summers; requires no fertilizing; becomes ragged and open if overwatered; not successful in southern Florida.

PESTS AND DISEASES: Spider mites are occasionally bothersome, and gummosis disease is possible if roots are not well drained.

VARIETIES AND CULTIVARS: Cultivar 'Glauca' with a compact habit and blue-green foliage; cv. 'Horizontalis', very broadly pyramidal with horizontal branching; cv. 'Indica' with bright green leaves; cv. 'Stricta' ('Pyramidalis') with somberly dark green foliage and the most rigidly erect and narrowest silhouette of *any* columnar tree known.

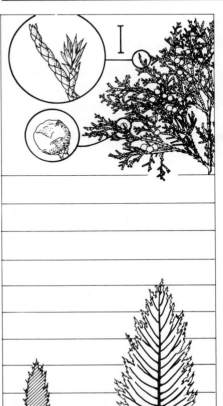

Juniperus chinensis   (Chinese juniper)

Zones 4 to 10   30' to 60'   Cypress family

Far better known as the parent of many hybrid tree forms and shrubby cultivars, the Chinese juniper has long been established natively throughout most of eastern Asia. It has the unique asset, for a generally sunloving group of evergreens, of being tolerant (along with most of its progeny) to goodly amounts of filtered shading. All junipers adapt successfully to drought and wind without complication.

HABIT: Variable in outline but generally erect and conical; moderate to slow growth, depending on the hardiness zone.

SEASONAL APPEARANCE: Carries two kinds of foliage; its dark green juvenile leaves are needle-like, three-pointed, and prickly with chalky white banding on the topside; the paired, mature foilage is scale-like, blunt-tipped, tightly arranged, and also dark green on its cord-like twigs; flowering is separated on different plants with male trees carrying tiny, yellow cones of pollen often located on juvenile growth; the female plants develop clustered, gray-brown to purple-brown, berry-like cones up to a third-inch wide requiring two years for maturity; its bark is gray-brown and irregularly scaly.

PREFERENCES AND PROBLEMS: Full sun best but is tolerant to consistent light shading; adapts well to dry, rocky sites and to slightly acid soil but prefers alkaline and well-drained, good soil; dislikes waterlogged conditions; foliage of all junipers is especially sensitive to damage from wind-drifted sprays of chemical weed killers.

PESTS AND DISEASES: All junipers are prone to some degree of attack from spider mites, aphids, and twig dieback (phomopsis); they are also the alternate host of a disfiguring rust disease common to many rose-family members; any large, dark orange, spore-housing galls found on juniper twigs are visual evidence that this problem is active in the neighborhood; prune off and destroy all such galls to interrupt the disease cycle.

VARIETIES AND CULTIVARS: (only the tree forms are listed here): Cultivar 'Ames' with mostly prickly, juvenile leaves emerging blue-green but changing to all green later; dwarfed at first, then tightly upright, zone 5; cv. 'Aurea', male, slow-growing with light gold (if in full sun), mostly juvenile foliage, zone 6; cv. 'Columnaris' with dense, silver-green mostly juvenile, prickly foliage, narrowly columnar with rapid growth, zone 5; cv. 'Iowa', erect but informal with blue-green, mature foliage throughout, free-fruiting, zone 4; cv. 'Keteleeri', pyramidal, loosely dense, slow-growing with dark green, scale-like foliage and generous annual fruiting of half-inch, gray-green cones, zone 5; cv. 'Mas', densely columnar, male with yellow-green leaves, zone 5; cv. 'Mountbatten', dense, narrowly pyramidal with gray-green, mostly juvenile foliage, heavy-fruiting, zone 4; cv. 'Obelisk', slow-growing, narrowly columnar, neatly dense without pruning, and foliaged with very blue-green prickly leaves, zone 5; cv. 'Pyramidalis', slow-growing male with half-inch silver blue-green, prickly foliage in a dense, pyramidal shape with strongly upright branching, zone 5; cv. 'Stricta', similar in all respects to 'Pyramidalis' except all leaves are mature in form and soft to the touch, zone 6; cv. 'Tortulosa' ('Kaizuka') with bright green, all-mature leaves and angular, silver-blue, third-inch fruit; if single-trunked, apt to be narrowly erect but leaning to one side with twisted foliage; if multistemmed, likely to be only a meandering, contorted shrub; zone 7; cv. 'Variegata' with juvenile growth cream-tipped, otherwise resembles 'Pyramidalis', zone 5.

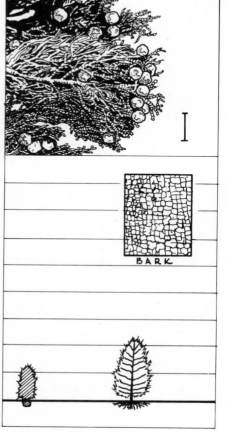

BARK

Juniperus deppeana pachyphlaea   (Alligator juniper)

Zones 7 to 10   35' to 50'   Cypress family

Native to the arid regions of southwestern Texas and Arizona into central Mexico, the alligator juniper has exceptional drought resistance, sluggish growth, and a remarkable potential of surviving up to 500 years. The oddly checked bark provides a noticeable landscape bonus on older specimens, while its adaptability to difficult sites proves useful for erosion control plantings.

HABIT: Conical when young, becoming open and round-topped with stout branching when older; very slow to develop.

SEASONAL APPEARANCE: Juvenile leaves are pale blue-green and grouped often in threes; mature foliage is minute, scale-like, waxy, and blue-gray; both appear on four-angled, blue-green twigs; flowering is separated but on the same plant with inconspicuous male stamens but female cones becoming round, half-inch, and red-brown; its noteworthy older bark divides into 1- to 2-inch, squarish plates and varies from red-brown to gray-brown in color.

PREFERENCES AND PROBLEMS: Thrives in full sun on moist, average, well-drained soils out of high winds; greatly tolerant of dry, sterile, rocky soils; adaptable only to the hardiness zones of the western United States.

PESTS AND DISEASES: See *J. chinensis.*

VARIETIES AND CULTIVARS: Cultivar 'Silver' with bright, gray-blue foliage.

Juniperus scopulorum (Rocky Mountain juniper, Colorado red cedar)

Zones 4 to 10   30' to 50'   Cypress family

Providing an attractive habit and coloring as a long-lived specimen or hedge for areas with very dry, high-temperature summers, this native of the Rocky Mountains grows wild from British Columbia to Arizona and Texas. Parent of many fine hybrid selections, it is rarely planted in today's landscapes, except as a novelty.

HABIT: Narrowly upright and dense when young, maturing to a broadly pyramidal or openly round-topped specimen with both a stout trunk and branching but usually without lower limbs; slow to moderate growth.

SEASONAL APPEARANCE: Minute, gray-green to light blue, scale-like, pointed leaves appear on squared, juvenile stems that become rounded with age; flowering is separated on the same plant but the male ones are inconspicuous; oval female cones take two years to develop fully and are bright or dark blue and about a half-inch wide; its dark red-brown to gray-brown, stringy bark is persistent even when later cracked and furrowed.

PREFERENCES AND PROBLEMS: Best in sun on a well-drained, average soil; tolerant of great dryness; unsuitable in the usually wet summers of the eastern United States.

PESTS AND DISEASES: See *J. chinensis;* prone to troublesome twig blight in areas with high humidity and consistent summertime rainfall.

VARIETIES AND CULTIVARS: Cultivar 'Argentea', narrowly conical with silver-gray foliage; cv. 'Blue Heaven' ('Blue Haven'), very hardy, neatly pyramidal, and dense with deep blue-green leaves; has reliable, annual, silver-blue fruit generously produced; cv. 'Chandleri', compact and pyramidal with silver-blue leaves; cv. 'Gray Gleam', male, slow-growing, narrowly pyramidal with silver-gray foliage becoming showiest in winter; cv. 'Pathfinder' with blue-silver leaves and a dense, narrowly conical shape; cv. 'Pendula', very drought-resistant, upright with drooping branches and green foliage; cv. 'Platinum' with bright, silver-blue leaves, neatly dense and pyramidal without pruning, somewhat slow-growing; cv. 'Welchii', narrowly pyramidal to columnar with silver-green leaves.

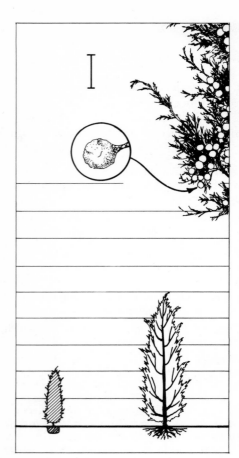

Juniperus virginiana (Red cedar, Eastern red cedar)

Zones 3 to 9   30′ to 90′   Cypress family

Widely and generously distributed naturally, this very hardy juniper grows freely along most of the Atlantic Seaboard well into the Great Plains and has an enduring appeal for hedges, groves, backdrops, and specimen use. Commercial use of its pungent, red-toned wood for moth-proof chests as well as for pencil making is almost traditional, while the capital of Louisiana, Baton Rouge ('red stick'), derives its name from the abundance of these evergreens found there by early French explorers.

HABIT: Slenderly conical to densely pyramidal with ascending branches when young and horizontal ones later; slow to moderate growth rate depending on its hardiness zone.

SEASONAL APPEARANCE: Juvenile needles are sharp-pointed, awl-shaped, and blue-green; adult foliage is scale-like, heavily overlapped on the twigs, and persistent even when dry and browned; the winter coloring is purplish to brown-red; plants usually have flowering on separate trees with inconspicuous male blooms balanced by noticeable female crops of eighth-inch, fleshy, highly aromatic, berry-like, dark blue cones covered with chalky powder; heavy fruiting occurs only every two or three years; its thin, light red-brown to gray bark peels in slender, fibrous strips.

PREFERENCES AND PROBLEMS: Grows well almost anywhere except in true swamps; adaptable from full sun to semishade in any soil type; self-seeds freely.

PESTS AND DISEASES: See *J. chinensis;* alternate host for the destructive apple-cedar rust fungus, which generally prohibits its planting near any commercial apple orchards; bagworms often devour its foliage.

VARIETIES AND CULTIVARS (many are grown commercially and these selections are but a sampling): Cultivar 'Burkii', male, narrowly pyramidal and dense with steel-blue foliage turning slightly purplish in winter; cv. 'Canaertii', generously fruiting female erectly compact with cord-like branching; summer foliage yellow-green but turns dark green in winter; cv. 'Glauca', narrowly columnar and dense with very gray leaves; cv. 'Hillii' ('Pyramidiformis hillii'), tightly conical with slightly prickly, gray-green summer foliage turning plum-colored in winter; cv. 'Manhattan Blue', male, very compact with blue-green leaves; cv. 'Nova' with gray-green leaves and a narrowly columnar form; cv. 'Pendula', showing an open silhouette of drooping branches, male; cv. 'Skyrocket' erect, pencil-thin, and flexible (requires staking in snowy areas) with blue-green leaves.

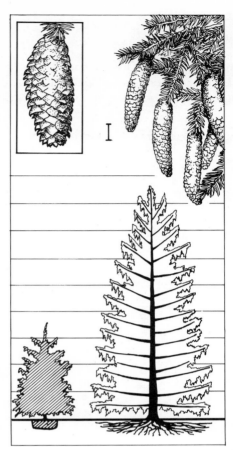

Picea abies [*excelsa*] (Norway spruce)

Zones 3 to 8   100' to 150'   Pine family

Spruces are look-alikes with firs in growth habits of being stiff-needled and pyramidal with regular whorls of branching. They differ (see *Abies concolor*) by having down-hanging, slender cones persistently intact even when they drop, roughened twigs with squared (in cross section), sharp-tipped needles, and a wider adaptability to cold and wind.

Generally fast-growing in a large range of soil types, they have several drawbacks: sizable spread and invasive rooting, the loss of lower limbs from crowding or shading, and a marked thinning out of the crown with age. Few spruces adapt well to parched, compacted soil or to the hot, low-rainfall summer weather of the midwestern and southwestern parts of the United States. All are prone to red spider and spruce gall aphid infestations in some degree, along with rust and honey fungus attacks.

The species listed here comes from northern and central Europe and has a wide popularity as a specimen or windbreak for its rapid growth with little care. Sporting the largest cones of any spruce, it quickly expands widely and soon develops a graceful appearance with age from its fringe-like, pendant branchlets. Unfortunately, it also becomes noticeably open and thin in its top regardless of cultural watering or fertilizing procedures.

HABIT: Stiffly upright and dense when juvenile but broadening sizably and becoming open-crowned with horizontal branching and pendulous twigs later; fast-growing.

SEASONAL APPEARANCE: Shiny, rigid, dark green needles up to three-quarters inch long carry faint white lines and grow along all sides of the twigs but point upward and forward; its leaves persist up to seven years; sexes are separated on the same tree with nondescript male flowering but with rosy red females followed by variable collections of light brown, glossy cones up to 7 inches in length; the thin, scaly bark is dark red-brown.

PREFERENCES AND PROBLEMS: Prefers full sun in almost any location—including seashores—but thrives on a well-drained, sandy loam with reasonable moisture; adapts poorly to compacted, very dry soil conditions or to high heat and dry summer weather.

PESTS AND DISEASES: See introductory remarks.

VARIETIES AND CULTIVARS (only some of the many tree forms provided here; intriguingly dwarfed, shrubby types of this plant are derived from either the seeds or stem cuttings of branches taken off normal-sized plants infected with the witches'-broom disease): Cultivar 'Aurea' with foliage golden yellow if in full sun, moderate growth habit; cv. 'Aurescens' with leaves yellow-gold when juvenile but fading to yellow-green with age; cv. 'Compacta', dwarfed, broadly conical, and dense with shining green foliage; cv. 'Finedonensis' with almost horizontal branching even when young, yellow-white new growth turning bronze and then green; cv. 'Inversa' densely branched and columnar with all growth pendulous and eventually spreading across the ground; cv. 'Pendula', a medium-growing plant with drooping twigs and branches.

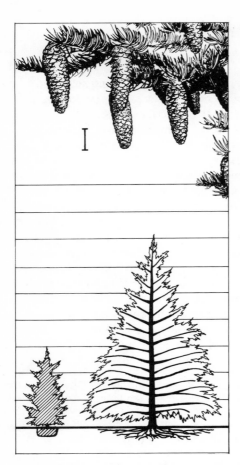

Picea asperata (Chinese spruce, Dragon spruce)

Zones 5 to 8   70′ to 150′   Pine family

Abundantly wild in western China, this fir is the Oriental counterpart of the European *P. abies* for its wide distribution and easy adapatabilitiy to diverse growing conditions as either a lawn specimen or a wind barrier, especially at the shore.

HABIT: Erect and dense when young, broadening into a wide pyramid with age; moderate in growth rate.

SEASONAL APPEARANCE: Very rough-textured, horizontal branches carry rigid sometimes pubescent twigs with densely set, stiff, sharp needles of dull gray to blue-green about three-quarters inch long; male flowering is visually unimportant, but females are scarlet and develop into 4-inch cones of fawn-gray changing later to chestnut brown; the gray bark peels in thin flakes.

PREFERENCES AND PROBLEMS: Best grown in full sun on an acid, well-drained, moist soil; tolerant of seaside spray and winds; dislikes alkaline soils and dryness.

PESTS AND DISEASES: See *P. abies.*

VARIETIES AND CULTIVARS: None.

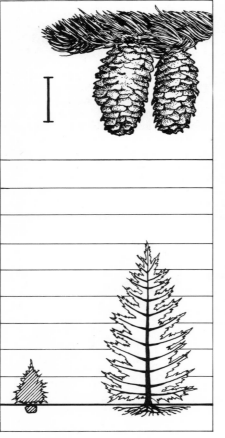

Picea engelmannii (Engelmann spruce)

Zones 3 to 8   70′ to 150′   Pine family

Well liked for its narrow silhouette and foliage color, this very hardy native of the mountain areas of British Columbia down to Arizona and New Mexico grows surprisingly well in almost any soil type while holding its lower branching far longer than most other spruces.

HABIT: Narrowly conical and dense when young, developing into a slender pyramid later; slow to moderate growth, depending on available soil moisture.

SEASONAL APPEARANCE: New twigs slightly hairy with 1-inch, blunted foilage somewhat soft to the touch; leaves are variable from deep or pallid blue-green to gray with a highly disagreeable odor if bruised; male flowering inconspicuous but females are bright red; light brown cones with noticeable, papery scales grow from 1 to 3 inches long; the thin, purple-brown to russet-red bark is composed of loosely attached scales.

PREFERENCES AND PROBLEMS: Enjoys full sun on a moist, acid, clay-loam soil but is adaptable to almost every other kind of soil except dry, chalky ones; highly cold-tolerant; shallow-rooted and unsuited for very windy sites; usually not found cultivated except in the western United States.

PESTS AND DISEASES: See *P. abies;* likely to be afflicted also by the spruce budworm.

VARIETIES AND CULTIVARS: Cultivar 'Argentea' with silvery gray leaves; cv. 'Glauca' with steel-blue foliage; cv. 'Microphylla', dwarfed, compact with shorter needles.

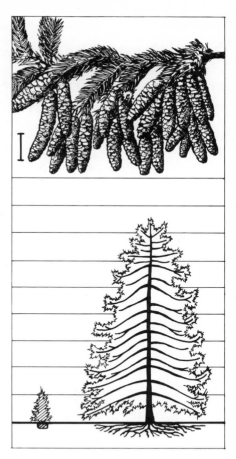

Picea glauca (White spruce, Cat spruce, Canadian spruce, Skunk spruce)

Zones 2 to 6   40′ to 80′   Pine family

Extreme hardiness is the chief asset of this native spruce from Alaska, most of Canada, and the northern boundaries of the United States. It withstands the oppressive heat and drought of most city conditions satisfactorily as well, but its ornamental value is less than stellar when compared with the visual appeal of other similarly adaptable evergreens.

HABIT: Narrowly conical and upright in its juvenile stage but becoming more pyramidal with age; develops a uniform silhouette of long, thick, drooping branches; moderate-growing.

SEASONAL APPEARANCE: Slender stems carry many blunt-ended, three-quarter-inch, gray-green to blue-green needles with a distinctively rank odor of skunk when crushed; male flowers are pale red while females are brighter red; its cones are slender, glossy, light brown, and about 2 inches long; the thin, relatively smooth bark is gray-brown and scaly.

PREFERENCES AND PROBLEMS: Does best in full sun on a moist, well-drained, gravelly soil; tolerant of moderate shading, high heat, and drought.

PESTS AND DISEASES: See *P. abies;* also susceptible to European sawfly, spruce bud-worm, and trunk and root fungi.

VARIETIES AND CULTIVARS: Variety *albertiana,* a narrowly pyramidal form native from British Columbia to Montana; often confused with cv. 'Densata', which has longer, cylindrical cones and tighter foliage; cv. 'Caerulea' with very silvery blue, short leaves densely crowded on the stems; cv. 'Conica', very slow-growing, dwarfed, narrowly conical, and dense with light gray-green needles; cv. 'Densata', very hardy, compact, densely symmetrical with light green to blue-green foliage and a slow rate of growth.

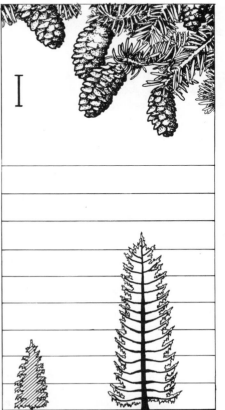

Picea omorika (Serbian spruce)

Zones 4 to 8   60′ to 100′   Pine family

A handsome, slender evergreen with upturned branch tips, this inhabitant of the mountains of eastern Yugoslavia grows in any moist soil, has reasonable adaptability to polluted city air, and also shows good cold tolerance.

HABIT: Narrowly columnar and spire-like with dense foliage and gracefully ascending branch tips; slow to medium growth rate.

SEASONAL APPEARANCE: Overlapping, forward-pointing, half-inch, glossy, very dark green needles are uniquely flattened (for a spruce) and carry conspicuous, gray-white lines on the under surface; flowering is unimportant; its cones are somewhat egg-shaped, bluish black, changing to cinnamon-brown, and up to $2^{1}/_{2}$ inches long; the thin, scaly bark is orange-brown to medium brown.

PREFERENCES AND PROBLEMS: Full sun on a well-drained, moist soil is best; tolerant to almost any soil, to city conditions, and to cold winds.

PESTS AND DISEASES: See *P. abies.*

VARIETIES AND CULTIVARS: Cultivar 'Borealis', in form very much like the silhouette of *P. abies* but with longer and narrower leaves; cv. 'Pendula' with long, slender, drooping branches and slow growth.

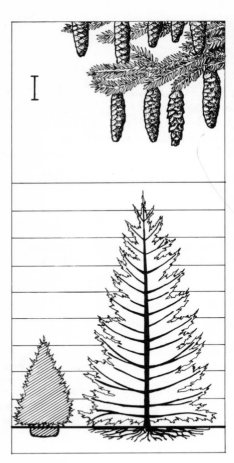

Picea orientalis (Oriental spruce, Eastern spruce)

Zones 5 to 7   80' to 120'   Pine family

Native to the Caucasus Mountains and northern Asia Minor, this tree is liked for its glossy, dark green needles, slow growth, down-to-the-ground foliage, and graceful silhouette.

HABIT: Densely conical when young, changing to a pleasantly open, widely pyramidal outline with ground-hugging, gently upturned branching often with pendulous branchlets; slow-growing.

SEASONAL APPEARANCE: Glistening, dark green, crowded needles up to a half-inch long appear from densely hairy new growth; all flowering is deep red; the slender young cones are purple but become ashy brown and over 3 inches long when mature; its gray-brown bark exfoliates in thin scales.

PREFERENCES AND PROBLEMS: Likes full sun and a consistently moist, well-drained site; tends to a short life on dry, shallow soils; install away from strong and cold winter winds to avoid needle discoloration.

PESTS AND DISEASES: See *P. abies;* more susceptible to damage from the spruce budworm than other species.

VARIETIES AND CULTIVARS: Cultivar 'Aurea', slow-growing with cream-white to gold-colored new shoots and bronze-gold foliage; cv. 'Gracilis', dwarfed, densely conical with lustrous, grass-green needles, very slow-growing.

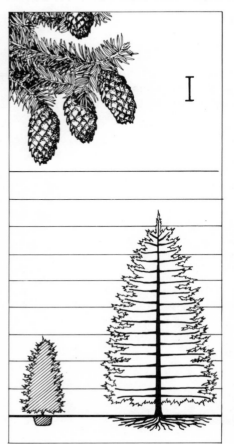

Picea pungens (Colorado spruce)

Zones 3 to 8   80' to 100'   Pine family

Not commonly cultivated today because more stimulating color choices are readily available in most nurseries, this North American native is found in Wyoming, Utah, Colorado, and New Mexico, becoming the only successful spruce to grow in the dry, hot southwestern and midwestern parts of this country. In silhouette it is probably the best-looking species for its first twenty years, but then it ages less gracefully. Oddly, but reasonably apt, the nursery selections of its bluest cultivar seedlings are called "shiners."

HABIT: Densely pyramidal and stiff at all ages with unbending, horizontal branching; slow to moderate growth depending on the zone location.

SEASONAL APPEARANCE: Very stiff, harsh-tipped, green to gray-green needles vary from 1/2 to 1 1/4 inches in length on smooth, yellow-brown new stems; older twigs are noticeably rough from stub bases left when needles fall after about eight years; flowering is not a color asset; the 2- to 4-inch cones are oblong and shiny in a noticeable, light chestnut-brown coloring; its thick bark is ash-brown and deeply grooved with irregular, vertical ridges.

PREFERENCES AND PROBLEMS: Grows thriftily in full sun on a moderately rich, well-drained, gravelly soil that is either moist or somewhat dry; very tolerant to shore conditions and arid, warm climates; loss of lower limbs inescapable with aging; troublesome to arrange well in gardens from its uncompromising stiffness; for good health it requires many insecticide sprays.

PESTS AND DISEASES: See *P. abies;* also bothered by the European spruce sawfly.

VARIETIES AND CULTIVARS (selected here for general availability and color quality): Cultivar 'Argentea' with silver-white needles; cv. 'Bakeri', slow-growing with longer, deep blue foliage; cv. 'Glauca', very drought-resistant and the most commonly sold cultivar for its light blue new growth and gray-blue leaves; cv. 'Hoopsii', densely pyramidal with very silvery foliage; cv. 'Koster' with drooping branchlets and brightly silvered needles, especially in winter; cv. 'Moerheimii', compactly dense with waxy, noticeably silver-blue leaves slightly longer than the parent; cv. 'Thompsonii' with very long, thick, silvery foliage.

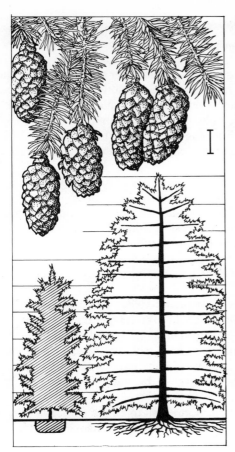

Picea sitchensis (Sitka spruce, Coast spruce, Tideland spruce)

Zones 6 to 9   100' to 160'   Pine family

By far the tallest spruce known, this decorative inhabitant of the Pacific coastal regions from Alaska to northern California is also extremely rapid-growing, but only when planted in a cool, humid location similar to its home grounds.

HABIT: Narrowly conical at first, then enlarging to a broad pyramid; very fast-growing in the correct climate.

SEASONAL APPEARANCE: Spiny-pointed, thick, flattened, bright green to blue-green needles range up to 1 inch in length and are set at 90-degree angles to the twigs; uniquely, the foliage is banded with white lines on the *upper* surfaces; its flowering is nondescript; the oval cones appear on the stiff, terminal shoots in colorings from pale yellow or reddish brown; young bark is scaly and dark gray-brown, but older trunks, which splay widely at the base with age, are dark purple to deep red-brown with thin, easily flaked scales.

PREFERENCES AND PROBLEMS: Demands a year-round, cool, humid climate; grows best in full sun on a constantly moist, acid, average-fertility soil, yet is tolerant of poor, ill-drained, or sandy conditions; transplants easily up to 15 feet; keeps its lower branching longer than many other spruces and holds it best when grown in the open; does not perform well along the eastern coast of the United States.

PESTS AND DISEASES: See *P. abies.*

VARIETIES AND CULTIVARS: Cultivar 'Speciosa' ('Glauca') with slower growth, a more compact habit, and gray-toned foliage.

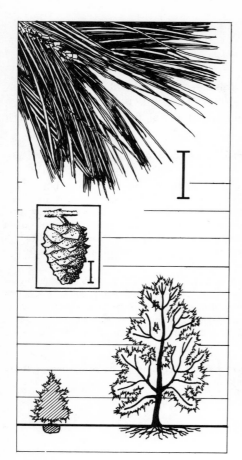

Pinus bungeana (Lacebark pine)

Zones 5 to 9   40′ to 75′   Pine family

Pines are exceptional evergreens. They lead all other cone bearers in their number of species, their varied range in world distribution, their sizable forests, and their multiple usefulness as both decorative specimens and valuable lumber. Found natively only in northern hemispheres, the ninety species of known pines spread from the Arctic Circle to the equator. Curiously, more types are concentrated in Mexico than anywhere else on earth.

Pines carry their needles in bundles or fascicles of two, three, or five, and they are the only conifers with a papery sheath enclosing these clustered leaves. Pine foliage offers diversity in size from 1 inch to 1 foot, plus textural contrasts from finely soft to stiffly rugged. If wanted, pine growth can be controlled easily by removing the central new-growth spire (called a "candle") when it fully emerges in the spring. Such pruning stimulates the ring of secondary buds beneath these main shoots for greater plant density.

Pines grow best in full sun on an average-fertility, well-drained soil. They do not need additional feeding and benefit from having their normal needle drop kept as a resiliant, cooling mulch. Scale and aphid infestations are common problems to all pines, but those with five-needle clusters are usually pestered as well by the disfiguring white pine blister rust (carried by wild currants). Even with separated sexes on the same plant, no pine has noticeably decorative flowering.

This uniquely attractive pine from northwestern China carries flaking bark mottled in cream, red, and green, making it ornamentally useful from several standpoints.

HABIT: Conical with mostly heavy branching but may become widely pyramidal and round-topped since it often develops multiple stems; slow-growing.

SEASONAL APPEARANCE: Needles usually remain for five years and are clustered in threes on shiny, gray-green twigs; the leaves are stiff, light green, up to 4 inches long and smell like turpentine if bruised; its 2- to 3-inch, egg-shaped, light brown cones appear either singly or in pairs; the smooth, dull gray bark scales off in patches much like a sycamore *(Platanus)* to reveal mottlings of cream, green, and red beneath; old trees may develop mostly chalk-white trunks in some areas.

PREFERENCES AND PROBLEMS: See introductory remarks; likes limed soils; may remain only bushy in cold areas.

PESTS AND DISEASES: See introductory remarks.

VARIETIES AND CULTIVARS: None.

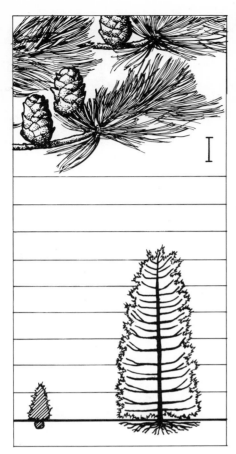

Pinus cembra   (Swiss stone pine, Russian cedar, Arolla pine)

Zones 3 to 8   45' to 75'   Pine family

Handsome as a columnar specimen, this slow-growing, densely compact evergreen from the central European Alps as well as Siberia attractively retains its lowest branches into maturity and has great hardiness.

HABIT: Narrowly conical and dense; slow-growing.

SEASONAL APPEARANCE: Needles are in bundles of five and remain up to five years; new stems emerge orange-brown and pubescent with stiff, dark blue-green, 3- to 5-inch leaves finely toothed along the slim edges and with white lines on the inside of each leaf; the oval cones are terminal, about 3 inches long, and purple-brown when mature; its bark is smooth and green-gray when juvenile but reddish gray later.

PREFERENCES AND PROBLEMS: Full sun and average, well-drained soil are best.

PESTS AND DISEASES: See *P. bungeana;* also susceptible to white pine weevil damage and honey fungus disease.

VARIETIES AND CULTIVARS: None.

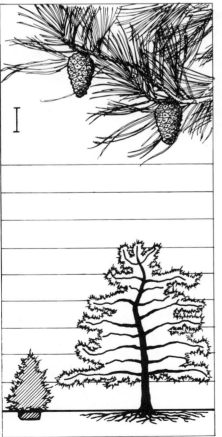

Pinus densiflora   (Japanese red pine)

Zones 5 to 9   60' to 100'   Pine family

Generally more durable in the western sections of the United States, this Japanese evergreen develops a wide-spreading, irregular crown with picturesque, elongated branching and showy, reddened bark.

HABIT: Conical when juvenile but quickly developing a contorted trunk and broad, flat-topped silhouette with strongly horizontal branching; may be multistemmed; slow to moderate growth rate.

SEASONAL APPEARANCE: Needles appear in bundles to twos and remain for only two seasons; they are 3 to 5 inches long, sharp-tipped, and brightly blue-green but turn yellowish green in winter; the cones are long-lasting, purple-toned or tawny, oval to oblong, and about 2 inches in length; its bark is orange-red when young, peeling in thin scales, but turning gray on the lower level with age.

PREFERENCES AND PROBLEMS: Enjoys full sun on an average-fertility but well-drained soil; its elongated branching may suffer breakage from ice storms or wet snow-falls in zone 5.

PESTS AND DISEASES: None of serious importance.

VARIETIES AND CULTIVARS: Cultivar 'Alboterminata' with needles yellow-white at the tips'; cv. 'Oculus-draconis', having foliage ringed with two yellow bands; cv. 'Um-braculifera' ('Tanyosho'), an upright, multistemmed, and wide-spreading low dwarf of very sluggish growth with dark green, slender needles; dislikes consistent cold winds and desert conditions.

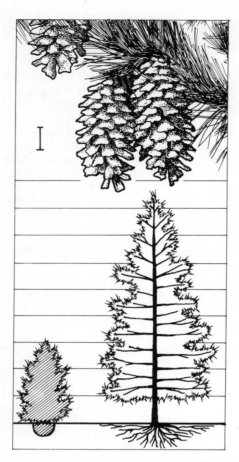

Pinus monticola (Western white pine, California mountain pine)

Zones 6 to 9   60′ to 200′   Pine family

In garden developments this hardy, serviceable evergreen tolerates drought well and keeps a respectable size, but in its native wilds of British Columbia to California it can expand to the 200-foot limits. It is greatly similar to *P. strobus* except for its narrower silhouette.

HABIT: Narrowly columnar and open when young, changing to a more rounded and spreading outline with slightly drooping branches when older, fast-growing when juvenile but slowing down when mature.

SEASONAL APPEARANCE: Stout, yellow-brown to red-brown twigs carry the white-lined, blue-green, 2- to 4-inch, flexible but stiff needles in groups of five; its cones are long and slender, between 5 and 8 inches in length, and droop from the branches; its variable young bark is thin and smooth with a gray tone, while older trees have deeply divided, squarish plates and purple or cinnamon-colored scales.

PREFERENCES AND PROBLEMS: Deep, porous soil and full sun are preferred for older plants, but young trees will develop well in greater shading; very drought-tolerant; its visual similarities to the popular *P. strobus* forestall its large-scale use in the eastern parts of the United States.

PESTS AND DISEASES: See *P. bungeana;* white pine blister rust remains a major affliction.

VARIETIES AND CULTIVARS: None.

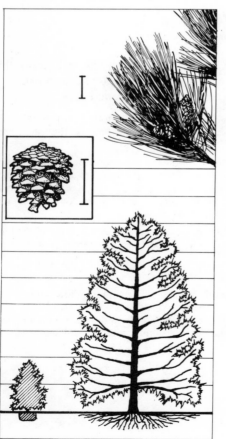

Pinus nigra (Austrian pine, Austrian black pine)

Zones 4 to 8   60′ to 100′   Pine family

One of the most conveniently adaptable pines in existence, this stolid native of central and southern Europe, plus Asia Minor, has the unflagging ability to adjust to almost any growing condition with full sun from windswept airport sites to noxious pollution in city parklands. It also shrugs off the influence of cold, blustery winds.

HABIT: Stays densely pyramidal, stiffly branched, and wide-spreading until maturity, when it becomes flat-topped; moderate-growing.

SEASONAL APPEARANCE: Its bundles of two needles are dark, shiny green on yellow-brown twigs; the recurved leaves range between 3 and 6 inches and are both unbendingly stiff and very sharp-pointed; its winter buds have a pineapple-like silhouette and are very hairy; the glossy, yellow-brown, oval cones can be up to 4 inches long; its rough bark is dark brown-gray and noticeably grooved.

PREFERENCES AND PROBLEMS: Adaptable to just about every atmospheric condition and soil type available—except wet—as long as it has full sun; suitable for windy shore sites and topsoil-denuded locations; dislikes reflected heat from pavements or buildings.

PESTS AND DISEASES: Inconsequential.

VARIETIES AND CULTIVARS: None with full botanical credentials.

Pinus parviflora (Japanese white pine)

Zones 6 to 8   30' to 60'   Pine family

Decoratively interesting for its elongated silhouette and tufted foliage, this slow-growing Japanese import provides an exotic garden accent where it is allowed sufficient space for its wide-spreading growth.

HABIT: Openly pyramidal but squat when juvenile; becoming broadly horizontal and moderately dense when older; usually slow in growth.

SEASONAL APPEARANCE: Its tufted bundles of needles persist for two years and come in groups of five mainly at the tip ends of the very long, green-brown branches; its ornamentally twisted leaves are blue-green to blue-gray and between 1 and 2 inches long; the oval cones are rust-colored, about 1¹/₂ inches long, and appear in clusters; young bark is smooth and gray-black, but older trunks become fissured with many flaking scales.

PREFERENCES AND PROBLEMS: Plant in full sun on a well-drained, moist site away from excessive wind.

PESTS AND DISEASES: See P. bungeana.

VARIETIES AND CULTIVARS: Cultivar 'Glauca', more upright in form with silvery blue needles.

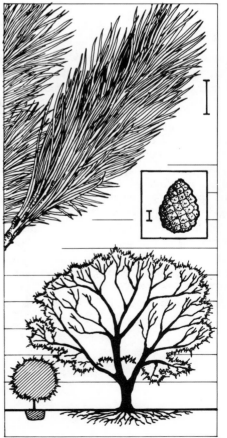

Pinus pinea (Italian stone pine, Umbrella pine, Stone pine)

Zones 8 to 10   80' to 100'   Pine family

Instantly recognizable when mature by its wide-spreading, umbrella shape, this drought-tolerant, Mediterranean-area pine is common to most Italian scenery and carries a sought-after, half-inch, edible, nut-like seed called "pignolia" in southern Europe.

HABIT: Stoutly globular and very dense when young; becoming picturesquely dome-shaped or flat-topped with a wide spread when older; generally moderate in growth.

SEASONAL APPEARANCE: Slender, gray-green twigs carry clusters of two, bright green, slightly twisted, stiff, and sharp-pointed needles up to 8 inches long; its broadly oval, pale brown cones measure almost 6 inches in length; the bark ranges between red-brown and gray-brown.

PREFERENCES AND PROBLEMS: Enjoys the greatest amount of sun on a well-drained, average soil; greatly tolerant of dryness and high heat but seems to thrive especially well on the shore; very space-consuming in the average garden from its low-branching habit.

PESTS AND DISEASES: None of importance.

VARIETIES AND CULTIVARS: None.

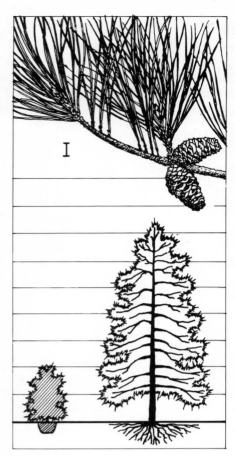

Pinus ponderosa (Western yellow pine, Ponderosa pine, Blackjack pine)

Zones 5 to 9   100′ to 150′   Pine family

Widely distributed from British Columbia to Mexico and west to Nebraska and Texas, the tree dominates any space it occupies in a reasonably short time. Unfortunately, it is not at its best much beyond its natural growing area, especially so in the eastern parts of the United States.

HABIT: Narrowly conical and full-foliaged when juvenile with a very straight trunk; more open and loose when older; fast-growing when younger but slows to moderate later.

SEASONAL APPEARANCE: Its sharp, stout needles usually come in threes but may be in fives because of its wide natural distribution; these leaves are from 5 to 11 inches in length and vary from dark green to yellow-green; the clustered cones have prickly scales, are almost oblong, and vary between 3 and 8 inches long; they modify in color from bright green to purple to light reddish brown at maturity; its young bark is almost black but changes with aging to cinnamon-brown with noticeably plate-like fissures.

PREFERENCES AND PROBLEMS: Likes a well-drained site in a very sunny location; benefits from extra watering when young; adapts to many soil types, including alkaline, with ease; drought-tolerant but still not suitable for desert heat and wind; often encumbered with parasitic mistletoe growths.

PESTS AND DISEASES: See *P. bungeana;* also troubled by the destructive Dendroctonus bark beetle and the caterpillar of the Pandora moth.

VARIETIES AND CULTIVARS: Variety *arizonica* has almost-black bark, cones no longer than 3 inches, and 4- to 7-inch needles most often seen in groups of fives; variety *scropulorum* is smaller in every aspect with greater hardiness and a narrower silhouette than the parent; its branches droop and carry 3- to 6-inch leaves in bundles of threes.

Pinus radiata (Monterey pine)

Zones 8 (warm) to 10   75′ to 100′   Pine family

A billowy, rapid-growing native evergreen from southern California, it is capable of a spectacular 6-foot expansion annually when fully established. Health problems often plague it, however, and limit its ornamental placement on a widespread basis.

HABIT: In youth it is a vigorous, dense cone of foliage, enlarging later to a generously wide-spreading, attractively open, rounded outline without lower branching; capable of a remarkable 6-foot growth yearly if favorably located.

SEASONAL APPEARANCE: Slender, sharp-tipped, 4- to 6-inch, grassy green, flexible needles are arranged in groups of three; the clustered, lopsidedly oval, persistent cones can be up to 7 inches long and appear first as bright green but mellow to a warm brown later; its thick bark is dark brown and deeply grooved when older.

PREFERENCES AND PROBLEMS: Provide full sun and a well-drained site; adaptable to wide range of soil types; especially tolerant to shore conditions but dislikes hot, dry summer weather and smoggy air.

PESTS AND DISEASES: See *P. bungeana;* especially prone to spider mites, scale attacks, and the depredations of the five-spined engraver beetle.

VARIETIES AND CULTIVARS: Variety *binata* has stouter needles in fascicles of twos.

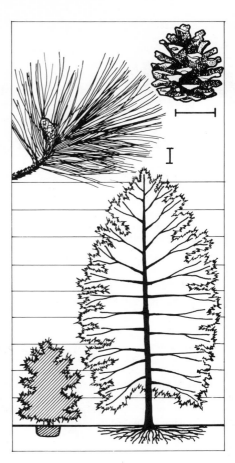

Pinus resinosa (Red pine, Norway pine)

Zones 3 to 8   60' to 90'   Pine family

Even though this hardy, red-barked tree from Newfoundland to Pennsylvania and west to Minnesota is native only to the North American continent, one of its common names received European credentials early from visual associations made by Spanish explorers who erroneously believed they were identical with trees seen along the Norweigian coasts. Easily moved and highly adaptable to a wide range of growing conditions, this pine is usually incapable of retaining its lower branching for screening purposes.

HABIT: Broadly pyramidal but open when young with a slender stem and stout branching; becomes densely and symmetrically oval with age but without many lower limbs; moderate to fast in growth, depending on the hardiness zone.

SEASONAL APPEARANCE: Very similar (and too often confused) in needle appearance to *P. nigra,* but here the two-clustered leaves are flexible and snap easily if bent between the fingers; its leaves are dark, glossy green and between 5 and 6 inches in length; the broadly oval, light brown cones measure up to $2^1/_2$ inches long and come tightly attached at right angles to the twigs; its thick, roughened bark becomes noticeably reddish brown with aging and divides into shallow fissures.

PREFERENCES AND PROBLEMS: Widely adaptable in full sun to any number of soil conditions from wet to dry, poor to rich, and gravelly to sandy; readily transplanted; adjusts well to urban situations; unsatisfactory when planted in the dry, summer heat of the Great Plains or the southwestern United States.

PESTS AND DISEASES: See *P. bungeana;* also disfigured by the pine bud moth.

VARIETIES AND CULTIVARS: Cultivar 'Globosa', dwarfed and round-headed with dense branching and crowded tufts of foliage.

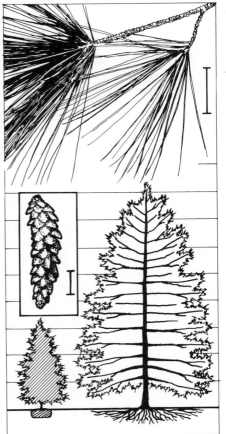

Pinus strobus (White pine, Eastern white pine, Weymouth pine)

Zones 3 to 7   100' to 150'   Pine family

Well established for centuries as the monarch of the eastern North American forests, this delicately foliaged but very hardy pine is one of the most serviceable evergreens known. Its majestic size and notably straight trunk encouraged the eighteenth-century viscount Weymouth to plant it extensively on his English estate at Longleat, since Great Britain had long been denuded of stately trees suitable for ship's masts, but it failed to develop quickly or grandly there. For today's landscapes we find it highly suitable as a graceful specimen, sturdy windbreak, or trimmed hedge.

HABIT: Narrowly conical and symmetrically dense with tiered branching in its juvenile stage; becomes irregular in outline and bare-branched at the bottom toward maturity; moderately rapid in growth.

SEASONAL APPEARANCE: Carries slim, flexible, 3- to 5-inch, bluish green needles with faint white lines on the underside in bundles of five, mostly bunched at the outer reaches of the twigs; the leaves remain for three years; its narrowly cylindrical, 4- to 8-inch, yellow-gray cones have a slight curvature; young bark is smooth, greenish brown to ashy gray, but older trunks are dark gray and ridged vertically.

PREFERENCES AND PROBLEMS: Best grown in full sun on a sandy loam with consistent moisture; tolerant to many soil types if moist; transplants easily; apt to show leaf scorch on very windy sites; may also grow satisfactorily in some western parts of zone 8.

PESTS AND DISEASES: See *P. bungeana;* the larva of the white pine weevil quickly destroys the central leader, spoiling the tree's outline.

VARIETIES AND CULTIVARS: Cultivar 'Compacta' with slow, dense growth; cv. 'Contorta' with twisted branching and tufts of densely set needles; cv. 'Dawsoniana', dwarfed and spreading; cv. 'Fastigiata' with upright branching (catching snow in some growing areas) and a narrowly conical head; cv. 'Nana' ('Densa'), a sluggish-growing, low, dense shrub; cv. 'Pendula' with stiff but drooping branches to ground level; cv. 'Pyramidalis', markedly conical.

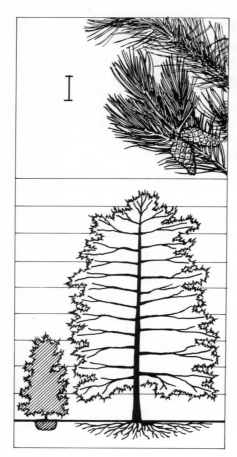

Pinus sylvestris (Scots pine, Scotch pine, Scotch fir)

Zones 3 to 8   70' to 100'   Pine family

One of the handsomest pines in existence, it is also one of the hardiest with a natural range from Siberia throughout Europe and the British Isles. Growing colorfully picturesque with aging, it adjusts well to many soil types and resists city pollution.

HABIT: Openly pyramidal when juvenile and becoming pleasantly irregular and round-topped with age; moderate in growth rate.

SEASONAL APPEARANCE: Its blue-green, up to 3-inch, twisted, and stiff needles come in clusters of two; occasionally the leaves may become yellowish green during winter on some soils; the oblong, dull, brown-gray cones range up to $2^{1/2}$ inches in length and are often set pointing backward toward the trunk; its colorful bark in the upper branching is bright orange-red and flaky, but that on the lower trunk is generally rough, chunky, and either gray-brown or reddish brown.

PREFERENCES AND PROBLEMS: Provide generous sunshine and an average-fertility, well-drained site; adaptable to a wide range of soils but is less content on wet, acid or dry, chalky soils; transplants better when young; tolerant of urban conditions.

PESTS AND DISEASES: See *P. bungeana;* seriously afflicted by dry rot fungus of the trunk.

VARIETIES AND CULTIVARS: Cultivar 'Argentea', taller and heftier with silvery needles; cv. 'Aurea', slow-growing with yellow-green summer color and noticeably golden yellow needles in winter; cv. 'Beauvronensis', very dwarfed, bushy, and slow-growing with colorful red-brown winter budding; cv. 'Compressa', dwarfed, narrowly columnar with mostly straight needles of gray-green coloring; cv. 'Fastigiata' with tightly ascending branches and a slender, columnar form; cv. 'Nana', a low mound of dense branching; cv. 'Pendula' with drooping branches; cv. 'Watereri', columnar at first but eventually spreading with very blue-green needles.

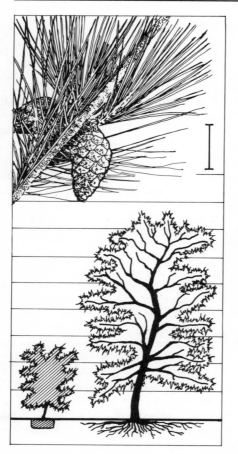

Pinus thunbergiana [*thunbergii*] (Japanese black pine)

Zones 5 to 8   60' to 130'   Pine family

Valued as a durable specimen for shore conditions of salt spray, cold winds, and low-fertility soils, its highly contorted silhouette and sharp needles do not always gain this Japanese native an enthusiastic response. It always looks weatherbeaten, yet sturdy.

HABIT: Asymmetrical and conical at all ages with a crooked trunk and generally irregular branching and dense foliage; slow to moderate in growth, depending on soil moisture.

SEASONAL APPEARANCE: Winter buds are very hairy, grayish tan, and up to 2 inches tall; the sharp, stiff, bright green needles come in twos, vary from 3 to $4^{1/2}$ inches, and funnel around the buds; its oval cones are medium brown and up to $2^{1/2}$ inches long; the bark is a dull, blackish gray.

PREFERENCES AND PROBLEMS: Enjoys full sun and a cool, moist atmosphere but tolerates wind, drought, seaside conditions, and neglect very well; usually devoid of lower branching with age; sluggish on arid sites; usually adaptable to zone 9 in the western United States.

PESTS AND DISEASES: See *P. bungeana;* currently has an unexplained disease causing severe branch loss on Cape Cod in Massachusetts.

VARIETIES AND CULTIVARS: Cultivar 'Oculus-draconis', foliage marked with two yellow bands; cv. 'Variegata', leaves mottled with yellow-white.

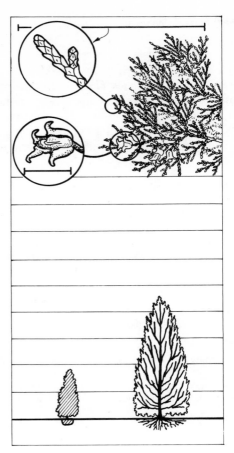

Platycladus orientalis [Thuja orientalis]
(Oriental arborvitae)

Zones 6 to 10   **40' to 50'**   **Cypress family**

Very popular in the U.S. southland, especially for its many attractive shrub forms, this native of northern and western China, plus Korea, offers both a thick mass of upright stems and foliage useful as a screen, hedge, or formal specimen. It substitutes well for arborvitae *(Thuja)* in warm, dry regions.

HABIT: Mostly conical at all ages with upright branching and usually multiple stems; moderate-growing.

SEASONAL APPEARANCE: Differs from its relative *Thuja* by having its branchlets in a vertically upright position; the tiny foliage is scale-like, grooved on the backside, bright green, and without the very pungent smell of *Thuja;* flowering is separated on the same plant, but the males remain inconspicuous; its 1-inch, female cones are erect, fleshy, and blue-toned when young but become woody with noticeable horn-like endings; the thin, red-brown bark peels in papery scales.

PREFERENCES AND PROBLEMS: Thrives in full sun and on a moist, rich soil out of sharp, cold winds; tolerant to light shading, summer drought, and high heat; dislikes extremely acid soil conditions; adaptable for growing in some areas of zone 10; prone to stem damage from ice and snow since the plant becomes more brittle with age.

PESTS AND DISEASES: Occasionally bothered by red spider mites.

VARIETIES AND CULTIVARS (a sizable list with only the tree forms given here): Cultivar 'Argenteus' with tips of new growth whitened; cv. 'Aureus' with springtime foliage golden yellow; cv. 'Azureus', having very gray-blue leaves; cv. 'Bakeri', dense, broadly conical with bright green foliage, well adapted to hot, dry sites; cv. 'Beverleyensis', pyramidal with deep yellow leaves; cv. 'Caesius' with blue-gray foliage; cv. 'Columnaris', having a columnar silhouette and green leaves; cv. 'Conspicuus', narrowly compact with golden yellow leaves having a greenish overcast; cv. 'Elegantissimus', compact with yellow spring foliage and possibly brownish red winter coloring; cv. 'Flagelliformis' ('Pendulus') with drooping branches and thread-like foliage; cv. 'Glaucus', pyramidal in outline with blue-green leaves; cv. 'Gracilis', slenderly pyramidal; cv. 'Howardii', pyramidal but only 10 feet tall; cv. 'Intermedius' with both juvenile and mature foliage obvious on drooping branchlets; cv. 'Maurieanus', green-leaved with a very narrowly columnar form; cv. 'Mayhewiana' with a pyramidally compact outline and yellow-tipped branchlets; cv. 'Meldensis', carrying mostly needled, blue-green leaves and a narrowly pyramidal shape; cv. 'Strictus' ('Pyramidalis'), densely pyramidal; cv. 'Tataricus' with yellow-toned branchlets; cv. 'Texanus Glaucus' with blue-green foliage and a pyramidal outline.

Podocarpus macrophyllus (Southern yew, Japanese yew, Buddhist pine)

Zones 7 (warm) to 10   45' to 60'   Podocarpus family

Closely allied botanically to the shorter-needled yew *(Taxus), Podocarpus* offers the same landscape advantages of container culture, topiary training, and specimen use as its multistemmed, shrub cousin. Its new growth is noticeably reddish as it emerges, creating a novel color contrast during most of the seasons. This species originated in central and southwestern Japan.

HABIT: Somewhat irregular when young but narrowly upright and dense with stiffly horizontal branching later; slow-growing.

SEASONAL APPEARANCE: Flattened, glossy, leathery, bright to dark green, half-inch-wide leaves often extend up to 4 inches; flowers appear on separate plants, and neither male nor female is noticeably interesting; the somewhat innocuous fruit on female plants is a fleshy, purple cup surrounding a hard seed; the bark is gray with shallow grooves.

PREFERENCES AND PROBLEMS: Shelter from bright sun and wind in areas with hot summers; otherwise, full sun and a moist, acid, well-drained soil are satisfactory; usually shows chlorosis yellowing if grown in either alkaline or damp and very heavy soils; avoid planting anywhere that reflected light and heat are excessive.

PESTS AND DISEASES: Generally untroubled.

VARIETIES AND CULTIVARS: Variety *angustifolius* has a narrower, denser silhouette and light green new growth with occasionally curved leaves; its fruit is blue-toned and appears on quarter-inch stalks; variety *maki* carries smaller, dark green foliage in heavy quantities and makes a more upright specimen but at a slower growth rate than *angustifolius.*

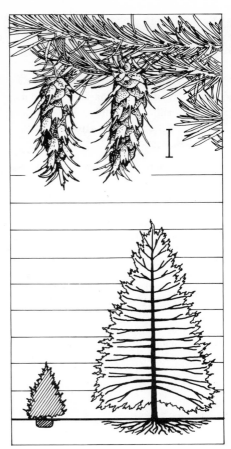

Pseudotsuga menziesii [douglasii, taxifolia] (Douglas fir)

Zones 6 to 8   70′ to 200′   Pine family

Discovered twice in its native habitat of the Rocky Mountains and the Pacific coastal regions, this fir had the distinction of being seen first on Vancouver Island in British Columbia by Menzies in 1791, who made little promotion of it, surprisingly; it was rediscovered—and appreciated more fully—by Douglas in another area of the West and introduced into England by him in 1827. The botanic and common names now obligingly give shared acknowledgment to both. We benefit from its special ornamental qualities today in specimen, windbreak, and hedge use.

HABIT: Highly variable in form because of its wide distribution, it usually is broadly conical and symmetrically dense at all ages with horizontal upper branching and gracefully curving lower limbs; becoming bare-branched at the lower level with age; moderate to fast in growth.

SEASONAL APPEARANCE: Sharply pointed buds produce new growth with soft, heavily set, 1- to 1½-inch, dark green to gray-green needles showing faintly white lines beneath; when crushed, the needles give off the odor of camphor; its nondescript flowers are separated on the same tree; the 3- to 4-inch slenderly oval, light brown cones become distinctive by having three-pronged, projecting bracts at each scale; its juvenile bark is brown and rigid, but is rough and corky-ridged with dark red-brown or gray coloring when mature.

PREFERENCES AND PROBLEMS: Best grown in full sunlight and on a moist, acid, well-drained site; does not succeed on either waterlogged or chalky soils; tolerant to semishading and wind at a slight loss in density; adaptable to zone 9 in western United States.

PESTS AND DISEASES: Aphids, mealy bug, fungal root rot, and canker disease are the main difficulties.

VARIETIES AND CULTIVARS: Variety *glauca* has greater hardiness to grow well into zone 4 with smaller, gray-toned foliage (with a turpentine odor if crushed) and somewhat shorter cones; cv. 'Argentea', needles are silvery white; cv. 'Brevibracteata' with smaller, overall dimensions, especially in the protruding bracts on the cones; cv. 'Caesia', having branchlets at right angles and grayish green leaves; cv. 'Compacta' with dark green, shorter needles and a compactly conical form; cv. 'Densa', flat-topped with deep green foliage and dwarfed; cv. 'Fastigiata', slenderly conical with reddened winter buds; cv. 'Glauca Pendula' with bluish foliage on drooping branchlets; cv. 'Globosa', a rounded, green-leaved dwarfed form; cv. 'Pendula' with green needles on pendulous branching; cv. 'Pyramidata', semidwarfed, slow-growing, and conical in outline with bright green foliage; cv. 'Viridis' with green leaves and larger cones.

Sciadopitys verticillata (Umbrella pine, Japanese umbrella pine)

Zones 6 to 8   35' to 50'   Taxodium family

Uniquely beautiful for its glossy, whorled foilage of up to thirty fat needles arranged on the twig like the spokes of an umbrella, as well as for its substantially dense and slowly expanding silhouette, this native of central and southwestern Japan is a truly choice specimen for any sheltered garden development not engulfed by polluted air.

HABIT: Very densely symmetrical and narrow when juvenile with a more openly pyramidal shape later; may develop several trunks readily; slow-growing.

SEASONAL APPEARANCE: Its fleshy, blunt-tipped, 3- to 5-inch, stiffened needles (actually two leaves anciently joined) are separated by a thin groove on both sides; they are dark, waxy green with whitened lines beneath and come crowded at the ends of the yellowish twigs in attractive whorls of between twenty and thirty; curiously, there is also a second set of leaves present, but these are all unnoticeably scale-like and appear flattened on the twig between the larger sets of foliage; this tree has the flower sexes separated on the same plant with unimportant male blossoming matched by noticeably erect, 2- to 4-inch, oval, woody cones requiring two years to mature; bark color varies from dark red-brown to gray-brown and exfoliates in long, slender strips.

PREFERENCES AND PROBLEMS: Enjoys a fertile, acid, consistently moist, well-drained, cool site in full sun or light shading; intolerant of alkaline or dry, sandy soils and air pollution; protect from excessive wind, especially in locations with high summer heat.

PESTS AND DISEASES: Admirably free of both.

VARIETIES AND CULTIVARS: None with botanic credentials.

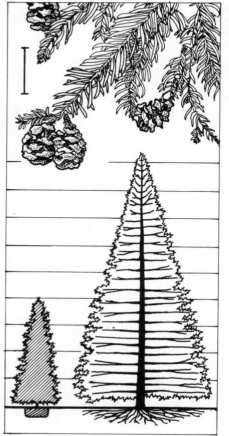

Sequoia sempervirens (Redwood, Coast redwood)

Zones 7 to 10   90' to 360'   Taxodium family

Long acknowledged as the world's *tallest* living thing (*Sequoia wellingtonia* is the largest), the wild redwood has an immense, straight trunk and a massive crown of foliage. It is native only to coastal southern Oregon and the high-humidity sections of northern and central California, but it transfers well as a nursery-grown, landscape ornament since its growth habit is refined and not likely to overwhelm any site quickly. A striking accent at any age, it appears at its symmetrical best when grown openly as a specimen.

HABIT: Variable since most stock comes from seed, the typical form is narrowly conical when young; older trees are more open and pyramidal with straight trunks and mostly horizontal branching; growth is rapid if consistently watered.

SEASONAL APPEARANCE: Carries two foliage types; terminal, juvenile growth is scale-like; older leaves are similar in shape to the yew *(Taxus)* with curved, flat, pointed needles from one-third to 1 full inch long, dark green above and gray-toned beneath; its flowering is separated on the same plant, but the male parts are non-showy; the oval, terminal cones are pendulous, red-brown, and about 1 inch in size; they ripen in one season but persist for several; its young bark is reddish brown to cinnamon-red and fibrous; old specimens have uncommonly thick bark (up to 1 foot) that is spongy and deeply fluted.

PREFERENCES AND PROBLEMS: Grows well in either full sun or semishade on a consistently moist, good soil with average drainage; prefers shelter from strong winds; enjoys high-humidity sites; foliage likely to yellow from iron deficiency, especially on alkaline soils; generally adaptable only to zone 8 in the eastern United States; dislikes crowding.

PESTS AND DISEASES: Neither makes any serious inroads.

VARIETIES AND CULTIVARS: Cultivar 'Adpressa' ('Albospica'), slow and dwarfed with young leaves and tips of twigs noticeably creamy white in spring but fading by winter; cv. 'Glauca' with conspicuously blue-toned leaves; cv. 'Nana Pendula', having some pendulous branching and carrying gray-toned needles; cv. 'Pendula' with arched, drooping branches.

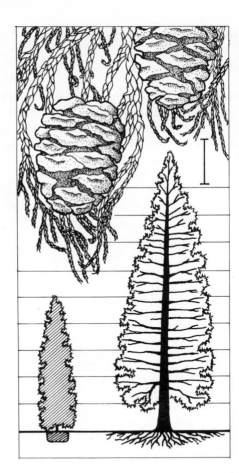

Sequoiadendron wellingtonia [*giganteum*] (Giant sequoia, Big tree, Giant redwood, Sierra redwood)

Zones 6 to 10   150′ to 300′   Taxodium family

With estimates of age for some venerable wild specimens coming close to 4000 years, this mammoth tree from the western slopes of the Sierra Nevada mountain areas of the United States hardly seems likely as a candidate for landscape use. Yet it transplants well from nurseries, is neatly symmetrical, and has greater hardiness than *Sequoia sempervirens*. It expands selfishly, however, to dominate any small space in a hurry, but when used for ornament in a large-scaled, open area, it offers the splendor of luxuriant foliage and impressive height.

HABIT: Slenderly conical with a very straight trunk and usually persistent, drooping lower branches at all ages; occasionally these lowest limbs root where they touch the ground and intensify the bulkiness of the outline; fast-growing.

SEASONAL APPEARANCE: Twigs are rope-like and are covered tightly with sharp-pointed, overlapping scale leaves in bright, deep green or bluish green; flowering is on different parts of the same tree with nondescript male portions gathered at the tips of branches; the female cone is almost 4 inches long, egg-shaped, very solidly woody, a dull, yellow-brown, and persistent for many years; its young bark is dark red-brown with thin, fibrous scales; older trunks have craggy, spongy bark up to a mind-boggling 20 inches thick.

PREFERENCES AND PROBLEMS: Provide full sun and a deep, acid, sandy to gravelly, fertile soil, plus abundant moisture until fully established; water deeply but only occasionally when older; prefers a cooler climate than *S. sempervirens;* tolerant of lime but dislikes shallow, chalky soils; tends to stay confined into zones 6 to 8 in the eastern United States.

PESTS AND DISEASES: A high tannin concentration in the trunk and stems forestalls either from causing problems.

VARIETIES AND CULTIVARS: Cultivar 'Pendulum', very narrowly columnar with long, drooping branches held very close to the trunk, slow-growing and rare; cv. 'Pygmaeum', dwarfed and shrubby with crowded branching and gray-toned needles.

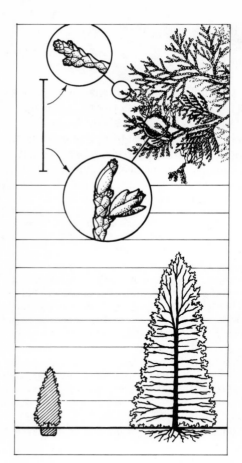

Thuja occidentalis (American arborvitae, White cedar, Northern white cedar)

Zones 3 to 9   40′ to 60′   Cypress family

This almost-columnar native evergreen of moist woods from Nova Scotia to North Carolina (and west to Ontario and Illinois) was the first known tree from North America to be planted ornamentally in Europe; it all happened in the sixteenth century and in Paris. Since then the fast-growing arborvitae has been used so often in landscapes that it is now considered common and perhaps not worth consideration for today's layouts. Nevertheless, its great hardiness, ease in transplanting, freedom from insect and fungus attacks, and newer cultivars suggest that a closer look at this "workhorse" of the plant world is in order.

HABIT: Has a narrowly conical and upright silhouette with flat and crowded sprays of dense foliage to ground level at all ages; carries mostly short, horizontal branching with upturned tip ends when older; trunk often divides into several stems; fast-growing if kept moist.

SEASONAL APPEARANCE: Its pleasantly aromatic foliage is composed of tightly flattened, quarter-inch scales held in horizontal, fan-like sprays; individual leaves are dark green on the upper side and yellow-green beneath, but consistently turn an unsatisfactory brown tone in winter; flowers appear on separated parts of the same tree, and the males are almost invisible; its oblong, erect, female cones are usually less than a half-inch long, light to cinnamon-brown in color, and open in a bell shape with upturned ends like a pagoda; the thin, scaly bark has narrow ridges and a light brown to red-brown coloration.

PREFERENCES AND PROBLEMS: Grows to its full potential in a cool atmosphere with high humidity, full sun, and a consistently moist soil of average fertility; tolerant of semishading and some drought; adapts well to limestone and heavy, clay soils; usable only in zones 6 to 9 in the western areas of the United States.

PESTS AND DISEASES: Generally untroubled, but red spider mites can be problematic at times.

VARIETIES AND CULTIVARS (many are desirable shrubs but only tree forms are identified here): Cultivar 'Alba' with year-round, whitened tip growth; cv. 'Buchananii', narrowly pyramidal with thin, gray-green foliage; cv. 'Columbia' with pale green leaves and all-year silvery white tips; cv. 'Conica', cone-shaped with green needles and slender foliage sprays; cv. 'Douglasii Aurea', slenderly pyramidal with summer foliage golden yellow, becoming bronzed in winter; cv. 'Douglasii Pyramidalis', densely pyramidal with spirally twisted foliage remaining green in winter; cv. 'Elegantissima' with shiny, dark green needles lightly tipped in yellow and a narrowly pyramidal tree shape; cv. 'Fastigiata' ('Columnaris'), short-branched and mostly pyramidal with down-spreading, light green foliage; cv. 'Lutea' ('George Peabody'), the strongest growing cultivar yet known with a narrowly conical silhouette and golden yellow needles, but only if in full sun; cv. 'Nigra', compactly pyramidal and slower-growing than most with dark green leaves all year; cv. 'Pendula' with drooping branchlets, green foliage and an open form; cv. 'Pyramidalis', dense, narrowly pyramidal with fan-like, bright green needles; cv. 'Riversii', broadly pyramidal with yellow foliage in summer, turning yellow-green in winter; cv. 'Rosenthalii' with shining, dark green leaves and a slow-growing, compact, pyramidal shape; cv. 'Semper Aurea', dense and broadly pyramidal with lustrous foliage tipped with deep yellow, changing to brownish yellow in winter; cv. 'Spiralis', best in full sun to maintain sturdy, slender growth; densely set, twisted branching with fern-like, dark green leaves; cv. 'Vervaeneana', short-growing, pyramidal, dense with greenish yellow, variable foliage that is distinctively bronze-toned in winter; cv. 'Wareana', dense, slow, stout with ascending branches and a pyramidal shape, retains its bright green leaves all year.

Thuja plicata (Giant arborvitae, Giant cedar, Western red cedar)

Zones 5 to 9   100′ to 200′   Cypress family

For a rich ornamental display, this sizable inhabitant of the Pacific coast from Alaska to northern California is unmatched. It does not turn brown in winter like *Thuja occidentalis,* has no bothersome pests or diseases, is easily pruned to any height, and is nondemanding about constant moisture or a particular soil type. Its only serious handicap is a shallow but vigorous root system that prevents much underplanting of other material.

HABIT: Broadly pyramidal, dense, and fully symmetrical at all ages with lower branches recurved and usually held to ground level; rapid-growing when given sufficient water.

SEASONAL APPEARANCE: Its slender, drooping branches carry flat, lacy sprays of year-round, dark green, glossy, scale-like foliage; the leaf undersides are paler green with distinctive white markings like some *Chamaecyparis;* when bruised, the needles produce a pleasantly tangy scent; male flowering is not noticeably interesting; the oval, half-inch female cones first are green and later become brown and leathery; the shredding fibrous bark is thin but tough and can be from cinnamon-red to brown.

PREFERENCES AND PROBLEMS: Thrives in full sun on any fertile, moist, well-drained, acid or alkaline soil; tolerant of semishading, dryness, and occasionally strong winds; discourages much variety of underplanting because of its heavy shade and surface rooting; nursery stock grown from seed of coastal plants fail to be as hardy as those from mountain selections; generally unsatisfactory in zone 9 of the eastern United States.

PESTS AND DISEASES: Greatly resistant to both.

VARIETIES AND CULTIVARS: Cultivar 'Atrovirens' with needles a shining, dark green; cv. 'Aurea' ('Zebrina'), slower-growing than the parent with golden to lemon yellow, striped foliage usually similarly colored in winter; cv. 'Fastigiata', narrowly columnar with slender, ascending branches much like a Lombardy poplar and with finer, densely set leaf sprays; cv. 'Hogan' with a tightly compact silhouette; cv. 'Pendula', slender-trunked with drooping branches and noticeably upturned ends; many attractive shrub forms of *T. plicata* are also in cultivation.

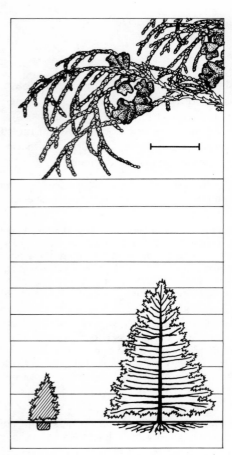

Thuja standishii [japonica]   (Japanese arborvitae)

Zones 6 to 8   40' to 50'   Cypress family

At first glance, it would seem to be only a smaller version of *T. plicata,* but this native of the mountains of central Japan offers a wider, more open silhouette, a slower habit of growth, and the distinctive smell of lemons when the foliage is crushed. It becomes a definitive specimen in large, open spaces.

HABIT: Broadly pyramidal but irregularly open with mostly horizontal branching becoming more noticeably upthrust with age; slow to moderate rate of growth.

SEASONAL APPEARANCE: Its scale-like foliage is yellowish green with triangular white dots below and is carried in graceful, drooping sprays; if bruised, the leaves have a lemon scent; the sexes are separated on the same tree, but the males are non-showy; its female, ovoid, half-inch cones are greenish yellow when young and become light brown later; the deep red-brown bark peels in papery rolls.

PREFERENCES AND PROBLEMS: Takes either full sun or light shade equally well and enjoys a rich, consistently moist, average soil with good drainage; dislikes windy sites.

PESTS AND DISEASES: Unbothered.

VARIETIES AND CULTIVARS: None.

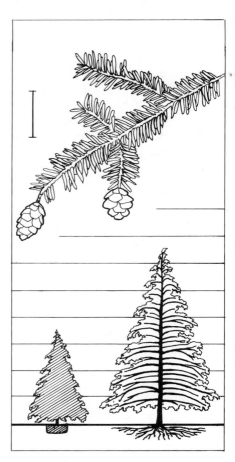

Tsuga canadensis (Canada hemlock, Eastern hemlock)

Zones 3 to 7   60' to 80'   Pine family

For popularity as a graceful, shapely, fine-needled evergreen useful for sun or shade, the hemlocks win hands down. As a plant group they are native to North America and the Orient, but none is wild in Europe. All are shallow-rooted and transplant with ease; all dislike drought; and all have a preference for cool, nonwindy sites with consistently moist, acid soils and reasonable humidity. They are not truly at home in the parched, windswept, polluted conditions of most urban areas.

Because they have ground-hugging foliage and accept heavy shearing with aplomb, they are greatly valued as hedges and screens. Generally pest- and disease-free if grown well, all have some tendency, however, to be troubled by red spider mites during prolonged hot, dry weather. For dependable attractiveness in all seasons, though, hemlocks are landscape essentials.

The very hardy species described here is distributed generously in nature from Nova Scotia to Alabama and west to Minnesota. This is unusual since it is the only hemlock with a broad range of cultivar forms and foliages, including an intriguing collection of dwarfed shrub types. Surprisingly, it adjusts readily to either acid or alkaline soils throughout the United States.

HABIT: Broadly pyramidal, dense and feathery with long, slender, horizontal or nodding branches with gracefully drooping ends at all stages of growth; often develops multiple stems; generally moderate in its rate of expansion.

SEASONAL APPEARANCE: Flattened rows of blunt-tipped or notched, narrow, third- to half-inch needles are shiny, dark green with two whitened bands beneath; they come densely crowded on thin, somewhat hairy, yellow-brown stems and remain up to four years; male flowering is nondescript and separated from the female; its stalked, pendulous cones are up to three-quarters inch long, oval in form, annual in appearance, and gray-brown when ripe; young bark is often cinnamon-red and grooved, but older trunks become dark brown, deeply grooved, and scaly.

PREFERENCES AND PROBLEMS: See introductory remarks; possibly adaptable into zones 8 and 9 on cool sites.

PESTS AND DISEASES: See introductory remarks.

VARIETIES AND CULTIVARS (only tree forms are listed here): Cultivar 'Albospica', compact and slow-growing with whitened branch tips showiest in summer; cv. 'Atrovirens', having an irregular silhouette with foliage medium green with a yellowish margin; cv. 'Aurea', dwarfed with tightly compressed leaves emerging first golden yellow but fading in summer to yellow-green; cv. 'Fastigiata', narrowly ascending with short, erect branching and fern-like leaves; cv. 'Fremdii', slow-growing, moderately tall, compactly pyramidal with dark green foliage; cv. 'Gracilis' with very tiny leaves on drooping branches; cv. 'Macrophylla', a small, slow-growing, densely branched tree or heavy shrub with larger needles than the parent; cv. 'Microphylla' with extremely small leaves resembling heather; cv. 'Pendula' (T. sargentii), very popular as a slow-growing, pendant, wide-spreading shrub with densely arching branches and an eventual height of about 12 feet; cv. 'Westonigra' with very dark green, closely set leaves and a raggedly open outline.

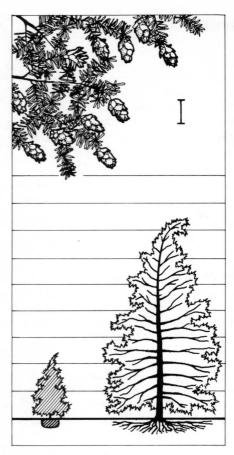

Tsuga caroliniana (Carolina hemlock)

Zones 5 to 7   40' to 70'   Pine family

With spirally arranged, projecting needles instead of the usual flat-planed ones common to other hemlock, this more gracefully shaped plant from the mountain areas of southwestern Virginia to northern Georgia is seemingly able to adjust better to the soot and dust prevalent in cities. It still has a cultural need, however, for the general preferences given under *T. canadensis* to gain its best performance, and it needs an acid soil.

HABIT: Compactly conical with a less rigidly symmetric outline than *T. canadensis;* usually carries pendulous branchlets; growth is at a moderate pace.

SEASONAL APPEARANCE: Twigs are usually smooth and light red-brown when young with slender needles spirally radiating on all sides; the blunt-tipped, up to three-quarter-inch foliage is glossy green above (and variable from dark to medium intensity) with two distinct white bands beneath; flowering is decoratively unimportant; the annual crops of oblong cones are up to 1¹/₂ inches long and show widely spreading scales when mature; its dark red-brown bark has large, yellowish pores which darken to purple-gray later.

PREFERENCES AND PROBLEMS: See *T. canadensis;* more tolerant of city conditions.

PESTS AND DISEASES: Red spider mites are the worst problem.

VARIETIES AND CULTIVARS: Cultivar 'Compacta', a dwarfed, low, and very dense shrub with a rounded top; may outgrow this habit in time to become tree-like.

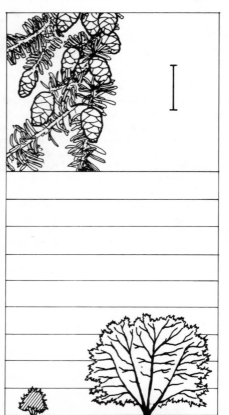

Tsuga diversifolia (Japanese hemlock, Northern Japanese hemlock)

Zones 6 to 8   25' to 80'   Pine family

Usually multistemmed, very slow-growing, and dome-shaped, this unusual native from the high mountain reaches of central and southern Japan has a very dense silhouette from retaining its needles up to nine years. It is probably best placed for specimen use, but only on acid soils.

HABIT: Varies by location to being either broadly pyramidal or dome-shaped with mainly horizontal branching and dense foliage; often develops multiple stems; very slow-growing.

SEASONAL APPEARANCE: Has pubescent, red-brown new twigs with half-inch, slender, very glossy, dark green, blunt-ended or notched needles carrying a grooved topside and two noticeably wide, white bands beneath; male flowering is rusty red but inconspicuous; the oval cones are shiny brown and up to three-quarters inch long; its trunk color is conspicuously reddish brown.

PREFERENCES AND PROBLEMS: See *T. canadensis.*

PESTS AND DISEASES: None of consequence except red spider mites.

VARIETIES AND CULTIVARS: None with botanic credentials.

Tsuga heterophylla (Western hemlock)

Zones 7 to 9   100' to 200'   Pine family

Tallest of all the hemlocks, this stately tree thrives only in its coastal habitat from Alaska to California as well as in the northern parts of Idaho. It wants high humidity, cool air, and a rich, very moist soil at all times and therefore does not grow at all well in the less humid parts of the eastern United States. Resembling a *Cedrus deodara* in its pendulous branchlets and general outline, it looks best in a landscape providing ample room for viewing and for its own expansion. This species is still often misnamed *T. mertensiana,* which is another type with the same native distribution but with blue-green foliage and a shorter size.

HABIT: Fine-textured with gracefully spreading branches and an unforked, straight trunk; young trees often show a broad outline, but older plants have a narrow, pyramidal shape with a spire-like crown; fast-growing.

SEASONAL APPEARANCE: New twigs are light brown, turning gray, and dense with bristly hairs; the soft, round-ended leaves are between one-third and three-quarters inch long, either lustrous dark green or yellowish green, grooved above, and with two white lines beneath; its flower production is of no visual importance; the acutely pointed, oval cones are up to 1 inch in length and vary from light to reddish brown; they are usually produced in sizable and showy quantities each year; the thin, dark russet-brown bark is narrowly fissured.

PREFERENCES AND PROBLEMS: See *T. canadensis;* also requires a constantly moist atmosphere and soil; prefers shelter from wind since its great size and shallow roots make it susceptible to easy uprooting; can extend its adaptation to zone 5 in the western United States with plants grown from seeds originally taken from those areas.

PESTS AND DISEASES: Suffers greatly from many types of both.

VARIETIES AND CULTIVARS: Cultivar 'Argentea' with blue-white needles.

Deciduous

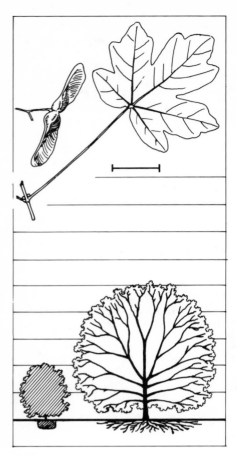

Acer campestre (Hedge maple, Field maple, English corkbark maple)

Zones 5 to 8   25' to 35'   Maple family

Maples have extensive distribution throughout the north temperate growing areas of the world. Generally dense in habit, they carry an international appeal either for a wide range of sizes, silhouettes, and seasonal colors or for their remarkable adaptability to many exposures and climates. As a group they grow freely on average soil in a hardiness range from zones 3 to 9 and provide some of the showiest autumn color found in any plant type. Since at least 150 different species are known, you can usually expect to find some maple to suit your landscape needs.

All maples are fibrously shallow-rooted, which makes them easy to transplant but also susceptible to damage in prolonged drought. For the most part they prefer to have good drainage and full sun, but they adapt to less than the best conditions without major difficulty. They are deservedly popular as sturdy street and shade trees, especially in difficult urban situations. Because maples are heavy with sap in winter and spring, prune only in summer. If provided with more than the minimal conditions for growth, maples excel as long-lived specimens of distinction.

All maples have leaves oppositely arranged on the twigs. Most have simple leaves, but a few carry compound foliage. Their fruit clusterings are uniquely distinct from other trees by being winged and in pairs, and many species are clearly separated by the special angle of these fruit wings. Maples often produce vast quantities of viable seeds annually, and the crush of new seedlings can be a maintenance problem of concern on many developed sites. The limited portfolio of maple species provided here represents only those with the most enduring appeal and reliability for landscape purposes. Personal investigation will likely introduce you to others of merit with such a long list of identified types.

Native to a vast area that includes Great Britain, Europe, northern Turkey, the Caucasus, and northern Iran, this particular tree is a twiggy maple that takes heavy pruning very well for rustic screens and formalized hedges. It is also valued for its high tolerance to air pollution, poor or alkaline soils, and dry conditions. The foliage remains in good condition until late in the autumn, but while it commonly turns a clear, golden yellow, it also may drop without changing color in some areas.

HABIT: Dense, compactly twiggy, and generally round-headed; may take a shrub form occasionally; slow-growing.

SEASONAL APPEARANCE: Its light brown, often corky twigs carry minute, woolly, red-brown, pointed buds; the 2- to 4-inch leaves have three to five rounded lobes and are smooth, dull green above with some hairiness beneath; the petioles are unusual for having milky sap; its small, greenish yellow, upright flowering in early spring has no decorative value; the pubescent fruit carry horizontal wings and measure up to $1^{1}/_{2}$ inches across; the bark is gray-brown and shallowly cracks into rectangular plates.

PREFERENCES AND PROBLEMS: Enjoys either full sun or light shade on a rich, well-drained, acid soil; very tolerant to either dry, alkaline or low-fertility soils and to air pollution; takes shearing well; not always common in nurseries of the United States.

PESTS AND DISEASES: None of importance.

VARIETIES AND CULTIVARS: Cultivar 'Compactum', bushy and low with a fully rounded outline; cv. 'Postelense' with new foliage golden yellow, fading to green; cv. 'Pulverulentum', scarce, its leaves are heavily covered with specks and blotches of white; cv. 'Schwerinii' with purple-toned foliage when young but later becoming green.

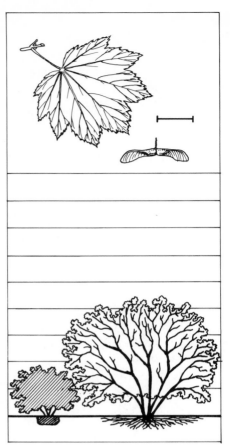

Acer circinatum (Vine maple)

Zones 5 to 9   25' to 35'   Maple family

Highly ornamental in flower, this sprawling, twisted, shrubby tree of Pacific coast stream banks from British Columbia down to northern California is well suited for garden use from its reasonable size and good tolerance to semishade, especially near tall evergreens.

HABIT: Displays contorted and meandering stems with upward and outward thrusts much like a vigorous vine; usually multistemmed and densely round-headed when cultivated; in the wild it tends to become tangled and fully interlaced with itself from new rooting where branches hit the ground; generally fast-growing.

SEASONAL APPEARANCE: Smooth, limber, reddish twigs carry thin, almost-round, 2- to 7-inch leaves with seven to nine shallow, pointed lobes; emerging foliage is red-tinged, but summer leaves become light green; they change to autumnal tints of red or orange in sunshine but are mostly yellow-toned when in shade; the small, drooping clusters of springtime flowers are unusually bright for a maple in reddish purple and white; the young fruit is bright red, smooth and has horizontally divergent, narrow wings with downturned ends; its smooth bark varies from greenish to bright red-brown.

PREFERENCES AND PROBLEMS: Likes full sun on sites with moist soil well enriched with organic matter; tolerant to some root competition and semishade, even from nearby evergreens; can be trained as a wall espalier; prefers some midday shading if grown where summers are hot and dry; probably tolerant only to zone 8 in the eastern parts of the United States.

PESTS AND DISEASES: No difficult problems known about either.

VARIETIES AND CULTIVARS: None.

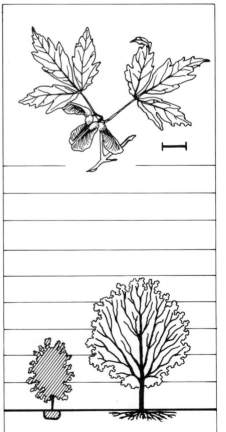

Acer griseum (Paperbark maple)

Zones 6 to 9   20' to 40'   Maple family

Its outstandingly colorful, red-toned bark is the special attraction of this unusual visitor from central China. Trunk and branches peel and flake in odd-sized patches to make a showy but refined specimen that carries a distinctive appeal when displayed openly against a darker, perhaps evergreen backdrop.

HABIT: Upright branches form a neatly open, rounded outline; slow growth rate.

SEASONAL APPEARANCE: Pointed, brown-black buds bring pubescent, bronze new growth; young twigs generally bark-peel by the third season; the foliage is compound with $1\frac{1}{2}$- to 3-inch leaflets coarsely blunt-tipped and colored dull, dark green above with noticeably silvered undersides; its glowing autumn color ranges from rich red to orange; the midspring flowering is yellow-toned but not outstanding; the very downy fruit is up to $1\frac{1}{4}$ inches long with downturned wings and has no ornamental value; its cinnamon-brown, thin bark peels and curls in papery layers to reveal a smooth, glistening trunk.

PREFERENCES AND PROBLEMS: Best grown in full sun on a moist, average, well-drained soil; difficult to propagate in quantity because most of its seeds fail to produce an embryo for germination; usually unsatisfactory in growth beyond zone 8 in the eastern United States.

PESTS AND DISEASES: Inconsequential.

VARIETIES AND CULTIVARS: None.

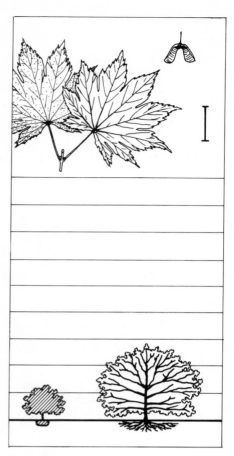

Acer japonicum (Full-moon maple)

Zones 5 to 9   20' to 30'   Maple family

Generally similar in shape to *Acer palmatum,* this Japanese native is larger and more rounded when mature but is still mostly horizontal in branching. It develops slowly enough to be a useful garden ornament, especially in sheltered locations. The common name derives from its full, roundish foliage.

HABIT: Broadly spreading and rounded with tiered, horizontal branches; often shrubby; very slow-growing.

SEASONAL APPEARANCE: Smooth twigs carry nearly rounded, 3- to 5$\frac{1}{2}$-inch bright green leaves with seven to thirteen pointed lobes turning a rich crimson or orange-red in autumn; the early spring, pendulous, red flower clusters are small but noticeable; its 1- to 2-inch fruit is also red-toned but somewhat hairy when young with mostly downturned wings (occasionally horizontal); the bark is greenish brown.

PREFERENCES AND PROBLEMS: Suited best for full sun on a moist, well-drained, average soil with shelter from cold wind blasts.

PESTS AND DISEASES: Of no importance.

VARIETIES AND CULTIVARS: Cultivar 'Aconitifolium' with leaves divided almost to the base and from nine to thirteen divisions, coloring a deep ruby in autumn; cv. 'Aureum', slower-growing than the parent with all-season, pale, golden yellow foliage that usually scorches in full sun; cv. 'Vitifolium' a vigorous type with broader, fan-shaped leaves having ten to twelve lobes and red-toned fruit.

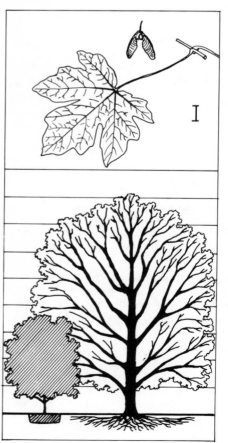

Acer macrophyllum (Oregon maple, Califoirnia maple, Canyon maple, Bigleaf maple)

Zones 7 to 9   75' to 100'   Maple family

Native from southeastern Alaska to California, the maple with the largest leaves of all appears to enjoy growing only on the Pacific side of the United States. Long popular there as a sizable shade tree, it offers a brilliant autumn show when its enormous leaves turn a bright orange.

HABIT: Dense, broadly round-headed with upright, spreading branches and short trunk; fast-growing,

SEASONAL APPEARANCE: Blue-toned, stout, smooth twigs produce glistening, dark green, mature leaves with paler undersides and three to five deeply divided lobes; while leaf sizes vary, even on the same tree, they can normally be up to 1 foot across; the autumn color is usually a strong orange or may also be a rich yellow in some growing areas; its deep yellow, fragrant, 4- to 6-inch flower clusters (occasionally greenish yellow) appear as the leaves unfold; the long, drooping sprays of winter-persistent fruit are vigorous enough at times to carry three wings instead of the normal two; they first are reddish and hairy but soon become smooth, yellow-brown and up to almost 2 inches long; the thin bark is broadly ridged and varies from brown-gray to brown tinged with red.

PREFERENCES AND PROBLEMS: Full sun is best on a rich, moist, gravelly site; does not endure in the eastern part of the United States.

PESTS AND DISEASES: Usually resistant to both.

VARIETIES AND CULTIVARS: None.

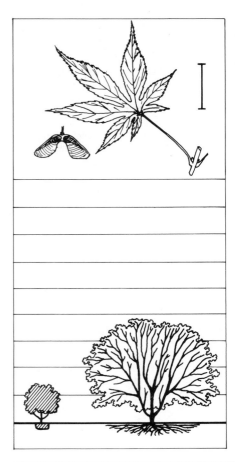

Acer palmatum (Japanese maple)

Zones 5 to 9   20′ to 50′   Maple family

A fine-textured and popular accent tree, the Japanese maple actually has an ancestral background from Korea, China, and Japan. It provides an airy, graceful note in wind-protected landscapes needing a special refinement. A wide variety of cultivars are commonly available.

HABIT: Often shrubby, multistemmed, and mound-like, the usual form is slenderly erect with a shortened trunk and mostly ascending branching showing a layered appearance; slow-growing.

SEASONAL APPEARANCE: The very slender green and smooth twigs (occasionally reddish when young) have thin, bright green, palmately formed, 2- to 4-inch, deeply lobed leaves with five to eleven separations; when grown in shade, they do not conspicuously color in the autumn, but if raised in sun, they are likely to turn deep scarlet; the midspring, tiny flowering is red-toned and not conspicuous; the small, three-quarter-inch, smooth fruit is bunched in tight clusters; its green bark is smooth and thin and ages with silvery, vertical stripes.

PREFERENCES AND PROBLEMS: Enjoys a moist, well-drained, average-fertility, humusy soil in full sun (but prefers semishade if on drier sites); requires protection from hot, dry winds and salt-filled air to avoid leaf scorch; apt to be less successful in zone 9 of the eastern United States.

PESTS AND DISEASES: Few bother it.

VARIETIES AND CULTIVARS: A generous list exists with such exhaustive differentiations of leaf colors, foliage patterns, mature sizes, and ranges of hardiness far too numerous to be described here; available nursery offerings and personal preference are often the only guidelines for proper choices from this wealth of attractive material.

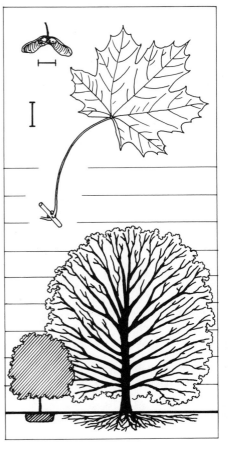

Acer platanoides (Norway maple)

Zones 4 to 9   60′ to 90′   Maple family

Native to Europe and most of western Asia, this stalwart species of street trees is adaptable to the widest range of growing conditions without difficulty. It has drawbacks for ordinary garden use, however, with its greedy surface rooting and very dense shading; those must be balanced with its rugged hardiness and attractive form. It is one of the last deciduous trees to show autumn coloring, and it has an identifying characteristic of exuding milky juice from the petiole when one of its large leaves is snapped off.

HABIT: Wide-spreading and dense with either a dome-shaped or rounded crown; moderate to rapid growth rate.

SEASONAL APPEARANCE: Carries egg-shaped, purple-toned winter buds of noticeable size on smooth, reasonably stout twigs; the summer foliage varies from 3 to 6 inches in width and is thin, medium green, and glossy with five doubly serrated lobes that are sharply pointed; the autumn color comes late in the season and appears as bright yellow to dull gold; its midspring flowering is showy from sizable, upright, rounded clusters of chartreuse blossoms appearing before the foliage, making the entire tree outline attractively conspicuous; the plentiful, up-to-2-inch fruit develops on long stalks and has gently recurved wings; its dark gray bark is tightly set on the trunk and becomes only shallowly ridged with age.

PREFERENCES AND PROBLEMS: Thrives in full sun or light shading on any average, well-drained soil; completely tolerant of befouled city air, meager soil, and seashore conditions; readily transplanted at any age; takes wind and cold with aplomb; has invasively dense surface rooting and heavy shade, forestalling any success with underplanting; prone to sizable aphid infestations in spring and early summer that produce a sticky, soot-collecting sap residue on stems and leaves as well as on pavements and cars below.

PESTS AND DISEASES: Stoutly resistant to most insect and fungal attacks, but aphids are a consistently bothersome nuisance; verticillium wilt occasionally disfigures new growth; foliage usually scorches in zones 8 and 9 on some sites.

VARIETIES AND CULTIVARS (few large trees have produced more cultivar selections and only a select list is offered here): Cultivar 'Aureo-marginatum' with light green foliage lightly brushed with pink; cv. 'Charles F. Irish', a large, round-topped form with upswept branching and smaller leaves than the parent; cv. 'Cleveland', upright and oval with large, dark green foliage; cv. 'Columnare', smaller-leaved and noticeably twiggy with a narrowly conical shape; cv. 'Crimson King', slower-growing than the parent with dark maroon foliage all season; cv. 'Crispum', having leaves with crinkled edges; cv. 'Drummondii' with leaves edged in silver-white; cv. 'Emerald Queen', carrying leathery, glossy, dark green foliage; cv. 'Erectum', slow-growing with larger, darker foliage than 'Columnare' but with a pyramidal outline and thinner branching; cv. 'Faassen's Black' with a deeper maroon leaf than 'Crimson King' and a pyramidal silhouette; cv. 'Harlequin', a round-headed tree with variegated leaves; cv. 'Improved Columnar', a gracefully columnar form; cv. 'Laciniatum', a slenderly erect, large tree with leaves having wedge-shaped bases and lobes reduced to claw-like points; cv. 'Olmsted', a dwarfed columnar form about 25 feet tall; cv. 'Palmatifidum' ('Lorbergii') with light green leaves almost divided to the base and long-pointed tips; cv. 'Reitenbachii', medium in size with deeply divided bronze-green new growth turning dark purple by summer and showing red autumn color; cv. 'Royal Red' with persistently glossy, rich red foliage; cv. 'Rubrum' with green summer foliage changing to glowing red in autumn; cv. 'Schwedleri', slow-growing with light red new growth turning bronze-green in summer and red in autumn; cv. 'Stollii', new growth red-toned with shallowly three-lobed, very broad leaves up to 9 inches across; cv. 'Summer Shade', a rapid-growing, heat-resistant, upright form, with very leathery, large, deep green leaves, adapts well to the southern United States; cv. 'Walderseei', a weak-growing type carrying foliage densely speckled with white for a gray-toned, overall appearance.

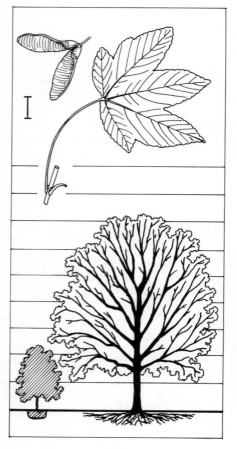

Acer pseudoplatanus (Sycamore maple, Mock plane, Sycamore)

Zones 5 to 9   70′ to 100′   Maple family

Durable and picturesque with flaking, lavender-tan bark much like an orchard apple tree as it ages, this commonly cultivated tree from Europe and western Asia adapts well to any exposed situation and grows easily in any soil. It firmly withstands the full force of salt-laden, coastal winds and shows dependable hardiness on all sites. Its popularity is somewhat diminished, however, by its dingy brown autumnal coloring.

HABIT: Similar in outline to A. platanoides with a broad-spreading, rounded crown and generally dense foliage, it is not quite so compact or stiff-trunked; fast to moderate growth, depending on age.

SEASONAL APPEARANCE: Noticeably large, emerald-green winter buds appear on smooth, gray-toned twigs and produce five-lobed, wavy-margined, dull-surfaced, dark green leaves between 3½ and 6 inches across; there is no worthwhile autumn color unless you prefer muddy brown; its pendulous, greenish yellow flowering can be up to 5 inches long but is often hidden by the emerging springtime leaves; the tan 1½- to 2-inch fruit is sometimes winter-persistent and comes clustered in long chains with wings divergent at a right angle; the dull, metallic-gray bark of young trees later becomes attractively lavender-tan and breaks into broad, flaky scales.

PREFERENCES AND PROBLEMS: Succeeds in any soil that is well drained and adjusts from full sun to light shade easily; very sturdy on exposed, windblown sites, especially at the shore; tolerant of salt spray; dislikes high heat and will probably grow better if limited to zone 8 on the eastern coast of the United States; not so long-lived as A. platanoides.

PESTS AND DISEASES: Prone to several trunk-boring insects and to various leaf-spotting diseases.

VARIETIES AND CULTIVARS: Cultivar 'Albo-varegatum' with foliage blotched and streaked with white; cv. 'Atropurpureum', a form with maroon foliage when young and turning in summer to dark green with noticeably deep red undersides; cv. 'Erectum', a large tree with upright branching; cv. 'Erythrocarpum' with smaller leaves and bright red fruit until fully ripe; cv. 'Flavovariegatum' with leaves variegated in yellow; cv. 'Leopoldii' with dark rose emerging growth and mature leaves variegated with yellowish pink; cv. 'Purpureum' with noticeably purple-toned undersides of foliage; cv. 'Pyramidale' with green leaves and a pyramidal shape; cv. 'Quadricolor', having new green growth spotted with stark white and rose-tan; cv. 'Rubrum' with dark green foliage showing wine-red undersurfaces; cv. 'Spaethii' with leaves deep green on top and rich purple-crimson beneath; cv. 'Variegatum', young leaves reddish but changing to all green later with white variegations; cv. 'Worleei', a medium-sized tree with new foliage orange-yellow but changing to deep yellow by summer if in full sun.

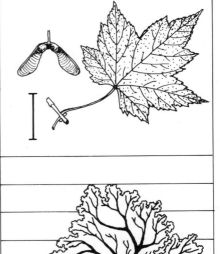

Acer rubrum (Red maple, Scarlet maple, Swamp maple)

Zones 3 to 9   70' to 120'   Maple family

Wide-ranging in natural distribution from Newfoundland to Florida and west to Minnesota, Oklahoma, Iowa, and Texas, the red maple is a common occurrence in lowland wet spots and even swampy areas, yet it is perfectly adaptable to drier conditions, too. Offering a relaxed silhouette and strikingly attractive gray bark, it serves as a specimen or shade tree with good hardiness.

HABIT: Usually taller than broad with a densely oval or globular outline and a rounded crown when mature; fast-growing.

SEASONAL APPEARANCE: Small, red-toned winter buds produce lustrous, bright to dark green, three- to five-lobed leaves with silver-haired undersides in dimensions between 3 and 6 inches; the autumn color is predominately scarlet, but orange and yellow are not uncommon; its very early spring flowering of red or reddish brown appears well before the leaves from profuse clusters of small buds scattered along the tips of the smooth twigs; the pendulous, almost inch-long fruit come in heavy bunches and are usually bright red when young; its smooth, pale gray young bark later darkens to blackish gray and becomes scaly with shallow furrows on the lower trunk, but the upper limbs long retain their rich pewter tone.

PREFERENCES AND PROBLEMS: Flourishes in full sun on consistently moist, rich soil but adapts well to semishade and to drier conditions; grows equally on acid or alkaline soils yet colors best in autumn on acid ones; prone to weak-woodedness and is easily damaged by ice and heavy, wet snowfalls; sometimes confused with *A. saccharinum* in the juvenile age.

PESTS AND DISEASES: None of consequence.

VARIETIES AND CULTIVARS: Variety *drummondii* has leathery, five-lobed leaves with deeper clefts; variety *trilobum* has smaller, rounded foliage with only three lobes near the tip; cv. 'Armstrong', a narrowly columnar form; cv. 'Autumn Flame', a dense, round-headed type with earlier autumnal coloring of scarlet and persistence beyond the norm; cv. 'Bowhall', a pyramidal form; cv. 'Columnare' with a slow-growing, upright shape and deep green foliage turning bronze to red in autumn; cv. 'Gerling', a broadly pyramidal form; cv. 'Globosum', a dwarfed, compact tree with bright red, spring flowering; cv. 'October Glory' with shiny foliage turning brilliant crimson in autumn and holding longer; cv. 'Palmatum', a male plant with drooping twigs and sizable, five-lobed leaves; cv. 'Paul E. Tilford', a compact, globose type; cv. 'Scanlon', a medium-sized tree with a compactly pyramidal outline plus combined orange, amber, and red autumnal colors; cv. 'Schlesingeri', a vigorous type with early, brilliant scarlet autumn color.

Acer saccharinum [*dasycarpum*] (Silver maple, Soft maple, White maple, River maple)

Zones 3 to 9   90' to 130'   Maple family

Despite its enormous size, graceful silhouette, and exceptional hardiness, this native maple from low wetlands of Quebec to Florida (and west to Minnesota and Oklahoma) has severe landscape handicaps. Since it grows very rapidly, it produces weak, brittle wood highly susceptible to important storm damage from wind, snow, and ice. Also, its vigorous surface roots can easily crack and lift paving and are quickly able to clog underground drainage lines. Further, the wet inner wood is highly prone to attacks of fungi and insects. With all these drawbacks, it is included here because it is splendidly adaptable for very poor soils and to harsh climates where little else of size will grow. Otherwise, use it with great caution.

HABIT: Upright and broad with strong-looking, spreading branches having gracefully drooping ends and somewhat contorted twigs; generally develops an oval shape and a doomed crown; very rapid in growth at all ages.

SEASONAL APPEARANCE: Tiny, brown-red winter buds on irregular twigs (with a strong, disagreeable smell when bruised) carry five-lobed, deeply cleft, doubly toothed, thin leaves from 4 to 6 inches in length with a bright green top and a silver-white coating beneath; the autumnal color is usually clear yellow but occasionally can have an orange tint; the generously produced small clusters of pinkish brown to green-yellow flowers appear in either late winter or very early spring and are not noticeably showy; its sizable, nearly right-angled fruit can measure up to 2½ inches and is the largest of all the maples; the thin, light gray to tan-gray bark of juvenile plants is often unhappily confused with that of *A. rubrum;* older trunks have a spirally twisted appearance, a silvery gray-brown color, and broad, flaky scales with the ends lifted outward.

PREFERENCES AND PROBLEMS: Excels for speedy growth on any consistently damp soil in full sun; acid soil preferred for best autumn color; tolerant of drier, shadier sites and frigid exposures; readily transplanted; extremely brittle and weak-wooded as it matures; may show leaf scorch on foliage in prolonged drought; has an invasive surface rooting able to hoist pavements as well as obstruct drain lines.

PESTS AND DISEASES: Many of both, especially aphids and cottony maple scale infestations, plus heart rot fungus.

VARIETIES AND CULTIVARS: Cultivar 'Albo-variegatum' with foliage flecked in pink and white; cv. 'Blairii', well-shaped with stronger branching and a rapid growth rate; cv. 'Crispum' with yellowish green foliage; cv. 'Heterophyllum' with an upright shape and irregular leaves cut almost to the base; cv. 'Longifolium', carrying three-lobed, very deeply cleft leaves; cv. 'Lutescens', emerging foliage is orange-toned but later becomes a soft yellow-green when in full sun; cv. 'Pyramidale', a columnar form; cv. 'Silver Queen', a *male* tree with sizable and rapid growth; cv. 'Skinnen', pyramidal and only semiweeping; cv. 'Tripartitum' with twigs carrying prominently large, white breathing pores and sizable, deeply cut leaves having only three points; cv. 'Wieri', a medium-sized, pyramidal form with deeply dissected, lacy foliage.

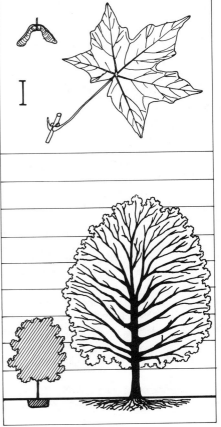

Acer saccharum (Sugar maple, Rock maple, Hard maple)

Zones 3 to 9   60' to 100'   Maple family

One of the most attractive deciduous trees known, the sugar maple has no peer for spectacularly beautiful autumn color. Its dignified and sturdy silhouette, moderate growth rate, general freedom from pests and diseases, plus its bonus of producing sugary sap worth converting to maple syrup, make it a choice selection for any landscape development not in the polluted atmosphere and soils of cities. Native from Quebec to Florida and west to Texas, it displays its features best in generously moist, fertile land uncrowded by other planting.

HABIT: Slenderly and usually symmetrically oval to globular with upswept branching and mostly horizontal twigs; moderate in growth.

SEASONAL APPEARANCE: Delicately sharp-pointed brown buds on smooth, gray-brown twigs produce three- to five-lobed, thin, dark green leaves (paler beneath) with undulating margins and widths between 4 and 6 inches; the autumnal colors are vivid and range between orange, gold, scarlet, and crimson; its midspring flowering is creamy yellow in drooping clusters of moderate showiness; the smooth fruit measures between 1 and 2 inches and has slightly divergent wings; its juvenile bark looks smooth and silvery tan, but the older trunk becomes ash-gray and breaks into hard, flinty scales.

PREFERENCES AND PROBLEMS: Easily moved when young, it enjoys full sun on an evenly moist, well-drained, moderately acid, fertile soil; tolerant to light shading, gravelly soil, and slightly alkaline conditions; does not adapt at all well to polluted city air, reflected heat, ice-melting chemicals on pavements, high-wind locations, or drought; its surface rooting and heavy shade usually forestall good response from any underplanting; appears to dislike conditions in zone 9 on the east coast of the United States.

PESTS AND DISEASES: None is a serious affliction.

VARIETIES AND CULTIVARS: Cultivar 'Globosum', a shrubby form often broader than tall; cv. 'Green Mountain' with leathery, dark green foliage and an oval crown; cv. 'Newton Sentry', a columnar form with a strong, central leader and stubby, ascending branches carrying very thick, wavy, dark green leaves; cv. 'Sweet Shadow' ('Laciniatum') with deeply divided, lacy leaves; cv. 'Temple's Upright' ('Monumentale'), often confused with 'Newton Sentry' but has no defined central leader, only many ascending branches, plus yellow-green foliage; the subspecies *nigrum* (which some authorities consider a true species) differs by developing a dark gray bark and by carrying brown twigs mottled in gray; its broader foliage has only three lobes and usually shows drooping margins with persistent hairs along the veins on the undersides.

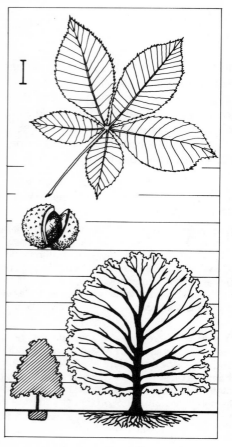

Aesculus × *carnea* (Red horse chestnut)

Zones 4 to 9   30' to 40'   Horse chestnut family

Ornamentally conspicuous when flowering, this hybrid created over 120 years ago by crossing *A. hippocastanum* and *A. pavia* has proved durably satisfying as a landscape specimen, especially in small spaces. As with all horse chestnut types, it is prone to many insect pests and diseases and offers no autumn color, but at least here the showy, red-toned blossoms and smaller fruiting give it an edge. In Europe it can often stretch to 80 feet.

HABIT: Generally pyramidal when juvenile but becoming oval and round-headed at maturity; moderate to fast in growth, depending on its hardiness zone.

SEASONAL APPEARANCE: Large, oval, dark brown, winter buds develop into compound, fan-like foliage normally with five leaflets almost equally 5 inches long; the leaves are deep, dark green with sunken veins and moderate glossiness; its midspring blossoming appears in terminally spired clusters to 8 inches high of red tones from flesh to scarlet generously produced (usually) on all portions of the tree; it lacks interesting autumn color; the slightly spiny seed capsule holds several rounded, brown fruit between 1 and 1¹/₂ inches in diameter; its thin, shallowly grooved bark is dull black-brown.

PREFERENCES AND PROBLEMS: Best suited to full sun on a deep, consistently moist, average soil; adapts well to light shade, urban conditions, and shore sites; starts flowering when only 6 to 8 feet tall; foliage scorches badly in drought and then drops early.

PESTS AND DISEASES: Has many noticeable problems with both, especially Japanese beetles, mildew, and rust disease.

VARIETIES AND CULTIVARS: Cultivar 'Briotii' has more compact growth, deep scarlet flowers, and taller (up to 10-inch) blossoms; cv. 'Rosea' carries pink-toned flowering.

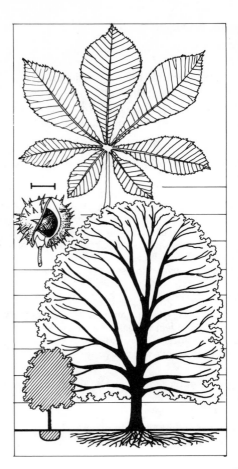

Aesculus hippocastanum (Common horse chestnut, European horse chestnut)

Zones 3 to 8   75' to 100'   Horse chestnut family

While generally held in low esteem nowadays because of its tendency to carry greatly disfigured summer foliage from insect and disease nuisances, this cold-tolerant native from the Balkan peninsula still presents an impressively large silhouette, exotic summertime foliage, and noteworthy flowering. Since its sizable fruit litter is often exasperating, consider the sterile double-flowered, nonfruiting type as a wise alternative in public spaces. In England these formidable fruit are aptly called "conkers," a corruption, it is said, of "conquerors."

HABIT: Upright and broadly oval with spreading lateral branching; usually fast-growing.

SEASONAL APPEARANCE: Noticeably sticky, rich brown, large winter buds appear on stout twigs with sizable breathing pores; the palmately compound foliage has between five and seven leaflets, each between 4 and 8 inches in length of medium to dark green color with slightly wrinkled margins; the autumn color is shabby brown; its prominent, late spring flowers are erect, densely conical, possibly to 1 foot tall, and composed of large, creamy white florets with blotches of red and yellow; the brown, 2- to 3-inch fruit comes wrapped in prickly outer coverings; its rough but thin bark at maturity turns scaly and dark gray or brownish gray.

PREFERENCES AND PROBLEMS: Grows best in full sun on a well-drained, deep, always-moist, average-fertility soil; intolerant of drought; adaptable to light shading, city pollution, and salt spray from coastal locations; fruit drop is a constant hazard in public spaces; starts to bloom only when about 20 feet tall.

PESTS AND DISEASES: The Japanese beetle and the caterpillar of the tussock moth are especially problematic as defoliators; mildew and rust diseases are common in summer.

VARIETIES AND CULTIVARS: Cultivar 'Alba' with pure white flowering; cv. 'Baumannii' with longer-lasting and larger, double, white, sterile blossoms producing no fruit; cv. 'Rosea', showing pink-toned flowers; cv. 'Rubricunda' with red flowers.

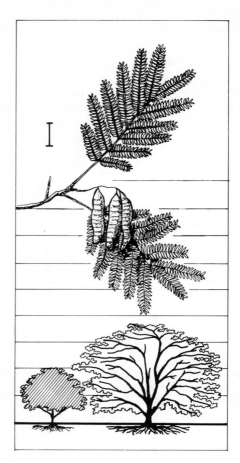

Albizia julibrissin (Silk tree, Mimosa, Mimosa tree)

Zones 7 (warm) to 10   25' to 40'   Pea family

Often erroneously spelled *Albizzia* in print, this feathery-foliaged tree is native from Iran to Japan and offers unusual, persistent, late summer flowering and a special attraction for hummingbirds. Unfortunately, it never seems to reach a venerable age or be free of destructive pests and diseases. Where it thrives, it makes a novel, late-flowering specimen.

HABIT: Often multitrunked with a flat-topped, broadly spreading crown and gracefully horizontal branches; rapid-growing.

SEASONAL APPEARANCE: Carries smooth and slender, tan branches and twigs; its doubly compound, feathery foliage is composed of quarter-inch, light green leaflets in a total size between 9 and 12 inches long and 4 to 5 inches wide; there is no autumn coloring; its long-lasting summer flowering is showy for several months from clusters of 1- to 2-inch, light pink, pin-cushion-like masses of stamens in rounded heads crowded toward the branch tips; the thin, yellow-tan fruit pods can be up to 6 inches long and show gentle constrictions between the seeds; the smooth bark is greenish tan.

PREFERENCES AND PROBLEMS: Likes full sun and high summer heat on a well-drained, average soil; tolerant of partial shade, wind, poor or sandy soils, and drought; adapts better if moved when no more than 8 feet tall and if also trunk-wrapped when young with paper or burlap for protection from cold during the winter months (at least until fully established); older plants may die to the ground level in severely cold winters.

PESTS AND DISEASES: Seriously damaged (if not killed) by a stem wilt from a widespread soil fungus at the root level, especially in the southern parts of the United States; webworms are highly destructive to its foliage.

VARIETIES AND CULTIVARS: Cultivar 'Alba' with white blossoming; cv. 'Rosea', much hardier than the parent with smaller, bright pink flowers; cv. 'Tryon', a form highly resistant to the soil fungus wilt.

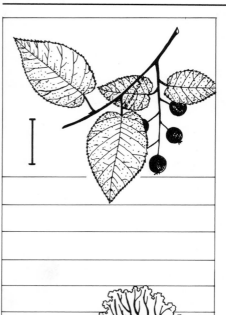

Amelanchier canadensis (Shadbush, Shadblow, Downy serviceberry)

Zones 4 to 8   20' to 50'   Rose family

Native to swampy woodlots from Quebec to Georgia, this reliable, easily grown, attractive spring tree offers landscape interest in all seasons. One of the first trees to bloom, it may unfortunately have only a week of fleeting glory if temperatures and wind velocities climb rapidly during that time. Its bright autumn color helps balance this seasonal inequality.

HABIT: Usually slenderly multistemmed with an upright, conical shape and a twiggy but open appearance; often suckers readily at the base to form a shrubby thicket; moderate-growing.

SEASONAL APPEARANCE: Slender, gray twigs produce oval, finely toothed, 1- to 2-inch, bright green leaves very downy on the undersides when young (becoming smooth later); upright but nodding clusters of snow-white, 1-inch, hairy flowers appear generously in early spring when the foliage is half emerged; its edible, tiny fruit appears in midsummer as a sweet but somewhat dry berry changing from green to red to maroon-purple when ripe; the showy autumn colors vary from rich yellow to apricot-orange and rusty red; its smooth, dark gray bark is marked with lighter streaks especially noticeable in winter.

PREFERENCES AND PROBLEMS: Grows equally in full sun or light shade on either acid or alkaline soils which are consistently moist and well drained; requires no supplemental fertilizing; its edible fruit is often quickly stolen by birds.

PESTS AND DISEASES: Red spider mites, lacewing flies, and fireblight are the worst afflictions.

VARIETIES AND CULTIVARS: None.

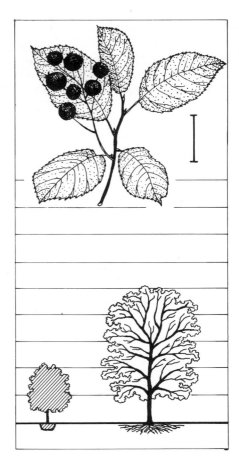

Amelanchier laevis (Allegheny serviceberry)

Zones 5 to 8   25' to 40'   Rose family

Generally found wild in the same moist woods as *A. canadensis,* this native of eastern North America is a tree form which grows from Newfoundland to Ontario and south to Georgia, Ohio, and Iowa. Its richly bronze-toned new foliage is one of its main distinctions; the other is fragrant flowering.

HABIT: Upright, single-trunked, and oval in outline with mostly horizontal branching; moderate growth rate.

SEASONAL APPEARANCE: Slim, gray twigs display drooping clusters of fragrant, white, three-quarter-inch, springtime blossoms interspersed with emerging deep bronze-purple, smooth, oval foliage; the leaves eventually turn dark green; its edible, early summertime fruit is reddish black when fully ripened and is enjoyed by birds; the autumn foliage varies from yellow to red; the smooth, light gray, young bark eventually matures to a dark reddish brown.

PREFERENCES AND PROBLEMS: See *A. canadensis.*

PESTS AND DISEASES: See *A. canadensis.*

VARIETIES AND CULTIVARS: None.

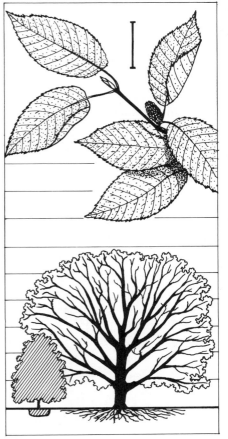

Betula lenta (Sweet birch, Cherry birch, Black birch, Mahogany birch)

Zones 4 to 8   50' to 75'   Birch family

Birches are famed for their delicate gracefulness and the unique variations of color in the decorative, peeling bark: On some species it is shimmering white; on others, silver-gray, apricot-pink, or even golden brown; on still others it is satiny mahogany or rough gray-black. Birch trunks and limbs are also usually lined with horizontal rows of conspicuous breathing pores (lenticels) similar to that on many cherries, but there is no botanic relationship between these different plants.

Birch flowering is always separated on the same tree. The noticeable but small, male, tubular catkins are evident in winter at the tips of the branching; they all become yellow-toned in spring as they expand downward toward the just emerging, green, female catkins starting from the buds below. Neither its flowering nor its cone-like seeds are very showy, but all birch at least have bright yellow autumnal foliage.

Birches enjoy a constantly moist, sandy soil and colonize with ease in their wild state. Because they are laden with sap in spring, they are best pruned at any other season. Unfortunately, no birch is exceptionally long-lived even with good care.

Two insects are debilitating to birch health. The bronze birch borer, a tiny grub which tunnels under the bark and invisibly girdles the upper stems, can quickly bring great loss to a plant's shapeliness. In both the northeastern and the northwestern parts of the United States another pest, the birch leaf miner, can also wreak havoc by consuming the chlorophyll cells between the leaf surfaces, causing almost complete browning of the new foliage in a short time. Severe attacks can lead to the death of a tree.

Even with these special difficulties to overcome, however, you can expect birches to maintain a colorful appeal as effective landscape features not easily matched by any other trees. Beauty sometimes has a price in maintenance requirements.

The birch described here is native to moist woods from southern Maine to upper Alabama and is probably the best for the richness of its golden autumn color. The strong fragrance of oil of wintergreen in the twigs provides a reason for naming it "sweet." It makes a handsomely wide-spreading specimen for large spaces.

HABIT: Dense and pyramidal when juvenile but becoming wide-spreading, more open, and dome-shaped with age; moderate in growth.

SEASONAL APPEARANCE: Young twigs carry a pleasantly aromatic, oil-of-wintergreen odor; its oblong, $2^1/_2$- to 5-inch, dark green, glossy leaves are covered with silky hairs beneath when young; the autumn foliage is bright, golden yellow; very slender, 1- to $1^1/_2$-inch, male catkins are in groups from seven to thirteen (the most generous in the genus); its female catkins are erect and about 1 inch high; the non-peeling bark is glossy and rich mahogany when young; when older, it becomes reddish brown or almost black and cracks into thick, irregular plates.

PREFERENCES AND PROBLEMS: Does very well in full sun on deep, rich, well-drained, moist, moderately acid soils in cool locations; adapts to semishade and to drier and heavier soils.

PESTS AND DISEASES: See introductory remarks.

VARIETIES AND CULTIVARS: None.

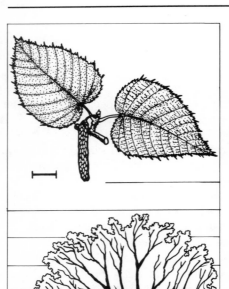

Betula maximowicziana (Monarch birch)

Zones 6 to 10   80' to 100'   Birch family

With the largest leaf of any birch, this native of central and northern Japan is also impressive for its tall growth and colorful bark. It is assuredly not a tree for small-scaled spaces.

HABIT: Stiffly erect with a rounded, loosely arranged, and wide-spreading crown; fast-growing.

SEASONAL APPEARANCE: Carries lustrous, dark green leaves close to 7 inches long and about 5 inches wide with noticeably fine-toothed margins and heart-shaped bases; the autumnal color is a clear, golden yellow even in warm areas; the winter-obvious, male catkins are nearly 4 inches long, while the female fruit later appear in two to four drooping clusters 3 inches in length; the flaking bark is orange-brown when juvenile, later becoming light gray.

PREFERENCES AND PROBLEMS: Grows satisfactorily in sun or light shade on any reasonably moist, average soil with good drainage; very suitable for cold, exposed sites as well as for dry, sandy locations.

PESTS AND DISEASES: See *B. lenta.*

VARIETIES AND CULTIVARS: None.

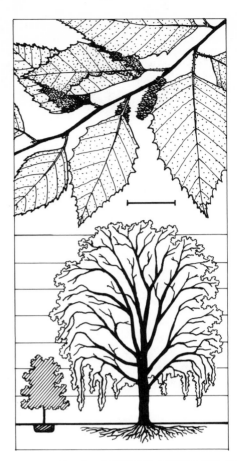

Betula nigra [rubra] (River birch, Black birch, Red birch)

Zones 5 to 10   50' to 100'   Birch family

So naturally adapted it can succeed in hot, dry locations as well as on very moist sites which are occasionally flooded, this graceful, native birch of wetlands from Massachusetts to Florida and west to Kansas has unusually heavy layers of pink-toned, peeling bark. Unfortunately, this decorative feature keeps moving exclusively into the upper branching as the plant matures. The tree is also unique for having its female cones ripen only in spring.

HABIT: Pyramidal with strongly ascending and horizontal branching when young; alters to an irregular, round-topped tree carrying slenderly weeping outer branches with age; reasonably fast-growing depending on soil moisture.

SEASONAL APPEARANCE: Its slender twigs have sharp-toothed, 1- to 3-inch, diamond-shaped, glossy leaves with a wedged base colored medium to dark green with whitened undersides; the autumn foliage varies from an ineffectual, dull gold to a clear yellow; its male catkins are brown, slender, and between 2 and 3 inches long; the erect female cones mature only in the spring and are covered wtih downy scales; these fruiting cones measure about 1½ inches in length; the young bark exfoliates in heavy layers of papery folds from pale salmon to red-brown or even silvery gray; the lower trunk and branches become dark, reddish brown and shaggy with thick, curly scales at maturity.

PREFERENCES AND PROBLEMS: Enjoys a moist, deep, well-drained, rich soil in full sun; readily adaptable to drier sites as well as to very wet ones; relatively short-lived; prone to ice breakage because of brittle wood; easily transplanted; takes prolonged flooding very well.

PESTS AND DISEASES: See B. lenta; usually more disease-resistant than other birches.

VARIETIES AND CULTIVARS: None.

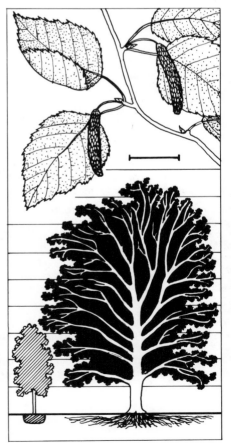

Betula papyrifera (Paper birch, Canoe birch, White birch)

Zones 3 to 8   60' to 100'   Birch family

Plants with white stems are rare indeed, and to find large trees so intriguingly colored is an especially attractive bonus for landscape use. Very hardy and widely distributed naturally from Newfoundland to Alaska, this beautiful tree shows less blackening of the lower trunk than other white-barked birches, has flexible wood for withstanding ice and snow damage, and is usually less afflicted by the bronze birch borer. All in all, this is a remarkable landscape asset with a deserved popularity.

HABIT: Narrowly pyramidal when young with an erect trunk; later more openly wide-spreading and round-topped; often with multiple or very low-branched stems; moderate in growth rate.

SEASONAL APPEARANCE: Warty, red-brown new twigs carry oval, 1½- to 4-inch, dull dark green leaves with coarse teeth and a light-colored underside; autumnal foliage is a medium yellow; the winter male catkins usually come in threes, which are slender and stiffly held apart and can measure up to 2 inches; female seed cones are smooth, pendulous, and about 2 inches long also, its strikingly white bark begins as deep brown when juvenile and soon becomes chalky, then peels in papery layers along the horizontal lines of the lenticels, and eventually darkens and furrows at the base; crude stripping of the bark (common in public spaces) is both disfiguring and highly damaging to the tree's future growth.

PREFERENCES AND PROBLEMS: Thrives in full sun on gravelly or sandy, acid soils with reasonable moisture; its best performance is in colder climates; northern trees grown far south of their natural range are often killed by borers.

PESTS AND DISEASES: See B. lenta; less infested, generally, with the bronze birch borer but highly prone to damage from the birch leaf miner.

VARIETIES AND CULTIVARS: Variety commutata [lyalliana] has foliage only up to 3 inches long and tighter bark with a red-brown tone; variety *cordifolia,* smaller in overall size and occasionally shrubby with foliage showing double teeth on the margins; variety *humilis* [*neoalaskana*] originated in the Yukon and has red-brown, exfoliating bark; variety *kenaica* is an Alaskan native with orange-toned, white bark later becoming deep brown-black and furrowed; carries smaller leaves about 2 inches long; variety *minor,* a shrubby form or occasionally a small, bushy tree; variety *subcordata,* a smaller form having 2-inch leaves and silver-gray bark with a purple overtone.

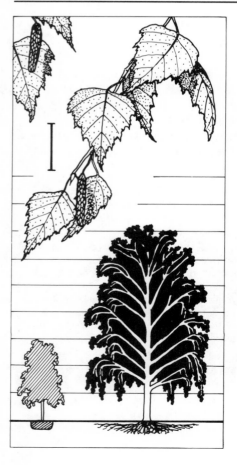

Betula pendula [*alba*] [*verrucosa*]
(European white birch)

Zones 3 to 9   40′ to 60′   Birch family

Native to the high-altitude areas of Europe and Asia Minor, this white-barked tree is probably the most widely planted of all the birches. Especially graceful in appearance, it offers some special silhouettes and leaf forms not available from *B. papyrifera,* but it is very short-lived and highly susceptible to great damage from the bronze birch borer. Rely on it for landscape interest but not for durability.

HABIT: Upright, open-foliaged, and generally pyramidal or oval at all ages; outer branching likely to become somewhat weeping with maturity; moderate-growing.

SEASONAL APPEARANCE: Golden brown, gracefully pendant twigs produce smooth diamond shaped, glossy, usually dark green leaves up to 2¹/₂ inches long; the autumn coloring varies from a noticeable yellow to yellow-green; the slim male catkins appear in odd-numbered clusterings and can range up to 1¹/₄ inches long; its female cones are narrowly cylindric and roughly 1 inch in length; young bark is golden brown, but older trunks and limbs turn a showy silver-gray with conspicuous black markings but with less peeling than *B. papyrifera;* the lower trunk eventually becomes dark gray and ridged in diamond-shaped patches.

PREFERENCES AND PROBLEMS: Best planted in a very sunny location on a moist, well-drained, sandy or gravelly soil; adjusts to either very wet or very dry sites and to acid and alkaline conditions; tolerant of polluted city air; not recommended, however, for the hot, dry conditions of desert areas; appears to be only fair to middling for growth in zones 9 and 10; begins to decline in about thirty years even with good care.

PESTS AND DISEASES: See *B. lenta;* this species is highly favored for destructive attacks from the bronze birch borer; cut-leaf forms are prone to aphid infestations.

VARIETIES AND CULTIVARS: Cultivar 'Dalecarlica', elegantly slender with gracefully pendulous twigs and deeply cleft foliage; cv. 'Fastigiata', densely columnar with stiffly upright branching when young but modifying to a broader, oval outline with age, has very deep green foliage and is prone to branch disfigurement from ice and wet snow; cv. 'Gracilis' with very finely dissected leaves on drooping branches and a narrow shape; cv. 'Purpurea', a slow-growing form with weak branching and maroon-purple new growth, has bronze-green summer leaves; cv. 'Tristis', narrowly symmetrical with very slender, pendulous branching; cv. 'Youngii', a smaller form with thin, weeping branches and an irregular, dome-shaped head, requires staking to establish a sturdy trunk.

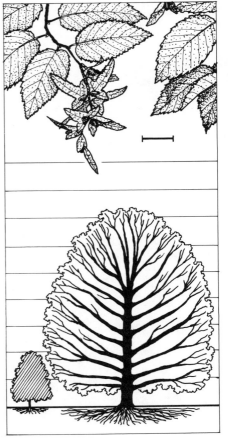

Carpinus betulus (European hornbeam)

Zones 4 to 9   50′ to 70′   Birch family

A reliable, durable, slow-growing tree native from Europe to Iran, this hornbeam species is twiggy enough to become a dense screen, and since it takes shearing very well, it is used often for topiary displays. If left untouched, however, it often can consume as much space as a beech and therefore belongs in large-scaled, open areas.

HABIT: Conical to oval when juvenile, it later spreads widely into a pyramidal shape; foliage is dense at all ages; slow-growing.

SEASONAL APPEARANCE: Foliage is oval, up to 4 inches long, dark green above with noticeable ribbing and downy beneath; dried leaves occasionally remain through the winter; its autumn color is yellow; the spring flowers are separated on the same plant but are nonshowy; its drooping female catkins are up to 5 inches long and in summer produce an unusual string of small nuts enclosed by 2-inch-long, papery bracts (or wings) with three sections that are attached to zigzag stalks; the sturdy trunk is smooth, bluish gray, and very tightly attached.

PREFERENCES AND PROBLEMS: Prefers full sun, a consistently moist, average soil with good drainage; tolerant to light shade and a wide range of soil types; readily pruned to particular landscape shapes; best moved when no more than 8 feet tall.

PESTS AND DISEASES: Apparently free of both.

VARIETIES AND CULTIVARS: Cultivar 'Carpinizza' with smaller foliage and mostly heart-shaped leaves; cv. 'Columnaris', a narrowly upright, single-trunked, dense form eventually becoming oval in outline; cv. 'Fastigiata', multistemmed with all erect branching and a more open appearance than 'Columnaris'; cv. 'Incisa' with deeply cleft, narrow leaves; cv. 'Pendula' with wide-spreading, drooping branches; cv. 'Pupurea', having purplish new growth; cv. 'Quercifolia' with deeply toothed leaves.

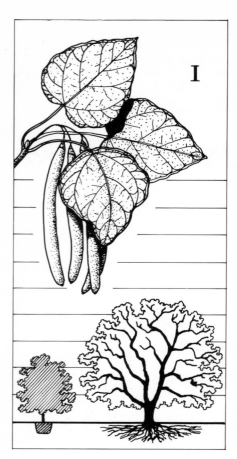

Catalpa bignonioides (Common catalpa, Indian bean, Southern catalpa)

Zones 5 to 10   25' to 60'   Bignonia family

Both this species and *C. speciosa* are very similar in all their main attractions, except that here the leaves are somewhat smaller, the height shorter, and the northern hardiness not as pronounced. It is native to Georgia, Florida, and Mississippi. They both make showy flowering specimens in early summer, when most other trees have already finished blooming.

HABIT: Wide-spreading and rounded with an eventually crooked trunk and coarse-looking foliage; fast-growing.

SEASONAL APPEARANCE: Both species have novel foliage arrangements by having three heart-shaped leaves whorled around the stout twigs at any one junction (except the flowering end); the leaf sizes vary, too, from two large and one small to one large and two small down the stems; here the leaves are abruptly tip-ended, about 8 inches long, dark green with some hairiness on the undersides, and ill-scented when bruised; there is no autumnal color; the conspicuous late spring to early summer flowering is terminally erect in pyramidal clusters up to 10 inches tall with 2-inch-wide, bell-shaped, frilled florets in white with two yellow streaks and many brown spots on the throats; the dangling clusters of persistent fruit are pencil-thick, brown pods from 6 to 15 inches in length containing overlapping, flat seeds having tufted ends; the bark is light gray-brown with scaly, flat ridges.

PREFERENCES AND PROBLEMS: Grows well in almost any condition from sun to shade, wet or dry, and in acid or alkaline soils in any climate; it performs better if given a deep, consistently moist, fertile soil, full sun, and protection from high winds; occasionally new growth is damaged by late frosts; appears to withstand hot, dry climates very well but leaves may scorch if humidity is too low.

PESTS AND DISEASES: Sometimes defoliated in the eastern parts of the United States by the larva of the sphinx moth; mildew is often a foliage problem in muggy summer weather anywhere.

VARIETIES AND CULTIVARS: Cultivar 'Aurea' with richly yellow, velvety foliage all season; cv. 'Nana' (the so-called umbrella tree), a dwarfed form usually grafted to upright trunks of the parent for a dense, dome-shaped head, rarely flowers.

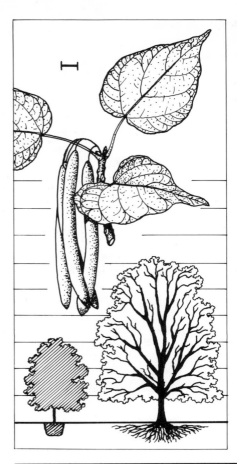

Catalpa speciosa (Western catalpa, Northern catalpa, Cigar tree)

Zones 5 to 10   50' to 100'   Bignonia family

This catalpa is found wild from southern Indiana and southeastern Iowa to Arkansas and Texas. Its greater size and upright shape offer a landscape alternative to *C. bignonioides,* although both species carry relatively the same foliage, flowering, and fruiting effects.

HABIT: Narrowly pyramidal but irregular at all ages; rapid in growth.

SEASONAL APPEARANCE: The whorled leaf arrangement is the same as that detailed under *C. bignonioides* except that here the densely pubescent, heart-shaped foliage stretches from 8 to 12 inches in length and has long, tapering tips; the leaf color is from light to medium green, and there is no odor from them when crushed; autumnal color is either yellow-green or brown; the late spring or early summer blossoming displays conspicuous, upright, closely-packed, $2^{1}/_{2}$ inch, creamy white florets with faint purple-brown spots and light yellow streaks arranged in 6-inch-tall, terminal clusters; the bunches of persistent dark brown fruit are from 10 to 20 inches long and between one-half and three-quarters-inch wide; they contain many seeds with fringed ends; its pale, red-brown to gray-brown bark cracks into thick scales.

PREFERENCES AND PROBLEMS: See *C. bignonioides.*

PESTS AND DISEASES: See *C. bignonioides.*

VARIETIES AND CULTIVARS: None.

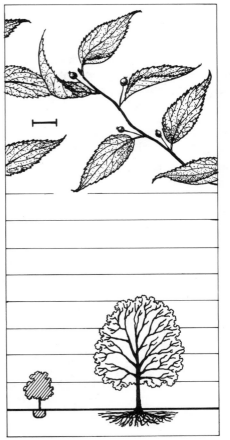

Celtis australis (Mediterranean hackberry, European nettle tree, Lote tree, Honeyberry, European hackberry)

Zones 7 to 9   40' to 80'   Elm family

Long valued for its enviable adaptation to desert conditions, this inhabitant of the Mediterranean shores of southern Europe has a neat appearance, deep roots, and freedom from most pests and diseases. It is a wise choice for street and highway planting where drought is a problem.

HABIT: Round-topped with spreading branches; usually narrower when older; reasonably fast-growing when juvenile but moderate- to slow-growing with age.

SEASONAL APPEARANCE: The toothed, elm-like leaves are rough to the touch, between 2 and 6 inches long, dark green above, and gray-green with dense hairs beneath; the foliage color is yellow in the autumn; male and female flowers are separated on the same tree, and both are inconspicuous; the female fruit is globose, about a quarter-inch wide on long stalks, edibly sweet (birds like them, too), and dark purple when ripe; the smooth, beech-like, gray bark gains corky warts and ridges with age.

PREFERENCES AND PROBLEMS: Performs best in full sun with reasonable moisture on an average-fertility soil; highly tolerant to desert heat, strong winds, and dry, alkaline soils once established; has a much slower growth rate if the soil is too dry.

PESTS AND DISEASES: None of consequence.

VARIETIES AND CULTIVARS: None.

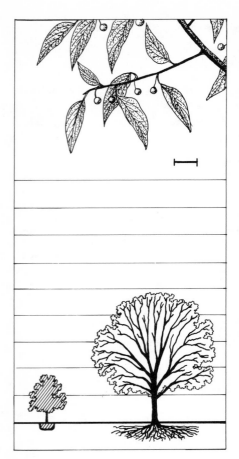

Celtis laevigata [*mississippiensis*] (Sugarberry, Mississippi hackberry)

Zones 6 to 9   60' to 100'   Elm family

Tall-growing in its natural habitat from Florida west to Texas and northeastern Mexico, in man-made developments it usually keeps to a lower size limit. It shares the same easy adaptation to dryness as *C. australis* (and most other species), making it a good candidate also for the parched conditions found in city streets and highways. It usually holds its foliage in good condition right to the edge of winter.

HABIT: Round-headed with somewhat drooping, spreading branches; quick-growing when young (if kept moist) but usually moderate later.

SEASONAL APPEARANCE: Its smooth-margined foliage is thin, between 2 and 4 inches long, oval to lance-shaped, slick to the touch, and dark green; its greenish brown flowering by either sex is nonshowy; the egg-shaped, juicy, edible fruiting is almost a half-inch in diameter and is first orange, then red, and finally dark purple when ripe; young bark is smooth and pale gray, but older trunks develop vertically narrow, sturdy ridges as well.

PREFERENCES AND PROBLEMS: See *C. laevigata.*

PESTS AND DISEASES: Very resistant to the branch distortions and deadwood resulting from the mite-spread disease called hexenbesen or 'witches'-broom', which seriously deforms *Celtis occidentalis,* a well-liked, additional species not represented here for that reason.

VARIETIES AND CULTIVARS: None.

Cercidiphyllum japonicum (Katsura tree)

Zones 4 to 9   60' to 100'   Cercidiphyllum family

Few trees are as elegantly neat, dependable, and so puzzling in their final shape as is this native of Japan and China. When young, all saplings are narrowly upright; but when older, the silhouette becomes either greatly rounded and openly wide-spreading or reasonably pyramidal and narrow. Female plants tend to be the broadened trees, while male trees push vigorously upward more sleekly. Unfortunately, until a plant blossoms (a long wait), there is no way to know which sex is on hand. Too, many trees tend to be sold either multistemmed or very low-branched, creating even more difficulties for an early determination of the final outline. Yet whatever their curious growth problems, these are choice plants for specimen use in many large-scaled landscapes.

HABIT: See above; moderate to fast in growth when young but only moderate-growing with age.

SEASONAL APPEARANCE: Very slender, stiff, brown-red twigs carry deep red budding in neatly parallel rows; the emerging 3- to 4-inch foliage is bronze-toned, smooth, and broadly heart-shaped; its leaves resemble *Cercis* (redbud), which accounts for the genus name; mature foliage is dark, bluish green with gray-toned undersides; the minute flowers are on separate trees with male plants showing little color value, but females, especially older ones, fairly glow with magenta or brownish red hues in early spring before the leaves arrive; the slender, boat-like fruit is lavender-brown, about a half-inch long, and appears in clusters of two to four in the axils of the leaves; the voluminous crops of very tiny, papery seeds rarely germinate; its autumnal colors range from bright yellow to scarlet (occasionally apricot); the young bark is brownish red, turning with age to a silvery brown, and older trunks become spirally twisted with shaggy, furrowed bark.

PREFERENCES AND PROBLEMS: Thrives in full sun or light shading on a constantly moist, rich, well-drained soil; tolerant of moderate drought; older trees with heavy, low branching are prone to stem damage from ice storms and snowstorms; somewhat troublesome to transplant when older; does not appear to thrive beyond zone 8 in the eastern United States.

PESTS AND DISEASES: Unbothered by either.

VARIETIES AND CULTIVARS: Variety *sinense* has greater height and usually a single trunk, plus foliage with persistent small hairs on the undersides.

Cercidium floridum [*torreyanum*] (Palo verde, Blue palo verde)

Zones 8 and 9   15′ to 30′   Pea family

In the desert regions of southern California, Arizona, and northeastern Mexico, any tree with size has significance. This is one of those picturesque and colorful plants native to these regions, and it is welcomed for its ability to survive long drought and still be reliably durable.

HABIT: Shrubby and wide-spreading with a very open crown; very slow to expand if kept consistently dry, but reasonably lively with irrigation.

SEASONAL APPEARANCE: Generally leafless most of the year and awaits rainfall to show its scattered compound, tiny leaves with pale blue-green or dull gray-green leaflets; the entire leaf measures only a scant $1^1/_2$ inches at best; its slender twigs usually are accompanied by stiff, thorn-like spurs; the pea-like flowers in midspring are bright yellow and fragrant and appear in clusters up to 2 inches long; the flat, smooth fruit pods are between 2 and 4 inches long and mature in a yellow-brown color; its smooth bark is blue-green or pale olive when young but becomes reddish brown and scaly with age; there is no possibility of autumn coloring here.

PREFERENCES AND PROBLEMS: Needs full sun to exist and grows on any desert soil within its hardiness range; prone to litter leaves and spent flowers; requires regular irrigation and fertilizing to grow with any size and appeal.

PESTS AND DISEASES: None.

VARIETIES AND CULTIVARS: None.

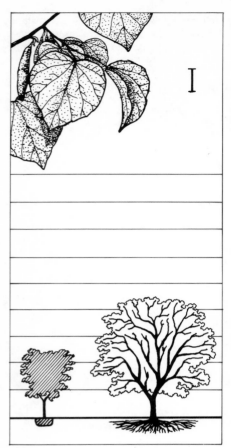

Cercis canadensis (Redbud, Eastern redbud)

Zones 5 to 9   25' to 40'   Pea family

Wild in most of the moist woodlots of the eastern United States, this harbinger of spring is the hardiest species and usually glows with its tiny, magenta flowers at the same time as the more showy native dogwood *(Cornus florida).* It adds a pleasant accent note to both rustic and formalized garden spaces.

HABIT: Openly thin with an irregular trunk and angular, thin branching; matures with a flat-topped, spreading appearance; moderate to rapid in growth, depending on soil moisture.

SEASONAL APPEARANCE: Dark purple-brown, zigzagged, slender twigs carry broadly heart-shaped, glossy, dark green leaves between 3 and 6 inches wide; the early spring flowering is held close to the leafless twigs and branches in small clusters of rosy pink or magenta-colored, pea-shaped, half-inch flowers; the flat, narrow, seed pods measure up to 3½ inches but are dull gray and not decorative; the thin, young bark is often smooth and gray, but older bark becomes purple-toned and scaly with narrow plates.

PREFERENCES AND PROBLEMS: Enjoys full sun or light shading on a fertile, sandy loam (acid or alkaline) with good drainage and reasonable moisture; has long roots and requires a year to recover from transplanting; in the eastern United States its hardiness range seems to be zones 4 to 8.

PESTS AND DISEASES: Suffers from coral spot fungus on twigs, leaf spot disease, and canker of the stems.

VARIETIES AND CULTIVARS: Variety *alba* is slower-growing with ivory-white blossoms but lacks the hardiness of the parent; cv. 'Forest Pansy', a form with purple-toned leaves on red twigs; cv. 'Oklahoma' has wine-red flowers; cv. 'Pinkbud' with brightly true-pink flowering; cv. 'Plena', a double-flowered, upright form with less blooming conspicuousness than the parent; cv. 'Rosea', a pink-toned form; cv. 'Royal' with generous bloom from white flowers; cv. 'Wither's Pink Charm', a type with soft pink blossoms.

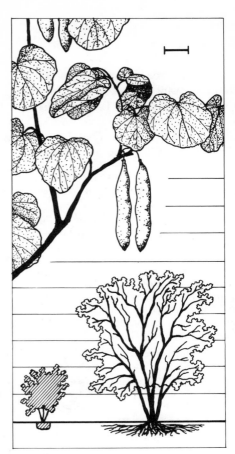

Cercis siliquastrum (Judas tree, Love tree)

Zones 7 to 9   25′ to 35′   Pea family

If you would like to believe it, historically this is the tree from which Judas Iscariot hanged himself after betraying Christ. Its white blossoming then turned to rose as it blushed in shame. In any case, it is a popular spring-flowering plant throughout its native habitat of southern Europe and western Asia. It is not, however, a wise choice for windy locations since it has brittle twigs.

HABIT: Usually multistemmed and bushy with a rounded outline but a flattened top; fast-growing.

SEASONAL APPEARANCE: Foliage is waxy, bluish green, 2 to 5 inches long, and deeply cleft at the base but with a blunted tip; its bright, purple-rose, three-quarter-inch blossoms are in clusters of three to six along the thin twigs and appear in midspring before the foliage; the persistent fruit pods are up to 4 inches long and mature to a full red-brown color; its smooth bark is gray.

PREFERENCES AND PROBLEMS: Best in full sun on a moist, average-fertility, acid or alkaline soil with good drainage; shelter to protect from late spring frost; avoid windy sites since the brittle twigs readily drop if abused; pruning attention is necessary to achieve single-trunked specimens.

PESTS AND DISEASES: Coral spot disease is the worst affliction.

VARIETIES AND CULTIVARS: Variety *alba* has pure white flowering.

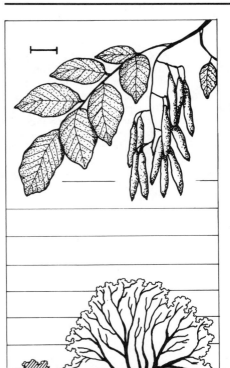

Cladrastis lutea [tinctoria] (Yellowwood, Virgilia)

Zones 4 to 9   30′ to 50′   Pea family

There is some similarity here to a beech in its mature trunk's gray color and smoothness, but this native of the southeastern United States greatly differs in late spring when it is strung with long chains of perfumed, wisteria-like flowering. Deep rooted and adaptable, yellowwood provides a specimen attraction for large spaces even out of bloom.

HABIT: Generally rounded at all ages with wide-spreading branches as it matures; moderate-growing.

SEASONAL APPEARANCE: Light gray, somewhat zigzagged, thin twigs produce compound foliage about 1 foot long composed of seven to eleven bright green leaflets; autumn color is golden yellow to orange; in late spring, after leaves are fully extended, its pendant, slightly fragrant, foot-long chains of white, pea-like flowers drape the entire tree; the nonshowy fruit later form clusters of brown, flat, narrow pods between 3 and 4 inches long; its smooth, young bark is light brown but ages to silver-gray and develops horizontal wrinkles; its inner bark is a bright yellow.

PREFERENCES AND PROBLEMS: Likes full sun and any fertile, deep, well-drained, reasonably moist soil, whether acid or alkaline; tolerant to some drought when fully established; wood is brittle, and ice or heavy snow can cause damage; prune only in summer or early autumn since stems bleed sap profusely in spring; flowering displays are generous and showy only every second or third year.

PESTS AND DISEASES: Very resistant to both.

VARIETIES AND CULTIVARS: Cultivar 'Rosea' has pale pink blossoms.

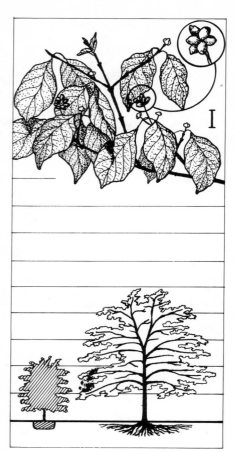

Cornus florida (Flowering dogwood)

Zones 5 to 9   30' to 40'   Dogwood family

This is one of the most remarkable small trees because of its special attractiveness in all seasons. Naturally distributed over much of the eastern United States, and even as far west as Kansas and Texas, this showy plant has consistent public appreciation for its winter silhouette and bark, spring flowering, summer fruit and autumn foliage. Not many other trees can claim that amount of noticeability—besides being easy to grow.

HABIT: Somewhat upturned branching in youth gives way to horizontal layering with age; mature plants have a dense, flat-topped crown; moderate- to slow-growing depending on its age.

SEASONAL APPEARANCE: Juvenile twigs are purple-red to dull green and carry oval, opposite leaves between 3 and 6 inches long and about 2 inches wide; older branching is dull gray; the glossy summer foliage varies between bright and dark green, while its autumn color is a glowing scarlet; flowering comes in midspring before the leaves and emerges from tiny, button-like, elevated winter buds at the ends of the twigs; its true flowers are a central mound of tiny, yellowish blossoms surrounded by four petal-like, white, modified leaves or bracts with notched ends; total flower expansion falls between 3 and 5 inches; its clustered, raised fruit is oval, shiny, scarlet, and about a half-inch long; young bark is smooth and light gray; older trunks become checkerboard-furrowed and dark reddish brown or silvery.

PREFERENCES AND PROBLEMS: Grows well in either full sun or light shade on a deep, rich, acid, consistently moist but well-drained soil; dislikes both excessive wind and wetness along with prolonged drought; benefits from extra humus around the roots when transplanted; pruning and bark wounds are slow to heal; requires reasonably dry, late summer and early autumn weather conditions to form proper budding for the next season.

PESTS AND DISEASES: Especially prone to stem borers (usually at the branch junctions); occasionally bothered by leaf spot disease and crown canker.

VARIETIES AND CULTIVARS (its great popularity annually increases the rate of discovery of "new" types by nurseries and arboreta): Cultivar 'Cherokee Chief' with dark pink or ruby-red bracts; cv. 'Cloud 9' with noticeably generous flowering; cv. 'Fastigiata', narrowly upright when young but apt to revert to mostly horizontal branching with age; cv. 'Gigantea', a form with a total blossom spread of 6 inches; cv. 'Hohman's Golden' with foliage attractively streaked in yellow and rich red with bronze autumnal color, not prolific for bloom; cv. 'Nana', a dwarfed form to 6 feet with a compact head and skimpy flowering; cv. 'Pendula', a form with drooping branches; cv. 'Pluribracteata' ('Alba Plena') with somewhat double flowers; cv. 'Rainbow' with summer foliage mottled in deep yellow and pink on a green base, turning bright crimson in autumn; cv. 'Rubra', a commonly available form with bracts ranging from pale pink to rose; cv. 'Salicifolia', having narrow, willow-like foliage; cv. 'Sweetwater Red' with deep red flowering and a reddish cast to the foliage; cv. 'Welchii', a sparse-flowering type with leaves nicely variegated in green, cream, and deep rose; cv. 'White Cloud' with creamy bracts and abundant bloom even when juvenile; cv. 'Xanthocarpa', a type with yellow fruit.

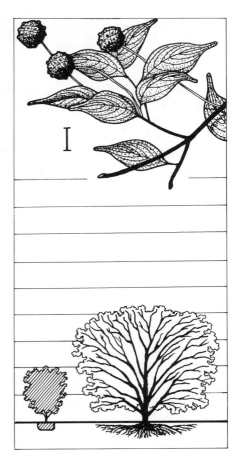

Cornus kousa (Kousa dogwood)

Zones 5 (warm) to 9   15′ to 25′   Dogwood family

Becoming more popular yearly, this smaller species from Japan and Korea has the attractive quality of blooming at least a month later than *C. florida.* Its intriguing silhouette, pendulous fruit, and peeling bark give it specimen status in almost any landscape where it is hardy. As a bonus, its creamy bracts may become pink-toned and persistent through the summer if weather conditions are not extremely hot and rainy.

HABIT: Branching is upright, forming a dense, inverted pyramid shape; longer, older stems may become somewhat horizontal or pendulous; often seen as a multistemmed shrub; slow-growing when juvenile but moderate-growing later.

SEASONAL APPEARANCE: Warty, tan-gray twigs carry small, dark brown, peaked, dome-shaped flower buds terminally; its foliage is lustrous on top and slightly hairy beneath, oval, long-tapered, between 3 and 4 inches long, and medium or dark green; the early foliage often has a bronzed tint; autumn leaves are bronze-red; summer flowering is star-like and extends above the fully developed foliage; the true flowers are very small, greenish yellow, and set in a tight head surrounded by four creamy white, 1- to 2-inch, pointed bracts often persistent through the summer months (and perhaps changing with age to a pink-cream); the fleshy, three-quarter-inch, globose fruit has a slight resemblance to a raspberry in shape and mature coloring; the young fruit begins upright on ever-elongating stalks that eventually become pendulous as the fruit grows larger and heavier; its older bark becomes attractively mottled at the base with exfoliating brown and gray patches to reveal a cream-toned inner bark.

PREFERENCES AND PROBLEMS: Grows best in full sun but is tolerant to light shading on an acid, rich, deep, consistently moist, and well-drained location; sulks if placed in poor, shallow, dry, or chalky soils; dislikes high winds.

PESTS AND DISEASES: None of consequence.

VARIETIES AND CULTIVARS: Variety *chinensis* is usually more hairy on the undersides of the leaves, carries longer flower bracts, and may be less hardy in some cold locations; cv. 'Milky Way' a profuse-blooming type; cv. 'Rubra' with light pink bracts; cv. 'Variegata' has variegated leaves; cv. 'Xanthocarpa' with yellow fruit.

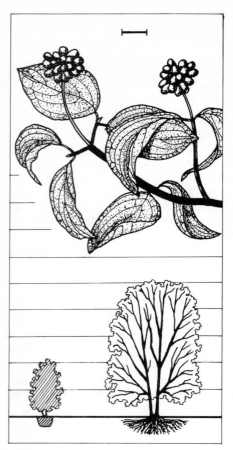

Cornus nuttallii (Mountain dogwood, Pacific dogwood, Nuttall's dogwood, Western dogwood)

Zones 7 to 9 (limited) **50′ to 75′** **Dogwood family**

Taller and showier in flower than other tree dogwoods, this inhabitant of the Pacific coast from British Columbia to the mountains of southern California seems to be limited mainly to its home grounds since it fails to develop satisfactorily away from the cool, moist, moderate climate of its native habitat. Where it will grow well, it is a handsome specimen of note.

HABIT: Usually narrowly conical with a straight trunk (often several) but becoming more pyramidal in outline with age; slow- to moderate-growing.

SEASONAL APPEARANCE: Slender, grooved, dull purple-red twigs carry small, greenish mounds of true flowers half enclosed in the dormant season by green leaf bracts; in midspring, before leaves have fully emerged, the four to six bracts unfold to become about 6 inches in total spread and are white, greenish white, or pale pink and resemble a large clematis blossom; reflowering is very likely in late summer or early autumn; the leaves are between 3½ and 5 inches long, thin, oval with sharp tips, and bright green above but gray-green beneath; its autumnal leaves are in shades of red or yellow; the attractive, red to orange, very tiny, oval, shiny fruits are densely clustered in 1-inch bunches atop long stalks; its thick bark is smooth and varies from reddish brown to light gray.

PREFERENCES AND PROBLEMS: Seemingly limited for zones 7 to 9 and only in its native range, but if tried elsewhere, it wants a deep, moist, coarse-textured, well-drained soil away from heat and cold extremes of climate; dislikes regular irrigation; difficult to move when large because of deep tap roots; bark scalds if unprotected from strong, summer sun.

PESTS AND DISEASES: Nothing of consequence.

VARIETIES AND CULTIVARS: Cultivar 'Eddiei', a form with variegated foliage.

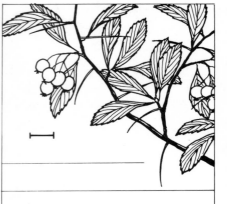

Crataegus crus-galli (Cockspur thorn, Cockspur hawthorn)

Zones 5 to 9 **20′ to 30′** **Rose family**

There are far too many (perhaps 1000) identified hawthorns growing wild or in cultivation to hope to be fully selective here; the limited choices offered represent only those with satisfactory (separate or combined) characteristics of habit, flowering, fruiting, or leaves for a wide geographic area of expected availability in nurseries. Personal discovery of other quality hawthorns is to be expected with a plant as prolific as this.

Hawthorns are small trees that are usually thorny, dense-foliaged, mostly white-flowered, and often multistemmed, very twiggy, and bushy. (The word *haw* is Anglo-Saxon and means "fence" or "hedge," a first use for these barrier plants.) They grow in any well-drained soil and are generally tolerant of wind, drought, cold, and the sooty grime of city air. Neither their flowering nor fruiting is consistently decorative, and the autumn leaf color of many is often dull. They are also prone to a host of pests and diseases (as are other members of the rose family), including caterpillars, borers, scale, leaf miners, lacebugs, spider mites, rust diseases, and fire blight. In consequence, hawthorns seem best used discreetly as isolated specimens.

The species described here is native from Quebec to Michigan and south to North Carolina. It is dense, long-thorned, and bright-colored with persistent fruit and glowing autumn foliage. It is now very much favored for planting in the dry climates of the southwestern United States, where it grows quite well.

HABIT: Wide-spreading with horizontal, thorny branching; very densely twiggy and becoming round-topped; slow to moderate in growth depending on its locale.

SEASONAL APPEARANCE: Slender twigs carry thin, curved, stiff thorns between 1¹/₂ and 3 inches long (these may be branched on older wood and extend up to 8 inches); the 1- to 3-inch, alternate foliage is leathery, shiny, slender, and dark green; it changes to scarlet or orange in the autumn; the late spring flowers are white, about a half-inch wide, and appear in clusters no broader than 3 inches; they carry a highly disagreeable odor; the hard, globose, half-inch, dark red, glossy fruit comes in bunches and persists well into winter (most birds seem to avoid it); its bark is dark brown to dark gray and scaly.

PREFERENCES AND PROBLEMS: Best grown in full sun on a well-drained, average soil; adjusts better if transplanted when quite small; apt to be blown askew in windy locations because of its denseness; takes well to shearing; thorns can be hazardous in public spaces.

PESTS AND DISEASES: See introductory material.

VARIETIES AND CULTIVARS: Variety *inermis,* an almost thornless, vigorous type that is currently uncommon in cultivation.

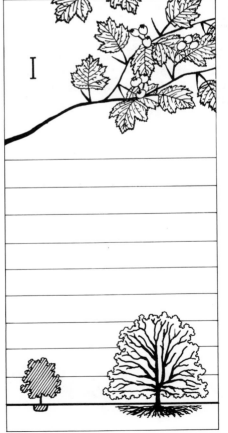

Crataegus laevigata [*oxyacantha*] (English hawthorn, White thorn)

Zones 5 to 9   15′ to 25′   Rose family

This species from Europe, north Africa, and western Asia is basically white-flowered like so many other hawthorns, but it has given rise to a wealth of brighter-colored cultivars highly useful for many landscape purposes.

HABIT: Dense with low, spreading branches and an eventual round-headed shape; often shrubby in form; slow-growing.

SEASONAL APPEARANCE: Thin, zigzagged twigs carry stout, half- to 1-inch thorns and alternate, glossy, deep green, deeply cleft leaves with three to five lobes in a size between three-quarters and 2 inches; there is no pertinent autumn color; the half-inch flowers are white in loose clusters no larger than 1¹/₂ inches across; its oval fruit is deep red at maturity and between a quarter- and a half-inch long; young bark is greenish gray, but older bark is dark gray.

PREFERENCES AND PROBLEMS: Does best in full sunlight on an average-fertility soil with good drainage; resents transplanting when its size is above 10 feet; foliage scorches in prolonged drought; not very long-lived in the midwestern United States.

PESTS AND DISEASES: See *C. crus-galli;* leaf spot fungal disease causes severe and continual defoliation throughout the summer.

VARIETIES AND CULTIVARS: Cultivar 'Alba' with pure white flowers; cv. 'Autumn Glory', a form with white flowers, large fruit that persists, and leathery leaves — but with less hardiness than the parent; cv. 'Masekii' with pale pink-and-white flowers; cv. 'Paulii', a popular type carrying double, bright scarlet or deep rose blossoms that is very prone to leaf spot and twig blight; cv. 'Plena' with double white flowers fading to pink with age; cv. 'Punicea', a form with single, carmine blossoms having a white center; cv. 'Rosea' with single bright pink flowers centered in white; cv. 'Superba', single-flowered and noticeable in bright red with a white center; also has glossy, red fruit and very good resistance to leaf spot disease; the very hardy (zone 3) Canadian cultivar 'Toba' (a hybrid of *C. laevigata* 'Paulii' and *C. succulenta*) is very similar in habit and general appearance to *C. laevigata* but has double pink flowers turning deep rose with age, plus winter-persistent (but few) fruit and leathery, glossy leaves; it might be logically substituted in cold areas where the English hawthorn form is wanted but does not grow.

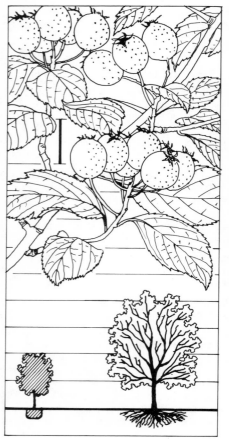

Crataegus × *lavallei* [× *carrieri*] (Lavalle thorn)

Zones 5 to 9   15′ to 30′   Rose family

One of the handsomest hawthorns in foliage, flowering, and fruit, this hybrid of *C. crus-galli* and *C. pubescens* is very resistant to air pollution damage and is essentially thorn-free. It would make an attractive specimen or terrace tree almost anywhere.

HABIT: More erect and open than other hawthorns with an oval-headed outline; moderate in expansion.

SEASONAL APPEARANCE: Its narrow foliage is dark green, leathery, glossy above but hairy beneath, between 2 and 4 inches in length, and usually tapered at both ends; the autumnal coloration is between copper-red and bronze-red; only a few thorns appear along the twigs and branches, but those will be about 1 inch long; its late spring, three-quarter-inch, white flowering appears in clusters approximately 3 inches wide; the orange-red, brown-speckled, mostly half-inch fruit is slightly pear-shaped and persists through the winter; its bark is dark gray-brown.

PREFERENCES AND PROBLEMS: Likes abundant sunshine and a well-drained soil with average fertility; does not move well unless small-sized; fails to grow uniformly on some sites; very tolerant of city pollution; apt to be blown out of plumb in windy locations.

PESTS AND DISEASES: See *C. crus-galli.*

VARIETIES AND CULTIVARS: None.

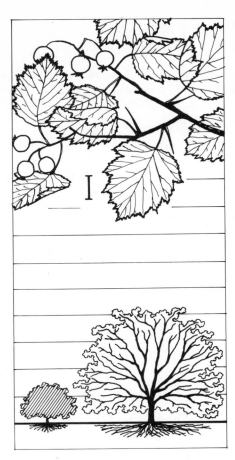

Crataegus mollis (Downy hawthorn)

Zones 5 to 9   20' to 35'   Rose family

Native from Ontario to Minnesota and south to Arkansas and Alabama, it has the advantage of wholly noticeable, large fruiting in late summer and a tolerance for very difficult soil conditions. While not a truly refined plant, it offers the dependability and adaptability which many other hawthorns cannot supply. Unfortunately, its flowers are ill-smelling.

HABIT: Densely branched and wide-spreading, it eventually becomes round-headed; moderate-growing.

SEASONAL APPEARANCE: Unique and variable by showing ashy gray new twigs with and without stiff, curved thorns between 1 and 2 inches long; new leaves are alternate and heavily covered with downy hairs; this pubescence erodes by midsummer to show an almost-smooth, somewhat triangular, 3- to 4-inch, medium green leaf appearance; the color in autumn is reddish bronze; its very large, 1-inch, profusely clustered white flowers in midspring are objectionable for their strong scent; the early-ripening, palatable fruit is between three-quarters and 1 inch in length, spherical, bright red with some slight hairiness at both ends; it tends to drop completely by midautumn; the bark can be either red-brown or yellow-brown with shallow furrows and blocky ridges.

PREFERENCES AND PROBLEMS: Deserves full sun and good drainage on a reasonably fertile soil; tolerant of heavy, infertile soils without difficulty; may be considered just too coarse-looking for some landscape sites; fruiting is useful for preserves and jellies.

PESTS AND DISEASES: See *C. crus-galli;* susceptible to leaf disfigurement from the cedar hawthorn rust disease.

VARIETIES AND CULTIVARS: ·None.

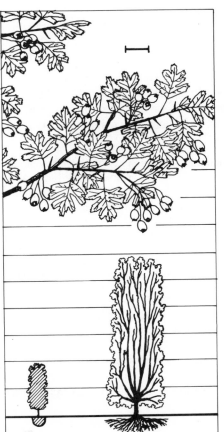

Crataegus monogyna 'Stricta' (Fastigiate single-seed hawthorn)

Zones 5 to 9   20' to 30'   Rose family

The parent tree is native to Europe, north Africa, and Asia, but it has little landscape value of itself and no autumn coloring. It has, however, been the source of many interesting variants, and this upright selection seems to have wide appeal for its mostly columnar growth, heavy fruiting, and delicate foliage. For a tight, erect hedge or narrow specimen accent, this is a hawthorn worth considering.

HABIT: Very dense and columnar with upswept branching until maturity, when it becomes more bulging in its outline; moderate in growth.

SEASONAL APPEARANCE: Foliage appears in a rich, polished green with deeply lobed, almost 2-inch-long leaves on slender stems with 1-inch thorns; there is no interesting autumnal color; its bunched, white, spring flowers are generously produced, sweet-scented, and about a half-inch across with noticeable red anthers; the bright red, half-inch fruit ripens in early autumn; its dark brown bark eventually becomes cracked with rectangular plates.

PREFERENCES AND PROBLEMS: Give it full sun and an average soil that drains easily; transplants better than many other hawthorns at a reasonable size; takes shearing well for hedge use; can adjust to confined spaces satisfactorily.

PESTS AND DISEASES: See *C. crus-galli.*

VARIETIES AND CULTIVARS: None.

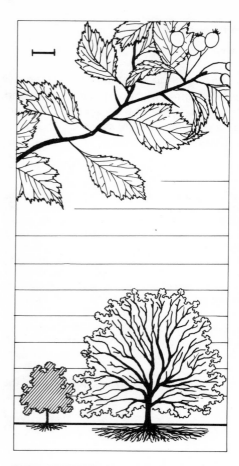

Crataegus nitida (Glossy hawthorn)

Zones 5 to 9   20' to 30'   Rose family

Almost completely thornless, this native of much of the midwestern United States from Ohio to Arkansas has attractive flowers and persistent fruit. It also has a rustic appearance perhaps better utilized only in naturalistic settings.

HABIT: Densely but irregularly branched with both ascending and horizontal limbs; its mature shape is a broadly rounded silhouette; moderate growth rate.

SEASONAL APPEARANCE: Its leaves are between 1 and 3 inches in length, somewhat narrow, dark green, very glossy on the upper surface, but dull and pallid beneath; these are carried on thin twigs mostly without thorns (if seen, they will be over 1 inch long); the showy autumnal color is a very bright orange to red; its late spring flowering comes as three-quarter-inch, white blossoms in loose clusters; the round fruit develops to almost a half-inch wide in shades between orange-red and deep red, persisting through the winter months; its close, dark gray bark has tan markings and eventually splits into thick, plate-like scales.

PREFERENCES AND PROBLEMS: Provide a sunny location on average-fertility soil having quick drainage.

PESTS AND DISEASES: See *C. crus-galli*.

VARIETIES AND CULTIVARS: None.

Crataegus phaenopyrum [cordata]
(Washington hawthorn)

Zones 5 to 9   20' to 30'   Rose family

Attractiveness is apparent throughout the year with this native hawthorn from the southeastern parts of the United States. Its good resistance to fireblight, glowingly colored autumnal foliage, bright fruit crop, and generally neat habit make it a ready candidate for just about any landscape location with bright sun.

HABIT: Mostly upright and broadly columnar with much twigginess but yet an open crown of foliage; eventually round-topped with some irregularity in its outline; often multi-stemmed; moderate growing.

SEASONAL APPEARANCE: Its slender, zigzagged twigs are red-brown with a coating of silver and carry slim, straight thorns between $1^{1}/_{2}$ and 3 inches long; the three-to five-lobed leaves are somewhat triangular, a lustrous bright green, and measure between 2 and 3 inches in length; its bright autumn coloring ranges from rich scarlet to orange; the profuse flowering is later to arrive than most hawthorns and appears in June as clusterings of half-inch, white blossoms with pale yellow anthers; the equally generous, quarter-inch fruiting is shiny, vividly red-orange, and persists well into winter (if birds do not get it first); its bark is grayish tan and scaly.

PREFERENCES AND PROBLEMS: Performs its best growth in full sun on a moist, well-drained, average soil; not favored for the hot summer climate of the lower midwestern United States.

PESTS AND DISEASES: See *C. crus-galli;* appears to be more resistant to fireblight than many other hawthorns.

VARIETIES AND CULTIVARS: Cultivar 'Clark', a form with even heavier fruit crops; cv. 'Fastigiata', a narrowly columnar type.

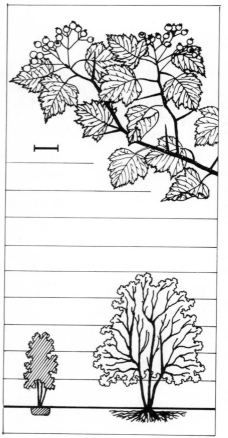

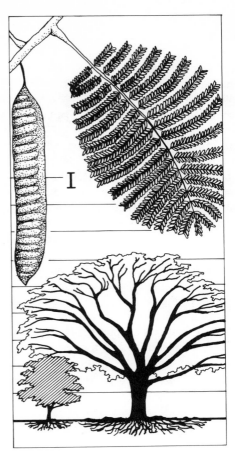

Delonix regia [Poinciana regia] (Royal poinciana, Flamboyant, Peacock flower, Flame of the forest)

Zone 10 (warm)   25′ to 40′   Pea family

Dramatic when in bloom, this native from the island country of Madagascar is now widely planted in semitropical locations throughout the world for its unbelievably vivid flower color and rapid growth. It also offers attractive filtered shading from its lacy foliage for parks and other large-scaled spaces.

HABIT: Very wide-spreading and dome-shaped with heavy branching and a broad trunk; rapid-growing.

SEASONAL APPEARANCE: The airy, feathery leaves are almost 2 feet long and pinnately compound with perhaps hundreds of quarter-inch, medium green leaflets soft to the touch; the spectacular flower display appears over the entire tree in early summer just as new foliage emerges; the 4-inch blossoms have a bright scarlet color with a yellow tint, five wedge-shaped petals, and a central mass of stamens; in some situations older plants occasionally rebloom sporadically within another six months; the giant seed pods which follow are flat, deep brown, woody, up to 30 inches long, and about 2 inches wide; this fruit often noticeably persists on the tree for more than a year; the smooth bark is grayish brown.

PREFERENCES AND PROBLEMS: Enjoys full sun and a deep, moist, sandy soil; intolerant of frost; appears to adapt well to salt-air locations but has brittle wood readily damaged in high winds; adjusts better to transplanting if moved when very small; develops a buttressed trunk with age as well as heavy surface rooting that can lift adjacent pavements.

PESTS AND DISEASES: Generally pest- and disease-free.

VARIETIES AND CULTIVARS: None.

Erythrina caffra [constantiana] (Coral tree, South African coral, Kaffirboom coral tree)

Zones 9 and 10   25′ to 40′   Pea family

Unusual in behavior by delaying its foliage drop to early winter, the South African coral tree then covers its bare outline with vivid flowering for the next month or so. While its quick growth habit and surface rooting may be undesirable at times, at least this species has proved the most adaptable for coastal planting, where growing any showy tree easily is not commonplace.

HABIT: Broadly spreading and dense with low, irregular, stout, thorny branching; expands rapidly.

SEASONAL APPEARANCE: The foliage is compound with three broadly wedge-shaped leaflets on very long petioles, light green and about 7 inches in its total width; old leaves drop about January, and flowering replaces them for the next four to six weeks; the blossoms are generous, terminal clusters of 2-inch, tubular florets radiating thickly from the stem from deep orange to bright vermillion; these flowers drip watery honey; all young growth has disagreeable thorniness, but it eventually disappears with age; its dark fruit pod is about 4 inches long, semiwoody and contains red seeds poisonous to people and other animals; the somewhat thorny bark is gray-brown.

PREFERENCES AND PROBLEMS: Provide full sun and a constantly moist but well-drained, average soil; highly tolerant of seashore conditions; does not transplant well unless very small; develops conspicuous, vigorous surface rooting with age.

PESTS AND DISEASES: Apparently free of both.

VARIETIES AND CULTIVARS: None.

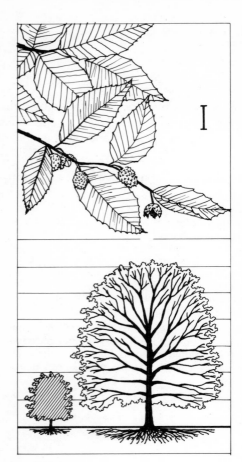

Fagus grandifolia [*americana*] (American beech)

Zones 4 to 10   75′ to 100′   Beech family

There is a wise old saying that installing a beech is planting a memory tree for the grandchildren. It takes many generations of patience to achieve the full potential inherent in these majestically imposing plants, and a venerable well-grown beech—with its life span measured by hundreds of years—is a priceless asset to any landscape.

Beech are hardy, pest-free, and sturdy trees with potentials of great size and spread. If left unpruned, any one of them can completely cover the ground with low, sweeping, graceful branching. They obviously make splendid specimens for large lawn areas, but their fibrous surface rooting and dense shade soon prevent having any other planting beneath them. How to resolve, attractively, the bare-earth inevitability around the trunk, as well as to prevent the harmful compaction that comes from repeated walking in this surface root zone, might be simply to avoid any pruning of lower limbs at all. Retaining the full naturalness of beech can have aesthetic advantages coupled readily with the horticultural ones.

Beech dislike winter or spring pruning since they bleed sap heavily then. They all dislike wet locations and prolonged drought, heavy and compacted soils, and being planted too low or transplanted carelessly. They are quickly and negatively sensitive, when established, to having more than a few inches of fill placed over their roots; any greater amounts will surely kill even the most rugged-looking specimen. As you can now tell, the king of the forest has a few finicky restrictions to being happily enthroned; otherwise, it might abdicate.

The species described here is natively scattered through most of the eastern woodlots of the United States and may even develop solid stands where conditions meet its exacting standards. Usually somewhat troublesome to transplant at any age—the smaller the better—its well-appreciated attractiveness comes from its strikingly silvered bark, attractive foliage, and imposing silhouette, all of which are more likely to be seen only in arboreta or parkland reservations today than in nurseries or suburban house lots. Wherever found, these splendid trees should be carefully preserved since they are not easily replaced.

HABIT: Broadly oval or pyramidal in outline producing dense shade and low branching which may be lost with aging; often sends up many root suckers around the base of an older trunk; slow-growing.

SEASONAL APPEARANCE: Round, slender twigs of pale, silver-brown carry tapered, pointed, 1-inch, chestnut brown, slightly hairy buds; the narrow, glossy foliage varies between 3 and 5 inches in length, is coarsely toothed, and emerges silvery green but turns dark green by summer; the autumn color is golden brown, and some dehydrated leaves often remain throughout the winter; the flowering is inconspicuous, and the sexes are on different parts of the same tree; the female fruit is a four-sided, prickly, half-inch overcoat for several sweet, brown, three-sided, edible nuts (much favored by squirrels); its smooth, tight-fitting bark is light bluish gray with dark banding as it matures.

PREFERENCES AND PROBLEMS: See introductory remarks; does well in either full sun or semishade on a deep, fertile, acid, humusy, well-drained soil; very difficult to transplant and establish even when very young; the smooth, sensitive but publicly attractive bark is prone to continual vandalism from initial-scratching boobs of both sexes; usually better if not grown beyond zone 9 in the eastern United States.

PESTS AND DISEASES: Normally free of both, but aphids often become seasonally damaging to new, soft growth.

VARITIES AND CULTIVARS: None.

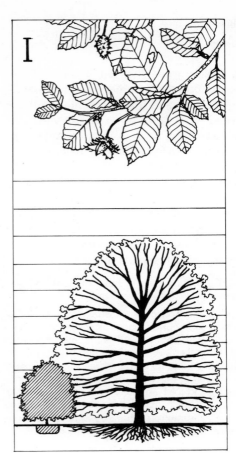

Fagus sylvatica (European beech)

Zones 5 to 10   50' to 80'   Beech family

More popular than *F. grandifolia* because it transplants easier and offers many interesting variants of outline, foliage, and coloring, this inhabitant of central and southern Europe takes shearing well, retains its lower branches to ground level naturally, and can endure for several centuries as a specimen of stately proportions.

HABIT: Densely oval or pyramidal with retained, ground-hugging, graceful branching; generally heavier-trunked than *F. grandifolia;* slow in growth rate.

SEASONAL APPEARANCE: Brown twigs have long-pointed, 1-inch, brown buds with mostly gray, hairy scales; the leaves are oval and up to 4 inches long of a shiny, dark green color above but paler beneath with fine teeth along the margins; its color in autumn is reddish brown to golden bronze; the female fruit is almost identical with that of *F. grandifolia;* its smooth, tight bark is dark gray with deeper-colored banding.

PREFERENCES AND PROBLEMS: See *F. grandifolia;* does well on limestone soils; not for dry areas of zone 10; restrict to zones 5 to 8 in the eastern United States.

PESTS AND DISEASES: Aphid infestation on new growth is the worst affliction.

VARIETIES AND CULTIVARS (many are now available of which these are the most well-known): Cultivar 'Albo-variegata' with leaves margined and streaked with white; cv. 'Asplenifolia', a form with finely divided, fern-like, dark green, very narrow foliage; cv. 'Atropunicea' ('Atropurpurea', 'Cuprea', 'Purpurea', 'Riversii') with persistently copper-red or purple-toned leaves (much variation here when raised from seed); cv. 'Borneyensis', a fountain form with a straight trunk and symmetrically equal, pendulous branching; cv. 'Cristata', slow-growing with small, clustered foliage deeply toothed and curved; cv. 'Fastigiata' ('Dawyckii', 'Pyramidalis'), a narrowly columnar, tall form; cv. 'Laciniata' ('Heterophylla', 'Incisa'), wide-spreading with age and has narrow leaves (larger than 'Asplenifolia') deeply cut to look almost regularly lobed; cv. 'Latifolia', with larger leaves up to 6 inches long and 4 inches wide; cv. 'Luteo-variegata' with foliage variegated in yellow; cv. 'Pendula', carrying its larger limbs horizontal to the main trunk but with outer branching totally drooping to the ground; cv. 'Purpurea Pendula' a small form with purple-toned foliage on weeping branches; cv. 'Rohanii', a slow-growing form with purple leaves mostly deep-cut like an oak; cv. 'Roseo-marginata', a type with purple foliage edged nicely in pink; cv. 'Rotundifolia' with noticeably upright branching and 1-inch, rounded leaves; cv. 'Tortuosa', an extremely slow-growing, low, and spreading type with twisted branches and drooping twigs often reaching ground level; cv. 'Tricolor', a novel form with leaves faded to white with green spotting and pink edges; cv. 'Variegata', showing white or yellow variegations on the leaves; cv. 'Zlatia', a slow-growing form with new growth pale yellow but turning light green by summer.

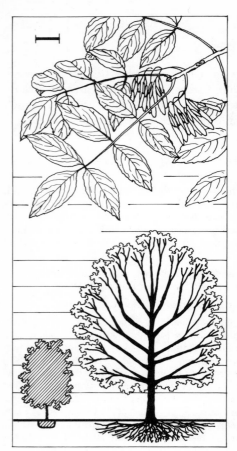

Fraxinus americana [alba]   (White ash)

Zones 4 to 9   75' to 120'   Olive family

Ashes are vigorous, fast-growing, prolific in seeding, tough, and generally undemanding. They transplant easily, grow well in many soil types and exposures, and have deep-enough rooting and only moderate shade to allow grass beneath them to succeed. They have no excitingly vivid autumn color and tend to be somewhat prosaic in fruit and outline, yet their large, opposite, compound leaves readily disintegrate when fallen, and they require no serious maintenance attention to thrive. Since flowering is often on separate plants, selection of only the sterile male types is worthwhile for landscape purposes.

The species here described is native from Nova Scotia to Florida and west to Texas and is the tallest of all the ashes. It requires no special consideration for good growth except consistent soil moisture. It is especially deep-rooted and shows vigorous response quickly.

HABIT: Upright and oval in outline with a rounded top (if not crowded) and with usually regular, upthrust branching; rapid-growing.

SEASONAL APPEARANCE: The stout twigs have a noticeable, V-shaped leaf scar beneath the rusty-brown buds; the pinnately compound foliage can measure between 8 and 12 inches long and has five to nine oval, pointed leaflets that are dark green above and gray-toned beneath; the autumnal color varies between purple-bronze and dull yellow, sometimes with both colors on parts of the same tree; the clusters of tiny, early spring, greenish yellow flowering—on separate plants—are inconspicuous; the female fruiting is lavishly produced annually and comes as large, drooping bunches of straw-colored, 1- to 2-inch, narrow propellor-like, winged seeds with a high germination rate; the ash-gray, tight bark eventually becomes thick and deeply furrowed in an elongated diamond pattern.

PREFERENCES AND PROBLEMS: Grows best in full sun on a deep, rich, well-drained, constantly moist soil; tolerant to a great variety of other soil conditions readily as well as to semishade.

PESTS AND DISEASES: Plagued by oystershell scale, canker, ash borer, and ash flower gall.

VARIETIES AND CULTIVARS: Cultivar 'Ascidiata' with leaflets showing a pitcher shape at the base; cv. 'Autumn Purple', a seedless male plant with deep purple autumn color; cv. 'Pendula' with drooping branches; cv. 'Rosehill', another seedless male that is especially worthwhile on low-fertility, alkaline soils, has a bronze-red autumn color.

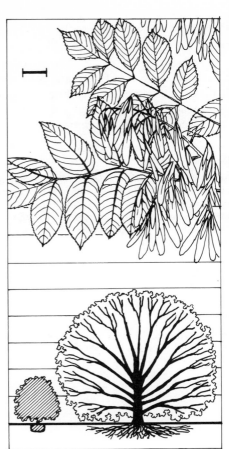

Fraxinus ornus (Flowering ash, Manna ash)

Zones 6 to 8   40' to 60'   Olive family

Native to much of southern Europe and western Asia, this highly fragrant ash is low-branched and dense naturally. It has been appreciated in European landscapes since the seventeenth century.

HABIT: Broadly globose with both dense foliage and branching at all ages; moderately fast in growth.

SEASONAL APPEARANCE: The foliage is luxuriantly thick and is composed of glossy, bright green, compound leaves between 6 and 10 inches long with wavy-margined, toothed leaflets only 1 inch wide; the autumn foliage is variable from soft yellow to lavender; its midspring flowering is showy from abundant, perfect flowers (sexes are not separated) that are pleasantly fragrant and held in fluffy, 3- to 5-inch, terminal clusters of tiny, cream-white, blossoms; its fruit develops as thick bunches of green, then brown, 1-inch, narrowly winged seeds often persisting into winter; the smooth bark is gray-toned.

PREFERENCES AND PROBLEMS: Enjoys a fertile, moist, deep soil and full sun for best flowering; tolerant of more dryness.

PESTS AND DISEASES: Oystershell scale is its worst problem.

VARIETIES AND CULTIVARS: None.

Fraxinus pennsylvanica lanceolata (Green ash)

Zones 3 to 8   40' to 60'   Olive family

Another sturdy ash with great dependability in many locales—and with prolific annual seed crop—this native from Nova Scotia to Georgia and Mississippi has enduring popularity for its vigor, easy culture, and dense crown of foliage. It is also very drought-resistant.

HABIT: Narrowly upright when juvenile, later changing to being round-topped with spreading, slender but irregular branching; moderately fast-growing.

SEASONAL APPEARANCE: The compound leaves are almost 1 foot in length and have five to nine glossy, almost inch-long, yellow-green leaflets; they appear on smooth twigs [the only noticeable difference between this species and *F. pennsylvanica* (red ash) is its lack of gray pubescence on new twigs and foliage; they are interchangeable for landscape use]; the autumnal color is yellowish brown; flowering appears on separate trees and is visually unimportant; the female fruiting comes in clusters of narrow, tan-colored, winged seeds about $2^1/_2$ inches in length; the gray-brown bark may have a touch of red in it and becomes slightly ridged and vertically furrowed with age.

PREFERENCES AND PROBLEMS: Best in full sun on a well-drained, fertile soil with reasonable moisture; very adaptable to alkaline, poor-fertility, and salty soils and very drought-resistant when established; transplants with great ease; unfortunately prolific in its annual seed production and wealth of new seedlings.

PESTS AND DISEASES: Borers and oystershell scale are the major problems.

VARIETIES AND CULTIVARS: Cultivar 'Aucubifolia' has leaves mottled in yellow; cv. 'Marshall Seedless', a sterile male with dark green, glossy foliage turning yellow in the autumn.

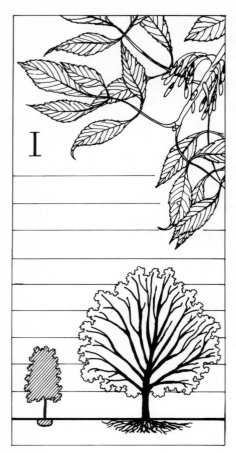

Fraxinus velutina (Velvet ash, Arizona ash)

Zones 6 to 10   30' to 50'   Olive family

Valuable for its tolerance to high heat, drought, and to alkaline soils, this native of Arizona and New Mexico has now extended itself into the upper sections of Mexico proper. It offers a reliability for those difficult growing situations in desert areas where large trees are a rare commodity.

HABIT: Pyramidal and dense when juvenile and becoming more open with a rounded silhouette with age; moderate in growth rate.

SEASONAL APPEARANCE: Its ash-gray twigs carry 6- to 8-inch, yellow-green, pinnately compound foliage with three to five narrow, oval, dull leaflets with wavy margins and gray hairiness beneath; greenish flowers appear in early spring on different trees, and both sexes are nonshowy; the notched, tan, female fruits are less than 1 inch long and typically slender; its autumnal foliage is golden yellow; the dark gray bark has broad ridges and breaks into scales with aging.

PREFERENCES AND PROBLEMS: Wants full sun and a well-drained, moist, reasonably fertile soil but is tolerant of both dry and alkaline soils without provoking problems; improved color in the foliage can be gained by providing regulated solutions of chelated iron during the growing season.

PESTS AND DISEASES: None of consequence.

VARIETIES AND CULTIVARS: Variety *coriacea* has leathery foliage and less pubescence on its twigs, plus broader leaves; variety *glabra* has glossy foliage.

Ginkgo biloba (Maidenhair tree, Ginkgo)

Zones 5 to 10   60' to 100'   Ginkgo family

Calling this native of southeastern China "the living fossil" is quite apt since some rocks dated to be 150 million years old have carried fossilized impressions of the same leaf outline you can find by looking at today's trees. It is the oldest cultivated nut tree in the world, but the female fruiting is so terribly ill-smelling that it must have some logical correlation to its longevity in history: Perhaps the awful odor discouraged animal consumption, and the tree then routinely continued producing itself as itself with no need for modifications. For all intents and purposes, this pest-free tree is an intriguing novelty for landscape use.

HABIT: When young, it has long, upright, asymmetric branching and a very open habit; with age it develops a more solid appearance and a somewhat pyramidal shape; moderate in growth.

SEASONAL APPEARANCE: The fan-shaped, leathery, wavy-edged, bright green (but dull) foliage is irregularly cleft and measures 2 to 3 inches wide; it resembles a leaflet of a maidenhair fern; the leaves grow in open clusterings from short spur growth along the smooth, grayish tan stems; the autumn leaf is a bright gold and has the unusual habit of dropping as a totality within a brief period; male and female flowering parts are on separate plants and are not showy; the plum-like female fruit can be up to 1 inch long and contain an edible seed considered a delicacy by Oriental people; the outer flesh, unfortunately, has such a rancid, persistent odor when ripe that this tree is being willingly removed from cultivation by nurseries; the thick, ash-brown bark is somewhat corky and becomes deeply furrowed and fluted with age.

PREFERENCES AND PROBLEMS: Wants full sun and perfect drainage on a deep, rich, sandy or gravelly soil; exceptionally tolerant of all types of growing conditions from hot, cool, dry, moist, and windy on either coastal or inland sites; it is late to leaf out, and young trunks may sunburn in very hot locations; it is very suitable for city grow-ing since it is remarkable in its adjustment to ice, wind, dust, and smoke; female plants do not set fruit for up to fifty years, and this delay can prove hazardous if a well-grown specimen turns out to be female (the better process is to buy only a known male cutting); intolerant of desert conditions in zone 10; appears to flourish best in zones 5 to 9 on the east coast of the United States.

PESTS AND DISEASES: None known for millions of years.

VARIETIES AND CULTIVARS: Variety *fastigiata* is narrowly columnar; variety *pendula* has weeping branches; cv. 'Autumn Gold' has a broadly spreading silhouette; cv. 'Fairmount' shows a pyramidal outline and very rapid growth.

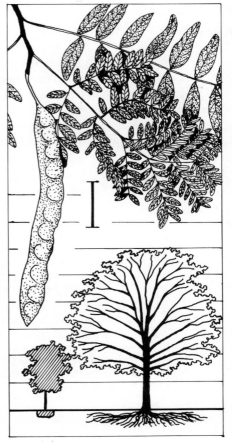

Gleditsia triacanthos inermis (Thornless honey locust, Thornless sweet locust, Thornless honeyshucks)

Zones 5 to 9   60′ to 100′   Pea family

The viciously branched thorns of ordinary honey locust should eliminate it from consideration in any landscape today, and with this naturally thornless variety (and its many cultivars) always nursery-available, there is no valid reason to use any other type. Its ready adaptability (much like *Ginkgo*) to a wide array of growing conditions, soils, and climates make this long-lived tree a wise decorative choice for much landscape work.

HABIT: Conical to flat-topped in outline with an erect trunk and broad-spreading, somewhat horizontal branching; the airy, fern-like leaves provide an open, see-through crown; fast-growing when young but moderate-growing later.

SEASONAL APPEARANCE: Dark, purple-brown, glossy, zigzagged twigs carry two types of pinnately compound, alternate foliage in one season; the sunken winter buds first produce 4- to 6-inch, once-pinnate leaves in tufted clusterings (fascicles) with small, slender, bright green leaflets; toward the close of the growing season the terminal leaves become twice-compound and between 8 and 10 inches in length (in the following season once-compound foliage will again sprout at these loca-tions); the autumn color is clear yellow; yellowish to green-white flowers of both sexes are on the same plant and open in midspring but are not decoratively con-spicuous; the purple-brown, flat but twisted, leathery fruit pods, often clustered, can stretch to 18 inches and persist into winter (for some, the wind movement of these pods creates an unwelcome, dismal, cracking sound); the young bark is smooth, purple-brown, glossy, and flecked with silver; older trunks becomes deep brown-black with stiff, recurved ridges.

PREFERENCES AND PROBLEMS: Grows best in full sun on a deep, moist, average-fertility, well-drained soil in climates with definite seasonal changes; remarkably adaptable to the widest variety of soils, including alkaline, as well as to drought, smog, dust, polluted air, hot summers, frigid winters, and neglect; late to leaf in spring and relatively early in autumn shedding; its filtered shade and deep roots allow lawn and shrubs to coexist amicably right to the trunk; foliage disintegrates quickly when fallen; relatively easy to establish when moved at any age; often promoted as a suitable replacement for the American elm, but its visual similarity is remote at best.

PESTS AND DISEASES: Unusually free of both, except for the mimosa webworm and borers (mostly in hot, humid areas).

VARIETIES AND CULTIVARS: Cultivar 'Imperial', a form with stiff, right-angled branching, dark green foliage, and a 35-foot height; cv. 'Majestic' with compact growth, few seed pods, deep green leaves, and a height of 65 feet; cv. 'Moraine', one of the first cultivars, seedless, broadly wide-growing with a 60-foot height but showing a weak, curved stem needing staking for many years when young; cv. 'Rubylace', a seedless form 60 feet tall with wine-red new growth; cv. 'Shademaster' with ascending branches and a vase-shaped form to 50 feet with dark green leaves persisting longer into autumn; cv. 'Skyline', narrowly pyramidal with upswept branching to 60 feet and very few seed pods; cv. 'Sunburst' with golden yellow new growth, seedless, and broad-headed to 60 feet.

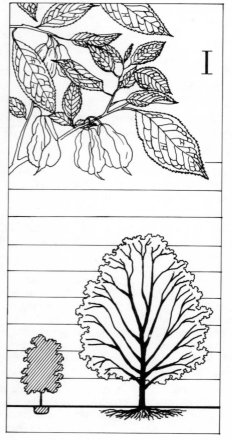

Halesia monticola   (Mountain silverbell, Snowdrop tree)

Zones 5 to 9   60' to 100'   Storax family

With its pendulous bell-like flowers lining all the stems in spring, this decorative tree from North Carolina to Georgia (and west to Tennessee) has a sparkling appearance for background or specimen landscape use. When seen from below, the blossoms show their golden centers to advantage. Its name honors Stephen Hales, a seventeenth-century botanist, which gives a good clue to the proper pronunciation of the plant name.

HABIT: Pyramidal to conical in outline with upright branching and an open crown; fast-paced in growth.

SEASONAL APPEARANCE: The alternate foliage appears on gray twigs and is dark yellow-green, elliptic, and can stretch to 7 inches; it tends to color as soft gold before shedding; the midspring flower clusters come with the leaves and have two to five bell-shaped, white, inch-long blossoms with bright gold stamens; by late summer its odd-shaped, four-angled, 1- to 2-inch, long-pointed fruit appear and become dry, light brown, and persistent (if squirrels do not strip them first); its gray-brown bark eventually becomes even darker and develops furrows and ridges.

PREFERENCES AND PROBLEMS: Grows well in full sun or light shade on an acid, rich, well-drained but moist, humusy, cool soil; is deep-rooted enough to allow other planting beneath to grow well (especially acid-loving rhododendrons and azaleas); transplants easily; prefers shelter from brisk winds; tends to lose its foliage early in the autumn; apt to become less upright and more shrubby in the northerly parts of the United States; does not grow satisfactorily in the desert regions of zone 9.

PESTS AND DISEASES: Highly resistant to both.

VARIETIES AND CULTIVARS: Variety *vestita* has leaves with mostly rounded bases; cv. 'Rosea' carries pale pink flowers.

Jacaranda mimosifolia   (Green ebony, Jacaranda)

Zones 9 and 10   25' to 50'   Bignonia family

Often confused with *J. acutifolia,* which is a dwarfed form only 10 feet tall, this inhabitant of northwestern Argentina (and perhaps some southerly parts of Brazil) is well appreciated for its attractive, prolific, lavender-blue flowering in early summer. There are over fifty different species known, and all originate in Central or South America.

HABIT: Variable in outline from upright with a stout trunk and pronounced horizontal branching to irregular, shrubby, and multistemmed; carries thin, fern-like leaves; fast-growing.

SEASONAL APPEARANCE: The opposite, pinnately compound leaves are up to 18 inches in length and dark green in color with oblong, about half-inch-long leaflets shining above and gray-toned beneath; there is no color change when leaves finally shed in early spring; the conspicuously showy, 2-inch blossoms appear terminally by late spring on older, leaf-less twigs and are lavender-blue to lilac, pendant in clusters up to 8 inches long, trumpet-shaped with a broad mouth and slightly fragrant; some trees carry a habit of flowering intermittently throughout the year; its decorative, disk-like seed pods are about 2½ inches long, dark brown, woody, and persistent; these are often collected for indoor ornament; the young bark is smooth and light brown but soon becomes rough and fissured.

PREFERENCES AND PROBLEMS: Thrives in full sun or light shading on an acid, deep, sandy, well-drained soil with reasonable moisture; prone to become dwarfed if constantly dry and becomes weak-headed if consistently wet; intolerant of frost and dislikes cool, foggy sites; has brittle branching and requires some sheltering from strong winds.

PESTS AND DISEASES: Apparently unbothered by either.

VARIETIES AND CULTIVARS: Variety *alba* has white blossoms.

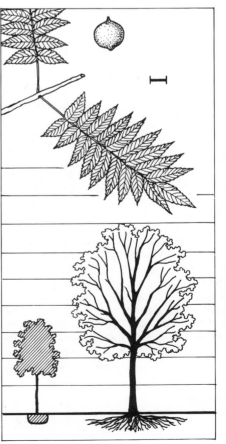

Juglans hindsii [*californica hindsii*]   (Hinds black walnut)

Zones 7 to 9   30' to 50'   Walnut family

Popular as a reliable shade tree for its drought tolerance and good resistance to the damaging oak root fungus, this native of central California carries a notably straight trunk, attractive foliage, and pleasant autumn color.

HABIT: Narrowly upright and symmetrical (but usually unbranched for about 10 feet of its lower height) with fine-textured foliage (for a walnut) and an open crown; fast in growth.

SEASONAL APPEARANCE: Its alternate, pinnately compound leaves are between 9 and 14 inches long with fifteen to nineteen narrow, up to 4-inch, medium green, toothed leaflets showing downy undersides; the greenish, midspring flowers are separated on the same plant, but the long catkins have no decorative value; its dark brown, almost-2-inch, female nut becomes thick-skinned and has a sweet taste but no commercial value; its desirable autumn color is clear yellow; the mostly smooth barks shows gradations of gray and brown.

PREFERENCES AND PROBLEMS: Best grown in full sun on a rich, deep, well-drained site with moderate moisture; drought-tolerant when fully established; bleeds sap profusely if pruned in spring; appears to grow better on the Pacific coast areas of its hardiness range; fruit drop may become a maintenance nuisance.

PESTS AND DISEASES: Occasionally bothered with aphid infestations; has good resistance to *Armillaria,* the oak root fungus disease.

VARIETIES AND CULTIVARS: None.

Koelreuteria elegans [formosana, henryi] (Flamegold, Chinese flame tree)

Zones 9 and 10   25′ to 40′   Soapberry family

For two-season attractiveness, this native of Taiwan and Fiji (and naturalized now in Florida) has few peers. The yellow glow of its early summer flowering is matched by the handsome seed pods later, while the tree maintains interestingly compound foliage and a neat habit in the other seasons. It contributes specimen appeal and, if pruned, can be a small shade tree of merit.

HABIT: Upright and spreading with a rounded outline often becoming flat-topped with age; fast to moderate in growth depending on its age.

SEASONAL APPEARANCE: Tan-colored, warty twigs have red-toned new growth and twice-pinnately compound leaves up to 18 inches long with nine to sixteen lustrous, nearly entire, oval, medium green leaflets about 3 inches in length; its autumn color varies from bright to dull yellow; the late spring flowering appears as loose, terminal sprays of slightly fragrant, richly yellow florets about a half-inch long; the summer fruiting is color-variable from orange to rose to red and becomes conspicuous by its many lantern-shaped, papery, inflated capsules nearly 1½ inches long; the irregular trunk is light brown and shallowly grooved.

PREFERENCES AND PROBLEMS: Enjoys full sun and almost any soil type as long as it is quick-draining; has deep rooting and becomes fully drought-tolerant when established; dislikes strong winds and shoreline exposures.

PESTS AND DISEASES: None of consequence.

VARIETIES AND CULTIVARS: None.

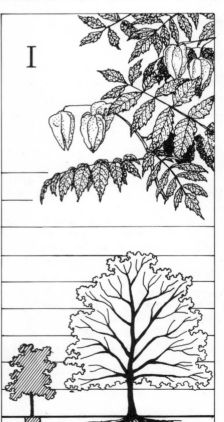

Koelreuteria paniculata (Varnish tree, Panicled goldrain tree)

Zones 5 to 9   30′ to 45′   Soapberry family

While not as spectacular in fruit as its kinsman *K. elegans,* this species from China and Korea (also naturalized in Japan now) does have the same adaptability to many soils and to drought while being advantageously more cold-tolerant. It is the most widely cultivated species of all.

HABIT: Dense, loosely and irregularly branched with a somewhat pyramidal form, becoming flat-topped with age; fairly rapid in growth.

SEASONAL APPEARANCE: Orange-brown twigs have raised, orange lenticels and produce alternate, once-compound, pinnate leaves to 18 inches in length with twelve to eighteen bright green, deeply cut leaflets (no two are alike) that have no autumn color of any worth; the early summer blossoming is variable from deep yellow to pale green-yellow and appears in loose, terminal, triangular strands up to 1 foot long; the 2-inch, three-sided, bladdery seed pods follow by late summer and are first light green, then red- or yellow-toned, and finally light brown; its light brown-gray bark becomes ridged with age.

PREFERENCES AND PROBLEMS: Thrives in full sun on a good, well-drained, moist soil but is very adaptable to less fertile and drier conditions; adjusts to air pollution, drought, great heat, wind, and alkaline soil; tends to be weak-wooded and may suffer branch damage in ice storms and snowstorms; deep-rooted and not likely to transplant well in a large size; apt to seed itself freely; usually lasts longer if grown no farther south than zone 8 in the eastern United States.

PESTS AND DISEASES: Unbothered by much except the coral spot fungus.

VARIETIES AND CULTIVARS: Cultivar 'Fastigiata', a narrowly erect type with tightly upright branching; cv. 'September', a form blooming in very late summer.

Laburnum × *watereri* (Golden chain tree)

Zones 5 to 9   15′ to 25′   Pea family

Often mislabeled *vossii*, this hybrid between *L. anagyroides* and *L. alpinum* has the best attributes of all the various types known. Its denser habit and deep-colored, longer flower clusters provide accent or specimen quality wherever it is installed.

HABIT: Stiffly upright and narrowly vase-shaped with long, pendulous flowering; often becomes either very low-branched or multistemmed; slow-growing.

SEASONAL APPEARANCE: New stems tend to be olive-green and thin with three-part, compound leaves covered in silvery hairs when emerging; the narrow, nearly 2-inch leaflets become glossy, bright green when mature; the late spring flowering hangs gracefully in long (10- to 20-inch), slender clusters of bright yellow, pea-like blossoms; the dull brown, 2-inch, flat pods (which contain poisonous seeds) are only infrequently produced; its brown-green, semiglossy bark is somewhat warty.

PREFERENCES AND PROBLEMS: Likes full sun or light shade (especially in the afternoon during hot weather) on a moist, well-drained, average-fertility soil; tolerant of highly alkaline conditions; roots are shallow and prevent use of this plant in very windy areas; rabbits are fond of the soft bark in winter; not adaptable to the hot, dry growing areas of the lower parts of the midwestern United States and is also unsuited for zones 8 and 9 in the eastern United States.

PESTS AND DISEASES: Black aphid infestations, leaf spot, and twig blight are the more common afflictions.

VARIETIES AND CULTIVARS: None.

Larix decidua [*europaea*] (European larch)

Zones 3 to 8   60′ to 100′   Pine family

Larch is unique as one of the few cone-bearing, needled trees with deciduous foliage. It grows easily and rapidly, has pendulous twigs, moves well [except the swamp-loving American larch or Tamarack *(L. laricina),* which does not take at all well to cultivation] and provides bright autumn color. This species is well distributed throughout the cooler and high-altitude regions of Europe, and it was once so popular in England in the seventeenth century that the 4th Duke of Atholl ordered and installed 17 million of them. It has the lightest green foliage of any larch.

HABIT: Narrowly pyramidal when young, becoming wide-spreading and irregular with age; fast in growth.

SEASONAL APPEARANCE: Buff-colored new shoots carry individual, spirally arranged, needle-thin, soft, 1-inch, bright green leaves; older twigs have short spur growths with tufts to three-quarters- to 1½-inch leaves; the autumn color is a bright, golden yellow; its springtime flowers are separated on the same plant, but neither the male nor female is very showy; the oval to round, female cone is woody brown, about 1½ inches long with scales opening much like a rose and persistent for a few years; the bark is deep gray with vertical cracks and scaly ridges.

PREFERENCES AND PROBLEMS: Prefers full sun but will tolerate light shading for brief periods; likes a consistently moist, deep, average-fertility soil and a climate where summers are cool and winters cold; intolerant of air pollution, drought, and shallow soil; easily transplanted; prefers summertime pruning, if needed; does not produce its first cones until it is at least twenty years old.

PESTS AND DISEASES: Can be seriously defoliated by the larva of the larch case bearer in late spring and is often deformed by canker diseases which are more easily spread in low, damp sites.

VARIETIES AND CULTIVARS: Cultivar 'Pendula' with noticeably drooping branches; cv. 'Pyramidalis', a narrow, conical form with ascending branching.

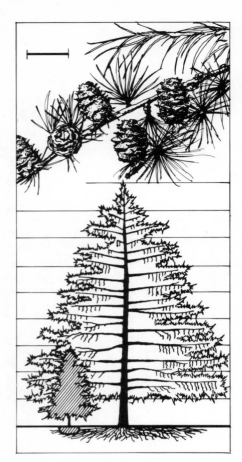

Larix kaempferi [*leptolepis*]   (Japanese larch)

Zones 5 to 8   70' to 90'   Pine family

This Japanese species is very broad in outline and appears to be much more resistant to canker diseases. It becomes a fine specimen quickly but is suitable only for large, open spaces.

HABIT: Narrowly pyramidal when juvenile but soon becoming very wide-spreading and open with long, horizontal branching; rapid-growing.

SEASONAL APPEARANCE: Twig growth here is a rich, reddish brown, and the soft needle foliage is about 1¼ inches long and mostly dark green with two noticeably white bands on the undersides; the separated flowering is not conspicuous; its 1-inch female cones are light brown, stalked, and have thin, rounded scales which recurve outward; its autumnal color is a yellowish or orange-gold; the dark, red-brown bark cracks into scales.

PREFERENCES AND PROBLEMS: See *L. decidua.*

PESTS AND DISEASES: See *L. decidua;* unusually resistant to canker diseases.

VARIETIES AND CULTIVARS: Cultivar 'Minor', a dwarfed form.

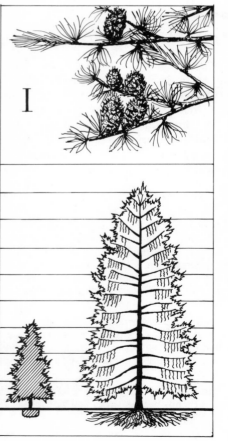

Larix occidentalis   (Western larch, Western tamarack)

Zones 5 to 7   60' to 180'   Pine family

In its native wilds of British Columbia to Montana this largest larch species will easily reach its upper height limits, but in cultivation it usually does not exceed the lower one. Its narrow silhouette can be a landscape asset in small areas.

HABIT: Slenderly pyramidal at all ages; branches recurve somewhat with age; may retain lower limbs to ground level under cultivation; fast-growing.

SEASONAL APPEARANCE: New twigs are orange-brown and pendulous with three-sided, stiff yet soft, 2-inch needles of bright green; the spring flowering is not noticeable; its deep brown, young female cones are egg-shaped and carry conspicuous, thread-like bracts between the scales; when ripe, the scales bend downward, releasing the bracts and seed; its autumn color is golden yellow; the young, scaly bark is dull, gray-brown and matures to become thick, deeply furrowed, and red-brown.

PREFERENCES AND PROBLEMS: See *L. decidua.*

PESTS AND DISEASES: See *L. decidua;* also suffers from brown heart rot.

VARIETIES AND CULTIVARS: None.

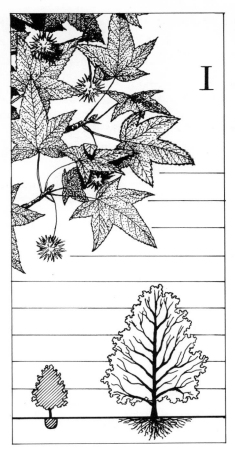

Liquidambar styraciflua (Sweet gum, American sweet gum, Red gum, Bilsted)

Zones 6 to 10   60' to 140'   Witchhazel family

Widely distributed on moist ground from southern Connecticut to Florida and west to Missouri and eastern Texas, this popular specimen tree has a pleasantly neat silhouette, novel foliage, intriguing fruit, and showy autumn color. Its curious name derives from the yellowish, clear, fragrant sap that resembles "liquid amber."

HABIT: Pyramidal and dense with a straight trunk but becoming broadly round-headed in time; fast to moderate in growth, depending on available soil moisture.

SEASONAL APPEARANCE: Smooth, gray-toned twigs have large, deep red buds that produce unusual, five-lobed, star-shaped (somewhat maple-like), glossy foliage between 3 and 7 inches wide in a rich green; the variable autumn color is scarlet to purple or yellow-toned; its older twigs often develop irregular, corky ridges; flowers are separated on the same tree but are green-toned and visually unimportant; the durable female fruit is a pendulous, woody ball between 1 and 1½ inches in diameter with conspicuous, hardened points surrounding tiny perforations; this fruit is first light green and eventually becomes deep brown; juvenile bark is brightly ash-gray, becoming red-brown with deep furrows at maturity.

PREFERENCES AND PROBLEMS: Grows best in full sun on a deep, fertile, consistently moist soil well supplied with humus; not suited for desert conditions; tolerant to light shade and wet soils (even occasional flooding from streams); leaves are apt to wilt in very windy locations and may develop chlorosis on very alkaline soils; deep taproot makes transplanting difficult except in small sizes; dropped fruit can be hazardous underfoot; ice storms in the northwestern United States usually damage branches readily; not as good in zone 10 of the eastern United States.

PESTS AND DISEASES: Occasionally wilt disease affects the twigs.

VARIETIES AND CULTIVARS (selections here are mainly for foliage improvements):   Cultivar 'Burgundy' with persistent, deep purple-red autumn leaves; cv. 'Festival' with mixed yellow, orange, and pink in autumn and a slenderly columnar form; cv. 'Palo Alto', also narrow but with especially rich autumnal tones of orange-red; cv. 'Variegata' with summer foliage streaked in yellow.

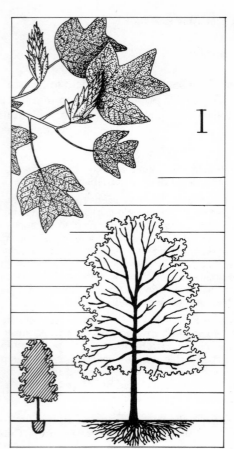

Liriodendron tulipifera (Tulip tree, Tulip poplar, Whitewood)

Zones 5 to 9   100′ to 200′   Magnolia family

One of the tallest of the hardwood trees in eastern North America, the tulip tree is long-lived, stalwart, and distinguished in all the native areas of its habitat from Massachusetts down to Florida and west to Mississippi. In landscape developments it offers good shade, unusual flowering, and colorful autumn foliage, plus a powerful trunk silhouette of lofty height when it matures.

HABIT: Narrowly conical in youth but maturing with a broadly pyramidal shape and hefty branching; tends to be asymmetric in its older outline; fast-growing when juvenile but moderate-growing later.

SEASONAL APPEARANCE: Twigs are shiny and olive-brown with odd, flattened buds much like a duck's bill; the broad, shallowly lobed leaves are unique by not having a center point or lobe but are indented noticeably in a saddle-like depression; the foliage appears on very long (up to 7-inch) stalks and is medium to yellow-green; the autumnal color is usually a rich, clear yellow; its special flowering is scented and tulip-shaped but not often showy since the late spring blossoming is often held high into the crown; these flowers are terminal, erect, cup-shaped, and up to 2 inches tall with greenish cream petals and a broad base of orange banding; the 3-inch high, spindle-shaped fruiting becomes tan and is made up of a host of narrow segments in a cone shape; by winter these seeds disperse and leave only a thin spike; the brown, young bark is smooth and thin but ages to deep gray-brown with long, vertical ridges.

PREFERENCES AND PROBLEMS: Does best on a deep, rich, consistently moist soil from acid to neutral in full sun; its deep tap rooting prevents easy transplanting unless quite young; tolerant to some poorly drained locations if not kept waterlogged; somewhat weak-wooded and can be damaged by severe ice storms or snowstorms; unsuited for street use in cities since it requires more soil water than most confined street planting allows; will not tolerate desert conditions at all.

PESTS AND DISEASES: Has few serious afflictions but is bothered occasionally by scale, aphids, and damage from a leaf gall insect.

VARIETIES AND CULTIVARS: Cultivar 'Aureo-marginatum' with foliage margined in yellow; cv. 'Fastigiatum', a narrower form with mostly upright branching; cv. 'Integrifolium' with totally unlobed leaves and a rounded leaf base.

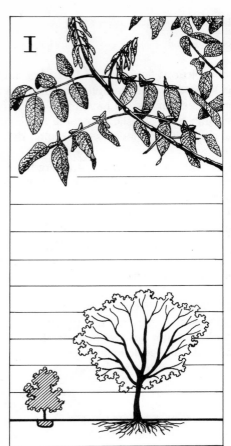

Maackia amurensis (Amur maackia)

Zones 5 to 8   20′ to 40′   Pea family

Few trees blossom conspicuously in late summer, but this native of Korea and Manchuria has the capacity. Regrettably, it has no fruit or autumnal coloring of note, but its hardiness and easy care suggest its landscape use as an undemanding tree of special seasonal interest.

HABIT: Irregular in outline when young with low branching and a shrubby appearance; usually requires some pruning to bring it into tree form; becomes flat-topped or gently rounded with age; moderate in growth.

SEASONAL APPEARANCE: Olive-brown twigs carry noticeable spring foliage entirely coated in glistening gray hairs; the pinnately compound foliage reaches from 7 to 10 inches in length and has thick, oval leaflets about 1½ inches long that are dull, dark green; there is no autumn coloring; its late summer flowers are cream-white spikes of densely crowded, tiny, pea-like blossoms held erect from the leaves in often generous clusterings up to 8 inches tall; its innocuous fruiting is 2-inch, flat, gray-brown pods; the bark develops to a rich, shining, brown-green that peels and curls thinly against the trunk with aging.

PREFERENCES AND PROBLEMS: Enjoys an average-fertility, loose, well-drained soil (acid or alkaline) in full sun; its greatest problem is a lack of nursery availability.

PESTS AND DISEASES: None.

VARIETIES AND CULTIVARS: Cultivar 'Buergeri' has leaves remaining noticeably hairy beneath.

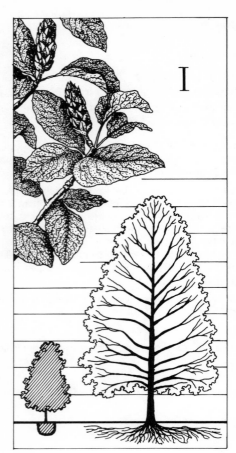

Magnolia acuminata (Cucumber tree)

Zones 5 to 10   60' to 100'   Magnolia family

Magnolias are valued for their conspicuous flowering and pest-free foliage; however, none of the types has bright leaf color in autumn, while the large fruit pods show only a short-term effectiveness. All have thick, fleshy roots difficult to move easily, and their thin bark is easily damaged. Since cuts take extraordinarily long to heal completely, unnecessary pruning should be avoided.

Magnolias prefer full sun but benefit from light shading where the sun is bright and summer temperatures rise appreciably. They grow their best when on a moist, deep, rich, well-drained, humusy soil that is acid or nearly neutral. For the most part they dislike constantly windy sites.

Reasonably tolerant to city air pollution, the early-flowering types are often greatly marred by late frosts. Many species form important, tall tree silhouettes, but others are broader and more shrub-like. In all, magnolias make sizable, reliable, and handsome specimens where they have sufficient room and consistent moisture.

The large-growing species here described is distributed natively from southern Ontario to Georgia and west to Louisiana. It is the only magnolia with deeply grooved bark when older, but it has less than noticeable, unfragrant flowers obscured by the developed foliage. It grows into a sturdy, vigorous lawn specimen with very attractive leaves.

HABIT: Narrowly pyramidal with stiff, upright branching for many years but becoming broadly rounded with age; foliage is dense, and its older branching often sweeps the ground from long, wide-reaching limbs; vigorous in growth.

SEASONAL APPEARANCE: Reddish brown stems carry thin, 4- to 10-inch, elliptic foliage with sharp-pointed tips that is dark green on top but lightly gray-pubescent beneath; its 2- to 3-inch, early summer flowers are not showy since they appear when foliage is fully developed and are greenish yellow to pale yellow; these are barely fragrant, fleshy, and loosely open-petaled; the cucumber-like seed head is 2 to 3 inches tall, turns from green to purplish red, and then shows tiny, red seeds which become suspended on white threads; the autumnal color is a pallid brown-yellow; its firm but thin, gray-brown bark is scaly and eventually deeply furrowed in vertical ridges.

PREFERENCES AND PROBLEMS: See introductory remarks; provide full sun or light shading and a fertile, well-drained, acid to neutral, loamy soil deep enough to accommodate its wide-spreading roots; trees first blossom only when about 20 feet tall; dislikes dry, alkaline soils; appears to behave better when limited to zones 6 to 8 in the eastern United States.

PESTS AND DISEASES: Unbothered except for an occasional scale infestation on the twigs.

VARIETIES AND CULTIVARS: Variety *cordata* has a lower height of 35 feet and smaller blossoms showing golden yellow outer petals with a canary yellow inner coloring; its curved fruit is dark red; not common; cv. 'Miss Honeybee', a form with larger flowers in pale yellow.

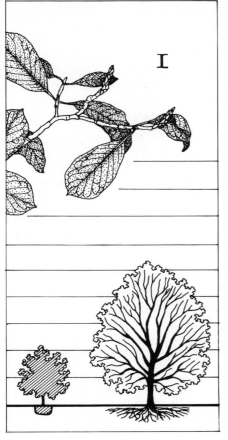

Magnolia heptapeta [*denudata, conspicua*] (Yulan magnolia)

Zones 6 to 10   35′ to 50′   Magnolia family

With sizable, clear white flowers blossoming well before the leaves, this native of China contributes a striking appearance to the midspring landscape. Its quick growth and capacity for young blooming, plus fragrant flowers, make it a popular landscape tree.

HABIT: Irregular when juvenile but becoming more rounded or pyramidal with age; carries many erect branches and gives dense shade; fast-growing when young but moderate-growing later.

SEASONAL APPEARANCE: Shiny twigs carry shaggy-hairy, gray winter buds that develop into 3-inch, thick-petaled (usually nine), fragrant, chalice-shaped, white blossoms opening to a 6-inch width and arriving before the leaves in early to midspring; the narrow, 3- to 7-inch leaves are medium to dark green above and slightly hairy beneath; its tapered fruit is brown-toned, about 5 inches tall, and carries orange seeds; the smooth bark is gray-brown.

PREFERENCES AND PROBLEMS: See *M. acuminata;* grows better if not crowded by other plant material.

PESTS AND DISEASES: None of consequence.

VARIETIES AND CULTIVARS: Cultivar 'Japanese Clone' with larger flowers and improved hardiness; cv. 'Lacey' with sizable blossoms opening to at least an 8-inch spread.

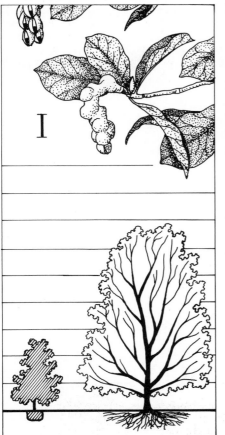

Magnolia × *loebneri* 'Merrill' (Merrill magnolia)

Zones 5 to 10   40′ to 50′   Magnolia family

The hybrid crossing of *M. stellata* and *M. kobus* first produced the *loebneri* strain, and from that development several interesting selections have now come such as cvs. 'Ballerina', 'Leonard Messel', 'Spring Snow', and 'Willowwood'; the selection 'Merrill' is the one most commonly available and offers greater height and spreads more quickly than these other forms. In time, of course, one of them may even supplant 'Merrill' in popularity.

HABIT: Openly pyramidal when young but becoming more symmetrical with age; fast-growing.

SEASONAL APPEARANCE: Slender, deep brown twigs produce heavy annual flowering of 4-inch-wide, fragrant, slender-petaled (between eight and fifteen) but floppy, spring blossoms before the leaves appear; its narrowly oval, rich green, glossy foliage averages 4 inches in length; cucumber-like fruiting is typical but infrequent; its bark is smooth and dark gray-brown.

PREFERENCES AND PROBLEMS: See *M. acuminata;* flowering starts when plants are very young.

PESTS AND DISEASES: None known.

VARIETIES AND CULTIVARS: See above.

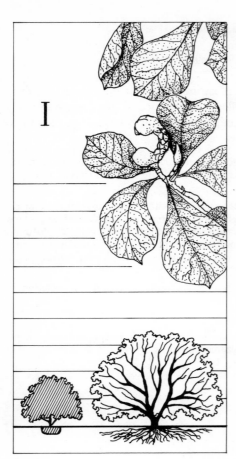

Magnolia × soulangiana (Chinese magnolia, Saucer magnolia)

Zones 5 (warm) to 9   20′ to 25′   Magnolia family

Surely one of the most popular of flowering trees, this pink-toned hybrid between *M. heptapeta* and *M. quinquepeta (liliflora)* is usually more shrubby than tree-like with its many main trunks and low-branching habit. Provide generous ground space for its wide spread wherever it is installed.

HABIT: Usually multistemmed and low-branched with a rounded silhouette at all ages; often matures nearly as wide as tall; moderate in growth.

SEASONAL APPEARANCE: Its gray-brown twigs have furry, 1-inch, winter buds that unfold to display heavy-textured, cup-shaped, six-petaled flowers opening into a flattened, saucer form in widths from 6 to 10 inches; they are slightly fragrant and show purplish pink streaking on the outside but are pure white inside; they appear before any of its leaves in midspring; its glossy, somewhat narrowed, heavy foliage ranges between 5 and 8 inches in length and from medium to dark green; the fruiting pods have typical red or deep pink seeds; its smooth bark is light gray.

PREFERENCES AND PROBLEMS: See *M. acuminata;* blossoms are liable to be quickly browned by late frosts; often proves highly variable in flower color when raised from seeds; begins to bloom when very young; avoid dryness and very windy sites.

PESTS AND DISEASES: Prone to serious attacks of scale insects.

VARIETIES AND CULTIVARS (there is a large selection available even beyond this list): Cultivar 'Alba Superba' with a more compact habit and large, almost-white blossoms; cv. 'Alexandrina', an earlier-flowering type having larger blooms with pure white interiors and a flush of purple-pink outside; cv. 'Andre Leroy' with pronouncedly cup-shaped flowering that is deep rose to purple outside and pure white inside; cv. 'Brozzonii', a late bloomer carrying wide-spreading (up to 10 inches), white flowers with very pale, purple-rose outer shading; cv. 'Burgundy', an early type having large blossoms mostly deep red-purple; cv. 'Grace McDade', a form with sizable light pink flowers showing reddish outer petals; cv. 'Lennei' carries very large, balloon-shaped blossoms that are deep purple outside and white inside; cv. 'Lombardy Rose', a long-blooming sort with petals dark rose on the lower end and white at the tips; cv. 'Norbertii', late-flowering with large, purple blooms; cv. 'Picture', an early bloomer with thick petals that are purple outside and white inside; cv. 'Rustica Rubra' with rounded flowers reddish purple outside and white inside; cv. 'San Jose' with early, scented flowering in white flushed with pink; cv. 'Verbanica', a slow-growing, late blooming form with long, slender buds and purplish pink blossoms.

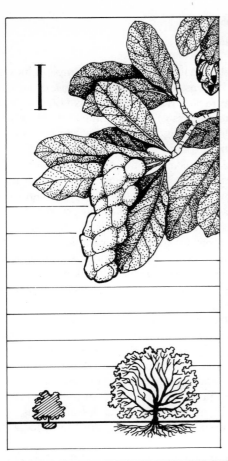

Magnolia stellata (Star magnolia)

Zones 5 (warm) to 9   15′ to 20′   Magnolia family

This early-flowering, hardy, diminutive species from central Japan is eager to bloom and begins quite young, but its perky blossom announcement of spring is often badly marred by late frosts. It is one of the few magnolias with any noticeable autumn coloring in the leaves.

HABIT: Compact and rounded with many small twigs and meandering stems; always dense in foliage; slow-growing.

SEASONAL APPEARANCE: Slim, gray-brown twigs carry small, furry, winter buds opening in very early spring to reveal pure white, fragrant, thin but slender-petaled (between twelve and eighteen), floppy-eared blossoms; the narrow, thick, dark green, glossy leaves appear on hairy new stems and measure between 1 and 5 inches long; they turn an attractive bronze tone in autumn; its contorted fruit is about 2 inches long with red-toned seeds; bark is brownish gray and smooth.

PREFERENCES AND PROBLEMS: See *M. acuminata;* its early blooming time may expose the flowers to complete browning from late frost.

PESTS AND DISEASES: Free of both.

VARIETIES AND CULTIVARS: Cultivar 'Centennial' with larger, more numerous flowers; cv. 'Rosea', non-fragrant with blush-toned flowering fading to white; cv. 'Rubra' with purple-rose blossoms; cv. 'Waterlily', more upright and bushy in appearance with pink buds and slender-petaled, white flowers.

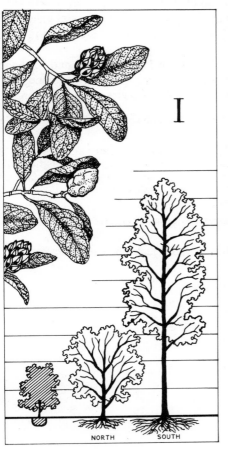

Magnolia virginiana [*glauca*] (Sweet bay, Laurel magnolia, Swamp magnolia)

Zones 5 (warm) to 9   20′ to 60′   Magnolia family

Because it is so widely distributed naturally in the United States (from Massachusetts to Florida and west to Tennessee and Texas), this fragrant-flowered, hardy tree offers both a shrubby and a deciduous nature—in the north—as well as a tall-growing, narrow tree form with fully evergreen foliage—in the south. It easily tolerates more variability in soil, climate, and available moisture than any of the other magnolias.

HABIT: Loosely open with infrequent branching at any age; is shrub-like and deciduous in colder areas but evergreen, slender-trunked, and narrowly columnar in warm sections; fast to medium in growth, depending on the locale.

SEASONAL APPEARANCE: Twigs are bright green with silky, white, small budding; the foliage is oblong, glossy, and leathery with dark green tops but silvered beneath and up to 5 inches long; the very late spring flowering is a cup-shaped, waxy, lemon-scented, creamy white blossom; its dark red summer cones are erect and about 2 inches tall; the smooth, light brown bark changes to gray and becomes slightly scaly with age.

PREFERENCES AND PROBLEMS: See *M. acuminata;* more shade-tolerant than other species; greatly dislikes drought but can readily accept very wet soils.

PESTS AND DISEASES: Unimportant.

VARIETIES AND CULTIVARS: Variety *australis* has larger, more silvery, evergreen foliage and may actually be the type most often seen wild in southerly locations; cv. 'Havener' has large, many-petaled flowering; cv. 'Mayer', a shrubby form.

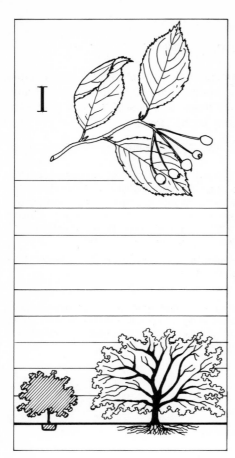

Malus × arnoldiana (Arnold crab apple)

Zones 5 to 9   15' to 20'   Rose family

When in doubt, plant a crab apple. That advice is not so simple-minded as it may first seem since these are the easiest, hardiest, and most ornamental flowering trees known, and the attractive nursery selections now available can be measured in the dozens regardless of where you live. Crab apples offer such splendid variation in flower, fruit, habit, and foliage that the world would indeed be drab without them.

Crab apples are closely related botanically to the apple but differ, primarily, by having fruit less than 2 inches in diameter. The common name supposedly derives from the taste of the sour fruit, which can give you a ''crabbed'' look after a few bites. They excel in the ornamental exuberance of their masses of spring flowers—single or double—and often by the persistence of their generous fruiting after the leaves drop. Some types, however, exhaust themselves after this much seasonal activity and pause for a full year before becoming showy again. Only a few crab apples have autumn color of any interest, but many contribute spring or summer foliage colors other than green. The selections presented here have normal green leaves and no autumn color change.

All crab apples grow with ease and like full sun on a fertile, well-drained, deep soil ranging from acid to slightly alkaline. While tolerant of drier, rockier—even wet—conditions, they do not prosper in desert locations. As members of the rose family, they are plagued with many diseases and insect pests requiring prompt and thorough attention, but they are not burdensome with their list of problems for most landscape situations. Asiatic forms, for some reason, seem to be more resistant to our local pests and diseases than the domestic types.

With a hundred known crab apples in cultivation, it is impossible here to evaluate even a small percentage of them. The selections discussed represent just a fair sampling of those with enduring seasonal values and landscape interest. Many other fine choices are obviously waiting for your personal discovery and use.

The species listed here is hybrid between *M. floribunda* and *M. baccata* and offers a greatly floriferous nature, fragrance, and good fruiting. For some growing areas it may prove to be only an alternate-year bearer.

HABIT: Dense-foliaged and mound-like in shape with mostly upright branching; fast to moderate growth, depending on its locale.

SEASONAL APPEARANCE: Its twigs tend to be zigzagged and carry 2- to 3-inch green leaves with noticeably wavy margins; the midspring, clustered flowers have dark red buds with long stalks and open into 2-inch, single, pink blossoms fading to white with age; the nearly round fruit is about a half-inch and yellow with a faint blush of red; its bark is reddish gray and scaly.

PREFERENCES AND PROBLEMS: See introductory remarks; prefers zones 5 to 8 in the eastern United States.

PESTS AND DISEASESS: Susceptible to both scab and fireblight in some areas.

VARIETIES AND CULTIVARS: None.

Malus baccata (Siberian crab apple)

Zones 2 to 9   35′ to 50′   Rose family

Extremely hardy and rugged, this species from eastern Asia is even further differentiated by its great height and profuse flowering every year.

HABIT: Pyramidal when juvenile but rounded with age; foliage is dense; fast-growing.

SEASONAL APPEARANCE: Smooth twigs carry slender leaves between 2 and 3 inches in length with long petioles; the midspring flower clusters have pink buds and pure white, single, annual blossoming that is very fragrant; individual flowers measure about 1½ inches across and carry five widely spaced petals: the long-persistent fruit varies but is usually close to a half-inch in diameter and colored yellow with red cheeks; its bark is dark gray-brown.

PREFERENCES AND PROBLEMS: See *M. arnoldiana;* appears limited to zones 2 to 8 in the eastern portions of the United States.

PESTS AND DISEASES: May be prone to scab in some areas.

VARIETIES AND CULTIVARS: Variety *jackii* is broad-crowned, vigorous, and upright with larger flowers, very deep green leaves, and bright red fruit; variety *mandshurica,* the first crab apple to bloom, has greater hardiness and resistance to scab than the parent and has pubescent leaf petioles, while the half-inch, yellow fruit is ellipsoidal; cv. 'Columnaris' with erect growth and yellow fruit showing a large red cheek but very prone to fireblight.

Malus floribunda (Showy crab apple, Japanese crab apple)

Zones 5 to 9   15′ to 30′   Rose familly

One of the oldest crab apples in cultivation, this vigorous Japanese native is wholly dependable for easy growth throughout its wide growing range. It performs annually with flowers and fruit and blooms at a very early age.

HABIT: Has a somewhat irregular outline when young, but becomes densely branched and dome-shaped with arched branching later; fast in growth rate.

SEASONAL APPEARANCE: Its new growth is very hairy on the emerging red twigs, and the dull green, 2- to 3-inch leaves maintain downy undersides; the midspring flower clusters come annually and are profuse with deep carmine budding and pale pink, 1½-inch, fragrant blossoms turning white with age; the round to oval fruiting is nearly one-quarter inch long and either all yellow or yellow with a sizable red cheek; its gray bark is scaly.

PREFERENCES AND PROBLEMS: See *M. arnoldiana;* apt to seed itself easily into other areas.

PESTS AND DISEASES: Slightly susceptible to scab and mildew.

VARIETIES AND CULTIVARS: None.

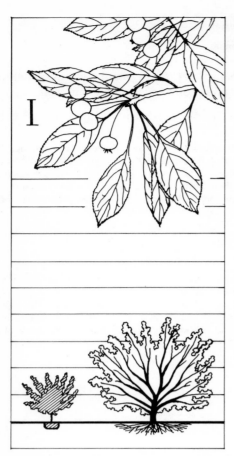

Malus hupehensis [*theifera*] (Tea crab apple)

Zones 5 to 9   20′ to 35′   Rose family

Often wildly irregular in outline, this Chinese native has no central leader and may develop only a series of long, unbranched stems gesticulating in the air; other selections can become neatly refined and very much vase-shaped. In any case, the tree is unique. The Chinese concoct a medicinal tea from the leaves, which accounts for its name.

HABIT: Variable (see above) from loose and open to stiff and vase-like; in either form the trunk is very short, and main stems have a multitude of short-spurred, lateral twigs which carry the generous flowering only every second year; moderate in growth.

SEASONAL APPEARANCE: New growth is hairy and carries purple-toned young foliage changing to glossy, dark green and a mature size of 2 to 4 inches; its deep pink, clustered buds develop into single, fragrant, white or pale pink blossoms about 1½ inches wide; heavy flowering is only in alternate years; the half-inch fruit is round and oddly nonshowy in this country with a pallid yellow-green color faintly brushed with rose (in Europe it usually is a bright scarlet); the bark is a deep gray-brown and eventually cracks into large flakes when older.

PREFERENCES AND PROBLEMS: See *M. arnoldiana;* usually is unsuitable in zone 9 in the eastern part of the United States.

PESTS AND DISEASES: Severely prone to fireblight but is very resistant to scab.

VARIETIES AND CULTIVARS: None.

Malus × 'Katherine'

Zones 5 to 9   15′ to 20′   Rose family

An unusually floriferous, double-blossomed hybrid between *M. halliana* and *M. baccata,* this crab apple offers an extraordinary landscape value as a picturesque specimen, even when out of flower. It bears annually.

HABIT: Upright when young but becoming outward-spreading, open, and irregular with maturity; may be multistemmed; slow to moderate growth.

SEASONAL APPEARANCE: Its dark green, 2- to 3-inch leaves appear on red-brown stems that also carry the heavy, midspring flowers; its clusterings of rosy red buds open into double, 2-inch, pink blossoms fading to white at maturity; the fruit does not balance the flowers for interest (and both occur annually) since they are a non-glossy, deep red, and only a quarter-inch wide; its dull bark is brownish gray.

PREFERENCES AND PROBLEMS: See *M. arnoldiana;* it is perhaps suited only to zones 5 to 8 in the eastern sections of the United States.

PESTS AND DISEASES: Resistant to both scab and fireblight.

VARIETIES AND CULTIVARS: None.

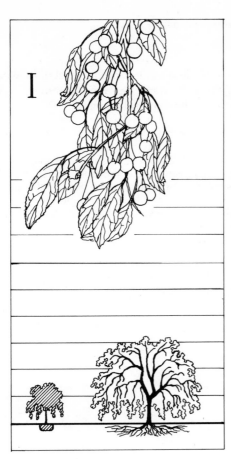

Malus × 'Red Jade'

Zones 5 to 8   15' to 20'   Rose family

Even though it comes to us with an unclear parentage, this introduction from the Brooklyn Botanic Garden in New York contributes the novelty of a graceful, weeping form with conspicuous fruiting not often seen in crab apples. It produces only every other year, unfortunately, but is well worth the delay.

HABIT: Upright with pendulous, slender branching at all ages; slow-growing.

SEASONAL APPEARANCE: The 2-inch leaves are bright green and appear on deep brown, weeping twigs also supporting drooping clusters of deep pink, midspring buds that become 1-inch, white flowers of no special distinction; the fruiting is spectacular, however (but only appears each second year), and fills all the branching with heavy bunches of bright red, egg-shaped, half-inch fruit with great persistence into the winter months; its bark is a light brown-gray.

PREFERENCES AND PROBLEMS: See *M. arnoldiana;* prefers not to exceed zone 8 in the easterly portion of the United States.

PESTS AND DISEASES: Moderately resistant to mildew and scab but is afflicted by fireblight.

VARIETIES AND CULTIVARS: None.

Malus sargentii   (Sargent crab apple)

Zones 4 to 8   6' to 10'   Rose family

This Japanese introduction is a broad but very low mound of plant twigginess and annual, showy fruiting. It commands attention for its unusually dwarfed specimen quality.

HABIT: Wide-spreading, irregular, and dwarfed when young but becomes more mound-like and noticeably dense-twigged at maturity; very slow-growing.

SEASONAL APPEARANCE: New growth is conspicuously hairy; older, zigzag twigs carry spur-like growths from which come the very abundant, springtime flower clusters of three-quarter-inch, white, fragrant blossoms with bright gold anthers; its flowering is dependably annual; the new leaves are usually covered on both sides with fine hairs but turn smooth and dark green; they range from 2 to 4 inches in length, often with cleft ends; its third-inch, rich red, generous fruiting persists long into the autumn; the bark is dark gray-brown.

PREFERENCES AND PROBLEMS: See *M. arnoldiana;* tends to sucker heavily at the base and early removal of this unneeded growth retains the good outline of the plant.

PESTS AND DISEASES: Slightly bothered by scab, leaf spot, fire blight.

VARIETIES AND CULTIVARS: Cultivar 'Rosea' has deep rose-pink buds.

Malus × scheideckeri (Scheidecker crab apple)

Zones 5 to 9   15' to 20'   Rose family

A double-flowered hybrid of long-standing virtue from a crossing between *M. floribunda* and *M. prunifolia,* this crab apple has annual, showy blossoming and an easy tolerance for shaping and pruning.

HABIT: Upright and dense-foliaged with an oval or pyramidal outline at all ages; slow growth rate.

SEASONAL APPEARANCE: The more or less oval, 2- to 4-inch, shiny foliage is a rich green above and hairy beneath; its annual flowering is produced generously all along the stems for a very showy, springtime appearance of mostly double blossoms heavily bunched; they are 1½ to 2 inches wide in pale pink; the orange-yellow, persistent, three-quarter-inch fruit is globose and slightly indented on the ends; the bark is deep brown-gray and scaly.

PREFERENCES AND PROBLEMS: See *M. arnoldiana;* adjusts better in the eastern United States to limits of zones 5 to 8.

PESTS AND DISEASES: Highly susceptible, unfortunately, to many diseases.

VARIETIES AND CULTIVARS: Cultivar 'Hillieri' has flowers only half-double.

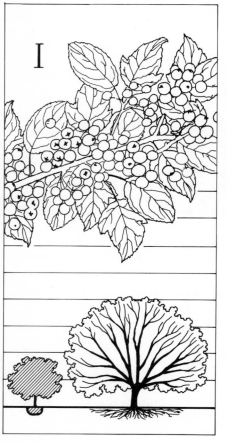

Malus × zumi calocarpa (Redbud crab apple)

Zones 6 to 9   20' to 25'   Rose family

Certainly one of the finest crab apples for showy, very persistent fruiting, this hybrid between *M. baccata mandshurica* and *M. sieboldii* also has fragrant, noticeable flowering and a handsome, spreading silhouette.

HABIT: Densely twigged and spreading at all ages; moderate in growth.

SEASONAL APPEARANCE: The broad, medium green foliage is between 1½ and 3 inches long with a tapered base; its many-clustered, tiny, midspring flower buds are rose-pink and open into 1-inch, fragrant, single flowers (but only in alternate years); the splendidly persistent, bright red, round fruit is about a half-inch in diameter; the bark is dark gray-tan.

PREFERENCES AND PROBLEMS: See *M. arnoldiana;* prefers zones 6 to 8 in the eastern sections of the United States.

PESTS AND DISEASES: Highly resistant to scab but is prone to contract fireblight.

VARIETIES AND CULTIVARS: None.

Melia azedarach (Chinaberry, Pride-of-India, Bead tree, Paradise tree, Alelailla)

Zones 7 (warm) to 10   30' to 45'   Mahogany family

This is one of those serviceable, easy-to-raise trees with both attractive and unattractive qualities. It has fragrant flowering, showy and persistent fruiting, dense shade, and a special adaptation to prolonged drought. On the other hand, it litters all the time, has brittle wood, carries poisonous seeds, and quickly volunteers seedlings everywhere. Originally from northern India and western China, it is now naturalized in much of the semitropical climates of the world.

HABIT: Carries upthrust branching and dense twigginess with heavy foliage; eventually becomes very wide-spreading and rounded; fast-growing.

SEASONAL APPEARANCE: Green twigs produce alternate, doubly compound, fern-like leaves varying between 1 and 3 feet in length; the thin, oval, dark green leaflets have noticeable teeth, are between 1 and 2 inches long, and emit a pungent odor if bruised; there is no autumnal coloring; its springtime flowering appears in 5- to 8-inch, loose, terminal clusters of fragrant, pale lavender, nonshowy, diminutive blossoms; these are followed by glistening, egg-shaped, three-quarter-inch, hard fruit usually persisting well into the winter months; this plentiful fruiting is poisonous but so sour-tasting that it has little attractive potential of being eaten by people or animals; the mostly smooth, young bark is dark brown or red-brown and becomes furrowed with age.

PREFERENCES AND PROBLEMS: Wants full sun and an average-fertility, deep soil, acid or alkaline, with good drainage; needs consistently hot summer weather to develop fully; adapts easily to dry, infertile soils and is readily drought-tolerant when established; not overly long-lived; wants wind protection since branching is brittle; persistently litters spent foliage, flowers, or fruit; produces an overly generous seedling crop annually, and all seem to germinate.

PESTS AND DISEASES: Amazingly free of both except for an occasional whitefly infestation on the foliage.

VARIETIES AND CULTIVARS: Cultivar 'Floribunda', a bushy form with generous blossoming; cv. 'Umbraculifera', a naturally umbrella-shaped tree with drooping leaves and a shorter mature height.

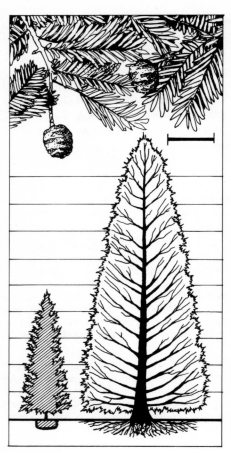

Metasequoia glyptostroboides (Dawn redwood)

Zones 5 (warm) to 10   75' to 100'   Taxodium family

Once believed to be totally extinct in the world, this dawn-of-history, cone-bearing, deciduous tree was inadvertently discovered alive and well in the eastern Szechuan province of China in the mid-1940s. Like its fossil counterpart *Ginkgo,* it has remained unchanged and unhampered for millions of years—perhaps only by being currently remote from people—and in cultivation now it is pest-free and able to grow easily at a startling rate. It makes a special feature of itself in large lawn areas.

HABIT: Very open when young but becoming densely twiggy and upright-branching with age; maintains a symmetrical, narrowly pyramidal outline to ground level; extremely fast-growing.

SEASONAL APPEARANCE: Its red-brown twigs develop bright green to bluish green, alternate, needled foliage about 1½ inches long on young trees but only to a half-inch long on older specimens; the foliage turns a rich bronze in autumn when the plant sheds both the needles and the twiglets holding them (new budding is directly beneath the separation); flowering is separated on the same tree but is not conspicuous; the deep brown, female cones are long-stalked and pendulous, about 1 inch long, and persist through the winter; its red-brown, juvenile bark matures to a furrowed gray and peels in long strips.

PREFERENCES AND PROBLEMS: Enjoys full sun and a deep, humusy, constantly moist, well-drained, slightly acid soil; will grow attractively in chalky conditions but is slower; suffers from drought and very cold, dry, winter winds; appears to thrive along streams and ponds; transplants easily but requires adequate open space for quick expansion.

PESTS AND DISEASES: None.

VARIETIES AND CULTIVARS: Cultivar 'National', a selection with a very narrow, pyramidal form.

Nyssa sylvatica (Pepperidge, Sour gum, Black gum, Upland tupelo)

Zones 5 to 9   50' to 100'   Tupelo family

Early and brilliantly glossy autumn color is its outstanding attribute. Readily adaptable to poorly drained and very wet soils, this native of the eastern United States is troublesome to move except when young because of its deep tap root. Its usual common names are provided above, but on the Massachusetts island of Martha's Vineyard it has another common name, *bung-hole tree,* from its nineteenth-century use as a nonshrinking wood for the plugs or bungs of liquid-filled barrels.

HABIT: Pyramidal when young but becoming broad-spreading and flat-topped with age; has many short, horizontal, but irregular branches downturned at the ends; slow to moderate in growth.

SEASONAL APPEARANCE: Stems are gray-brown with noticeably right-angled, stiff, short twigs and clustered, alternate foliage; the lustrous, oval, dark green, leathery leaves vary from 2 to 5 inches in length and often have red petioles; its tiny, clustered flowers appear on different trees (for the most part) but are not noticeable; the female fruiting is egg-shaped, between one-third and two-thirds inch long, and dark blue; the conspicuous autumnal color is mostly a vibrant scarlet but can also show as orange or coppery red; its red-tinged, dark gray bark eventually cracks into irregular ridges with lozenge-shaped plates.

PREFERENCES AND PROBLEMS: Likes full sun but will adapt to semishade on a deep, consistently well-moistened, lime-free soil; readily grows on poorly drained sites; its tap-rooting nature prevents easy transplanting except when young; prefers shelter from seashore winds and dislikes heavily polluted air and drought; not suitable for desert conditions; late in coming to leaf in the spring.

PESTS AND DISEASES: Unbothered except for occasional leaf blotch disease.

VARIETIES AND CULTIVARS: None; the related species *N. aquatica* of the swampy parts of the southern United States, however, is very similar in shape and growth habit but has inch-long, reddish purple fruiting and foliage between 7 and 10 inches in length; it could readily substitute in those growing areas for *N. sylvatica.*

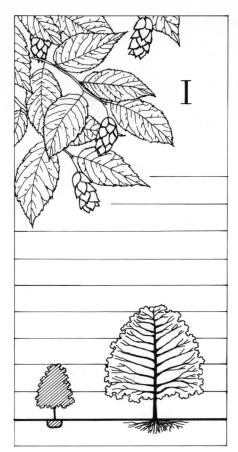

Ostrya virginiana (American hop hornbeam, Leverwood)

Zones 4 to 9   30' to 60'   Birch family

Attractive for its bright, flaky bark, break-resistant limbs and pest-free nature, this native of the eastern woods of North America has been oddly neglected for landscape use. Its slow, neat growth and pleasant summertime fruiting ought to encourage its planting more frequently, while its drought tolerance certainly can be put to good use.

HABIT: Pyramidal when juvenile but becoming rounded later with many slender, gracefully upright branches; slow-growing.

SEASONAL APPEARANCE: Slim winter twigs carry identifying clusters of three stiff, tiny, male catkins; the alternate leaves are dark yellow-green, egg-shaped, finely toothed, downy beneath, and between 3 and 5 inches long; the spring flowering is spearated on the same plant with neither sex very noticeable; its conspicuous female fruiting in midsummer becomes a 2-inch-long, pendant cluster of cream-colored, slightly inflated, papery shells resembling hops that turn light brown in autumn as the foliage becomes dull yellow; the bright gray-brown bark is thin and flaky and eventually splits into narrow, longitudinal strips free at both ends.

PREFERENCES AND PROBLEMS: Adapts well to both full sun and half shade on an average-fertility, well-drained, gravelly soil; has commendable tolerance for naturally dry soils, including slopes; its sturdy branches are rarely damaged by ice and snow; has a sparse root system and does not move well unless young.

PESTS AND DISEASES: None known.

VARIETIES AND CULTIVARS: None.

Oxydendrum arboreum [Andromeda arborea] (Sourwood, Sorrel tree, Titi)

Zones 5 to 8   35' to 80'   Heath family

Of the same family as rhododendron, mountain laurel, and andromeda, this tree form of the group is wild from Pennsylvania to Florida and west to Louisiana and southern Illinois. Its late summer flowering resembles sprays of the unrelated lily of the valley, and it also contributes bright autumn color to the landscape.

HABIT: Usually much lower in height with cultivation; slenderly pyramidal at all ages with older branches spreading and becoming slightly pendulous; slow in growth.

SEASONAL APPEARANCE: Red-brown twigs carry 3- to 8-inch, glossy, lance-shaped, heavy foliage with a long, bristle tip; new leaves emerge as bronze-red but later become dark green; the showy autumn color is a bright red with some yellowish overtones; its midsummer, terminal blossoming is composed of gracefully recurved, branched sprays of tiny, oval, white, somewhat fragrant florets similar to lily-of-the-valley flowers; the tiny, gray-tan fruit persists into winter; the bark is tan-gray with a tinge of red and becomes deeply grooved with aging.

PREFERENCES AND PROBLEMS: Best grown in full sun, but light shading is tolerated on an acid, very humusy, average-fertility, and constantly moist soil; performs better if summers are consistently cool; dislikes drought and high winds, and its new growth is easily damaged by late frost; usually needs some spring pruning since its late flowering keeps the end twigs soft longer than usual and therefore prone to drying out in winter; often has multiple stems; difficult to establish quickly even when young; intolerant of desert sites.

PESTS AND DISEASES: Nothing of importance.

VARIETIES AND CULTIVARS: None.

Paulownia tomentosa [imperialis] (Princess tree, Empress tree, Royal paulownia, Karri tree)

Zones 7 to 10   40' to 60'   Bignonia family

Although a native of China, this attractive tree is now naturalized in many mild areas of the United States. Related to *Catalpa,* it also has sizable flowering and large, coarse foliage, but here the showy blossoms are lilac-blue and pleasantly scented. Where it is fully adaptable, it makes a handsome specimen in the landscape.

HABIT: Generally low-branched and round-headed with an open crown at all ages; becomes wide-spreading with heavy limbs at maturity; rapid-growing.

SEASONAL APPEARANCE: The winter silhouette carries both the erect, brown, seed capsule stalks of the past year and the upright, terminal flower buds for the new season; these pendant, dormant new buds are velvety, rusty brown and about the size and shape of an olive; they eventually elongate in early spring (before the leaves) into yellow-throated, pale violet to lilac-blue, vanilla-scented, trumpet flowers about 2 inches long in upright, pyramidal clusters at least 1 foot or more tall; the heart-shaped, thick, dark green foliage varies from 5 to 12 inches in length, can be entire or with up to three lobes, and is downy with beige hairs beneath; its leaves appear on stout, warty twigs covered with soft, light brown hairs; the winter-persistent fruit develops in the summer as an inch-long, oval, long-pointed, glossy green capsule which matures to gray-brown; its dark brown bark is well mottled with shallow, light gray cracks.

PREFERENCES AND PROBLEMS: Thrives in full sun but accepts light shade on a deep, rich, moist, well-drained sandy loam; tolerant of city pollution and seaside locations but dislikes drought and probably does less well in the dry, windy summer weather of the lower midwest and southwest of the United States; flower buds are often severely winter-damaged north of New York City even though the plant may remain hardy; has brittle wood and is prone to litter through the year; cannot be transplanted well unless below 6 feet tall; its heavy shade and surface rooting discourage any successful underplanting as the plant matures.

PESTS AND DISEASES: None except occasional foliage mildew in very muggy weather.

VARIETIES AND CULTIVARS: None.

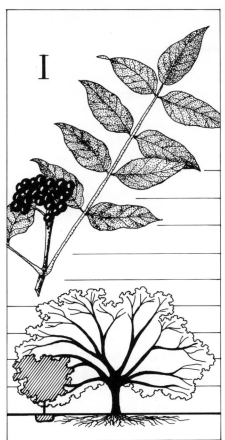

Phellodendron amurense   (Amur cork tree)

Zones 4 to 9   35′ to 50′   Rue family

A uniquely interesting tree when it develops its light tan, corky bark and the wide-spreading canopy of its mature form, this native of China and Japan is also valuable for its pest-free nature and tolerance to drought.

HABIT: Flat-topped with an inverted-pyramid shape when juvenile; wide-spreading with massive branching later; very open and more rounded with age; fast-growing.

SEASONAL APPEARANCE: Its long, slender, orange-brown twigs have bright yellow inner bark and carry opposite foliage that is pinnately compound, about 1 foot long, dark green, and glossy with five to thirteen oval leaflets; its autumn color is soft yellow; the terminal, late spring flowering is greenish and separated on different trees; female plants develop large clusters of berry-like, shiny, black, quarter-inch fruit on 3-inch stalks; the attractive buff-colored bark becomes thick, very corky, and deeply grooved with age.

PREFERENCES AND PROBLEMS: Grows rapidly in full sun on almost any soil type, including alkaline; fibrous roots make it simple to transplant at almost any age; well adapted to drought and greatly tolerant of air pollution; its crown is light-headed enough for grass to endure beneath it; female fruit can stain paving, and they readily overseed an area; its natural form is too low-headed to be pruned attractively for street planting.

PESTS AND DISEASES: Exceptionally free of both.

VARIETIES AND CULTIVARS: None.

Pistacia chinensis   (Chinese pistache)

Zones 6 (warm) to 10   40′ to 60′   Cashew family

Best grown where summers are very hot, this autumnally colorful inhabitant of China, Taiwan, and the Philippine Islands is a close relation to *Sumac,* a well-liked group of shrubs with long, pinnately compound leaves and vivid color changes in autumn. While not the nut of commerce, which is *P. vera,* this pistache provides other attributes such as a symmetrically neat appearance, a pest-free existence, and showy autumn foliage to serve handsomely as a specimen or street tree.

HABIT: Often irregular when young but maturing to a round-headed and broad silhouette with somewhat pendulous foliage; fast-growing when young but only moderate-growing later.

SEASONAL APPEARANCE: The alternatively set foliage is pinnately compound with an even number of leaflets; its leaves measure 12 to 16 inches long and are a bright green and shiny with six to ten pairs of narrow, entire leaflets about 2 inches in length; its blossoms appear on different trees near the ends of the twigs but are not conspicuous in the landscape; the female fruiting appears in 6-inch, loose clusters of oval, red-brown, inedible nuts which turn purple when ripe; the autumnal color is either bright red or orange-red; its bark is deep brown.

PREFERENCES AND PROBLEMS: Prefers full sun on any average, deep, well-drained soil, whether acid or alkaline; very tolerant of high heat and drought; often naturally shrubby and then requires pruning and staking to establish a high-headed tree form; male plants have denser-looking silhouettes; its best performance may be limited to zones 9 and 10 and the warm parts of zone 8.

PESTS AND DISEASES: Has been especially free of both but oak root fungus and verticillium wilt are now making inroads.

VARIETIES AND CULTIVARS: None.

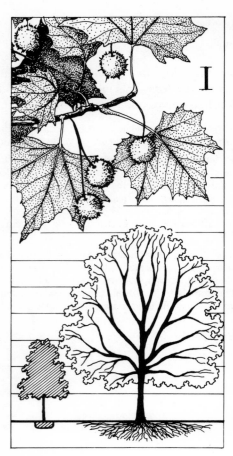

Platanus × *acerifolia* [*hybrida*] (London plane tree, Buttonwood, Sycamore)

Zones 5 to 10   80' to 120'   Sycamore family

As one of the most successful large trees for growing in heavily polluted city conditions, this hybrid between *P. occidentalis* and *P. orientalis,* developed in the eighteenth century, has proved itself time and again throughout the world. That it also has fascinating, peeling bark, attractive shade, massive limbs, and very long life only adds to its honors. Further, it also submits willingly to heavy shearing for hedges and screens. Not many other large trees offer such diversity.

HABIT: Pyramidal when young but maturing into a broad, well-balanced outline with a rounded crown and somewhat drooping branch ends; fast-growing.

SEASONAL APPEARANCE: Winter buds are large and conical, and the emerging new stem growth is densely covered for a long time with tiny hairs that can cause human irritation when finally shed in great quantities; the 5- to 8-inch, leathery foliage is maple-like (as its species name implies) with three to five shallow lobes, light green and covered with fuzz on both surfaces; the autumn color is yellow-brown or orange-brown; the midspring flowers are separated—but are near one another—on the same plant and appear in small clusters of red-toned or yellow balls that develop into pairs of 1½ inch, bristly, green-brown, seed heads suspended from the twigs by long petioles; this fruit persists long into winter and is generally infertile; its distinctive gray-tan bark exfoliates in large but thin plates to show smooth, creamy yellow patches beneath and a generally mottled appearance in time.

PREFERENCES AND PROBLEMS: Grows best in full sun or light shade on a rich, deep, moist but well-drained soil, whether acid or alkaline; adjusts well to just about any other soil type, high heat, drought, and city pollution; transplants well; benefits from biennial fertilizing to improve its resistance to diseases; its thick foliage does not disintegrate quickly after it drops; the leaves often develop chlorosis as well as scorch in desert sites.

PESTS AND DISEASES: None of serious importance except temporary disfigurement from anthracnose disease on emerging spring growth, but it has greater resistance than other species to this affliction.

VARIETIES AND CULTIVARS: Cultivar 'Pyramidalis', an upright form without drooping branch ends and with leaves having only three lobes.

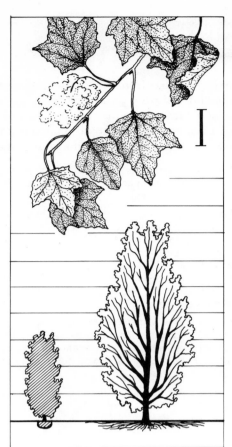

Populus alba 'Pyramidalis' ['Bolleana'] (Bolleana poplar)

Zones 4 to 10   40' to 70'   Willow family

Few poplars have either long life or attractive landscape values. This unusual native to many parts of Europe, however, offers a reasonable life span, colorful autumn foliage, and a columnar silhouette. It grows well in almost any difficult situation. While not quite stellar in the total complexity of dependable, interesting, and useful trees, it is worthwhile enough for many landscape situations to be included here.

HABIT: Narrowly columnar at all ages but never stiffly rigid; fast in development.

SEASONAL APPEARANCE: Its alternate leaves appear from twigs and winter buds noticeably covered with fine hairs; the foliage varies by the location: on vigorous shoots the deltoid leaves have three to five deep lobes but on less active, older twigs they are simple and triangular in outline; each, however, is deep gray-green on top and chalk white below from many fuzzy hairs; they flutter easily in wind because of their long, flexible petioles; the autumn color for this cultivar is a surprising deep red (most poplars become yellow-toned); the spring flowering is on different plants and appears before the leaves emerge, but neither sex has any significance; the female, fluffy seed heads, however, have more nuisance than landscape value; its light gray, smooth bark has an overtone of green with noticeable, horizontal streaks from prominent breathing pores; the deep gray, mature bark is deeply grooved.

PREFERENCES AND PROBLEMS: Enjoys either full sun or light shade on a moist, light loam but is tolerant of any soil; willingly accepts salty winds, wet sites, city pollution, and drought conditions; has invasive, shallow roots able to clog underground drains and heave pavements (much like its cousin *Salix*); tends to sucker heavily around the trunk and has brittle wood that may suffer branch damage in ice and heavy snow.

PESTS AND DISEASES: The list of both is sizable, but not all are either major afflictions or always locally troublesome.

VARIETIES AND CULTIVARS: None.

Prosopsis glandulosa torreyana (Western honey mesquite)

Zones 7 to 9   20′ to 30′   Pea family

Native to southern California, southeastern Arizona, northern Mexico, and Texas, this exceedingly deep-rooted desert plant grows only in very arid locations. It provides welcome shade necessary to making such harsh living areas hospitable. If kept too dry, it becomes a mere shrub, but consistent irrigation and occasional fertilizing improve its landscape image as a tree.

HABIT: Loose and irregular with either a very short trunk and low branching or with a multistemmed, shrubby nature in a generally pyramidal or mounded silhouette; exceedingly slow-growing unless given regular watering.

SEASONAL APPEARANCE: Has crooked branching and spiny twigs with alternate, pinnately compound foliage in a bright yellow-green; the feathery leaves range between 3 and 6 inches in length and have ten to fifteen pairs of slim, inch-long leaflets; there is no autumn coloring; the early spring 2- to 4-inch spiked flowering continues until the beginning of summer and is sweetly fragrant and greenish yellow in color; its slender fruiting pods are sugar-rich and between 2 and 6 inches long with some constrictions evident between the seeds; its dark brown bark is thick and rough with some peeling into narrow strips as it ages.

PREFERENCES AND PROBLEMS: Needs full sun and a deep, well-drained soil with regular irrigation to perform with any speed and tree shape; adjusts easily to both alkaline and dry conditions when established because of its extraordinary deep rooting (perhaps as much as 50 feet); apt to be merely a shrub on poor, rocky soil; cannot successfully be transplanted unless very small.

PESTS AND DISEASES: None.

VARIETIES AND CULTIVARS: None.

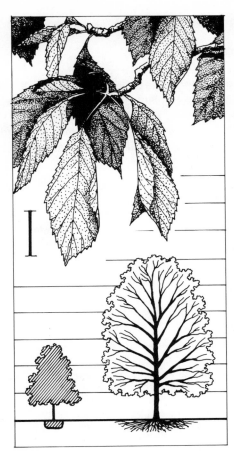

Prunus avium 'Plena' (Double-flowered mazzard cherry)

Zones 4 to 9   20' to 35'   Rose family

Prunus is a name used collectively for all those plants (perhaps 600 or more) with stone fruit (botanically, drupes) and includes the many tree and shrub forms of cherry, plum, peach, apricot, nectarine, almond, and cherry laurel. Obviously it is vital to have the species name correct when you order material with such special diversity.

All tend to bloom early—but briefly—in the spring with colors from white to deep pink, have little autumnal foliage effect, carry no persistent winter fruit, and possess relatively short life-spans. (Many, of course, have important commercial values for their fruiting.) All are sun-loving, of easy culture requiring only good, well-drained soil with reasonable moisture, and are readily transplanted. Unfortunately, this group is prone to a host of insect pests and diseases affecting every part of the plant at one time or another. Severe cold, ice, and wet snow, plus high winds, often damage or crack the weak wood, and they heal slowly from pruning. In all, their decorative values barely outweigh their disadvantages. Use them with some caution.

In this review only the cherries, plus one plum, are evaluated since these are by far the most decorative, sizable, and enduring of the group for landscape purposes. A year-round feature of some cherries is the shiny, colorful bark or an intriguing silhouette. Other values are the generous, annual flowering from either single or double (nonfruiting) flowers, attractive scents, and autumn foliage color. None on this list has any noticeable fruiting, and all dislike polluted air. These choices represent the types most often enjoyed in landscape plantings.

The species described is native to much of Europe and western Asia. The parent is dependable for its sweet, edible fruit and as a rootstock for grafting but is decoratively unimportant. This sterile, double-flowered form, however, has very early bloom with impressive showiness and, of course, no fruit.

HABIT: Tall and pyramidal when juvenile but changing to conical with age; fast-growing.

SEASONAL APPEARANCE: The alternate foliage is thin, oval, toothed, and deep green in sizes from 2 to 6 inches long; its petioles are identifiably distinctive by carrying two long-pointed, large, red or yellow nectar glands at the point of junction with the leaf blade; autumnal color varies from deep red to orange or yellow; its early spring blossoming comes well before the leaves as heavy, drooping clusters of fragrant, 1- to 1½-inch, double white flowers with up to thirty petals; there is no potential for fruit; its reddish to purplish brown, glistening bark has a metallic luster and is heavily marked with raised bands of corky, horizontal breathing pores.

PREFERENCES AND PROBLEMS: See introductory remarks.

PESTS AND DISEASES: Has a sizable catalog of each.

VARIETIES AND CULTIVARS: None.

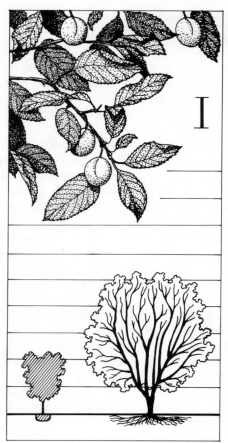

Prunus cerasifera 'Atropurpurea' [pissardii]
(Purpleleaf plum)

Zones 4 to 9   15′ to 25′   Rose family

Decoratively important for its summertime, purple-toned foliage, this plum selection comes from a nondescript parent plant native from central Asia to the Balkans. As one of the first deep-toned plants in this genus to gain international popularity, this cultivar has since been somewhat bypassed by other color variants of itself. Nevertheless, it is the more commonly available form in nurseries.

HABIT: Shows an upright, dense-foliaged, vase shape when young that alters with age to a more rounded silhouette; fast to moderate in growth depending on the climate.

SEASONAL APPEARANCE: Its new foliage emerges coppery red as the early spring flowering occurs; these single, fragrant, pale pink, three-quarter-inch blossoms appear in billowy masses but last only a brief time; its summer foliage is dark wine-red, 1 inch long, and finely toothed but does not change color in autumn; the edible, sweet, purple fruit is about 1 inch in diameter but nondecorative; its rough bark is dark purple-brown.

PREFERENCES AND PROBLEMS: See *P. avium* 'Plena'; tends to produce many crossing branches that blur the inner-stem outlines.

PESTS AND DISEASES: Susceptible to many of both and requires regular spraying maintenance to look its best.

VARIETIES AND CULLTIVARS (these are either selections from this cultivar or have been bred from it):   Cultivar 'Hollywood', a taller form with green, spring foliage turning deep red on the undersides later and with 2-inch, red-toned, edible fruit; cv. 'Newport' is a smaller type carrying purple-red leaves and pink blossoming; cv. 'Thundercloud' forms a round ball in silhouette with deep, copper-purple foliage, pink-to-white flowering, and few fruit; cv. 'Vesuvius' ('Krauter Vesuvius') is almost nonflowering but has the darkest leaves in a deep purple-black.

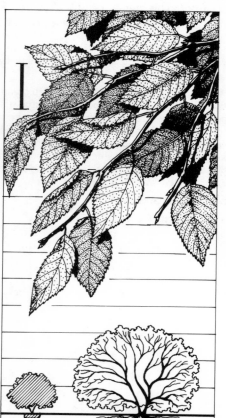

Prunus × 'Hally Jolivette'

Zones 5 to 8   10′ to 15′   Rose family

This cherry has an unusually complex genealogy since it was created by first crossing *P. subhirtella* with *P. yedoensis* and then recrossing the outcome with *P. subhirtella.* These botanic machinations were worth the wait since this is a double-flowered sort with a long blooming period, graceful branching and foliage, plus a wide-spreading, billowy nature.

HABIT: Fine-twigged and dense with irregular stems and a rounded outline at all ages; usually multi-stemmed and shrubby in appearance; fast to moderate in expansion depending on its locale.

SEASONAL APPEARANCE: Slender, tan twigs carry midspring, pink buds that open to 1½-inch, double white blossoms with a deep rose-colored center; its novel flowering continues for at least fourteen days (longer if the weather is cool) and appears in consecutive rhythms to have the plant long covered with flowers in various stages of bloom; the thin, narrowly oval leaves are between 2 and 2½ inches long and medium green; its autumn color varies from reddish to yellow-orange; it appears to set no fruit; the bark is a dull, silver-purple.

PREFERENCES AND PROBLEMS: See *P. avium* 'Plena'.

PESTS AND DISEASES: Appears less troubled than most cherries.

VARIETIES AND CULTIVARS: None.

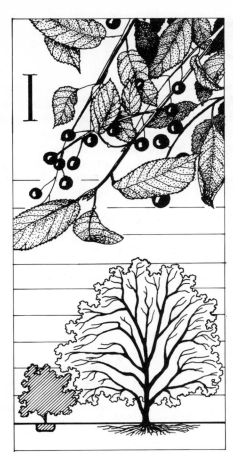

Prunus padus (Bird cherry, European bird cherry)

Zones 4 to 8   30' to 45'   Rose family

Widely distributed internationally from Europe across Asia to Japan, this is the first cherry to show foliage in the spring. Its fragrant blossoms are generously produced annually on long spikes, its foliage is consistently attractive, and it is less susceptible to inroads from the tent caterpillar.

HABIT: Has an irregular, open silhouette at all ages with upright branching; usually carries pendant end twigs; fast-growing.

SEASONAL APPEARANCE: Leafing first among the cherries, it has 2- to 4-inch, smooth, fine-toothed, somewhat oval leaves of dull, dark green with occasional hairy tufts on the undersides; the twigs are red-brown and give off a highly unpleasant odor if bruised; its autumn color varies from yellow to bronze; flowering comes in mid-spring as drooping, terminal spikes of half-inch, white, almond-scented blossoms; these flower stalks are from 3 to 6 inches long and support between ten and thirty half-inch blossoms; its egg-shaped, black fruit is about a quarter-inch wide and sharply astringent in taste; the thin, gray-black, peeling bark is dotted with light brown lenticels.

PREFERENCES AND PROBLEMS: See *P. avium* 'Plena'; unsuited for desert conditions.

PESTS AND DISEASES: Shares most of the problems of others but appears to be less nuisanced by the tent caterpillar.

VARIETIES AND CULTIVARS: Variety *commutata* blooms about three weeks earlier than the parent and has coarsely toothed foliage; cv. 'Plena' has larger and double flowers with a longer period of bloom; cv. 'Watereri', single-flowered with spikes up to 8 inches.

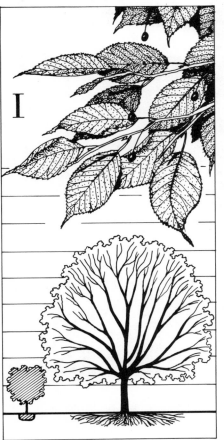

Prunus sargentii (Sargent cherry)

Zones 4 to 9   40' to 50'   Rose family

Impressive in its list of virtues, this native of northern Japan, Korea, and the Sakhalin Peninsula offers great size, good hardiness, showy flowering, autumn foliage color, and lustrous bark. It has a deserved popularity.

HABIT: Upright with a symmetrical form, dense foliage, and a rounded top; vigorous-growing.

SEASONAL APPEARANCE: The alternate, oval leaves are bronze-toned when young and turn glossy, dark green later; the foliage tends to be somewhat pendulous from its good size of 3 to 5 inches; the autumnal color appears early and is usually vivid red but may also be orange-red to bronze; the midspring blossoming appears before the leaves as clusters of 1¼-inch, single, deep rose blossoms; the nonshowy summer fruit is oval, a third-inch wide, and dark purple-black; its shiny, mahogany brown, trunk bark becomes dull gray-brown at the base with maturity and peels in coarse, curly strips.

PREFERENCES AND PROBLEMS: See *P. avium* 'Plena'; has proved to be highly intolerant of smog.

PESTS AND DISEASES: Suffers occasional bouts with most of the problems of its cousins.

VARIETIES AND CULTIVARS: Cultivar 'Columnaris', a narrowly upright form.

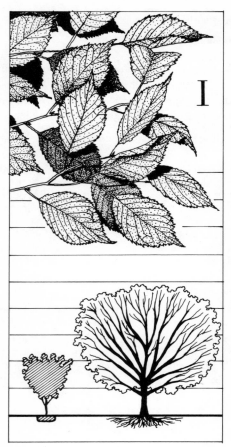

Prunus serrulata (Japanese flowering cherry, Oriental cherry)

Zones 5 to 9   20′ to 25′   Rose family

While the Japanese parent of these selections can reach to 60 feet, it is uncommon to find it now in cultivation since the more attractive hybrids readily surpass it for beauty and neat behavior. This process of selecting desirable forms has been pursued in Japan for hundreds of years, and the true origin of some types is now lost in history, but they still have worldwide appeal even without known pedigrees. Most nursery offerings today are grafted plants on *P. avium* roots, which accounts for the thick trunk.

HABIT: Variable by cultivar but usually compact; quick-growing.

SEASONAL APPEARANCE: The smooth, shining foliage is often red-toned when emerging but turns dark green by summer and can be from 2½ to 5 inches long; the autumn color varies from plant to plant in this list; most are fruitless, but if found, the fruit will be small and dark purple or black; the bark usually is nonpeeling and is often red-toned.

PREFERENCES AND PROBLEMS: See *P. avium* 'Plena'; not suited to desert growing; zones 5 to 8 are preferred in the eastern United States.

PESTS AND DISEASES: Susceptible to quite a few of both.

VARIETIES AND CULTIVARS: Cultivar 'Amanogawa', a narrowly upright form with light pink, semidouble flowers and a slight fragrance; cv. 'Beni Hoshi' ('Pink Star') has arching branches and a domed outline with vivid pink, single flowers; cv. 'Fugenzo' ('Kofugen', 'James H. Veitch'), a late-blooming sort with large, 2½-inch, soft pink, double blossoms and bronze new foliage; cv. 'Kwanzan', a popular, stiffly upright form with pendulous, deep rose-pink, double flowers about 2½ inches wide and reddish orange autumn color; cv. 'Shirofugen' ('White Goddess') has late-arriving, large, double pink flowers fading to white plus bronze new growth; cv. 'Shirotae' ('Mt. Fuji') with double or semidouble, fragrant, pure white flowers and usually yellow foliage in the autumn; cv. 'Shogetsu', a shorter type with 2-inch, very double, pale blush flowers; cv. 'Ukon' with bronze new growth and pendulous, semidouble, pale yellow flowers and often orange-red autumnal foliage.

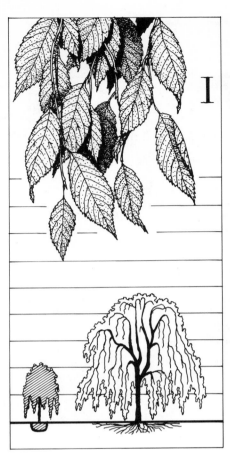

Prunus subhirtella (Higan cherry, Rosebud cherry)

Zones 5 to 9   20′ to 25′   Rose family

This species from Japan is not usual in cultivation for itself nowadays since the cultivars have more popular appeal. All its types have filmy, generous flowering well before leaves emerge but offer no autumn foliage color. The drawing shows the popular weeping form.

HABIT: Rounded with twiggy denseness and upright branching; moderate in growth.

SEASONAL APPEARANCE: Hairy, very slender twigs carry thin, medium green, toothed, oval leaves between 1 and 3 inches long without autumn coloring; flowering comes freely before the foliage in early spring as clusters of soft rose or almost-white, three-quarter-inch blossoms with notched petals; its infrequent fruit is round, shiny, black, and about a quarter-inch wide; the bark is tan-brown and somewhat shiny.

PREFERENCES AND PROBLEMS: See *P. avium* 'Plena'; intolerant of constant smog; perhaps at its best only in zones 6 and 7 in the eastern United States.

PESTS AND DISEASES: Has its full share of both.

VARIETIES AND CULTIVARS: Variety *ascendens* is fully erect with lance-shaped leaves and white flowers; cv. 'Autumnalis', a shorter type with partly double flowering and both a full spring and a partial autumn bloom; cv. 'Pendula', the very popular weeping form with single, pale pink blossoms and shiny, deep green leaves; cv. 'Rosea', an erect, pink-flowered type; cv. 'Yae-shidare-higan', similar in form to 'Pendula' but with double, pink flowering.

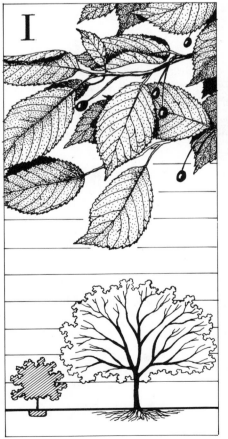

Prunus yeodensis (Yoshino cherry, Potomac cherry)

Zones 6 to 9   30′ to 45′   Rose family

One of the most widely planted ornamental cherries, this inhabitant of Japan is probably a natural hybrid of *P. subhirtella* and *P. serrulata* (or *P. speciosa*) since it will come true to form when grown from seed. Its gracefully open nature, glossy foliage, and breath-taking flowering masses have charmed people for generations. One of the most spectacularly well-known displays of them is around the Tidal Basin in Washington, D.C.

HABIT: Slender, wide-spreading, curved branching produces a dome-shaped outline at all ages; fast-growing.

SEASONAL APPEARANCE: Its 3- to 5-inch, oval to wedge-shaped leaves are dark, glossy green on the top and somewhat fuzzy beneath; they have no important autumn color; the early spring blossoming comes before the leaves and is composed of slightly fragrant, single, three-quarter-inch flowers of pale pink fading to white; its unimportant fruiting is small and shiny black; the bark is mahogany-brown.

PREFERENCES AND PROBLEMS: See *P. avium* 'Plena'; this is a relatively short-lived plant; prefers zones 6 to 8 in the eastern parts of the United States; does not thrive in desert situations.

PESTS AND DISEASES: Prone to a considerable number of them.

VARIETIES AND CULTIVARS: Cultivar 'Akebono' ('Daybreak'), a smaller form with double, soft pink blossoms.

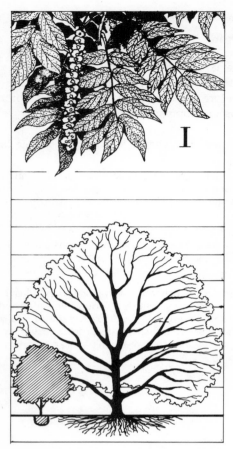

Pterocarya fraxinifolia [*caucasica*]   (Caucasian wingnut)

Zones 6 to 9   50′ to 100′   Walnut family

Uncommon yet to find in cultivation, this fast-growing tree from the Caucasus Mountains to northern Iran is unusual for its deep green, compound leaves and strings of light green fruiting in summer. Since it is also widely hardy, a good shade producer and pest-free, it deserves a little more public interest. They grow especially well near ponds and streams.

HABIT: Usually low-branched with a wide-spreading, pyramidal, dense crown; rapid in growth.

SEASONAL APPEARANCE: Round, stout, grayish twigs produce pinnately compound, alternate foliage up to 18 inches long with smooth, glossy, dark green, nonstalked leaflets changing to yellow-green in the autumn; its uninteresting flowers are separated on the same tree and are pendulous, light green catkins produced from the springtime leaf bud; the female fruit in summer is a lengthy (up to 20 inches) string of drooping nuts well surrounded by three-quarter-inch, circular, light green wings and generously produced throughout the plant; the bark is reddish brown and deeply furrowed with aging.

PREFERENCES AND PROBLEMS: Best grown in full sun on a consistently moist, deep soil; very tolerant of compacted soil, drought, and high winds; has aggressive surface rooting; occasionally develops heavy thickets of suckering stems around the base.

PESTS AND DISEASES: Currently untroubled by either.

VARIETIES AND CULTIVARS: None; the less-hardy (zones 8 to 10) *P. stenoptera* from China is very similar in appearance and is also very tolerant of dry, compacted, or sterile soil conditions.

Pterostyrax hispidus   (Epaulette tree, Fragrant epaulette tree)

Zones 6 to 9   20′ to 50′   Storax family

Its early summer bloom and its drooping flower clusters can remind you of the epaulette shoulder braiding on military uniforms, while the pleasant fragrance suggests a lot of other attractive things. Not common in cultivation, this visitor from Japan and China has a novel attractiveness for its late blooming and gray, bristly seed pods in winter. As a bonus, it seems to be completely trouble-free.

HABIT: Carries slender, spreading branches low to the ground at all ages; develops an open, rounded outline; moderate in growth.

SEASONAL APPEARANCE: Its alternate, toothed leaves are oblong, light green with silvery undersides, and between 3 and 7 inches in length; their autumn color is a nonconspicuous yellow-green; the early summer flowering is from clusters of small, bell-shaped, creamy white, fragrant blossoms with prominently extended stamens, all arranged on drooping, 5- to 10-inch panicles with the appearance of fringe; its tiny, gray, spindle-shaped, ten-ribbed, dry fruit pods are very densely bristly and remain dangling through the winter; the dark gray bark exfoliates in thin strips.

PREFERENCES AND PROBLEMS: Full sun is best on a moist, sandy, acid loam; has a distaste for shallow, chalky, or poorly drained sites; needs protection from strong winds and from sudden changes of temperature in winter.

PESTS AND DISEASES: Apparently unbothered.

VARIETIES AND CULTIVARS: None.

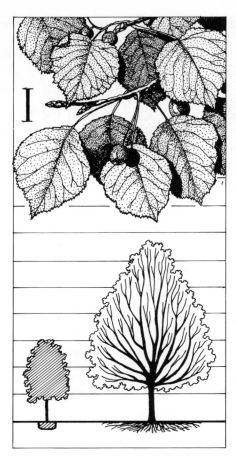

Pyrus calleryana selections (Callery pear)

Zones 6 to 9   30' to 50'   Rose family

The Chinese parent plant is not nearly as desirable in shape or size as any of the new cultivars, which have lately become highly popular as pest-free, hardy, city-tolerant, shapely, colorful introductions of great landscape value. All share the same basic descriptive information. 'Bradford' is shown.

HABIT: Generally conical and dense both in twigginess and foliage with a very upright trunk and branching; fast in growth.

SEASONAL APPEARANCE: Its prominent winter buds are tan, fuzzy, and a quarter-inch tall; flowering is in midspring before the leaves and literally covers all the tree with 3-inch clusters of pure white, inch-wide blossoms with noticeably black stamens; the hard, globe-shaped, half- to 1-inch fruit is russet-colored and prominently dotted brown; its broadly oval, wavy-edged, very glossy, alternate leaves are dark green and between 1½ and 3 inches long; they change in autumn to either a gleaming red-bronze or reddish orange and persist long into the season without damage; its gray-brown, smooth bark is tinged with red and becomes furrowed at the base with age.

PREFERENCES AND PROBLEMS: Prefers full sun on a damp, heavy soil but is remarkably tolerant of dryness; adapts well to polluted city air and to snow-melting chemicals on pavements.

PESTS AND DISEASES: None of importance; is reliably resistant to fire blight.

VARIETIES AND CULTIVARS: Cultivar 'Aristocrat', an open form with more horizontal branching and darker, narrower foliage than 'Bradford'; cv. 'Bradford', an egg-shaped form with noticeably ascending branches and twigs, long popular in cultivation as an accent or street tree; cv. 'Chanticleer' a narrow, conical type with tightly upright branching and a width equal to half its height.

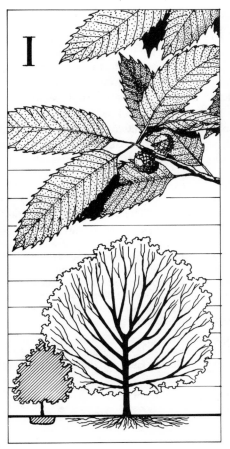

Quercus acutissima (Sawtooth oak)

Zones 7 to 9   35' to 50'   Beech family

With over 800 species and cultivars growing somewhere in the north temperate zones of the world, plus some few in tropical and subtropical parts of Asia, the oak is certainly a well-known plant. With all the expected diversity from such an international distribution, there has to be some unifying characteristic for identification. Its uniqueness is in its brown, acorn fruit; only an oak has them.

Yet beyond that simple botanic characteristic, the oak is characterized by other features perhaps not so totally exclusive but at least pertinent. Oaks have vaunted sturdiness, remarkably long life, unusually wide adaptability from icecap to jungle, diverse leaf outlines from simple to lobed to sharp-pointed, persistent or deciduous foliage, truly magnificent spread, and noble size. What other tree matches that varied range?

All oaks have clusters of terminal buds and nonshowy, pendant catkins for flowers. They are simple to grow and have few demands for culture. In general, they all like full sun and an average-fertility soil as long as it is acid. A few types want dry, gravelly conditions while others need swampy wetlands to survive. If some are snug in frigid climates, others tolerate only balmy breezes. Whatever the growing conditions, there is likely to be an oak to satisfy your needs.

Unfortunately, oaks are prey to some of the most devastating insect and disease afflictions known. In the eastern United States the gypsy moth larva can devour whole forests of foliage in a season, while in the western parts of the United States the oak moth has its own voracious eating habits on leaves. Then there is the oak wilt disease so prevalent in the north central United States, plus the devastating oak root fungus of the far western sections of the country. Each of these problems can bring either death or severe maiming within a short time.

Yet even with the most threatening handicap on its doorstep, the oak continues as always in adapting to its changing circumstances. The oak is not called durable in haste and will somehow continue to give pleasure to our landscapes for all the time that is left.

The species described here is native to China, Korea, and Japan but is not yet commonly known or used in the United States even though it has few pests, a glossily polished foliage, and a nonvigorous, neat habit of growth.

HABIT: Broadly pyramidal and dense in its juvenile stage but becoming broadly oval and more open with age; its branching is mostly curved and upright; moderate-growing when young but slow-growing when older.

SEASONAL APPEARANCE: Its new leaves are downy at first but become narrowly oblong, between 3 and 7 inches in length, shiny, dark green above and bright green beneath with bristle-like teeth along the margins (much like a true chestnut [*Castanea*] has) and turn a clear yellow in the autumn; the flower catkins are separated on the same tree and emerge from the leaf bud; neither sex is colorful or noticeable when in bloom; its acorns are without stalks, between one-half and three-quarters inch long; its cup encloses two-thirds of the fruit and has spiny, spreading scales; this fruit matures in the second year; the gray-brown bark is deeply ridged and furrowed with age.

PREFERENCES AND PROBLEMS: Rich, moist soil in full sun is best; tolerant to less favorable soils and is generally of easy culture; may be prone to iron chlorosis in some areas.

PESTS AND DISEASES: None of importance.

VARIETIES AND CULTIVARS: None.

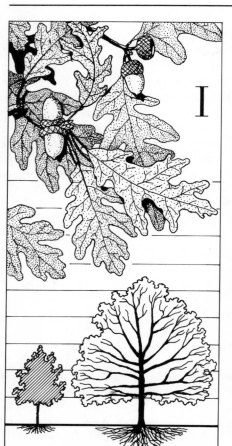

Quercus alba (White oak)

Zones 4 to 9   50′ to 100′   Beech family

More than likely you will never have time enough to raise a white oak to its full majesty in your own lifetime. Not only are they sluggish, but their deep roots make them poor risks to move unless very small. With a potential life-span of 300 years, this native to much of the eastern United States can be an imposing champion of oaks. Always preserve any found growing naturally well, especially since they are easily disturbed by any nearby construction activity. Its rugged outline and glimmering, silvery bark justify your particularity here.

HABIT: Irregularly pyramidal when young but becomes densely foliaged and broadly wide-spreading with mostly horizontal branching later; very slow-growing.

SEASONAL APPEARANCE: New foliage is pale pink and very densely hairy; the full-sized leaves are 5 to 9 inches long, have five to nine rounded lobes, and are blue-green or bright green in color with gray fuzz beneath; its autumnal change of color ranges from plain brown to purplish red; some dried foliage usually remains in winter; flowering is unimportant visually; the acorns are mostly short-stalked, usually over a half-inch long with a chestnut-brown cup that caps one-quarter of the sweet-tasting nut; these mature in one year; the young bark is light ash-gray and scaly, but older bark becomes deeply fissured with narrow, rounded ridges.

PREFERENCES AND PROBLEMS: Grows equally in full sun or light shade on a deep, consistently moist, well-drained, acid soil; adapts well to dry, gravelly, or sandy soils; intolerant to alkaline conditions (and fails to endure in Europe); difficult to transplant successfully unless very small.

PESTS AND DISEASES: Unfortunately it is prone to many of both.

VARIETIES AND CULTIVARS: None.

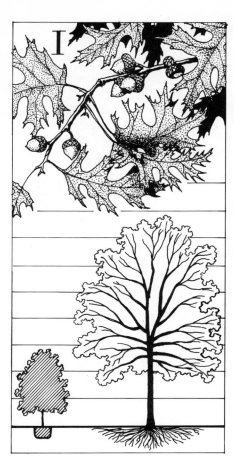

Quercus coccinea (Scarlet oak)

Zones 4 to 9   50' to 80'   Beech family

Troublesome to move with ease because of deep tap roots, this native of the eastern and central portions of the United States is more slim than many other oaks in general outline and offers a brilliantly showy, autumnal foliage display.

HABIT: Pyramidal in youth but altering to a rounded outline later with an open crown; growth can be rapid when fully established.

SEASONAL APPEARANCE: Its emerging growth is bright red and heavily pubescent; the summer foliage appears on slim twigs and is about 6 inches long with seven to nine, deep-cut lobes having bristle tips in a bright, glossy, olive-green color with a yellow midrib; the leaves turn brilliantly red in the autumn and persist for a long time; its blossoming is nondescript; the acorns are either stalk-less or have very diminutive ones and mature in two years; the half- to 1-inch fruit is enveloped by a light red-brown, shiny cup that captures up to half the nut; its smooth, light brown to gray-brown bark is seamed with thin, red streaks, while the older bark turns very dark gray and shows corrugation from irregular, shallow grooves that are lightly scaly.

PREFERENCES AND PROBLEMS: Enjoys full sun on a light, dry, sandy but fertile soil; intolerant of limed soils altogether; roots are close to the surface and sensitive to compaction; has proved troublesome to transplant except when small and must be given good pre- and aftercare to survive.

PESTS AND DISEASES: Not especially bothered by either.

VARIETIES AND CULTIVARS: Cultivar 'Superba' ('Splendens'), a form with higher gloss on the leaves.

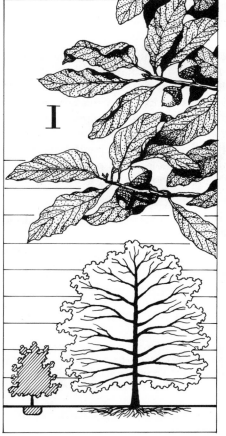

Quercus imbricaria (Shingle oak, Laurel oak)

Zones 5 to 9   50' to 60'   Beech family

Retaining its lower branching to ground level if well grown, this native of the central United States from Pennsylvania to Arkansas and south to Georgia transplants with far greater ease than most other oaks. It contributes good shade, makes a fine windbreak, and can even be readily trimmed into a topiary shape as a formal hedge or screen. Its main common name derives from the ease with which shingles for roofing were made from its wood by settlers.

HABIT: Irregularly pyramidal when juvenile, changing to a broadly round-headed and open silhouette when older with few major branches; moderate growth rate.

SEASONAL APPEARANCE: Its new twigs are dark green but convert to deep brown by the second season; the emerging foliage is bright red (yet in Europe it emerges, peculiarly, as soft yellow) but soon changes to deep, lustrous green with pale, fuzzy undersides; the leathery leaf outline greatly resembles a laurel and is between 4 and 6 inches long with entirely smooth margins; it becomes dark red to rusty yellow in the autumn; the springtime, green-brown flower catkins are separated on the same tree but have no colorful significance; its paired acorns are only three-quarters inch long and become enclosed to almost half their length by the red-brown cup; they mature in the second year; young bark is smooth, glossy, and light brown, but older bark is irregularly but shallowly cracked into gray-brown scales tinged with red.

PREFERENCES AND PROBLEMS: Best grown in full sun on a rich, acid, deep, constantly moist but well-drained soil; does not tolerate an alkaline condition; transplants with much less difficulty than many other oaks; can be tightly sheared easily for hedges.

PESTS AND DISEASES: Has few troubles.

VARIETIES AND CULTIVARS: None.

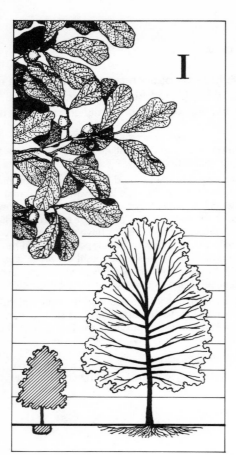

Quercus nigra [aquatica] (Water oak, Possum oak)

Zones 7 to 10   60' to 80'   Beech family

A fast-growing tree with an affinity for wet places, this native of the eastern United States from Delaware to Florida and west to Texas is usually partially evergreen in its southernmost locations. It moves with great ease and develops quickly into a sizable shade tree without problems.

HABIT: Generally conical at all ages with a straight trunk and gracefully slender, ascending branches; fast-growing.

SEASONAL APPEARANCE: The new twigs are reddish and carry wedge-shaped, slender, nontoothed leaves only 2 to 3 inches long; they are a dull, blue-green color above but lighter-toned below and may have several shallow lobes at the tip end; the autumn color is green since many leaves persist until late winter in their natural state; its flowers are on different parts of the twigs and have a reddish color; the acorn is about a half-inch long with a saucer-shaped, light red-brown cap covering up to one-third of the nut; they fully ripen in the second season; its light, red-brown bark has thin scales when juvenile but matures to nearly black with rough, wide ridges.

PREFERENCES AND PROBLEMS: Enjoys full sun on a rich, acid, sandy soil with plentiful moisture; able to exist satisfactorily on any wet soil that is not permanently under water; has no tolerance for an alkaline soil; transplants with simple ease.

PESTS AND DISEASES: Appears to be unbothered by either.

VARIETIES AND CULTIVARS: None.

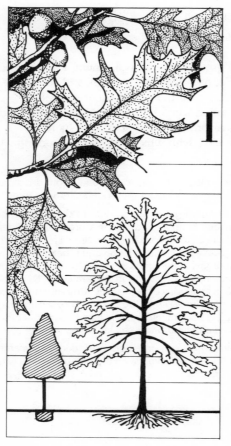

Quercus palustris (Pin oak, Spanish oak)

Zones 5 to 9   60' to 80'   Beech family

The foremost qualities of popularity for this inhabitant of moist woods from Massachusetts to Delaware and then west to Arkansas are the easily moved fibrous roots and its distinctive habit of carrying three types of branching. Upper limbs are upright, the middle branches are mostly horizontal, while the lowest limbs are downturned. Removing the bottom branching, a usual need when the tree is installed near to traffic of cars or people, soon triggers the horizontal ones to become pendulous in their stead. This oak is also an obvious good choice for a ground-hugging specimen where it can have both adequate room and freedom from pruning necessities.

HABIT: Pyramidal with a rounded, open top and carries slender main limbs with dense, twiggy branching; generally rapid in growth.

SEASONAL APPEARANCE: Has many short, spur twigs on slim branching; its smooth, glossy, bright green foliage is 3 to 5 inches long with broadly cleft lobes ending in bristle tips; the autumn color varies from scarlet to russet-bronze; the green flowering appears with the leaves and has no visual appeal; its half-inch female fruit is dome-shaped and squat with the cup enclosing one-third of the red-brown nut; it matures in two years; the tight bark changes from light gray to dark gray-brown with flat, scaly ridges.

PREFERENCES AND PROBLEMS: Thrives on a rich, consistently moist, well-drained, acid site in full sun but is adaptable to wetter, poorly drained, or clay soil situations; readily tolerant of the fumes of city air but will not accept an alkaline soil; transplants with ease because of its fibrous rooting; occasionally shows leaf chlorosis if soil conditions are not fully to its liking.

PESTS AND DISEASES: Relatively unhampered except for infrequent scale and caterpillar nuisances.

VARIETIES AND CULTIVARS: None.

Quercus phellos (Willow oak)

Zones 6 (warm) to 9   40′ to 60′   Beech family

Here is the finest textured oak of all with its very slender, unlobed foliage and the same transplanting ease of *Q. palustris*. Well distributed from New York to Florida and west to Texas, it is highly considered as an attractive shade tree with many desirable qualities. In its southernmost growing areas it may be partially evergreen.

HABIT: Neatly pyramidal when juvenile but altering later to a gracefully conical or round-headed mature specimen witn dense twigginess and slender branching; rapid-growing and long-lived.

SEASONAL APPEARANCE: Carries an abundance of short twigs with very slim, willow-like leaves between a one-quarter and 1 inch wide and from 2 to 5 inches in length with both ends tapered; the lustrous top surfaces are a bright green, but the undersides retain a dulled, fuzzy appearance; its color in autumn is either a pleasant pale yellow or russet, depending on its locale; the spring flowering has no appeal; the tiny, yellow-brown acorns are only a half-inch long with shallow, saucer-like, pale russet cups; they ripen in the second year; its very hard, smooth, light red-brown, juvenile bark ages to almost black with shallow, narrow grooves.

PREFERENCES AND PROBLEMS: Grows well in either full sun or light shade on an acid, constantly moist, average-fertility soil; will adapt to poorly drained sites and to occasional flooding; does not accept alkaline soil conditions well; is readily transplanted because of a fibrous root system but moves better if less than 15 feet tall.

PESTS AND DISEASES: Infrequently bothered with bark scale on young growth.

VARIETIES AND CULTIVARS: None.

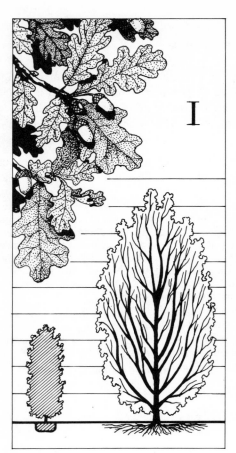

Quercus robur 'Fastigiata' (Pyramidal English oak)

Zones 5 to 8   40' to 60'   Beech family

The parent plant is a fast-growing native of Europe, the British Isles, northern Africa, and western Asia, but it is not a totally adaptable tree in many parts of this country since it has a haphazard response to cold and our too variable climate changes. The popular upright form here listed is far more cooperative and reliable but often is highly susceptible to summertime mildew disfigurement.

HABIT: Narrowly columnar with upright branching from ground level when young but becoming more broadly oval with age; may develop several main leaders; fast-growing, especially in mild climates.

SEASONAL APPEARANCE: Its 2- to 5-inch foliage is shiny, dark green on top, and pale blue-green beneath with six to fourteen rounded lobes and shallow clefts; the autumn coloring is usually nonexistent since the leaves shed green or change only to dull brown; it often retains some dried foliage through the dormant period; the yellow-green, spring catkins have no decorative value; its oval, yellow-green, 1-inch acorns are held uniquely on long, 1- to 3-inch stalks and are covered by cups that enclose one-third of the nut; they ripen in the first year; the dark gray bark is deeply furrowed.

PREFERENCES AND PROBLEMS: Prefers full sun but is adaptable to light shading on a well-drained, better than average, moist soil that is acid or even somewhat alkaline; transplants with relative ease when small; appears to be resistant to moderate city pollution; not suited for desert growing conditions.

PESTS AND DISEASES: Generally unaffected by insects but is prone to heavy mildew attacks in hot, muggy summers.

VARIETIES AND CULTIVARS: None.

Quercus rubra [*rubra maxima, borealis*] (Red oak, Northern red oak)

Zones 5 to 10   60' to 80'   Beech family

Native to much of eastern North America, this well-liked oak has attractive adaptability to city conditions, grows with ease and speed, is deep-rooted, and usually transplants without problem. It is frequently seen in quantity as a shade tree on streets and parkways.

HABIT: Usually broadly pyramidal when young but matures to a dome-shaped, wide-spreading, dense form with upcurved branching; vigorous-growing at all ages.

SEASONAL APPEARANCE: The lustrous, dark green leaves are between 4 and 9 inches long with seven to nine, tapered lobes having bristle tips; they can color in fall from rich red to russet or only plain brown; its very early spring, green-brown catkins are separated on the twigs and have nothing noticeable about them; the three-quarters to 1¼-inch, red-brown acorn is enclosed by a tight-scaled cap for about one-quarter of its length and matures only in the second season; the bark on young trees is smooth and slate-gray but matures to a deeper color with broad but shallow, vertical ridges; the upper limbs usually show noticeable, long, dark streaking over the gray, much as if paint had been spilled at a branch junction.

PREFERENCES AND PROBLEMS: Grows best in full sun on a rich, moist, acid loam with good drainage; adapts reasonably well to less agreeable conditions and adjusts very satisfactorily to city pollution; usually has deep rooting and accepts some drought when established fully; transplants easily in all growing areas but accepts very alkaline soil with some reluctance.

PESTS AND DISEASES: Maintains a good resistance to both.

VARIETIES AND CULTIVARS: None.

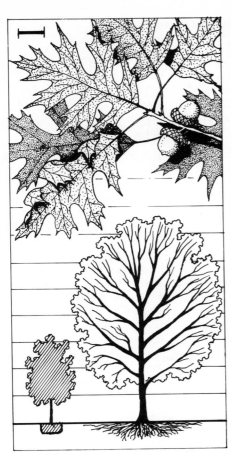

Quercus shumardii (Shumard's red oak)

Zones 6 to 9   75′ to 120′   Beech family

Able to be transplanted more successfully than *Q. coccinea*, this native oak from the southeastern portions of the United States is similar in foliage and general outline. Remarkably free of insect and disease nuisances, it differs botanically by showing tufts of light hairs on the undersides of the leaves.

HABIT: Somewhat irregular in outline when juvenile but developing an oval to round head when older; the stout branching is mostly upright with an open crown; fast-growing, especially in rich, moist soil.

SEASONAL APPEARANCE: New twigs are bright green and smooth; the dark, glossy, 6- to 8-inch leaves have whitish hairs in downy tufts along the axils of the veins on the undersides; each leaf is deeply cleft and ends with sharp-pointed, divided tips; the autumn color ranges from a predominant scarlet to dull gold; the springtime flowers are green-brown and not conspicuous; its acorn is light brown, about 1 inch in length, and carries a thick, light brown cup down one-quarter of the nut; young trunks have smooth, thin, light gray bark, while older ones develop thick, corky, rugged-looking bark in pale red-brown with scaly ridges.

PREFERENCES AND PROBLEMS: Likes full sun and a deep, moist, rich, and well-drained site; appears to tolerate moderately alkaline conditions without developing leaf chlorosis; produces many acorns but few seedlings; dislikes very cold or windy sites; transplants more easily than *Q. coccinea*.

PESTS AND DISEASES: Unusually free of both.

VARIETIES AND CULTIVARS: None.

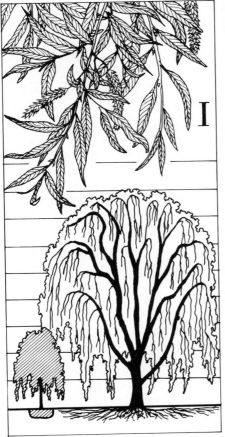

Salix alba tristis [*vitellina* 'Pendula'] (Golden weeping willow)

Zones 2 to 10   50′ to 75′   Willow family

All willows are water lovers, grow very fast, and have brittle wood, plus an invasive, dense rooting which easily clogs drainage lines. Their foliage is prone to many insect attacks, and there is little autumnal color worth noting. Nevertheless, they are consistently popular, especially the weeping types, and this graceful native from Europe, north Africa, and much of Asia is the hardiest of the lot. Its richly golden twigs add a bright note to a winter setting, making it superior to other tree forms for unusual landscape value.

HABIT: Sturdily upright with long, pendulous branching often touching the ground; very rapid-growing at all ages.

SEASONAL APPEARANCE: Bright yellow or tan-yellow slender twigs carry narrow, 1½- to 4-inch, shiny, bright green to yellow-green leaves with silvered undersides; the early spring flowers are greenish and appear on separate plants; autumn color is a weak yellow; the tiny fruit capsules are downy and have no ornamental value; its bark is smooth and greenish yellow when juvenile but ages to dark gray with deep furrows.

PREFERENCES AND PROBLEMS: Grows thriftily in full sun on any average, moist soil; dislikes shallow, chalky, or very dry locations; its brittle wood readily shatters in ice storms and windstorms; apt to litter constantly during the year; may require pruning and staking support to establish an attractive, upright habit when young; avoid late winter and springtime pruning since the cuts bleed excessively.

PESTS AND DISEASES: Susceptible to a wide array of both.

VARIETIES AND CULTIVARS: None.

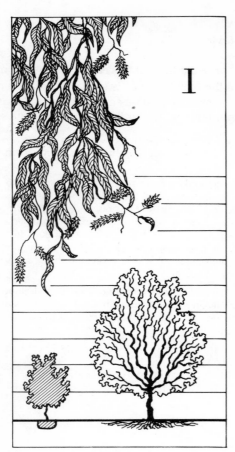

Salix matsudana 'Tortuosa' (Dragon-claw willow, Corkscrew willow)

Zones 5 to 9   25′ to 40′   Willow family

Perhaps best located where it can be seen in winter against open sky, this bizarre-looking plant is from a parent originally found in northern Asia. Its contorted branching and wavy leaves offer a novelty for special landscape situations. The foliage arrives late but lasts longer than other willows.

HABIT: Upright with spirally twisted branchlets; often multistemmed; irregular in outline when young but usually develops an oval to rounded silhouette later; moderate in growth.

SEASONAL APPEARANCE: Its waxy, bright green, 3- to 4-inch, slender, alternate leaves are wavy and curled with whitened undersides; the autumnal color is often golden yellow; its catkin flowers are pale yellow and nonshowy, while the fruiting in late spring is merely white, cottony, tiny seeds; the brownish green bark is generally smooth.

PREFERENCES AND PROBLEMS: Best situated in full sun on a consistently damp site of average fertility; adaptable to more dryness than many other willows; tends to be short-lived and to litter dead twigs most of the time; requires thinning out periodically if purchased as a thicket form.

PESTS AND DISEASES: Appears to be scab- and canker-resistant as well as reasonably free of major insect pests.

VARIETIES AND CULTIVARS: Cultivar 'Golden Curls' offers yellow-toned twigs and somewhat slower growth.

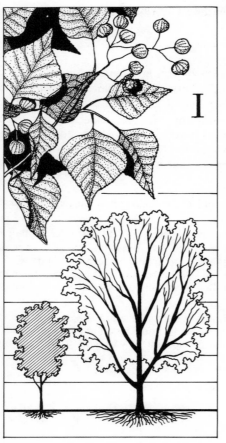

Sapium sebiferum (Chinese tallow tree, Vegetable tallow)

Zones 8 and 9   30′ to 40′   Spurge family

Showing the leaf form and quaking nature of an aspen, this native from China and Japan is happily free of insect and disease nuisances and tolerant of almost any soil condition where it is hardy. Its ready adaptability to city conditions ranks it high for street use.

HABIT: Upright with an oval crown when juvenile but changing to a wide-spreading, somewhat irregular and open head with stout branches later; often develops multiple stems at the base; fast-growing.

SEASONAL APPEARANCE: The 1- to 3-inch, light green, oval leaves taper sharply to a shallow point and flutter easily with any breeze; the autumn palette ranges from yellow to brilliant red but occasionally shows plum or orange in some growing areas; the 4-inch, catkin-like, terminal flower spikes are yellow; its hard fruiting capsules open to reveal waxy, white seeds persistent for many months; the bark is a dull gray-brown.

PREFERENCES AND PROBLEMS: Enjoys full sun on a consistently moist soil of average fertility; prefers a slightly acid soil but tolerates almost any conditions; best transplanted when very young; its milky sap is poisonous.

PESTS AND DISEASES: Outstandingly free of both.

VARIETIES AND CULTIVARS: None.

Sophora japonica (Japanese pagoda tree, Chinese scholar tree)

Zones 5 to 10   50′ to 80′   Pea family

Trees with bloom in late summer are scarce, and this inhabitant from China and Korea not only has that quality but also is undaunted by the pollution of cities and tolerant of both heat and dryness. For over 1000 years it has graced Oriental temple grounds, which accounts for its somewhat unusual common names.

HABIT: Generally round-headed at all ages with ascending but wide-spreading branches and a short trunk; moderate in growth rate.

SEASONAL APPEARANCE: The smooth, bright green twigs carry compound, fern-like, alternate foliage made up of three to eight pairs of oval leaflets about 2 inches in length; the entire leaf may measure between 6 and 10 inches and is medium to dark green on top with a gray-toned underside; the foliage drops green in the autumn; the late July to August flowering persists for roughly a month as terminal, open sprays of pea-like, yellow-white, half-inch florets capable of massing to a 15-inch length; its 3-inch, pendulous fruit pods are first green, then yellow-green, and finally brown-green with potential persistence into winter; these translucent, fleshy fruits show noticeable constrictions between seeds; the pale gray-brown bark darkens with age and becomes corrugated.

PREFERENCES AND PROBLEMS: Performs best in full sun on an average, sandy loam with good drainage; very adaptable to city conditions as well as to drought and high heat; blooming is often inconsistent if grown where summers are cool and damp; fallen blossoms can stain pavements; tends to branch low to the ground and cannot be pruned attractively for street use; fruit drop may create a maintenance nuisance.

PESTS AND DISEASES: Unbothered by either.

VARIETIES AND CULTIVARS: Cultivar 'Pendula', a seldom-flowering form with stiffly pendant branching and a smaller size; cv. 'Regent', a more erect, fast-growing type with glossy, deep green foliage and earlier bloom; cv. 'Tortuosa' with twisted branching and very slow growth; cv. 'Violacea', having late bloom and flowers with a purple tinge.

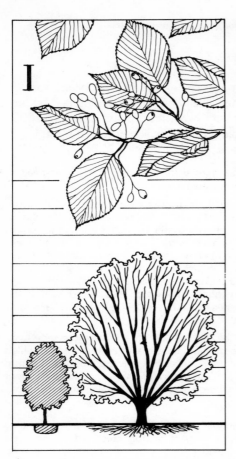

Sorbus alnifolia (Korean mountain ash)

Zones 5 to 7   40' to 60'   Rose family

The mountain ash group is famed for its vivid and generous fruiting and its cooperatively neat growth habits as lawn specimens or garden ornaments. Like their cousins, hawthorns, they have mostly bland flowering and some important pests, but they are difficult to surpass for the persistent, colorful clusterings of showy fruit in late summer and autumn. The species described here is native to most of the temperate regions of eastern Asia and contributes a novelty of simple foliage (most are compound-leaved) and very noticeable, glowing, reddish fruit with uniquely long persistence.

HABIT: Somewhat pyramidal when young but changing to a broadly oval, heavily twigged, symmetrical silhouette later; usually rapid in growth when juvenile but only moderate with age.

SEASONAL APPEARANCE: The new twigs are brownish red and have diamond-shaped breathing pores; its leaves are simple, broadly oval with an abrupt point, shining green, and between 2 and 4 inches long; autumnal color can be scarlet or almost-orange; the late spring flowering is in flat clusters of white, mainly half-inch blossoms well distributed over the tree; its conspicuous, half-inch, oval fruits are a vibrant scarlet or deep orange and last well into the winter; the smooth bark is a rich gray.

PREFERENCES AND PROBLEMS: As with other rose-family members, it prefers full sun and in this instance seems to grow better in a slightly alkaline soil; in general it prefers a well-drained, moist, average-fertility site; dislikes excessive heat and drying winds, along with concentrated urban pollution.

PESTS AND DISEASES: Susceptible to fire blight but is highly resistant to trunk borers common to most other species.

VARIETIES AND CULTIVARS: None.

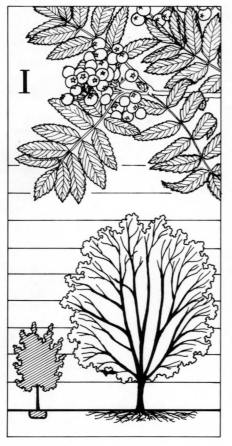

Sorbus aucuparia (European mountain ash, Rowan, Quickbeam)

Zones 2 to 7   30' to 60'   Rose family

Consistently popular for its bright fruit and wider range of hardiness, this mountain ash from Europe and Asia Minor performs best when in the colder parts of its climate zones. The berries are rich in vitamin C and can be prepared into a good-tasting jelly, but wily birds usually denude the tree well before the fruit can be harvested. It has been a landscape ornament here since Colonial times.

HABIT: Somewhat open but symmetrical when young with upright branching; the weight of fruit bends the outer stems gracefully with age, when it also develops an oval, dense crown; moderate to fast in growth depending on available soil water.

SEASONAL APPEARANCE: The gray-brown twigs are somewhat hairy when new with densely fuzzy, white, half-inch buds; the alternate, 4- to 10-inch, compound leaves are dull green with grayish undersides and are composed of thirteen to fifteen oblong leaflets; their autumnal color varies from deep red to rusty yellow; the 3- to 5-inch, terminal flower clusters sport mostly quarter-inch, cream-white, woolly florets; its globe-like, usually quarter-inch fruiting appears in late summer in tones of showy orange-red to rich red, pendulously clustered; the smooth bark is light gray or tan.

PREFERENCES AND PROBLEMS: Grows vigorously in full sun on an acid, amply moist, loamy, well-drained soil; tends to be short-lived with alkaline conditions and prefers colder sites for its best performance; excessive heat and dryness can cause trunk and stem scorch along with brown-edged foliage; its fruiting tends to be persistent but is usually devoured quickly by birds.

PESTS AND DISEASES: Unfortunately prone to trunk borers and fireblight.

Cultivar 'Asplenifolia' with deeply cut leaf margins and dense hairiness below; cv. 'Edulis', a larger-fruiting tree with almost-shiny leaflets and edible, sweet-tasting berries much utilized in Europe for preserves; cv. 'Fastigiata' with thick, stiff twigs and a narrowly upright habit along with showy, half-inch red fruiting; cv. 'Luteo-variegata', having foliage streaked with yellow; cv. 'Rossica', a form with blunt-tipped leaves; cv. 'Xanthocarpa', a type carrying yellow-orange fruit.

Styrax japonicus (Japanese snowbell)

Zones 5 to 9   20′ to 30′   Storax family

A choice small tree from China and Japan for specimen use, this late spring accent has fragrant, pendulous flowering all along the lower sides of the slender branching. They provide greater effect when seen from below.

HABIT: Generally low-branched and round-headed at all ages with pronounced horizontal branching when older; slow-growing.

SEASONAL APPEARANCE: The narrowly oval, glossy, dark green, alternate leaves are between 1 and 3 inches long and appear in upright positions along the slender stems; the weak autumnal color may be yellow-toned or somewhat reddish; its June flowering is prolific when the plant is fully established and comes as drooping clusters of star-shaped, mildly scented, three-quarter-inch, waxy, white-petaled blooms with noticeably yellow stamens; the nonshowy, grayish fruit splits open to reveal dark brown nuts; its gray-brown, smooth bark ages to show orange-brown, shallow grooves.

PREFERENCES AND PROBLEMS: Grows equally well in full sun or light shade on an acid, moist, well-drained, humusy soil well fortified with compost or peat moss; intolerant of limed conditions and may require protection from severe cold and strong winds in the northern limits of its hardiness; tends to become shrubby unless the lower branching is removed early; unsatisfactory in the dry, hot summers of the lower midwestern and southwestern United States.

PESTS AND DISEASES: Comparatively free of both.

VARIETIES AND CULTIVARS: None.

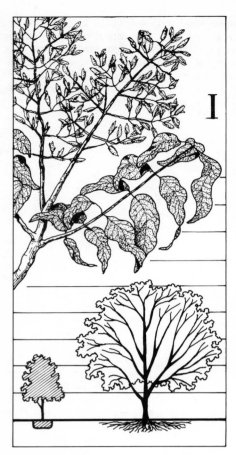

Syringa reticulata [*amurensis japonica*] (Japanese tree lilac)

Zones 4 to 8   20′ to 30′   Olive family

With attractively shiny bark similar to many cherries, this Japanese native contributes a late-flowering, showy habit plus an easy adaptability and hardiness for specimen and potential street tree uses. It also exhibits less susceptibility to the ailments common to other lilacs.

HABIT: Somewhat pyramidal when juvenile, it grows into an oval or rounded, open silhouette later with stiff, ascending branches; moderate in growth rate.

SEASONAL APPEARANCE: The opposite leaves vary between 2 and 5 inches in length and are dark green above with grayish hairs below. broadly oval, and often with long, tapering points; its autumn color is either nonexistent or an insipid yellow; the mid-June blossoming is terminal as loose, creamy, pyramidal heads up to 1 foot long with the strong scent of its relative, privet; the sizable, dry fruit capsules are warty and tan-colored with some persistence through the winter; its red-brown, smooth, glossy bark is cherry-like and has raised accents of horizontal breathing pores.

PREFERENCES AND PROBLEMS: Adapts from full sun to light shade on any fertile, consistently moist, humusy soil; behaves better where summers are cool and air moves through it consistently; may occasionally develop suckering stems at the base.

PESTS AND DISEASES: Generally free of foliage mildew but can be attacked by stem borers and scale insects.

VARIETIES AND CULTIVARS: Variety *mandschurica* has glossier foliage, smaller blossoms, and a 12-foot maximum height.

Taxodium distichum (Bald cypress)

Zones 5 to 10   50′ to 100′   Taxodium family

Similar in appearance to *Metasequoia glyptostroboides,* this deciduous U.S. native from Delaware to Florida and west to Texas and Arkansas has finer leaves on branchlets alternately arranged, noticeably buttressed trunks with raised "knees" in very wet locations, and brighter autumn color. It makes a distinctive and stately addition to large park or estate settings.

HABIT: Broadly pyramidal when juvenile, it later develops a densely twiggy, narrowly conical shape with mostly horizontal branching; moderate to fast in growth, depending on available moisture.

SEASONAL APPEARANCE: The medium green, feathery foliage comes in two styles: New leaves are soft and flat and about three-quarters inch long, while those on older twigs are spirally arranged and smaller; the autumnal changeover is to orange-yellow or dull orange; the twiglets drop along with the leaves; its flowering is separated on the same tree and is not conspicuous for either sex; the 1-inch, round to oval cones are first green, then purple-toned, and finally brown with some winter persistence on the tree; its light brown young bark later changes to a reddish or orange-brown and peels in long, vertical strips; in very wet or swampy locations the buttressed trunk may show hollow, breathing structures called "knees" rising to about 6 feet above the roots.

PREFERENCES AND PROBLEMS: Best placed in full sun on a deep, acid, very moist, sandy loam; adaptable with ease to transplanting as well as to drier conditions but has an aversion to alkaline soils; well suited to wet, even swampy, locations; extremely late to leaf out; tolerant of light shading as it ages; tends to be shallow-rooted but surprisingly wind-firm.

PESTS AND DISEASES: Susceptible to twig blight, heart rot fungus, spider mites, and cypress moth.

VARIETIES AND CULTIVARS: Variety *nutans* has spirally arranged, awl-shaped leaves on mostly ascending branchlets, plus a smaller size; cv. 'Pendens' carries horizontal main branching with noticeably drooping tips and slightly larger cones.

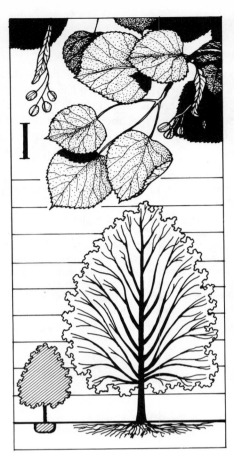

Tilia cordata (Littleleaf linden, Small-leaved European linden, Small-leaved lime)

Zones 4 to 9   60′ to 100′   Linden family

The lindens from Europe are superior in habit and foliage, especially autumn colors, to those from Asia and North America. This species is native throughout Europe and the British Isles and has great landscape value as a handsome specimen or street tree for its compact, stately habit and sweet-scented flowering in early summer. It is the latest linden to bloom.

HABIT: Pyramidal when young and densely compact with ascending, recurved branching at all ages; matures to a symmetrical, oval silhouette with ground-touching branches if left unpruned; fast-growing when juvenile but moderate-growing later.

SEASONAL APPEARANCE: Its 1½- to 3-inch foliage is heart-shaped, glossy, dark green above, and lighter beneath with tufts of rusty down at the base and along the leaf veins on somewhat zigzagged twigs; the early July bloom is very fragrant from terminal clusters of half-inch, pendant, creamy flowers held by a narrow, greenish leaf bract; in cold areas the autumn color is yellow, but in mild zones the leaves change only to a yellow-green; its tan-gray, felt-covered, hard, pea-sized fruit persists into winter; the bark is smooth and gray-brown, aging to deep gray with large cracks and ridges.

PREFERENCES AND PROBLEMS: Readily grown in full sun or light shade on almost any soil but prefers a deep, rich, constantly moist, well-drained location for exceptional performance; easily transplanted, pollution-resistant, readily pruned, very hardy, and tolerant of constricted root conditions; dislikes prolonged dryness and is not recommended for the lower midwestern United States; its prolific flowering invites great bee activity for several weeks; prone to collect much airborne soot on leaves and stems from aphid "honeydew" deposits of sticky sugar sap.

PESTS AND DISEASES: Many leaf-defoliating insects plague it, while in the northwestern United States a mite turns the summer leaves brown; aphid infestations on new growth produce excess sap droplets, encouraging sooty fungal growths.

VARIETIES AND CULTIVARS: Cultivar 'Greenspire', a straight-trunked, regularly symmetrical form well adapted to difficult sites; cv. 'June Bridge', an earlier-blooming discovery; cv. 'Pyramidlis', a narrowly pyramidal type; cv. 'Rancho' with mostly upright branching and smaller, glossier leaves; cv. 'Swedish Upright', a narrowly upright form with short, main branches having downturned ends.

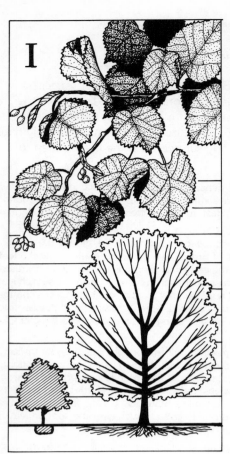

Tilia tomentosa [*argentea*] (Silver linden)

Zones 4 to 9   50' to 90'   Linden family

Imposingly symmetrical with strongly upright branching and silver-coated leaf undersides, this striking introduction from southeastern Europe and southwestern Asia is difficult to propagate and is unfortunately not seen enough in local nurseries. As a desirable lawn specimen or street tree, it is ornamentally difficult to surpass. Curiously, the strong-scented flowers have a narcotic effect on foraging bees.

HABIT: Broadly pyramidal when juvenile but changing later to a round or oval crown with stiffly upright branching and a dense, symmetrical head; fast-growing when young but moderate-growing later.

SEASONAL APPEARANCE: The gray-green, fuzzy twigs produce slightly wrinkled, heart-shaped leaves ranging from 2 to 4 inches in both length and width; the top surfaces are deep, lustrous green while the undersides show silver-white from downy hairs; autumnal color is yellow; its early summer, yellowish, half-inch blossoms are in clusters of seven to ten and carry rich perfume along with a slender, light green leafy bract; the oval, warty, down-covered fruit has a terminal point and some durability into the winter months; juvenile bark is light gray and smooth like beech but changes later to gray-brown with prominent ridges.

PREFERENCES AND PROBLEMS: See *T. cordata;* appears to be more heat- and drought-tolerant than many lindens.

PESTS AND DISEASES: See *T. cordata.*

VARIETIES AND CULTIVARS: Cultivar 'Fastigiata', an upright, narrower form.

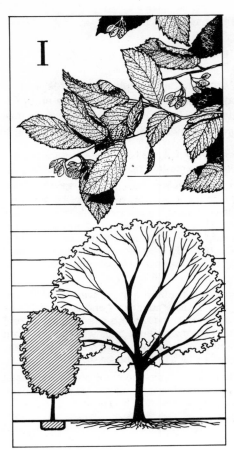

Ulmus americana (American elm, White elm, Water elm)

Zones 2 to 9   60′ to 120′   Elm family

The almost complete devastation of this magnificently canopied tree, which is an inhabitant of most of the eastern and central portions of the United States, by both the Dutch elm disease and the phloem necrosis virus immediately cautions against its generous use where these quick-killing afflictions are rampant. Since there is no other large tree with such a graceful silhouette and lofty branching, its loss is immeasurable to our landscapes, especially along avenues and in parklands. Existing trees are worth preserving with diligence toward insect spraying and deadwood sanitation pruning; and while many serious efforts to combat the disease problems have continued for decades, no certain cure is yet available. Although other elm species have less destructive drawbacks, none has the unique outline of this special tree.

HABIT: Unusually variable throughout its native growing range from vase-shaped to wide-spreading to narrow; develops a massive trunk with limbs high off the ground and upper branching noticeably divided into equally V-shaped crotches; may develop short, leafy twigs on the lower trunk; generally fast-growing at all stages.

SEASONAL APPEARANCE: Dense clusters of tiny, purple-brown flowers clothe the twig ends in very early spring, followed quickly by bunches of wafer-thin, oval, half-inch, light green fruit with a brown-toned center as the leaves emerge; the double-toothed semiglossy foliage is between 2 and 6 inches in length, dark green with a sandpapery feel on the tops and with soft, downy undersides; the leaf base is typically lopsided (an elm characteristic); the autumnal color is between bright, clear yellow and golden yellow; the dark, ash-gray bark shows interlocking, flaky ridges.

PREFERENCES AND PROBLEMS: Prefers full sun and a rich, deep, moist, well-drained, loamy soil but adapts to almost any soil conditions; has surface, fibrous rooting, discouraging much success with underplanting; transplants readily and shows great hardiness but can heave pavements from its somewhat buttressed trunk when older; not recommended for the harsh dryness of desert areas; late in leafing out where winter weather is mild.

PESTS AND DISEASES: Dutch elm disease and phloem necrosis are major, fast-killing afflictions, but there are many other fungal infections also, plus a host of defoliating insects.

VARIETIES AND CULTIVARS: Cultivar 'Ascendens' with a narrow, oval crown and high-placed, ascending branching; cv. 'Aurea', a form with yellow-toned summer leaves; cv. 'Augustine' has a rapid-growing, vertical habit; cv. 'Columnaris', a low-branched type with a broad, columnar shape; cv. 'Incisa', having deeply cut, smaller leaves; cv. 'Littleford', a narrowly vase-shaped form with upright branching and larger, thicker leaves; cv. 'Moline', a disease-resistant discovery with a narrow head and mature horizontal branching; cv. 'Nigricans' with deep green foliage; cv. 'Pendula', a vase-shaped form with long, pendulous outer branches; cv. 'Pyramidata' ('Pyramidalis') with a pyramidal silhouette; cv. 'Vase' ('Urnii'), a vase-shaped type.

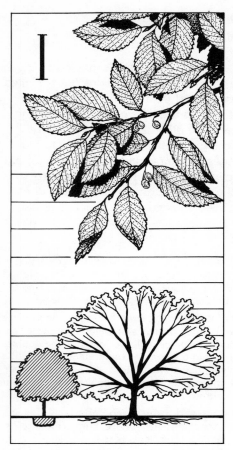

Ulmus parvifolia [*parvifolia sempervirens*] (Chinese elm)

Zones 5 (warm) to 10   40' to 60'   Elm family

Fascinatingly mottled bark is the ornamental highlight of this tree from China and Japan, plus its long-persistent, delicate foliage in the autumn. It has a close resemblance to its relative *Zelkova serrata* and functions well as a wide-spreading, low-headed, graceful specimen for large open spaces.

HABIT: Generally dome-shaped and open-headed at all ages with mature branching very elongated and often pendulous to the ground; reasonably fast-growing.

SEASONAL APPEARANCE: Wispy twigs carry leathery, smooth, dark green, glossy leaves between 1 and 3 inches long with a narrowly tapered base; the autumnal color is usually red-toned or purplish in cold areas but yellow in mild ones; this elm is partially evergreen in mild climates; the late summer blossoming appears as clusters of minute, greenish white flowers soon followed by quarter-inch, winged fruit in quantity; the irregularly flaking bark is basically gray-brown and has prominent orange breathing pores; the exfoliating bark pieces reveal green, gray, orange, and brown patches of trunk.

PREFERENCES AND PROBLEMS: Best planted in full sun on a moist, well-drained, rich, deep soil; tolerant of poor drainage and alkaline conditions and is adaptable to cold, wind, heat, high humidity, and dryness; young saplings need staking to form an upright silhouette; easily damaged in storms because of its weak wood; often confused with the inferior *U. pumila* (Siberian elm), an upright relative with vigorous, soft growth which is quickly smashed by high winds and ice storms.

PESTS AND DISEASES: Greatly resistant to Dutch elm disease but is prone to the fatal Texas root rot, especially in desert areas where this tree thrives; has recently been attacked by the witches'-broom disease that deforms new twig growth.

VARIETIES AND CULTIVARS: Cultivar 'Drake', a type with upright branching.

Ulmus × vegeta 'Camperdownii' [*glabra* 'Camperdownii'] (Camperdown elm)

Zones 5 to 8   15' to 25'   Elm family

An intriguing elm form for a special landscape site, this weeping tree is a natural hybrid between *U. carpinifolia* (Smooth-leaved elm) and *U. glabra* (Welsh or Scots elm). It is often grafted to other elm stock.

HABIT: Mushroom-shaped and densely twiggy with a sturdy trunk and many weeping branches; moderate in growth.

SEASONAL APPEARANCE: Its deep green to bluish green, smooth leaves are between 3 and 6 inches long and hang from zigzagged twigs; the color in the autumn is a deep yellow; spring flowering is ornamentally unimportant from minute, purple-green blossoms that develop into dense clusterings of pale green, oval, wafer fruit; the young bark is gray and smooth but changes to brownish gray with cracks and grooves later.

PREFERENCES AND PROBLEMS: Performs best in full sun on a rich, moist, average soil; easily transplanted and tolerant of many soil types; may be damaged by ice and snow because of its compactly dense head.

PESTS AND DISEASES: Somewhat prone to Dutch elm disease and elm leaf miner insects.

VARIETIES AND CULTIVARS: None.

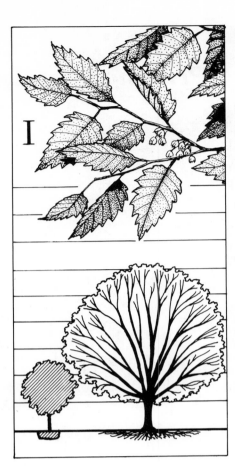

Zelkova serrata [keakii] (Japanese zelkova, Saw-leaf zelkova)

Zones 5 to 9   60′ to 100′   Elm family

Although long touted as a replacement for the American elm, its close relation, this graceful tree is more squat in outline and has a densely packed head of slender branches. It offers a handsome silhouette of its own for street tree and garden use. The attractively flaking bark is similar to *Ulmus parvifolia* and becomes an ornamental asset as it matures.

HABIT: Short-trunked with long, spreading, slim branching forming a broad or vase-shaped head; occasionally develops multiple stems; fast-growing when juvenile but moderate-growing with age.

SEASONAL APPEARANCE: The 2- to 5-inch, sharp-toothed, leathery leaves are oval and slightly rough on top; the autumnal colors vary from deep red to yellow-orange or even yellow-brown; its spring flowers are inconspicuous, and the sexes may be separated on some plants; the tiny, pea-like fruit is woody and nonshowy; its smooth, gray, young bark becomes brownish orange and flaky when older with many orange breathing pores.

PREFERENCES AND PROBLEMS: Enjoys full sun and a moist, deep soil; transplants easily when juvenile and requires little care; adapts to all soil types and becomes drought-tolerant when fully established; may be susceptible to damage from late frost when young.

PESTS AND DISEASES: Virtually pest-free and resistant to Dutch elm disease.

VARIETIES AND CULTIVARS: Cultivar 'Village Green', a very quick-growing and cold-tolerant form with a smooth, straight trunk and a somewhat vase-shaped silhouette like an American elm.

Guying Details

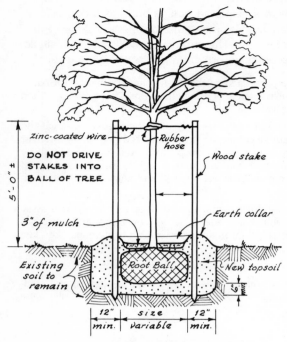

Zinc-coated wire

Rubber hose

Wood stake

DO NOT DRIVE STAKES INTO BALL OF TREE

5'-0" ±

3" of mulch

Earth collar

Existing soil to remain

Root Ball

New topsoil

6"

12" min. | size variable | 12" min.

Details for Double-Staking Trees Smaller than 3" in Caliper

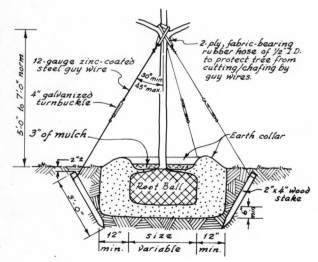

12-gauge zinc-coated steel guy wire

2-ply, fabric-bearing rubber hose of ½" I.D. to protect tree from cutting/chafing by guy wires.

30° min.
45° max.

4" galvanized turnbuckle

3" of mulch

Earth collar

5'-0" to 7'-0" norm.

2" ±

Root Ball

3'-0"

2" x 4" wood stake

6"

12" min. | size variable | 12" min.

NOTE: If tree to be guyed is planted on a slope, place 2 stakes uphill from tree in a line parallel to contours.

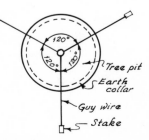

120°
120°
120°

Tree pit

Earth collar

Guy wire

Stake

Details for Guying Trees Larger then 3" in Caliper

Pruning

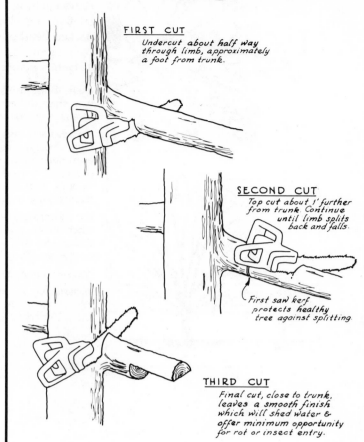

FIRST CUT

Undercut about half way through limb, approximately a foot from trunk.

SECOND CUT

Top cut about 1' further from trunk. Continue until limb splits back and falls.

First saw kerf protects healthy tree against splitting.

THIRD CUT

Final cut, close to trunk, leaves a smooth finish which will shed water & offer minimum opportunity for rot or insect entry.

TREES WITH POTENTIAL HEIGHTS FROM 15 TO 35 FEET

Broadleaf Evergreens

Acacia baileyana
Bauhinia variegata
Casuarina stricta
Citrus aurantiifolia
Citrus aurantium
Citrus limon
Citrus × paradisi
Citrus reticulata
Clethra arborea
Eriobotrya japonica
Ilex pedunculosa
Ilex pernyi
Ilex vomitoria

Leptospermum laevigatum
Melaleuca linariifolia
Metrosideros excelsus
Olea europae
Pittosporum phillyraeoides

Needle Evergreens

None included

Deciduous

Acer campestre
Acer circinatum
Acer japonicum

Cercidium floridum
Cercis siliquastrum
Cornus kousa
Crataegus crus-galli
Crataegus laevigata
Crataegus × lavallei
Crataegus mollis
Crataegus monogyna 'Stricta'
Crataegus nitida
Crataegus phaenopyrum
Laburnum ×watereri
Magnolia ×soulangiana
Magnolia stellata
Malus × arnoldiana
Malus floribunda

Malus × 'Katherine'
Malus × 'Red Jade'
Malus sargentii
Malus × scheideckeri
Malus × zumi calocarpa
Prosopsis glandulosa torreyana
Prunus avium 'Plena'
Prunus cerasifera 'Atropurpurea'
Prunus × 'Hally Jolivette'
Prunus serrulata
Prunus subhirtella
Styrax japonicus
Syringa reticulata
Ulmus × vegeta 'Camperdownii'

TREES WITH POTENTIAL HEIGHTS FROM 35 TO 60 FEET

Broadleaf Evergreens

Acacia dealbata
Acacia decurrens
Acacia pruinosa
Bauhinia blakeana
Brachychiton acerifolius
Castanospermum australe
Ceratonia siliqua
Chorisia speciosa
Cinnamomum camphora
Citrus sinensis
Crinodendron patagua
Cupaniopsis anacardiodes
Eucalyptus calophylla
Eucalyptus ficifolia
Eucalyptus rudis
Ficus benjamina
Ficus macrophylla
Ficus rubiginosa

Hymenosporum flavum
Ilex × altaclarensis
Ilex aquifolium
Ilex latifolia
Ilex opaca
Langunaria patersonii
Laurus nobilis
Melaleuca quinquenervia
Melaleuca stypheliodes
Pittosporum rhombifolium
Pittosporum undulatum
Prunus caroliniana
Prunus lusitanica
Quercus suber
Quercus virginiana
Quillaja saponaria
Schinus molle
Schinus terebinthifolius
Syzygium paniculatum

Needle Evergreens

Abies koreana
Abies nordmanniana
Cupressus arizonica
Juniperus chinensis
Juniperus deppeana pachyphlaea
Juniperus scopulorum
Pinus parviflora
Platycladus orientalis
Podocarpus macrophyllus
Sciadopitys verticillata
Thuja occidentalis
Thuja standishii

Deciduous

Acer griseum
Acer palmatum
Aesculus × carnea

Albizia julibrissin
Amelanchier canadensis
Amelanchier laevis
Betula pendula
Catalpa bignonioides
Cercis canadensis
Cladrastis lutea
Cornus florida
Delonix regia
Erythrina caffra
Fraxinus ornus
Fraxinus pennsylvanica lanceolata
Fraxinus velutina
Jacaranda mimosifolia
Juglans hindsii
Koelreuteria elegans
Koelreuteria paniculata
Maackia amurensis
Magnolia heptapeta

TREES WITH POTENTIAL HEIGHTS FROM 35 TO 60 FEET (Continued)

Magnolia × loebneri
Magnolia virginiana
Malus baccata
Melia azedarach
Ostrya virginiana
Paulownia tomentosa
Phellodendron amurense

Pistacia chinensis
Prunus padus
Prunus sargentii
Prunus yedoensis
Pterostyrax hispidus
Pyrus calleryana
Quercus acutissima

Quercus imbricarcia
Quercus phellos
Quercus robur 'Fastigiata'
Quercus rubra
Quercus shumardii
Salix alba tristis
Salix matsudana

Sapium sebiferum
Sorbus alnifolia
Sorbus aucuparia
Ulmus parvifolia

TREES WITH POTENTIAL HEIGHT BEYOND 60 FEET

Broadleaf Evergreens

Arbutus menziesii
Brachychiton discolor
Casuarina cunninghamiana
Casuarina equisetifolia
Eucalyptus camaldulensis
Eucalyptus citriodora
Eucalyptus cladocalyx
Eucalyptus cornuta
Eucalyptus leucoxylon
Eucalyptus polyanthemos
Eucalyptus robusta
Eucalyptus sideroxylon
Eucalyptus viminalis
Fraxinus uhdei
Grevillea robusta
Magnolia grandiflora
Quercus agrifolia
Quercus chrysolepis
Quercus ilex
Quercus laurifolia
Umbellularia californica

Needle Evergreens

Abies concolor
Abies homolepis
Abies pinsapo
Abies procera
Abies veitchii
Araucaria araucana

Araucaria bidwillii
Araucaris heterophylla
Calocedrus decurrens
Cedrus atlantica
Cedrus deodora
Cedrus libani
Chamaecyparis lawsoniana
Chamaecyparis nootkatensis
Chamaecyparis obtusa
Chamaecyparis pisifera
Cryptomeria japonica
Cunninghamia lanceolata
× Cupressocyparis leylandii
Cupressus glabra
Cupressus macrocarpa
Cupressus sempervirens
Juniperus virginiana
Picea abies
Picea asperata
Picea engelmannii
Picea glauca
Picea omorika
Picea orientalis
Picea pungens
Picea sitchensis
Pinus bungeana
Pinus cembra
Pinus densiflora
Pinus monticola
Pinus nigra
Pinus pinea

Pinus ponderosa
Pinus radiata
Pinus resinosa
Pinus strobus
Pinus sylvestris
Pinus thunbergiana
Pseudotsuga menziesii
Sequoia sempervirens
Sequoiadendron wellingtonia
Thuja plicata
Tsuga canadensis
Tsuga caroliniana
Tsuga diversifolia
Tsuga heterophylla

Deciduous

Acer macrophyllus
Acer platanoides
Acer pseudoplatanus
Acer rubrum
Acer saccharinum
Acer saccharum
Aesculus hippocastanum
Betula lenta
Betula maximowicziana
Betula nigra
Betula papyrifera
Carpinus betulus
Catalpa speciosa
Celtis australis

Celtis laevigata
Cercidiphyllum japonicum
Cornus nuttallii
Fagus grandifolia
Fagus sylvatica
Fraxinus americana
Ginkgo biloba
Gleditsia triancanthos inermis
Halesia monticola
Larix decidua
Larix kaempferi
Larix occidentalis
Liquidambar styraciflua
Liriodendron tulipifera
Magnolia acuminata
Metasequoia glyptostroboides
Nyssa sylvatica
Oxydendrum arboreum
Platanus × acerifolia
Populus alba 'Pyramidalis'
Pterocarya fraxinifolia
Quercus alba
Quercus coccinea
Quercus nigra
Quercus palustris
Sophora japonica
Taxodium distichum
Tilia cordata
Tilia tomentosa
Ulmus americana
Zelkova serrata

TREES WITH CONSPICUOUS FLOWERING

Broadleaf Evergreens

Acacia baileyana
Acacia dealbata
Acacia decurrens
Bauhinia species
Brachychiton species
Castanospermum australe
Ceratonia siliqua (female)
Chorisia speciosa
Clethra arborea
Crinodendron patagua
Eucalyptus species
Metrosideros excelsus

Prunus lusitanica
Quillaja saponaria

Needle Evergreens

None included

Deciduous

Acer circinatum
Acer platanoides
Aesculus species
Albizia julibrissin
Catalpa species

Cercis species
Cladrastis lutea
Cornus species
Crataegus species
Delonix regia
Erythrina caffra
Fraxinus ornus
Halesia monticola
Jacaranda mimosifolia
Koelreuteria species
Laburnum × watereri
Liriodendron tulipifera
Matuckia amurensis

Magnolia species
Malus species
Oxydendrum arboreum
Paulownia tomentosa
Prunus species
Pterostyrax hispidus
Pyrus calleryana cultivars
Sophora japonica
Sorbus species
Styrax japonicus
Syringa reticulata

TREES WITH ORNAMENTAL FRUITING

Broadleaf Evergreens

Brachychiton acerifolius
Castanospermum australe
Ceratonia siliqua (female)
Chorisia speciosa

Citrus species
Crinodendron patagua
Cupaniopsis anacardiodes
Eribotrya japonica
Ilex × altaclarensis cultivars

Ilex aquifolium (female)
Ilex opaca cultivars
Ilex pedunculosa (female)
Ilex perneyi (female)
Ilex vomitoria (female)

Pittosporum rhombifolium
Schinus species (female)
Syzygium paniculatum

TREES WITH ORNAMENTAL FRUITING *(Continued)*

Needle Evergreens

Abies koreana
Abies procera
Araucaria species *(female)*
Juniperus chinensis cultivars

Picea abies

Deciduous

Cornus species
Crataegus species

Delonix regia
Jacaranda mimosifolia
Koelreuteria species
Malus species
Melia azedarach
Ostrya virginiana

Paulownia tomentosa
Phellodendron amurense *(female)*
Platanus × acerifolia
Pterocarya fraxinifolia
Pterostyrax hispidus
Sorbus species

TREES WITH CONSISTENTLY COLORFUL FOLIAGE

Broadleaf Evergreens

Acacia baileyana
Eucalyptus polyanthemos
Ficus rubiginosa 'Variegata'
Ilex × altaclarensis 'Atrovirens variegata'
Ilex aquifolium cultivars
Ilex latifolia 'Variegata'
Laurus nobilis 'Aurea'
Prunus lusitanica 'Variegata'

Needle Evergreens

Abies concolor cultivars
Abies nordmanniana 'Aurea'
Abies pinsapo cultivars

Abies procera 'Glauca'
Cedrus atlantica cultivars
Cedrus deodora cultivars
Chamaecyparis lawsoniana cultivars
Chamaccyparis nootkatensis cultivars
Chamaecyparis obtusa 'Aurea'
Chamaecyparis pisifera cultivars
Cunninghamia lanceolata
Cupressus arizonica cultivars
Cupressus macrocarpa cultivars
Cupressus sempervirens 'Glauca'
Juniperus chinensis cultivars
Juniperus deppeana pachyphlaea 'Silver'

Juniperus scopulorum cultivars
Juniperus virginiana cultivars
Picea abies 'Aurea'
Picea glauca 'Caerulea'
Picea orientalis 'Aurea'
Picea pungens cultivars
Pinus parviflora 'Glauca'
Pinus sylvestris cultivars
Platycladus orientalis cultivars
Pseudotsuga menziesii 'Argentea'
Sequoia sempervirens 'Glauca'
Thuja occidentalis 'Lutea'
Thuja plicata 'Aurea'
Tsuga heterophylla 'Argentea'

Deciduous

Acer japonicum 'Aureum'
Acer palmatum cultivars
Acer platanoides cultivars
Acer pseudoplatanus cultivars
Catalpa bignonioides 'Aurea'
Cornus florida cultivars
Cornus kousa 'Variegata'
Fagus sylvatica cultivars
Fraxinus pennsylvanica lanceolata 'Aucubifolia'
Prunus cerasifera 'Atropurpurea'
Sorbus aucuparia 'Luteo-variegata'
Tilia tomentosa
Ulmus americana 'Aurea'

TREES HAVING NOTEWORTHY BARK WITH AGING

Broadleaf Evergreens

Chorisia speciosa
Eucalyptus species
Melaleuca species
Quercus suber

Needle Evergreens

Cryptomeria japonica
Cupressus glabra
Juniperus deppeana pachyphlaea

Pinus bungeana
Pinus densiflora
Pinus sylvestris

Deciduous

Acer griseum
Acer pseudoplatanus
Betula maximowicziana
Betula papyrifera
Betula pendula
Celtis australis

Cercidiphyllum japonicum
Cladrastis lutea
Cornus florida
Cornus kousa
Fagus grandifolia
Fagus sylvatica
Ginkgo biloba
Maackia amurensis
Metasequoia glyptostroboides
Phellodendron amurense
Platanus × acerifolia

Prunus avium 'Plena'
Prunus sargentii
Quercus alba
Salix alba tristis
Syringa reticulata
Taxodium distichum
Ulmus parvifolia
Zelkova serrata

TREES WITH NOTICEABLY FRAGRANT FLOWERS

Broadleaf Evergreens

Acacia baileyana
Acacia dealbata
Bauhinia blakeana
Cinnamomum camphora
Citrus species
Clethra arborea
Eriobotrya japonica

Hymenosporum flavum
Magnolia grandiflora
Olea europaea
Pittosporum species

Needle Evergreens

None included

Deciduous

Amelanchier laevis
Fraxinus ornus
Magnolia species
Malus species
Melia azedarach
Paulownia tomentosa
Prosopsis glandulosa torreyana

Prunus avium 'Plena'
Prunus cerasifera 'Atropurpurea'
Prunus padus
Prunus serrulata cultivars
Pterostyrax hispidus
Tilia species

TREES TOLERANT OF URBAN CONDITIONS

Broadleaf Evergreens

Ceratonia siliqua
Eucalyptus polyanthemos
Eucalyptus sideroxylon
Fraxinus uhdei
Ilex × altaclarensis 'Wilsonii'
Melaleuca species
Pittosporum rhombifolium
Prunus caroliniana
Quercus agrifolia
Quercus virginiana

Schinus terebinthifolius
Umbellularia californica

Needle Evergreens

Abies homolepis
Chamaecyparis pisifera cultivars
Picea glauca
Pinus resinosa
Pinus sylvestris
Tsuga caroliniana

Deciduous

Acer campestre
Acer macrophyllum
Acer platanoides
Acer saccharinum
Crataegus × lavallei
Crataegus nitida
Crataegus phaenopyrum
Fraxinus species
Ginkgo biloba
Gleditsia triacanthos inermis

Jacaranda mimosifolia
Juglans hindsii
Koelreuteria paniculata
Magnolia species
Malus species
Melia azedarach
Paulownia tomentosa
Phellodendron amurense
Pistacia chinensis
Platanus × acerifolia
Populus alba 'Pyramidalis'
Pyrus calleryana cultivars

TREES TOLERANT OF URBAN CONDITIONS *(Continued)*

Quercus species
Sapium sebiferum

Sophora japonica
Tilia cordata

Ulmus americana cultivars
Ulmus parviflora

Zelkova serrata

TREES WITH RAPID GROWTH HABIT

Broadleaf Evergreens

Acacia baileyana
Acacia dealbata
Acacia decurrens
Acacia pruinosa
Bauhinia species
Casuarina species
Chorisia speciosa
Eucalyptus species
Fraxinus uhdei
Ilex × altaclarensis
Quercus virginiana

Needle Evergreens

Abies procera
Araucaria bidwillii
Cedrus atlantica
Chamaecyparis obtusa 'Magnifica'
× Cupressocyparis leylandii

Cupresses arizonica
Picea abies
Picea sitchensis
Pinus radiata
Sequoia species
Thuja occidentalis
Thuja plicata

Deciduous

Acer macrophyllum
Acer platanoides 'Summer Shade'
Acer pseudoplatanus
Acer saccharinum
Aesculus hippocastanum
Betula maximowicziana
Betula nigra
Catalpa species
Cercidiphyllum japonicum
Cercis siliquastrum

Delonix regia
Erythrina caffra
Fraxinum americana
Ginkgo biloba 'Fairmount'
Gleditsia triacanthos inermis
Halesia monticola
Jacaranda mimosifolia
Juglans hindsii
Koelrueteria paniculata
Larix species
Liriodendron tulipifera
Magnolia acuminata
Magnolia heptapeta
Magnolia × loebneri 'Merrill'
Malus species
Melia azedarach
Metasequoia glyptostroboides
Paulownia tomentosa
Phellodendron amurense
Pistacia chinensis

Platanus × acerifolia
Populus alba 'Pyramidalis'
Prunus species
Pterocarya fraxinifolia
Pyrus calleryana cultivars
Quercus coccinea
Quercus nigra
Quercus phellos
Quercus robur 'Fastigiata'
Quercus rubra
Quercus shumardii
Salix alba tristis
Sapium sebiferum
Sophora Japonica 'Regent'
Sorbus alnifolia
Tilia species
Ulmus americana
Ulmus parvifolia
Zelkova serrata 'Village Green'

TREES TOLERANT OF SOME SHADING

Broadleaf Evergreens

Crinodendron patagua
Hymensporum flavum
Ilex species
Magnolia grandiflora
Quercus ilex
Umbellularia californica

Needle Evergreens

Abies concolor
Abies veitchii

Chamaecyparis lawsoniana
Chamaecyparis pisifera cultivars
Juniperus chinensis
Juniperus virginiana
Picea abies
Pseudotsuga menziesii
Sequoia sempervirens
Thuja species
Tsuga species

Deciduous

Acer species
Amelanchier species
Betula species
Carpinus betulus
Catalpa bignoniodes
Cercidiphyllum japonicum
Cercis canadensis
Cornus florida
Fagus grandifolia
Fagus sylvatica

Fraxinus americana
Halesia monticola
Jacaranda mimosifolia
Laburnum × watereri
Magnolia virginiana
Nyssa sylvatica
Ostrya virginiana
Quercus alba
Quercus phellos
Quercus robur 'Fastigiata'
Styrax japonicus
Syringa reticulata

TREES FAVORING CONSISTENTLY MOIST OR WET SITES

Broadleaf Evergreens

Arbutus menziesii (moist)
Brachychiton discolor (moist)
Castanospermum australe (moist)
Casuarina equisetifolia (moist to wet)
Casuarina stricta (moist to wet)
Crinodendron patagua (moist to wet)
Eucalyptus citriodora (moist)
Eucalyptus cornuta (moist)
Eucalyptus robusta (moist)
Eucalyptus rudis (moist to wet)
Ficus benjamina (moist)
Ficus macrophylla (moist)
Fraxinus uhdei (moist)
Grevillea robusta (moist)
Magnolia grandiflora (moist)
Melaleuca quinquenervia (moist to wet)
Quercus laurifolia (moist to wet)

Schinus molle (moist to wet)

Needle Evergreens

Abies nordmanniana (moist)
Abies pinsapo (moist to wet)
Abies procera (moist)
Cedrus deodora (moist)
Decrus libani (moist)
Chamaecyparis lawsoniana (moist)
Chamaecyparis nootkatensis (moist)
Chamaecyparis obtusa cultivars (moist)
Chamaecyparis pisifera cultivars (moist)
Cryptomeria japonica (moist)
× Cupressocyparis leylandii (moist to wet)
Juniperus virginiana (moist to wet)
Picea abies (moist)
Picea asperata (moist)

Picea sitchensis (moist to wet)
Pinus resinosa (moist to wet)
Pinus strobus (moist)
Sciadopitys verticillata (moist)
Sequoia sempervirens (moist)
Thuja standishii (moist to wet)
Tsuga species (moist)

Deciduous

Acer pseudoplatanus (moist)
Acer rubrum (moist to wet)
Acer saccharum (moist)
Aesculus species (moist)
Amelanchier species (moist)
Betula nigra (moist to wet)
Betula pendula (moist to wet)
Catalpa species (moist to wet)
Cercidiphyllum japonicum (moist)
Cornus kousa (moist)
Erythrina caffra (moist)
Fraxinus americana (moist)

Larix species (moist)
Liquidambar styraciflua (moist to wet)
Liriodendron tulipifera (moist)
Magnolia species (moist)
Metasequoia glyptostroboides (moist)
Nyssa sylvatica (moist to wet)
Oxydendrum arboreum (moist)
Populus alba 'Pyramidalis' (moist to wet)
Pterocarya fraxinifolia (moist)
Quercus imbricaria (moist)
Quercus nigra (moist to wet)
Quercus robur 'Fastigiata' (moist)
Salix species (moist to wet)
Sapium sebiferum (moist)
Sorbus aucuparia (moist)
Syringa reticulata (moist)
Taxodium distichum (moist to wet)
Tilia cordata (moist)

TREES WITH DROUGHT RESISTANCE

Broadleaf Evergreens

Acacia baileyana
Brachychiton acerifolius
Casuarina species
Ceratonia siliqua
Eucalyptus species
Ficus ribiginosa
Grevillea robusta
Ilex vomitoria
Lagunaria patersonii
Laurus nobilis
Leptospermum laevigatum
Melaleuca species
Olea europaea
Prunus caroliniana
Quercus suber

Needle Evergreens

Abies concolor

× Cupressocyparis leylandii
Cupressus arizonica
Cupressus sempervirens
Juniperus species
Picea pungens
Pinus monticola
Pinus nigra
Pinus pinea
Pinus ponderosa
Pinus resinosa
Pinus thunbergiana
Platycladus orientalis
Thuja occidentalis

Deciduous

Acer campestre
Acer platanoides
Acer pseudoplatanus
Acer saccharinum

Albizia julibrissin
Betula maximowicziana
Betula pendula
Catalpa species
Celtis species
Cercidiphyllum japonicum
Cercidium species
Crataegus species
Fraxinus velutina
Ginkgo biloba
Gleditsia triacanthos inermis
Juglans hindsii
Koelreuteria species
Maackia amurensis
Malus species
Melia azedarach
Ostrya virginiana
Phellodendron amurense
Pistacia chinensis

Platanus × acerifolia
Populus alba 'Pyramidalis'
Prosopis glandulosa torreyana
Pterocarya fraxinifolia
Pyrus calleryana cultivars
Quercus alba
Quercus palustris
Quercus rubra
Salix matsudana 'Tortuosa'
Sapium sebiferum
Sophora japonica
Tilia tomentosa
Ulmus parifolia
Zelkova serrata

TREES ADAPTABLE TO SEASHORE LOCATIONS

Broadleaf Evergreens

Acacia baileyana (protect from wind)
Casuarina cunninghamiana
Casuarina equisetifolia
Casuarina stricta
Cupaniopsis anacardioides
Eriobotrya japonica
Eucalyptus citriodora
Eucalyptus × ficifolia
Eucalyptus leucoxylon
Eucalyptus polyanthemos
Eucalyptus rudis
Eucalyptus sideroxylon

Eucalyptus viminalis
Ficus benjamina (protect from wind)
Ficus rubiginosa
Lagunaria patersonii
Leptospermum laevigatum
Melaleuca quinquenervia
Metrosideros excelsus
Pittosporum species
Prunus caroliniana
Prunus lusitanica
Quercus ilex
Quillaja saponaria

Needle Evergreens

Cryptomeria japonica
Cupressus macrocarpa
Juniperus virginiana
Picea asperata
Picea pungens
Pinus nigra
Pinus pinea
Pinus radiata
Pinus thunbergiana

Deciduous

Acer platanoides

Acer pseudoplatanus
Aesculus species
Amelanchier canadensis
Crataegus nitida
Delonix regia (protect from wind)
Erythrina caffra
Fagus sylvatica
Fraxinus pennsylvanica lanceolata
Gleditsia triacanthos inermis
Malus species
Paulownia tomentosa
Populus alba 'Pyramidalis'
Pterocarya fraxinifolia
Salix matsudana 'Tortuosa'
Tilia cordata

TREES FOR WINDBREAKS

Broadleaf Evergreens

Casuarina species
Cinnamomum camphora
Eucalyptus species
Leptospermum laevigatum
Melaleuca quinquenervia

Needle Evergreens

× Cupressocyparis leylandii

Cupressus arizonica
Cupressus macrocarpa
Juniperus species
Picea abies
Picea omorika
Pinus nigra
Pinus strobus
Pseudotsuga menziesii
Thuja species

Deciduous

Acer platanoides
Acer pseudoplatanus
Carpinus betulus
Crataegus phaenopyrum
Fagus sylvatica
Fraxinus americana
Fraxinus pennsylvanica lanceolata
Malus baccata

Populus alba 'Pyramidalis'
Quercus imbricaria
Quercus phellos
Syringa reticulata
Tilia cordata

TREES WITH COLUMNAR OR NARROWLY UPRIGHT HABIT

Broadleaf Evergreens

Acacia dealbata
Clethra arborea
Ficus rubiginosa 'Variegata'
Quillaja saponaria
Syzygium paniculatum

Needle Evergreens

Calocedrus decurrens
Cedrus atlantica 'Fastigiata'
Chamaecyparis nootkatensis
× Cupressocyparis leylandii cultivars
Cupressus arizonica
Cupressus sempervirens 'Stricta'
Juniperus chinensis cultivars

Juniperus scopulorum cultivars
Juniperus virginiana cultivars
Picea omorika
Pinus cembra
Pinus strobus 'Fastigiata'
Pinus sylvestris 'Fastigiata'
Platycladus orientalis cultivars
Podocarpus macrophyllus
Thuja occidentalis cultivars

Thuja plicata cultivars
Tsuga canadensis 'Fastigiata'

Deciduous

Acer platanoides 'Columnare'
Acer platanoides 'Improved Columnar'
Acer rubrum 'Columnare'
Acer saccharum 'Newton Sentry'

TREES WITH COLUMNAR OR NARROWLY UPRIGHT HABIT (Continued)

Betula pendula 'Fastigiata'
Carpinus betulus 'Columnaris'
Cornus florida 'Fastigiata'
Crataegus monogyna 'Stricta'
Crataegus phaenopyrum
  'Fastigiata'
Fagus sylvatica 'Fastigiata'

Ginkgo biloba fastigiata
Koelreuteria paniculata 'Fastigiata'
Larix decidua 'Pyramidalis'
Liriodendron tulipifera 'Fastigiatum'
Malus baccata 'Columnaris'
Metasequoia glyptostroboides 'National'

Populus alba 'Pyramidalis'
Prunus sargentii 'Columnaris'
Prunus serrulata 'Amanogawa'
Prunus subhirtella ascendens
Quercus robur 'Fastigiata'
Salix matsudana 'Tortuosa'

Sorbus aucuparia 'Fastigiata'
Tilia cordata 'Swedish Upright'
Tilia tomentosa 'Fastigiata'
Ulmus americana 'Ascendens'
Ulmus americana 'Columnaris'

TREES WITH WEEPING HABIT

Broadleaf Evergreens

Casuarina stricta
Eucalyptus camaldulensis
Eucalyptus viminalis
Melaleuca stypheliodes
Pittosporum phillyraeoides
Schinus molle

Needle Evergreens

Cedrus atlantica 'Pendula'
Cedrus deodora 'Pendula'
Chamaecyparis lawsoniana
  'Pendula'

Chamaecyparis nootkatensis
  'Pendula'
Juniperus scopulorum 'Pendula'
Juniperus virginiana 'Pendula'
Picea abies 'Inversa'
Picea abies 'Pendula'
Picea omorika 'Pendula'
Pinus strobus 'Pendula'
Platycladus orientalis
  'Flagelliformis'
Platycladus orientalis 'Intermedius'
Pseudotsuga menziesii 'Glauca
  Pendula'
Pseudotsuga menziesii 'Pendula'

Sequoia wellingtonia 'Pendulum'
Thuja occidentalis 'Pendula'
Thuja plicata 'Pendula'
Tsuga canadensis 'Pendula'

Deciduous

Betula pendula cultivars
Carpinus betulus 'Pendula'
Cornus florida 'Pendula'
Fagus sylvatica 'Borneyensis'
Fagus sylvatica 'Pendula'
Fagus sylvatica 'Purpurea Pendula'
Fagus sylvatica 'Tortuosa'

Fraxinus americana 'Pendula'
Ginkgo biloba pendula
Larix decidua 'Pendula'
Malus × 'Red Jade'
Prunus subhirtella 'Pendula'
Prunus subhirtella
  'Yae-shidare-higan'
Salix alba tristis
Sophora japonica 'Pendula'
Ulmus americana 'Pendula'

TREES DIFFICULT TO TRANSPLANT UNLESS YOUNG

Broadleaf Evergreens

Arbutus menziesii
Bauhinia blakeana
Bracychiton acerifolius
Cinnamomum camphora
Cupaniopsis anacardiodes
Quercus agrifolia
Quercus chrysolepsis

Needle Evergreens

Cedrus deodora
Pinus sylvestris

Deciduous

Albizia julibrissin
Carpinus betulus
Cercis canadensis

Cladrastis lutea
Cornus nuttallii
Crataegus crus-galli
Crataegus laevigata
Crataegus × lavallei
Delonix regia
Erythrina craffra
Fagus grandifolia
Koelreuteria paniculata

Liriodendron tulipifera
Nyssa sylvatica
Ostrya virginiana
Oxydendrum arboreum
Prosopsis glandulosa torreyana
Quercus alba
Quercus coccinea
Sapium sebiferum

Amherst, Garden Club of. *Trees in Amherst.* Amherst, Massachusetts. 1975.

Bailey, Liberty Hyde. *Cultivated Evergreens.* New York: The Macmillan Company. 1923.

Barber, Peter, and Phillips, C. E. Lucas. *The Trees Around Us.* Chicago: The Follett Publishing Company. 1975.

Bean, S. J. *Trees and Shrubs Hardy in the British Isles,* vols. 1 and 2. New York: E. P. Dutton & Co. 1915.

Beittel, Will. *Santa Barbara's Trees.* Santa Barbara, California: Santa Barbara County Horticultural Society, Inc. 1976.

Bloom, Adrian. *Conifers for Your Garden.* France: Sachets Floraiise. 1972.

Brockman, C. Frank. *Trees of North America.* New York: Golden Press. 1968.

Collingwood, G. H., and Brush, Warren D. *Knowing Your Trees.* Washington: The American Forestry Association. 1967 ed.

Conner, E. Wesley. *The Back Pocket Guide to Ornamental Plants.* San Luis Obispo, California: California Polytechnic State University Foundation. 1976.

Crockett, James Underwood. *Evergreens.* New York: Time-Life Books. 1971.

———. *Trees.* New York: Time-Life Books. 1972.

den Boer, Arie. *Flowering Crabapples.* Washington: The American Association of Nurserymen. 1959.

Dengler, Harry William. *Handbook of Hollies.* Washington: American Horticultural Society. 1957, vol. 36.

den Ouden, P., and Boom, B. K. *Manual of Cultivated Evergreens.* The Hague: Martinus Nijhoff. 1965.

Dirr, Michael A. *Manual of Woody Landscape Plants.* Champaign, Illinois: Stipes Publishing Company. 1977, rev. ed.

———. *Photographic Manual of Woody Landscape Plants.* Champaign, Illinois: Stipes Publishing Company. 1978.

Edlin, Herbert L. *Know Your Broadleaves.* London: Her Majesty's Stationery Office. 1973, rev. ed.

———. *Trees and Man.* New York: Columbia University Press, 1976.

Graves, Arthur Harmount. *Illustrated Guide to Trees and Shrubs.* New York: Harper & Row, Publishers, Incorporated. 1956, rev. ed.

Grimm, William C. *The Book of Trees.* Harrisburg, Pennsylvania: The Stackpole Company. 1957.

Harlow, William M. *Trees of the Eastern & Central United States and Canada.* New York: Dover Publications, Inc., 1957 ed.

Harrison, Charles R. *Ornamental Conifers.* New York: Hafner Press. 1975.

Hillier, H. C. *Hillier's Manual of Trees & Shrubs.* New York: A. S. Barnes and Company. 1973.

Hortorium, Liberty Hyde Bailey, Cornell University. *Hortus Third.* New York: The Macmillan Company. 1976.

Hosie, R. C. *The Native Trees of Canada.* Ottawa: Canadian Forestry Service. 1973, 7th ed.

Johnson, Hugh. *The International Book of Trees.* New York: Simon & Schuster, Inc. 1973.

Lancaster, Roy. *Trees for Your Garden.* New York: Charles Scribner's Sons. 1974.

Leathart, Scott. *Trees of the World.* London: The Hamlyn Publishing Group, Ltd. 1977.

Little, Elbert L., Jr., and Wadsworth, Frank H. *Common Trees of Puerto Rico and the Virgin Islands.* Washington: U.S. Department of Agriculture. 1964.

Mathias, Mildred E. *Color for the Landscape.* Arcadia, California: California Arboretum Foundation, Inc. 1973.

McMinn, Howard E., and Maino, Evelyn. *An Illustrated Manual of Pacific Coast Trees.* Berkeley, California: University of California Press. 1973, 2d ed.

Muller, Katherine K., Broder, Richard E., and Beittel, Will. *Trees of Santa Barbara*. Santa Barbara, California: Santa Barbara Botanic Garden. 1974.

Oakman, Harry. *Colourful Trees for Landscapes and Gardens*. Melbourne, Australia: Angus & Robertson, Ltd. 1967.

Phillips, Roger. *Trees of North America and Europe*. New York: Random House, Inc. 1978.

Pokorny, Jaromir. *A Color Guide to Familiar Trees*. London: Octopus Books, Ltd. 1974.

———. *Trees of Parks and Gardens*. London: Spring Books. 1967.

Pratt, Merritt B. *Shade and Ornamental Trees of California*. California State Board of Forestry. 1922.

Rogers, Matilda. *Trees of the West*. Pasadena, California: The Ward Ritchie Press. 1975.

Sacamano, Charles M., and Jones, Warren D. *Native Trees and Shrubs for Landscape Use in the Desert Southwest*. Tucson, Arizona: The University of Arizona. 1976 ed.

Sargent, Charles Sprague. *Manual of the Trees of North America*. Boston: Houghton Mifflin Company. 1922.

Stephens, H. A. *Trees, Shrubs and Woody Vines in Kansas*. Lawrence, Kansas: The Regents Press of Kansas. 1969.

Sudworth, George B. *Forest Trees of the Pacific Slope*. Washington: Government Printing Office. 1908.

Sunset Books, Editors of. *Garden Trees*. Menlo Park, California: Lane Publishing Company. 1975.

Vedel, Helge, and Lange, Johan. *Trees and Bushes in Wood and Hedgerow*. London: Methuen & Company, Ltd. 1968 ed.

Viertel, Arthur T. *Trees, Shrubs and Vines*. Syracuse, New York: Syracuse University Press. 1970.

Walden, Fred. *A Dictionary of Trees*. Petersburg, Florida: Great Outdoors Publishing Company. 1963.

Wyman, Donald. *Trees for American Gardens*. New York: The Macmillan Company. 1965, rev. ed.

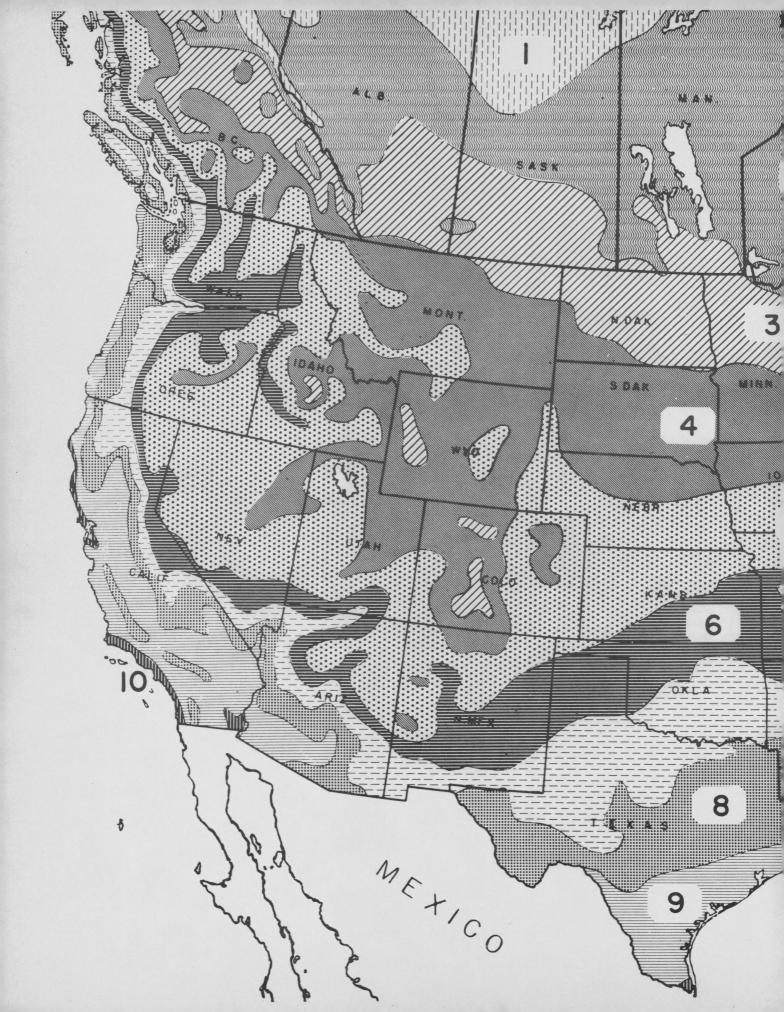